Judaism and Its Bible

University of Nebraska Press
LINCOLN

Judaism and Its Bible

A People and Their Book

FREDERICK E. GREENSPAHN

The Jewish Publication Society
PHILADELPHIA

Library of Congress Cataloging-in-Publication Data
Names: Greenspahn, Frederick E., 1946–, author.
Title: Judaism and its Bible: a people and their book / Frederick E. Greenspahn.
Description: Philadelphia: Jewish Publication Society; Lincoln: University of Nebraska Press, [2023] | "Published by the University of Nebraska Press as a Jewish Publication Society book." | Includes bibliographical references and index. | Summary: "Judaism and Its Bible explores the profoundly deep yet complex relationship between Jews, Judaism, and the Hebrew Bible, describing the extraordinary two-and-a-half-millennia journey of a people and its book that has changed the world"—Provided by publisher.
Identifiers: LCCN 2022049624
ISBN 9780827615106 (paperback)
ISBN 9780827619043 (epub)
ISBN 9780827619050 (pdf)
Subjects: LCSH: Bible. Old Testament—Criticism, interpretation, etc. | Bible. Old Testament—Criticism, interpretation, etc., Jewish. | Judaism—History—Post-exilic period, 586 B.C.-210 A.D. | BISAC: RELIGION / Biblical Studies / General | RELIGION / Judaism / Rituals & Practice
Classification: LCC BS1171.3 .G74 2023 | DDC 221.6—dc23/eng/20230524
LC record available at https://lccn.loc.gov/2022049624

Set in Adobe Text Pro by A. Shahan.

for Barbara

מרגלית דלית לה טימי

"a pearl that has no price"

(*j. Ber*. 9:1 12d)

Table of Contents

Preface

THIS BOOK WAS CONCEIVED IN 1984 AT a National Endowment for the Humanities seminar at Harvard University, where it became apparent that despite Judaism's seeming familiarity it is, as a prominent rabbi had put it thirty years earlier, "the unknown religion of our time."[1] That was not because there were no descriptions of Judaism, which has cultivated extensive scholarship throughout its existence, including an impressive body of academic research over the last two centuries. Nor was it attributable to the absence of study about religion, which has also flourished over the last hundred and fifty years. Rather, the problem was the lack of interaction between these two fields, a gap reflected in the existence of two separate (in both membership and approach) scholarly organizations, one devoted to religious studies (the American Academy of Religion) and the other to Jewish studies (the Association for Jewish Studies). Although these fields are now less separate than they once were, there are still bridges to be built. Nowhere is that more evident than with regard to the Bible, despite its commonly being perceived as a unifying feature of the "Judeo-Christian tradition."

As it happened, the project turned out to be more daunting than it first seemed, made even more so by a series of interruptions. Exploring the Bible's place in Judaism involves a wide array of disciplines that only begin with biblical studies and the history of Judaism. Other fields with much to contribute include comparative religion, sectarianism, ritual studies, and theology as well as Jewish-Christian and Jewish-Muslim relations, some of which are full-fledged academic disciplines of their own or even umbrellas for several. This book, therefore, leans heavily on the work of other scholars with whose insights I have tried to familiarize myself. Despite the limits of my own expertise, I hope that I have brought the fruits of their knowledge together in a comprehensible way, which will itself be a significant contribution to the various readerships I have in mind. Unless indicated otherwise, all translations are my own.

If this project can encourage a broad audience to rethink their assumptions and more scholarly ones to put their own work into a larger context, then the effort will have been a success. And if it can help people from diverse backgrounds appreciate the richness of the Jewish tradition over time and make them aware of how others' perspectives can be a valuable tool for understanding their own, then my goals will have been met.

I embarked on the study of the Bible with the expectation that understanding it would illumine the fundamental nature of Judaism. It was probably fortunate that I had not then heard of the genetic fallacy, that, in Wilfred Cantwell Smith's words, "if you wish to understand oaks, you should study more than acorns."[2] But in the process, I have come to recognize the depth and complexity of Judaism's relationship with the Bible. No one is more aware than I of the limitations and deficiencies of this study, which ultimately proved too big for one book or even one person. Still, I hope that I have been able to tie it all together in an accessible and suggestive way.

Acknowledgments

MANY COLLEAGUES, STUDENTS, AND FRIENDS have stimulated my thinking along the way. Wilfred Cantwell Smith convened the summer seminar mentioned above; he and the participants in that program so long ago provided both the inspiration and the intellectual framework for this study as a whole. Since then, I have tried out many of the ideas noted here in a variety of classes at several institutions and discussed various aspects of this topic both formally and in random conversations with colleagues far too numerous to mention. Those in Denver—Jeanne Abrams, Wallace Clift, Sandra Dixon, Cecil Franklin, William Gravely, Ginnette Ishimatsu, James Kirk, Carl Raschke, Gregory Robbins, Liyakat Takim, and Seth Ward—made me aware of the importance of raising these issues. Although I didn't realize it at the time, Samuel Sandmel and Nahum Sarna modeled both the importance of looking beyond the Bible (at "everything that came after," as Sandmel once put it) as well as the possibility of making sound scholarship comprehensible to a broad audience. The guidance and encouragement of Rabbi Barry Schwartz along with the support of the JPS and University of Nebraska Press staff have been central in enabling this project to reach fruition. And, most especially, Barbara Pearl, who has shared so much of this journey with me, supported my efforts to understand and articulate what I have learned. Words can hardly express my gratitude for all she has given and put up with so that I might reach this season.

Introduction

THE HEBREW BIBLE IS WIDELY REGARDED AS central to Judaism. The Qur'an speaks of Jews as "people of the book" (*ahl al-kitâb*), albeit while including Christians in the same category.[3] Christians, too, recognized the Bible's Jewish roots, leading the New Testament to characterize gentile Christians as "branches grafted onto a tree" (Rom. 11:13–24) and the McGuffey Reader to refer to Jews as "the keepers of the Old Testament."[4]

Jews regard the Hebrew Bible as the basis of their religion. Over 1000 years ago, the Babylonian Talmud used it to support practices mandated by rabbinic tradition.[5] Solomon Schechter, who is credited with having revived the Jewish Theological Seminary of America, spoke of it as Jews' "sole *raison d'être*," while Leo Baeck, leader of Berlin's Jewish community in the first half of the twentieth century, called it Judaism's "secure and immovable foundation, the permanent element amid changing phenomena."[6] Indeed, Jews consider themselves direct descendants of those whose experiences are described in its pages, its "natural and not adopted children."[7] Thus, Abraham is counted as the first Jew and the revelation at Mount Sinai as the basis for Jewish tradition. Christians recognize the Hebrew Bible (Old Testament) as the source for their religion, too, and therefore evidence of their shared heritage with Jews.

However, closer scrutiny reveals a more complex reality. Many Jewish practices are conspicuously different from those mandated in the Bible, while modern scholars question whether its theology is what it is commonly said to be. Nor are Jewish and Christian editions of the Bible identical. Not only are Jewish Scriptures only part of the Christian Bible, but many churches include books in their Old Testaments that are not in Jewish Bibles at all. Even the shared books are arranged differently in Christian and Jewish editions. Moreover, Christian tradition has long insisted that Jews misunderstand the Bible's contents. To be sure, Christians have often sought out Jewish Bible teachers and even identified the Bible's literal meaning as the *sensus judaicus*.[8] However, as Martin Luther put it, "Go to the Jew for the Hebrew grammar and to the [Christian] theologians for the sense."[9] Jews, of course, find such statements offensive. As comedian Lewis Black explained, "You called your book 'new' and said our book was 'old,' and yet every Sunday I turn on the television set, and there's a priest or a pastor reading from my book and interpreting it. And their interpretations, I have to tell you, are usually wrong. It's not their fault, 'cause it's not their book."[10]

In order to account for all this, Judaism's relationship to the Bible is deserving of more careful attention than it sometimes receives. That is the goal of this book—to explore the reality of the Bible's place in Judaism: how it came to be, how it is used, and how it has been understood.

To do this, we will adopt a descriptive approach, reporting what Jews do rather than what they say they do. We, therefore, begin with behavior—how Jews actually treat their Scripture, both in the synagogue and beyond—rather than with doctrine.

The Bible is pervasive in Jewish life. As the Labor Zionist leader A.D. Gordon observed, it "dominated everything."[11] Jewish martyrs have sometimes died with it at their side.[12] It is, therefore, not surprising that the Torah scroll, which contains the first five books of the Bible in the original Hebrew, occupies a place of honor in Jewish synagogues, where it is read sequentially over the course of the liturgical year, with each week identified by the section that is recited then. These are accompanied by selections from the Prophets and, on certain holidays, five smaller books. Moreover, virtually every Jewish practice is tied to a biblical passage, no matter how convoluted the logic needed to do so.

Whereas Christianity was born into a world that already had Scripture, ancient Israel was not. Judaism acknowledges as much when it traces its roots back to Abraham, Isaac, and Jacob, who lived centuries before the Torah was traditionally given at Mount Sinai. Since none of Israel's neighbors had what we would consider a Bible nor were any of the books in our Bibles written to be included in one, we must ask how this book (in Jewish terminology, the *Tanakh*, an acronym for its three components—*Torah*, *Nevi'im*, and *Ketuvim*) came to be and why certain books achieved that status while others did not. That process turns out to have taken longer and been more complex than is commonly thought. Although not all the details are completely understood, it probably took place in stages, beginning with the transcription of sacred traditions, which were then woven together into the books we have today. Only later were they recognized as authoritative and holy. Even then, it would be centuries before these separate books came to be regarded as parts of a single work ("the Bible"), a process that was probably not completed until the Middle Ages and possibly in Christendom before reaching the Jewish world. Nor is it necessarily over. The emergence of digital media in our own time may yet affect the Bible, as it has so many other written texts, transforming what is for us a single, unified work into something about which we can only speculate.[13]

Complicating matters further, much of Judaism is not biblical at all. As the early Zionist writer Yosef Brenner observed, "Biblical Judaism is far removed from modern Judaism."[14] The Passover holiday provides a dramatic example, since Jews do not observe it in the way the Bible prescribes, though many probably think they do. Rather than sacrificing a lamb as called for in the book of Exodus (12:1–20), they gather for a family meal (*m. Pesaḥim* 10).[15] Other Jewish practices, such as synagogue worship and Sabbath candles, are not mentioned in the Bible at all, though they are attributed to biblical verses. Instead, these practices are laid out in a set of later works, most prominently the sixth-century Babylonian Talmud. The resulting confusion was evident in a photograph that appeared on the cover of the Catholic magazine *The Bible Today*, which shows an Orthodox Jew poring over the pages of a large Hebrew tome, with the caption "Torah study in Safed, Israel"; however, it is not the Bible he is reading, but the Talmud.[16] Similarly, a sociological description of Orthodox Jewish study groups titled *The People of the Book* describes groups that engage in Talmud study.[17]

According to Jewish tradition, the Talmud contains a second Torah, a doctrine that has been been challenged several times over the course of Jewish history. This bipolarity and the resulting tension between the Written and the Oral Torahs mirrors that between the two parts of the Christian Bible: does the New Testament fulfill the Old as Jesus put it (Matt. 5:17) or replace it, as claimed by the second-century teacher Marcion and his intellectual heirs?

After exploring these issues, we will examine what Jews have said about the Bible. Although that might seem self-evident—it is the repository of God's instructions (the literal meaning of the word *torah*)–that is not the only way the Bible has been understood, a point often overlooked, in part because it differs from Protestant views of what a Bible should be. Jews have actually construed the Bible's importance in several different ways, sometimes emphasizing its status or its power more than its contents.

Because Judaism regards the Bible as complete and its contents fixed for all time, it has had to find ways to connect its Scripture with circumstances not addressed there, as must all communities that rely on fixed texts. Jewish authorities did that by producing an extensive body of biblical interpretation that links the written and the oral Torahs. We will examine the techniques they used to keep the Bible relevant and the breadth of the resulting interpretations.

Many of these interpretations have been incorporated into the remarkable number of translations of the Bible Jews have produced, some of which have even been considered inspired. These are often recited alongside the original, notwithstanding Judaism's emphasis on the Hebrew and occasional denials of its translatability. Surveying the variety of these renderings will help summarize Jewish attitudes towards the Bible.

One goal for this journey is that it lead us to appreciate the richness of Judaism's treatment of its Bible, the book from which Jews cannot escape.[18] As complicated as that relationship can be, Jews are, indeed, the people of that book, a product of something they themselves created. It is that complexity which we seek to explore in these pages in order to achieve an enhanced understanding and appreciation of this "unknown religion" by Christians, Jews, and any others who may find it valuable and informative.

Abbreviations

AJSL	*American Journal of Semitic Languages and Literature*
AJS Review	*Association for Jewish Studies Review*
ANET	*Ancient Near Eastern Texts Relating to the Old Testameont*, ed. J. B. Pritchard (Princeton NJ: Princeton University Press, 1969)
AZJ	*Allgemeine Zeitung des Judenthums*
b.	Babylonian Talmud (Bavli)
Bar	Baruch
BASOR	*Bulletin of the American Schools of Oriental Research*
Bib	*Biblica*
BJRL	*Bulletin of the John Rylands University Library of Manchester*
BJS	Brown Judaic Studies
BZAW	Beihefte zur *Zeitschrift für die alttestamentliche Wissenschaft*
CBQ	*Catholic Biblical Quarterly*
CCAR	Central Conference of American Rabbis
CD	Cairo Geniza copy of the Damascus Document
COS	*The Context of Scripture*, ed. W. W. Hallo (Leiden, 1997–)
DSD	*Dead Sea Discoveries*
EJ	*Encyclopaedia Judaica*, 2nd ed., ed. Michael Berenbaum and Fred Skolnik (Farmington Hills MI: Thomson Gale, 2007)
EM	*Encyclopaedia Mikra'it* (Jerusalem: Mosad Bialik, 1950–88).

ERE	*Encyclopedia of Religion and Ethics*, ed. J. Hastings (New York: 1908–27)
ErIsr	*Eretz-Israel*
Frag. Tg.	Fragment Targum
HE	Eusebius of Caesarea, *The Ecclesiastical History* (LCL 1926–32)
Ḥev	*Ḥever*
HR	*History of Religions*
HS	*Hebrew Studies*
HTR	*Harvard Theological Review*
HUCA	*Hebrew Union College Annual*
IEJ	*Israel Exploration Journal*
IOMS	International Organization for Masoretic Studies
j.	Jerusalem Talmud
JAAR	*Journal of the American Academy of Religion*
JAJ	*Journal of Ancient Judaism*
JANESCU	*Journal of the Ancient Near Eastern Society of Columbia University*
JAOS	*Journal of the American Oriental Society*
JBL	*Journal of Biblical Literature*
JBR	*Journal of Bible and Religion*
JCS	*Journal of Cuneiform Studies*
JE	*The Jewish Encyclopedia*, ed. I. Singer (New York, 1925)
JJS	*Journal of Jewish Studies*
JNSL	*Journal of Northwest Semitic Languages*
JPS	The Jewish Publication Society
JQR	*Jewish Quarterly Review*
JR	*Journal of Religion*
JSIJ	*Jewish Studies, an Internet Journal*
JSJ	*Journal for the Study of Judaism in the Persian, Hellenistic, and Roman Periods*
JSNT	*Journal for the Study of the New Testament*
JSOT	*Journal for the Study of the Old Testament*
JSS	*Journal of Semitic Studies*

JTS	*Journal of Theological Studies*
Jub	Jubilees
L.A.B.	*Liber Antiquitatum Biblicarum* (Pseudo-Philo)
LCL	Loeb Classical Library
Leš	*Leshonenu*
LXX	Septuagint
m.	Mishnah
Macc.	Maccabees
MGWJ	*Monatschrift für Geschichte und Wissenschaft des Judentums*
Mur	Murabba'at
Neof.	Targum Neofiti
ns	new series
NTS	*New Testament Studies*
os	old series
OTE	*Old Testament Essays*
OTS	Old Testament Studies
PAAJR	*Proceedings of the American Academy of Jewish Research*
PE	*Praeparatio Evangelica* (Preparation for the Gospel)
PG	*Patrologia Graeca*, ed. J.-P. Migne (Paris, 1857–86)
PL	*Patrologia Latina*, ed. J.-P. Migne (Paris, 1844–64)
Ps.-J.	Targum Pseudo-Jonathan
Q	Qumran
Rabb.	Rabbah
RB	*Revue biblique*
REJ	*Revue des études juives*
rprt	reprinted
RQ	*Revue de Qumrân*
RSV	Revised Standard Verison
SBL	Society of Biblical Literature
ScrH	Scripta Hierosolymitana
Sir	Wisdom of Ben Sira (sometimes called Ecclesiasticus)
SJOT	*Scandinavian Journal of the Old Testament*
t.	Tosefta

TDNT	*Theological Dictionary of the New Testament*, ed. G. Kittel and G. Friedrich, trans. G. W. Bromiley (Grand Rapids: 1964–76)
Tg.	Targum
Tg. Neb.	*Targum Nebi'im*
Tg. Onq.	*Targum Onqelos*
Tg. Ps.-J	*Targum Pseudo-Jonathan*
TLZ	*Theologische Literaturzeitung*
v.	verse
VigChr	*Vigiliae Christianae*
vss.	verses
VT	*Vetus Testamentum*
VTSup	Vetus Testamentum Supplements
vv.	verses
ZAW	*Zeitschrift für die alttestamentliche Wissenschaft*
ZDMG	*Zeitschrift der deutschen morgenländischen Gesellschaft*
ZKTh	*Zeitschrift für katholische Theologie*
ZNW	*Zeitschrift für die neutestamentliche Wissenschaft und die Kunde der älteren Kirche*

Judaism and Its Bible

ONE

Surrounded by Scripture

AT THE ENTRANCE TO THEIR HOMES, Jews often mount a small box called a mezuzah. Inside is a piece of parchment, inscribed with selections from the book of Deuteronomy that mandate placing "these words on the doorposts (*mezuzot*) of your house" (6:4–9 and 11:13–21) in Hebrew.[1] Some put *mezuzot* on the doorways inside their homes as well, kissing them each time they pass by.[2] Others wear them on chains around their necks. Jewish soldiers have even carried *mezuzot* in their pockets.[3]

The mezuzah's ubiquity is emblematic of Scripture's pervasiveness in Jewish life. Not only are biblical selections fastened to the entrance of Jewish buildings, but the text plays a prominent role in Jewish worship and is often used for decoration. On weekday mornings Jewish worshippers tie small boxes called *tefillin* (a plural form of the Hebrew word for "prayer"[4]), which contain the same passages as mezuzot along with selections from the book of Exodus (13:1–10 and 11–16) on their upper arms and foreheads. According to the Talmud, the sixth-century collection of rabbinic teachings, "Whoever has *tefillin* on his head, *tefillin* on his arm, fringes on his garment, and the *mezuzah* on his doorpost is fortified against sinning."[5]

Synagogues are often decorated with depictions of biblical events, such as Noah's ark or Daniel in the lions' den, and adorned with biblical quotations, such as the Ten Commandments.[6] A sixth-century building in the Galilee bore the blessings from Deuteronomy 28:6 and Isaiah 65:25, while one at Jericho included Psalm

125:5.[7] Toward the end of the twelfth century, Benjamin of Tudela (Spain) reported that Baghdad's "great synagogue of the Head of the Captivity has columns of marble of various colours overlaid with silver and gold, and on these columns are sentences of the Psalms in golden letters."[8] That practice may go back to antiquity if, as some scholars believe, the Hebrew term *mikhtam*, which is found in the introduction to several biblical psalms, refers to their being inscribed.[9]

Jewish children in Central and Eastern Europe were given eggs or cakes inscribed with biblical verses when they began school.[10] And an entire school of design, called micrography, creates pictures out of Hebrew texts written in tiny letters, some of which incorporate entire books of the Bible.

Jews have scoured the Bible for omens in a practice known as bibliomancy.[11] Moses Isserles, who incorporated Ashkenazi (Central and East European) teachings into the *Shulḥan Arukh* (the predominant code of Jewish law compiled by the Sephardic scholar Joseph Karo in the sixteenth century), allowed making decisions on the basis of whatever verses schoolchildren were studying.[12] Others sought guidance from the passage they found after opening a Bible at random.[13]

Magic

Biblical passages have often been used for magical purposes—inscribed inside bowls that were placed at the entrances to houses, apparently in order to cover angels and spirits, or placed in amulets—which was probably the original function of mezuzot and tefillin.[14] One such amulet quotes Genesis 49:22 as giving protection from the evil eye; another cites Exodus 11:8 in order to assist childbearing women; and several inscribed bowls invoke Zechariah 3:2 ("May the Lord rebuke you, O Satan; may the Lord who chooses Jerusalem rebuke you").[15]

The priestly blessing (Num. 6:24–27) has been especially popular for this purpose. An amulet with this passage dates from the time of Jeremiah in Jerusalem in the sixth century BCE.[16] A later amulet contains just the initial letters of its words (*yywyyp' wyyp'wlš*).[17]

Biblical passages have been recited over wounds and to ward off evil dreams.[18] The Talmud tells of people who tried to offset fevers by reciting Exodus 3:2–6 while making a notch in a twisted string that was tied to a thornbush.[19] In the sixteenth century, Rabbi Ḥaim b. Bezalel cited the talmudic teaching that reciting a verse that begins and ends with *'el* ("God") protects from enchantment and sorcery,[20] while the medieval *Sefer Ḥasidim* suggests placing a copy of Leviticus under a child's head in a cradle.[21] To this day, many Jewish homes mount wall plaques with Psalm 16:8 ("I keep the LORD before me"). Such inscriptions are sometimes arrayed in geometric formats, as in the case of a triangular plaque that includes Song of Songs 7:6 on the first line, then repeats it while removing one letter on each subsequent line.[22]

According to the medieval *Sefer Shimmush Tehillim*, the book of Psalms contains "awesome and wondrous secrets to protect and save a person from his evil."[23] Thus, it attributes protective powers to Psalm 1 (from bleeding), Psalm 7 (from enemies), Psalm 10 (from demons), Psalm 22 (when crossing a river), Psalm 45 (from wicked wives), and Psalm 58 (from threatening dogs).[24] It also advises reciting Psalm 37 over water and salt before placing them on the face of a drunk person, and reciting Psalm 16 ten times over river mud, ocean sand, and a bowl of water in order to identify a thief.[25]

These practices have ancient roots. Rabbinic texts describe numerous magical uses of psalms.[26] Psalm 91, which came to be called "a song of affliction," was so popular that even Rabbi Joshua ben Levi (third century, land of Israel), allowed it to be used for healing despite his belief that "one may not be healed with biblical verses."[27] Psalms 91 and 3 were both to be recited before going to sleep.[28] Psalm 121 was hung on a bed to protect against the demon Lilith and Psalm 116:6 to forestall miscarriage.[29] A nineteenth-century translation of the book of Psalms precedes each psalm with a rubric indicating its use, explaining that Psalm 1 is "against miscarriage," Psalm 2 "from a storm at sea," and Psalm 3 "for pains in head and shoulders."[30]

The Bible as Object

For many Jews the Bible is a powerful object. This idea underlies the Mishnah's claim that holy writings "defile the hands," a notion that paradoxically reflects their special sanctity.[31] Torah scrolls have therefore been kept in private homes and taken on journeys.[32] Others have been used as royal amulets, kept in birthing rooms, given to newborns, placed near sick babies or in public squares during times of drought, put on rooftops when under attack, taken to war, and put on public view after the death of religious leaders.[33] In the eighteenth century Jews took oaths using the Aleppo Codex, a famous copy of the Bible that had been endorsed by Moses Maimonides.[34] Jews presented Torah scrolls as gifts to non-Jewish rulers and displayed them in protests during the Holocaust.[35] Such veneration accounts, no doubt, for the desecration to which Torahs have been subjected by various opponents of the Jews, beginning already in pre-Christian times.[36]

Jews, therefore, treat Torah scrolls carefully. An early rabbinic code insists that nothing is to be placed on top of them, while the Talmud prohibits putting one on a bed (or any other place where sexual acts might take place) or letting them be touched by a naked person.[37] Worshippers are also expected to remain in a room until after the Torah has been removed.[38]

Jews have long discussed the proper response to dropping a Torah scroll.[39] In the fifteenth century the Jews of Ferrara, Italy, fasted after a page of the Bible had been accidentally torn.[40] Rather than being thrown away or destroyed, worn-out scrolls are left to decay naturally; often they are buried, like a dead person, and in some communities even mourned for.[41] Printed Bibles have occasionally been treated similarly.

The Bible in the Synagogue

Although synagogues often have several Torah scrolls, they all contain the first five books of the Bible (Genesis through Deuteronomy). Central and East European Jews draped their scrolls in cloth; Spanish Jews used metal covers.[42] The scrolls themselves are frequently decorated with silver crowns, bells, and breastplates, much like the priestly garments described in the Bible.[43] Modern scrolls are tied with cloth binders; in Western Europe these were often made of the cloth in which baby boys had been wrapped at their circumcisions and then stored for use at the child's bar mitzvah.[44]

Torah scrolls are kept in a closed cabinet at the front of the synagogue sanctuary. Whenever it is opened, worshippers rise, often without any visible cue.[45] On Monday, Thursday, and Saturday mornings as well as Saturday afternoons a scroll is removed as worshippers sing, pivoting in order to follow it while it is carried around the congregation, touching and kissing it as it passes by. This ritual is repeated when the Torah is returned to the cabinet.[46]

The Torah's five books are divided into fifty-four sections *(parashot* or *parashiyot)*, each read in sequence during Sabbath morning services over the course of a year, with additional passages added on special occasions. Because the number of weeks in a year varies according to the vagaries of the Jewish calendar, eight relatively short *parashot* can be combined. Selections from each week's portion are also read during the preceding Sabbath afternoon and on Monday and Thursday mornings.[47] Following the talmudic injunction that "One should always recite even if one does not understand," the selection is read in the original Hebrew.[48] Worshippers in some places stand during the reading; others rise only for certain passages, such as the Ten Commandments, which are chanted with a special melody.[49]

Although Jewish tradition insists that nothing in the Torah be skipped,[50] some communities read only part of each week's portion, following what is called a "triennial" cycle, in which each portion is divided into three parts, with the first being read in one year, the second in the next, and the third (final) in the last, thereby covering the entire text over three years.[51] The American Conservative movement's Committee on Jewish Law and Standards endorsed this procedure in 1988.[52]

The portions themselves are subdivided into several sections (seven on Sabbath mornings), containing at least three verses apiece, with special blessings recited before and after each section.[53] Following a traditional interpretation of Deuteronomy 31:9, the blessing for the first of these is reserved for a Jew of priestly descent (*kohen*) and the second for one who traces his descent from the tribe of Levi.[54]

The Torah portion is chanted in Hebrew, using distinctive melodies for special occasions. Modern readers use a pointer, called a *yad* (lit. "hand," reflecting its shape), in order to avoid touching the scroll directly.[55] An attendant (*gabbay*) follows the reading in a printed text in order to correct any errors.[56] Although a translation traditionally accompanies the reading, worshippers in many communities follow along by reading the translation silently.[57] On completing a book of the Torah, worshippers exclaim "*Chazak Chazak V'nitzchazek*" / "Be strong, be strong, and may we be strengthened."

After the reading is over, the scroll is lifted so that those present can see at least three columns. The worshippers rise, extend their little fingers toward it, and proclaim, "This is the Torah that Moses placed before the Israelites at God's command (Deut. 4:44) through Moses" (Num. 4:37, 4:45, 9:23, 10:13).[58] Although the reference may be intended to allude to the scroll's contents, the implication is that this very scroll is the one which God gave the people of Israel in the Sinai desert ("*This* is the Torah . . .")—an understanding reinforced by the Palestinian Talmud's requirement that worshippers treat the scroll exactly as was done at Sinai.[59] In that spirit, the nineteenth-century Hungarian rabbi Judah Aszod compared the synagogue *bimah* (pulpit) to Mount Sinai, with Israelites all around;[60] and the cabinet housing the scrolls is even called an *'aron*, the very word used for the chest in which the tablets were carried through the desert.[61]

A passage from the second section of the Bible ("Prophets") follows the Torah reading on Sabbath mornings and fast day afternoons.[62] These selections, called *haftarot* ("conclusion"; a list from the Cairo Genizah uses the term *ashlamta*, which means "supplement"[63]), are not read in sequence, but are based on thematic or linguistic links to the week's Torah portion.[64] A medieval tradition explains this practice as intended to ensure that Jews hear the Torah's message even when they are not allowed to read from the Torah itself.[65] However, that is not always the case, as is evident on holidays, when special readings relate to the occasion, and at the end of the liturgical year, when passages from the latter chapters of Isaiah, which emphasize consolation, are read in order to set the tone for the coming High Holy Days. The practice of reading prophetic passages originated separately from the Torah cycle, with varying biblical selections.[66]

According to several sources, passages from the Writings were read on the Sabbath and from the books of Job and Lamentations on the fast of Tisha b'Av.[67] However, except for the book of Esther, which already was connected with the holiday of Purim in Second Temple times, the present practice of reading the "Five Scrolls" on specific holidays is not attested until the Middle Ages, when Ruth and the Song of Songs were connected with Shavuot and Passover, respectively. Ecclesiastes' association with Sukkot seems to have come later.[68]

The Bible in Jewish Liturgy

Although the Torah reading is a central part of Jewish worship, it is not the only way in which the Bible is present. The liturgy itself includes several biblical passages, some of which are not prayers at all.[69] For example, the *Shema*, which proclaims the monotheistic belief that is central to Jewish theology and is recited in almost every worship service, comprises three paragraphs from the books of Numbers and Deuteronomy (Deut. 6:4–9, 11:13–21; and Num. 15:37–41). The story of Abraham's near-sacrifice of his son, Isaac (Gen. 22), and Moses's Song at the Sea (Exod. 15) are also included regularly. The additional (*musaf*) service for the morning of the Jewish New Year (Rosh Hashanah) includes three sections containing ten verses apiece—three from the Torah, three from the Writings (Psalms), three from the Prophets, and a concluding verse from the Torah—all devoted to themes central for that occasion: God's rulership, remembrance, and the ram's horn.[70]

Jewish liturgy includes several biblical passages, such as Exodus 31:16–17 ("the children of Israel shall keep the Sabbath"), which is recited on the Sabbath, in order to legitimize particular practices. This endorsement function is also visible in the way in which some biblical verses are introduced with the phrase "as it is written" (*kakatuv* or *shene'emar*). Still other verses decorate non-biblical passages. For example, Psalm 51:17 ("O LORD, open my lips and let my mouth declare Your praise") and Psalm 19:15 ("May the words of my mouth and the meditation of my heart be acceptable to You, O LORD, my Rock and my Redeemer") introduce and close the *Amidah* blessings, which constitute the core of most Jewish services.[71] Other passages have been used outside the synagogue. For example, sixteenth-century Jewish mystics recited the blessings in Genesis 48:20 ("May God make you like Ephraim and Manasseh") and the priestly blessing in Numbers 6:24–26 over their children, and Proverbs 31:10–31 ("What a rare find is a capable wife") over their wives at Sabbath eve dinners.[72] Traditional Jews recite the *Shema* immediately before death.

Routine prayers also draw heavily on the Bible, with the book of Psalms a particularly rich source; according to one count, nearly half of its contents are incorporated into the standard liturgy.[73] An entire section of the morning service, appropriately called "verses of song" (*pesuqei de-zimra*), comes from that book's last chapters. In addition, specific psalms are assigned for recitation on each day of the week,[74] and a group of Psalms (113–118, called *Hallel*) for the major ("pilgrimage") festivals—Sukkot, Passover, and Shavuot—as well as for Hanukkah, Purim, and the first day of each month.[75]

These practices follow the precedent established at the Jerusalem Temple, where the *Shema*, the priestly blessing, the daily psalms, and the Hallel were recited.[76] The ancient Greek translation of the Bible prefaces Psalm 29(28) with the words, "For the assembly of the tabernacle" (i.e., Sukkot), and rabbinic sources report that Levites recited Psalms 96 and 105 on holidays.[77] These were presumably brought into the synagogue, which came to be called a "small sanctuary" (cf. Ezek. 11:16) after the Temple fell to the Romans in 70 CE.[78] Conspicuously missing from this list are the Ten Commandments (Exod. 20 and Deut. 5), which had been part of the Temple service. Jewish tradition suggests that they were left out in response to heretics (perhaps Christians) who claimed that these were the *only* commandments God had given at Sinai.[79]

Several traditions report that the entire book of Psalms was recited in the synagogue, something that the patriarch Jacob is said to have done while away from his homeland.[80] According to the Ashkenazi memoirist Glikl of Hameln (1645–1724), ten learned men were sometimes hired to recite Psalms each morning.[81] Noting that "everything is contained in the Psalms," the twentieth-century Yiddish writer Shalom Asch describes a Psalm fellowship (*ḥevreh tehillim*), which met in a special room in the synagogue and recited psalms to help the poor and the lowly.[82] Several centuries earlier, Rabbi Isaiah Horowitz told of communities in which the entire book of Psalms was recited on the eve of the Day of Atonement—a practice which Rabbi Judah Loewe (the Maharal of Prague) believed could provide protection from seminal emissions.[83]

Biblical passages also comprise a major portion of the *tiqqunim* (lit. "repair") which some circles recite while staying up all night on special occasions, such as the holidays Shavuot and Hoshanah Rabbah.[84] On the latter, some recite the entire Torah.[85]

Many prayers that do not derive directly from the Bible comprise what one author describes as a daisy chain of biblical quotations (the formal term is "florilegium").[86] This practice, already evident in late biblical books, became prominent during the Second Temple period.[87]

The traditional liturgy surrounding the Sabbath morning Torah reading provides an excellent example, with its chaotic array of biblical verses: Pss. 86:8, 145:13, 10:16, 93:1 (= 97:1 / 99:1 / 1 Chron. 16:31), Exod. 15:18, Ps. 29:11, Ps. 51:20, Isa. 57:15, Isa. 10:35, Isa. 2:3, Deut. 6:4, Ps. 34:4, 1 Chron. 29:11, Ps. 99:5, and 99:9. The Torah reading is then followed by the recitation of Deut. 4:44, Num. 4:37(/45), 9:23, 10:13, Ps. 148:13–14, Num. 10:36, Ps. 132:8–10, Prov. 4:2, 3:18, 3:17, and Lam. 5:21, interspersed with a handful of nonbiblical phrases ("Father of mercy," "For we trust in You alone, O King," "Lord of all worlds," "Blessed be He who gave the Torah to His people Israel in His holiness," and "Our God is one, great is our Lord, holy His name"), which echo biblical style. A similar pattern is evident in the Passover seder, which intricately weaves the account of Israel's departure from Egypt in Deuteronomy 26 with supporting verses from the book of Exodus.

Although the Jerusalem Talmud prohibits using biblical verses as blessings,[88] the formula which opens most Jewish blessings—"Blessed are you, Lord, our God"—rests on biblical models (cf. Ps. 119:12 and 1 Chron. 29:10). In fact, the Babylonian Talmud's warning not to add adjectives to Moses' description of God as "great, powerful, and awesome" (Deut. 10:17) is based on a prohibition against making prayers more lavish than the Bible.[89]

Elsewhere, the Bible provides structure, as when different words from an individual biblical verse open each line of a poem or different verses close each stanza.[90] During the Middle Ages, secular poetry was also written in quasi-biblical style, a practice then extended to rabbinic and liturgical texts.[91] Even liturgical passages that do not come directly from the Bible often employ vocabulary that does. For example, the blessings over bread and fruit use the biblical words *leḥem* (bread) and *ʿeṣ* (tree) rather than the later synonyms *pat* and *ʾilan*.[92] This preference for biblical Hebrew extends to stylistic features, such as pronominal suffixes (e.g., *torato*) and the *vav* consecutive (e.g., *vattitten lanu*), both of which had fallen out of favor by the time these prayers were composed.[93] Thus, the sixth-century Palestinian liturgical poet Yannay used the parallelistic style that is a staple of biblical poetry for many of his works and drew on biblical imagery, as when he compared God to a shield and the sun (cf. Pss. 18:31 and 84:12).[94]

The printer Shabbatai Sofer of Przemysl strengthened this approach, incorporating several biblical features, such as the pausal form in the blessing over wine (*borei peri ha-gafen* instead of the normal *gefen*), into the 1610 "authorized daily prayerbook" sponsored by Poland's Council of Four Lands.[95] During the Jewish Enlightenment (eighteenth to nineteenth centuries), Jews extended that approach to non-biblical prayers, giving the prayerbook a distinctly biblical feel even when expressing ideas that were very much its own.[96]

A striking example of the use of biblical language is found in the second prayer of the daily *Amidah*. While its theme—that God will resurrect the dead—does not occur in the Bible outside of one isolated statement in the book of Daniel (12:2), much of its phraseology does, as demonstrated by the italicized words below:

> You are mighty forever, O Lord, You revive the dead and are *great in salvation* (Isa. 63:1), sustaining the living with loving-kindness, reviving the dead with great mercy, *supporting the fallen* (Ps. 145:14) and *healing* (Ps. 103:3) the sick, *freeing captives* (Ps. 146:7) and maintaining faith with *those who sleep in dust* (Dan. 12:2). *Who is like You* (Exod. 15:11), Master of mighty deeds, and *who resembles You* (Ezek. 31:2,18; Ps. 89:7), *King* (throughout the Bible), who *causes death and life* (1 Sam. 2:6) and makes salvation blossom. You are reliable to revive the dead. Blessed are you, O Lord (Ps. 119:12 and 1 Chron. 29:10), who revives the dead.

Even more dramatic is the prayerbook's treatment of the biblical list of divine attributes (*theologoumenon*)—"the Lord, the

Lord, a merciful and gracious God, patient and full of compassion and truth, keeping compassion for thousands, forgiving iniquity, transgression, and sin, but not cleansing," which occurs several times in the Bible[97] and is incorporated into the Torah service on major holidays. However, the prayerbook leaves out the closing words ("not cleansing"), thereby reversing the phrase's meaning so as to assert that God does cleanse from sin rather than that God does not.[98]

The *Kedushah* (lit. "sanctification"), sometimes called the *trislogion* on account of its threefold repetition of the term *kadosh* ("holy"), which Christians understood as alluding to the trinity, provides a final example. It is constructed around several biblical passages, most prominently Isaiah's vision of God (Isa. 6). However, unlike Christian practice, where the biblical verses are proclaimed in a straightforward way, Jewish worshippers recite each one in response to an introductory statement by their leader. Take, for example, this exchange recited during the traditional daily morning *Amidah*:

> LEADER: Let us sanctify Your name in the world just as they sanctify it in the heavenly heights, as written by Your prophet: And they cried out one to another, saying,
> WORSHIPPERS: "Holy, holy, holy is the Lord of hosts, the fullness of the entire earth is His glory" (Isa. 6:3).
> LEADER: In response to them, they say "blessed":
> WORSHIPPERS: "Blessed is the Lord's glory from His place." (Ezek. 3:12)
> LEADER: And in Your holy words it is written:
> WORSHIPPERS: "The Lord will reign forever, your God, Zion, forever and ever. Hallelujah." (Ps. 146:10).

The result is a miniature dialogue in which the leader acknowledges the biblical origin of the worshippers' lines ("as written by Your prophet" and "in Your holy words it is written"). However, the introduction, "Let us sanctify Your name in the world *just as they sanctify it in the heavenly heights,*" frames these words as imitating a heavenly proclamation. The introduction to Ezekiel's statement, which describes those words as what "*they* [i.e. angels] say," reiterates this idea. In so doing, the liturgy presents the congregation as reenacting a heavenly drama. The resulting words may come from the Bible, but the underlying idea—that earthly prayer imitates heavenly prayer—is not biblical, but rabbinic and kabbalistic.[99] By so doing, the prayerbook uses biblical passages to enact a later theological view.

Scripture Reading

In order to fully appreciate the significance of the Bible's pervasive presence in Jewish life, it is important to recognize that these prayers and practices were not constructed by a single person or at one time, but evolved over centuries. In other words, these are not the products of any individual or group, but of many different people, movements, and communities.

Consider the Scripture reading that is so central to Jewish worship. According to the Bible, public Torah reading began during the biblical period, when Joshua read Moses' laws to the Israelites as they made their way into the Promised Land (Josh. 8:30–35). Centuries later, King Josiah, who ruled the southern half of the Israelite nation, ordered the public reading of a scroll found in the Jerusalem Temple (probably a version of Deuteronomy) according to 2 Kings (23:1–3). Later still, Ezra read from "the book of instruction" (possibly the Pentateuch or, perhaps, just Deuteronomy) to the Judeans who had returned from Babylonian exile as they gathered in the Jerusalem market square on the first day of the seventh month (Neh. 8:1–8).

Although these have been cited as precedents for current Jewish practice, they are all described as one-time events. Even Moses' command that the Torah be read publicly during the holiday of Sukkot (Tabernacles) was to be carried out only every seventh (*shemiṭṭah*) year (Deut. 31:10–13). Moreover, rabbinic tradition holds that this custom of *haqhel* ("gathering"), which it understands as referring to the book of Deuteronomy, took place at the Temple in Jerusalem, as did readings from the books of Leviticus, Numbers, and Deuteronomy, whereas the biblical account of creation was recited in local centers that sent priestly delegations (*ma'amadot*) to officiate there.[100] These practices are obviously very different from what is done today.

An inscription from a first-century synagogue in Jerusalem reports that "Theodotus . . . built the synagogue for the reading aloud of the law and the study of the commandments."[101] That accords with the early rabbinic code, which insists that synagogues be equipped with copies of both the Torah and the Prophets.[102] Indeed, many of the oldest references to synagogues mention Torah scrolls as central features.[103] John Chrysostom, the fourth-century leader of the Christian community in Antioch, attributed the holiness of synagogue buildings to the fact that "the law and the book of the prophets can be found there."[104]

Both written and pictorial evidence suggest that these scrolls were kept in portable chests (*teivot*), from which they were brought in when needed.[105] Rabbi Obadiah of Bertinoro noted that the scrolls in the Palermo synagogue, which he visited in 1487, were "laid on a wooden shelf and not put into a chest as with us."[106] Several illustrations show the scrolls lying on their side.[107] Of course, that does not prove that the Bible was read on a fixed schedule or even during worship. Ancient synagogues were most likely study halls where the Torah was read for instruction and insight.

Synagogues became worship centers after the Jerusalem Temple was destroyed in 70 CE; some sources describe reading the Torah as a replacement for the sacrifices that had been performed in the Temple, a role usually attributed to the *Amidah* prayer.[108] Over time, permanent niches, much like those that held the statues and cult objects used by other religions, were built into synagogue walls to house the *teivah*. These eventually gave way to indentations (apses) that filled the entire wall.[109]

How and when the Torah came to be read in an annual cycle is not entirely clear. According to the New Testament book of Acts,

"Moses . . . is read every Sabbath in synagogues" (15:21),[110] but that does not prove that the Torah was read sequentially, much less according to a fixed schedule. That the Mishnah, compiled in the second-century CE, lists specific passages to be read on the four Sabbaths between Purim and Passover, along with other texts for various holidays,[111] suggests that relevant scriptural selections were initially read on special occasions.

The earliest reference to reading the entire Torah is found in the Tosefta, an ancient collection of rabbinic teachings that parallels the Mishnah and stipulates that the Torah should be read sequentially, beginning on Sabbath morning and then continuing that afternoon, with succeeding passages read on Monday and Thursday mornings.[112] Even then, there is no indication that the Torah cycle was connected to the calendar. Various sources identify 141, 154, 155, 167, and 175 such sections (called *sedarim*), suggesting that communities divided the Torah in different ways.[113] Reading one such portion each week, it would take about three years (hence the term "triennial") to complete the entire Torah, which is exactly how long our sources say Palestinian Jews needed; by reading longer passages, their Babylonian counterparts finished the Torah in a year.[114] However, that distinction may have not have been entirely geographical. Some twelfth-century Egyptian synagogues used the triennial readings associated with Palestine, while others followed the annual cycle, and the medieval Karaites read through the entire Torah twice each year.[115]

Around the year 1000, Babylonian Jews instituted an annual celebration to mark the completion of the Torah reading. This custom soon made its way to the land of Israel, where the closing chapters of Deuteronomy were read on the Sabbath before Yom Kippur (the Day of Atonement) and the reading of the book of Genesis was begun on the holiday afternoon.[116] There followed a celebration on the eighth day of Sukkot, the date on which King Solomon had dedicated the Jerusalem Temple (1 Kings 8:2). By the twelfth century, Jews living in Spain, Ashkenaz, and Provence read the opening of Genesis immediately after finishing the book of

Deuteronomy so as to avoid any break in the Torah reading cycle. This celebration, which came to be called *Simḥat Torah* ("rejoicing over the Torah"), has spawned a host of customs. In some communities the Torah scroll is dressed like a bride, with jewelry and silver or gold crowns.[117] Several communities remove all their scrolls from the ark and carry them around the synagogue seven times (*hakafot*), much like the willow branches (*aravot*) that were carried around the altar in the Jerusalem Temple on the holiday Hoshanah Rabbah.[118] In some places the blessings over the Torah are spoken collectively, a practice probably based on the *haqhel*; elsewhere, children recite them.

The prevalence of the annual cycle of Torah reading reflects the authority of Babylonian practice. Even the modern "triennial" format is plainly designed to convey the impression of covering the entire Torah over a single year, though not everything is read in that span. The Torah cycle thus serves a unifying function and ensures that all Jewish communities are reading from the same section each week. So powerful is its hold that Sabbaths are widely identified by the Torah portion read on them, with names typically drawn from the first word, such as *Shabbat Bereisheet* (the Sabbath of "In the beginning," Gen. 1:1–6:8), *Shabbat Vayera* (the Sabbath of "And he appeared," Gen. 18:1–22:24), and *Shabbat Beshalaḥ* (the Sabbath of "When he sent forth," Exod. 13:17–17:16).[119] Sermons are typically based on that week's passage. The Torah cycle thereby permeates Jewish consciousness both inside the synagogue and beyond.

This practice has profound religious consequences, enabling Jews to relive their sacred history each year, starting with the creation of the world, continuing through the patriarchal period and departure from Egypt, and concluding with their arrival at the Promised Land. Moreover, these events are read about in the same season as the holidays that commemorate them. For example, Rosh Hashanah, which takes place in the fall, is traditionally considered the anniversary of creation; and Passover, which celebrates the departure from Egypt, comes in the spring, close to when the book of Exodus is being read and several weeks before the revelation on Mount Sinai is commemorated on Shavuot. To be sure, the congruence is not exact, and the reading cycle is interrupted for special occasions, when selections from the Torah relating to those events are read instead. Moreover, some holidays, such as Purim and Hanukkah, commemorate events never mentioned in the Torah (although Purim is based on events described in the book of Esther). Still, the annual cycle dominates the Jewish year, guiding Jews through their sacred history on a recurring basis.

In reliving these events through the annual Torah cycle, Jews stop short of redemption, since Deuteronomy ends before the Israelite entrance into the Promised Land (an event recounted in the book of Joshua, which appears in a separate section of the Bible and therefore is not part of the annual cycle).[120] The Torah reading thereby correlates with Jewish theology which, though insistent that redemption is on its way, never allows it to arrive. It thus reflects Judaism's tradition of continuing hope in something that is always out of reach.[121]

Of course, Jewish worship itself is not scriptural. The Hebrew Bible never mentions regular prayer, much less rabbis or synagogues.[122] Instead, worship during biblical times centered around sacrifices performed by priests at the Temple, possibly in complete silence.[123] However, the plethora of biblical passages, phrases, and allusions that permeate Jewish practice impart an aura of antiquity and authenticity. So, too, synagogue architecture. The cabinet that holds the Torah scrolls is typically positioned at the top of several steps and, following a design dating back to antiquity, is often framed by columns and sheltered by a gabled roof under a decorative conch shell,[124] resulting in the image of a building façade. Although some scholars have suggested that this format was modeled on the portals of Greco-Roman temples, its placement on the Jerusalem-facing wall makes it reasonable to infer that the building it evokes is the ancient Temple.[125] Indeed, synagogue walls are frequently decorated with symbols of the Temple,[126] the doors of which were flanked by two columns (1 Kings 7:21). Sephardic Jews (those who trace their ancestry to medieval Spain and Portugal) call the ark *heikhal* (lit. "palace"), a term sometimes applied to the niche alone.[127] As worshippers pray, they therefore face both the Torah and Jerusalem. That connection is expressed liturgically when the ark is opened and worshippers recite the verse "*torah* shall go forth from Zion" (Isa. 2:3). Although the prophet meant that God's teaching (*torah*) is proclaimed in Jerusalem, presumably by priests, these words carry a very different message when proclaimed by Jewish worshippers as they see the sacred scroll on the Jerusalem-facing wall. A similar effect results from the recitation of Psalm 19, with its statement that God's Torah is perfect (v. 19) and Proverbs' insistence that it not be abandoned (4:2).

That impression is reinforced by the scroll itself. As archaic as it may seem, it is not what the Bible says Moses brought down from the mountain; the book of Exodus is quite clear about his having received tablets.[128] Furthermore, ancient Israelite scrolls were not normally written on parchment, as Torahs must be; biblical references to writing on both sides would have required papyrus.[129] Moreover, ancient scrolls were rolled around a single rod, not the two used for Ashkenazi Torahs.[130] Nor does the highly stylized font in synagogue scrolls match the usage in Moses' time, as Jewish tradition acknowledges when it describes the current font as coming into use among the Jews who returned to Jerusalem from the Babylonian exile.[131] Synagogue practice may evoke Sinai, but it is Ezra's reading (with its admitted echoes of the Sinaitic theophany) that Jews reenact.[132] It is telling, therefore, that the book of Nehemiah describes Ezra as reading from a scroll while standing on a raised platform (8:4), precisely as Jews do in the synagogue, where the Torah is read from the *bimah*, an architectural element found in the earliest known synagogues.[133]

The prophetic passages (*haftarot*) that accompany the Torah reading also reflect non-biblical views. As we have seen, only selections are read from these books and not *ad seriatim*. The Mishnah prohibits the reading of some prophetic passages, such as Ezekiel's vivid portrayal of the female Jerusalem (Ezek. 16) and his description of the divine chariot (Ezek. 1), although the Gemara, the rabbinic commentary on the Mishnah together with which it comprises the Talmud, mandates reciting the latter passage on Shavuot.[134] Even passages that are routinely read are occasionally adjusted, with specific verses left out or readings from two separate books combined in order to convey a particular message.[135] In addition, selections are chosen so as to begin and end on a positive note, a goal that sometimes necessitates omitting their final verses or repeating earlier ones.[136] Even cohesive passages may be selected in order to convey a specific view about the Torah portion, as when the triennial cycle assigns Isaiah 65:17 ("Behold, I am creating a new heaven and a new earth") to accompany the creation story, and Isaiah 33:7 ("messengers of peace weep bitterly") for the Sabbath when the story of the binding of Isaac is read, thereby allegorizing their messages.[137] Others all but contradict the Torah reading they accompany, as in the case of the haftarah for the morning of Yom Kippur, which taunts those who think that fasting will earn God's favor (Isa. 57:14–58:14) despite the Torah portion including the requirement to fast (Lev. 16:29).

Thus the paradox of the Hebrew Bible's role in Jewish life, where its ubiquity can obscure its occasional use to support messages very different from what it originally meant. On the one hand, the Bible describes the formative experiences of Judaism's classical tradition: creation, the exodus, and revelation at Sinai. Read publicly, it serves as a unifying focus for Jewish life and study, providing the skeleton and often the content for Jewish practice. It is front and center in the Talmud, the land of Israel, and the synagogue. However, it is often presented in ways that convey a very different message—the centrality of Jerusalem and its Temple, life always on the brink of fulfillment, and, as we will see, the teachings of post-biblical authorities, who used its words to convey their sometimes different ideas.

TWO

Creating the Bible

JUDAISM DID NOT ALWAYS HAVE A BIBLE. When the prophet Nathan criticized David for sleeping with Bathsheba, he didn't cite the Ten Commandments' prohibition of adultery (2 Sam. 12:1–4). Nor did Elijah avoid eating the carrion brought by ravens (1 Kings 17:6), even though that violates a law in Deuteronomy (14:21). Similarly, Amos (5:25) and Jeremiah (7:22) seem unaware of pentateuchal accounts about the Israelites having offered sacrifices during their forty-year sojourn in the desert.[1]

To be sure, biblical characters do know some *ideas* that are found elsewhere in the Bible. For example, Jeremiah's reference to Israel as the first fruits of God's harvest (2:3) presupposes her entitlement to the special treatment described in Leviticus (23:9–14). So, too, Jeremiah's description of Israel as "wayward and rebellious" (5:23) implies that she deserves the capital punishment Deuteronomy mandates for such behavior (21:18–21). He also cites the prohibition of remarrying an ex-wife after she has been married to someone else (Deut. 24:1–4) in order to emphasize that God's punishment of Israel (i.e., "divorce"), to whom God was symbolically married, means that their relationship is now over (Jer. 3:1). He even quotes the prophet Micah.[2] However, he could have known all of these without having read them in a book.

More importantly, those books that are in the Bible, with the possible exception of Deuteronomy, are unlikely to have been written in order to be included there, at the very least because the concept of a Bible didn't yet exist.[3] To be sure, other cultures had sacred traditions, some of which described past events. And various writings were attributed to gods or recited at sacred gatherings, as when the Babylonians recited the story of creation during their New Year celebration.[4] But that is not all we understand a Bible to be.

Over time, however, Judaism developed a strong doctrine of Scripture, as exemplified by the medieval philosopher Joseph Albo's conviction that the Torah "is found today in the hands of all Jews who are scattered throughout the world from east to west with one text without any difference."[5] Some claimed that even its accents had been given at Sinai.[6]

These ideas were not medieval inventions. Already the first century BCE philosopher Philo insisted that "the Jews never altered one word of what was written by Moses"; similar sentiments are found in a variety of hellenistic and rabbinic sources.[7] That conviction is rooted in the book of Deuteronomy, which reports Moses's command that the Israelites "observe everything which I command you; do not add to it or detract from it" (13:1).[8] To ensure that, Jewish tradition developed detailed regulations as to exactly how the Bible should be written, stipulating, for example, that all five books of the Torah be on a single scroll made out of sheets of parchment from ritually clean cattle with 3–8 columns of forty-two lines each.[9] One consequence of this injunction is that in some Torah scrolls, all but six columns begin with the Hebrew letter *vav*.[10] There are even rules governing the width of the spaces between words and the placement of hyphens and special marks,[11] as well as which words should have dots above or below them and where "isolated letters" should appear (at Numbers 10:35–36 and Psalm 107:21–40).[12] The text must also be written in a specific font, with letters hung from the line above.[13] Certain letters must have crowns over individual strokes, some with one and others with three; and five consonants must be written in a special way when they appear at the ends of words.[14] Moreover, some occurrences of specific letters must be written idiosyncratically, whether large, small, elevated, rolled, or curved.[15] As a result, rabbinic scholars were able to state the exact number of verses in both the Torah (5888) and other biblical books, as well as which word was in the exact middle and how many times certain words and phrases occur.[16]

Achieving this level of specificity took several thousand years that only began with the composition of the various books that have come to be included in the Jewish Bible. Modern scholars believe that the oldest passages—the songs attributed to Moses (Exod. 15) and Deborah (Judg. 5)—were composed around the twelfth or eleventh centuries BCE, but the process of composition continued through the second century BCE, when the book of Daniel was completed. Even then the books that would eventually become part of the Bible also had to be recognized as authoritative, official forms included in an accepted collection, and finally treated as a single corpus. As we will see, that process wasn't finished until the sixteenth century CE, after which it would take another century or two before the entire collection was given a specific name ("Bible"). In other words, as much as these books may have played a formative role in the development of Judaism, it was Jews who preserved, collected, and gave them authority. In one scholar's words, "Judaism is not founded on the Bible; the Bible is founded upon Judaism!"[17]

Writing

Although we are not sure how widespread literacy was in ancient Israel, writing was plainly an important part of its culture. The Bible requires a woman suspected of adultery to drink a ground-up copy of the charges against her that had been dissolved in water so that her innocence or guilt could be determined based on her body's reaction (Num. 5:11–28). Some of the prophets are said to have written down their teachings.[18] Others engaged in symbolic actions involving writing, as when Ezekiel ate a copy of his prophecies (2:8–3:3) and Zechariah saw an inscribed scroll flying through the air (5:1–4).

Both Israel and Judah had royal chronicles, and several of their kings are credited with having promulgated law books.[19] The Bible also mentions a Book of Adam's line (Gen. 5:1) and a Book of Yashar

(Josh. 10:13; 2 Sam. 1:18) as well as a collection of dirges (2 Chron. 35:25) and written regulations pertaining to governance (Deut. 17:18–20; 1 Sam. 10:25) and religious practice (1 Chron. 28:11).

Certain texts were considered holy. Although we do not know what was in the Book of the LORD's Wars (Num. 21:14), its contents were surely sacred, as must have been the Book of the Covenant (Exod. 24:7). Deuteronomy calls for God's teachings to be placed on doorposts and in the ark (Deut. 6:8 and 10:2; cf. Exod. 25:16 and 40:20).

Like their ancient neighbors, the Israelites believed that there were divine writings in heaven.[20] Some of these, such as a book listing human sins, apparently tracked events on earth.[21] So it is hardly surprising to read that God gave Moses laws in written form or that Moses and Joshua wrote down others.[22] These documents became a focal point in both the desert and, later, Jerusalem. However, that does not make them a Bible—a closed corpus of sacred works that serve as a community's ultimate authority.

An important step in that direction took place toward the end of the seventh century BCE, when a document called the Book of Instruction (*sefer hatorah*) was discovered in the Jerusalem Temple. This book was not a manual for a specific project, a sacred story, or a holy icon, but rather a repository of divine teaching. Most scholars think it was some form of Deuteronomy, which refers to itself as the "scroll of instruction (*torah*)," a term previously used for priestly teachings.[23] According to the book of Kings, Josiah, who ruled in Jerusalem at that time, responded to the discovery by enacting a dramatic reform that affected religious practice throughout his realm.[24]

Almost two centuries later, Ezra, who had come to Jerusalem from Babylonia, read a book to those gathered there (Neh. 8:1–8). Whether doing this was a new idea or the continuation of a practice that had developed during the exile, it marked an important step in the creation of a Bible. Biblical authors from this period make repeated references to *the book* of Moses's teaching (*sefer torat Moshe*) and frequently cite written instructions in support of specific practices.[25] As one example, the book of Chronicles tells of Solomon's recollection that God expected the royal family to follow God's *torah* (2 Chron. 6:16), where the earlier book of Kings had spoken of them as following God (1 Kings 8:25). Chronicles also supplements Kings' statement about Josiah's deeds being recorded in the Judean royal annals (2 Kings 23:28) with the assertion that they were recorded in God's *torah* (2 Chron. 35:26) and observes that the priest Jehoiada followed Moses's *torah* (2 Chron. 23:18), something not found in the earlier book of Kings (2 Kings 11:17–20).

The book of Daniel, which was written somewhat later, provides a valuable insight into the growing importance of sacred books when it attributes its expectation that the Babylonian exile would last 490 years to a passage in "the books" (9:2) rather than to the words of a living prophet.[26] That shift is also evident in the way the verb *d-r-sh,* which had previously been used for consulting God (presumably by means of an oracle), was now applied to consulting God's *torah.*[27] It is, therefore, not surprising that in the second century BCE, the Maccabees based their decision about going to war on sacred writings rather than on prophets, as earlier generations had.[28]

After defeating the Syrian Greeks, Judah Maccabee gathered copies of the books that had been lost (2 Macc. 2:13–15). Although his project is said to have been modeled on the precedent set by Nehemiah, there is no record of that having happened, making this the first reference to the collection of sacred works.

By the turn of the era, Scriptures were clearly a prominent part of Jewish life. Nearly a quarter of the Dead Sea Scrolls are biblical works, and even the non-biblical scrolls are filled with scriptural citations, as are the New Testament, the works of Philo, and the first-century CE Jewish historian Josephus.[29] Moreover, these books were important enough to be translated. The Greek version of the Pentateuch (the Septuagint) was produced during the third and second pre-Christian centuries, while the Dead Sea Scrolls include Greek versions of Exodus, Leviticus, Numbers, Deuteronomy, and the Minor Prophets, along with renderings of Leviticus and

Job in Aramaic, the Semitic language closely related to Hebrew that was prevalent at the time,[30] and commentaries on Psalms and several of the prophets.

Text

Several of the books that were included in this category existed in multiple forms. For example, the Greek edition of Jeremiah is structured differently than our Hebrew text, and the Greek versions of Esther and Daniel include several passages that are not found in Hebrew (or Aramaic) editions. Nor is that diversity limited to editions in different languages. The Jewish edition of the Pentateuch differs from that preserved by the Samaritan community, which traces its roots to the biblical period, as do the copies of Judges, Samuel, Isaiah, and Jeremiah that are preserved among the Dead Sea Scrolls. There are even variations between passages that are repeated in different parts of the Jewish Bible, such as 2 Samuel 22 and Psalm 18, 2 Kings 18–20 and Isaiah 36–39, and Psalms 14 and 53.

Clearly, biblical books existed in a variety of editions. It may, therefore, be misleading to speak of these as books rather than as collections or, as one scholar has put it, "larger, looser traditions of divinely revealed writing"[31] This is especially true for the book of Psalms, in which ancient manuscripts attest to a variety of arrangements; thus, traditions vary in how they divide the book of Psalms, with totals ranging from 146 to 159. Not until the Middle Ages was the dividing point between individual psalms firmly set.[32]

The later rabbis recognized that not all Hebrew scrolls were the same. They enumerate idiosyncratic readings in a scroll that belonged to Rabbi Meir and another that had been taken to Rome.[33] Even some of their biblical quotations differ from what is found in our editions.[34] They also mention scribal deletions (*'itturei soferim*), changes (*tiqqunei soferim*), readings (*mikra' soferim*), and corrections (*sevirin*), as well as places where the text should be read (*qĕrei*) differently from the way it is written (*kĕtiv*)[35]—modern Hebrew Bibles contain about fifteen hundred such cases.

Over time, certain editions apparently came to be normative. Thus, passages in a large copy of Isaiah found among the Dead Sea Scrolls that do not agree with our (masoretic) text have been corrected to bring them into conformity with our own, while biblical manuscripts from somewhat later that were preserved in nearby caves at Murabaat, Ḥever, and Tseelim all resemble our modern editions, as do several Greek translations from the same period.[36]

The process of establishing a normative text may have begun as early as the second century BCE, when a Greek document known as the Letter of Aristeas reports that the Greek translation of the Pentateuch was based on a copy from Jerusalem, presumably because it was believed to be more reliable than other scrolls.[37] Later rabbis tell of Temple funds being used to pay correctors, who inspected biblical manuscripts annually, and that the correct text was determined by comparing three scrolls in the Jerusalem Temple.[38] They also mention as particularly reliable a "book of the courtyard" (*sefer ha-azarah*), which was used for public reading, and *soferim*, whose job it was to count (*sfr*) the number of letters in Torah scrolls.[39]

It is noteworthy that during this same period, Greek scholars (*grammatikoi*) in Alexandria were establishing official texts of the Homeric writings.[40] Given hellenism's influence throughout the Mediterranean basin and the existence of a large Jewish community in Alexandria, such activities could have served as models for early Jews' interest in standardizing the text of their own holy books.

Lists and Categories

Although early Jews identified certain books as sacred, these were still not a Bible. Ancient references are consistently plural—"holy books" and the like—and our oldest copies are mostly individual books or small groups of works.[41] As one scholar observed, "The Hebrew Bible was a list before it was a book."[42] Evidence of that can be seen in the description of a trip that Melito, the second-century bishop of Sardis in western Anatolia, took "to the east" (i.e., Palestine) in order to find out which books were accepted there.[43] Two hundred years later, Christian authorities produced several such lists, as did the rabbis whose views are enshrined in the Babylonian Talmud.[44]

The Greeks had similar lists, called "canons," of writings they considered authoritative.[45] Athanasius, the fourth-century bishop of Alexandria, applied that term to the Christian collection, as did the fourth-century Synod of Laodicia, when it referred to "the canonical books of the New and Old Testament."[46]

According to the ancient rabbis, their sacred books had been inspired by the Holy Spirit, which they believed had left Israel shortly after the exiled Judeans returned from Babylonia in the sixth century BCE.[47] That may be why they were uncomfortable with a second-century BCE collection of wisdom teachings known as the Wisdom of Ben Sira and also Ecclesiasticus, since its author was known to have lived several centuries later. Although the book of Daniel had been completed in the same period, its acceptance was presumably due to its attribution to a survivor of the Babylonian exile.

Ancient Jewish sources group sacred books into several categories—most often "law" (*torah*) and "prophets," to which they sometimes add "hymns," "writings," "writings of David," "precepts," "wisdom," or just "others."[48] For much of the last century these groupings were seen as evidence that the process of canonization had taken place in three stages, with the Pentateuch (Torah) regarded as sacred by the time of Ezra, followed by the Prophets several centuries later, and then the more diverse Writings.[49] That would certainly account for the various names given the last section, as well as the fact that several books whose sanctity was disputed are included there. It would also explain why Chronicles and Daniel are in the last section of Jewish editions despite their resemblance to Samuel-Kings and the Major Prophets, alongside which they appear in fourth- and fifth-century Christian codices, as well as the different way each section is treated in Jewish liturgical practice. The fact that the Christian Old Testament included books not found in Jewish Bibles was then attributed to differences between the Jewish canons in Palestine and in Egypt, where the Greek Bible, which was adopted by Christianity, had been produced.[50]

However, all these conclusions have proven problematic. For example, archeologists' discovery of Greek translations of biblical books in Palestine raises doubts about the view that these versions originated in Egypt. In addition, several ancient sources refer to only two categories of Scripture—law and prophets or law and tradition (*kabbalah*)—rather than three.[51] Moreover, those terms can be ambiguous. Some writers use the word *torah* (or the Greek *nomos*) for all Scripture, or even the entirety of Jewish teaching, and not just the Pentateuch.[52] And many biblical figures, including Enoch, Samson, David, and Daniel, were considered prophets, suggesting that that term refers to a fluid category of non-pentateuchal works.[53] Judaism's three categories, like Christianity's four, may therefore refer to the arrangement of books that were already considered sacred rather than reflect the process whereby they achieved that status.

In any case, it would be a mistake to speak of a "Bible" in this period, at least in the sense of "a single book with a front cover and a back cover and a definite table of contents."[54] What ancient sources describe is a *category* of books that were deemed holy and authoritative (some scholars distinguish these two criteria), not a single, albeit composite, work.

Closure

Enumerations of books that belong in this category entail the recognition that other books do not. As the first-century historian Josephus explained, "We [Jews] do not possess myriads of inconsistent books, conflicting with each other. Our books, those which are justly accredited, are but two and twenty."[55] Early Church fathers cite that same number, though 4 Ezra and several rabbinic texts say there were twenty-four.[56] (Not coincidentally, Homer's *Odyssey* and *Iliad* and Hesiod's *Theogony* were each divided into twenty-four books, while both the Mesopotamian Gilgamesh epic and Rome's earliest legal tradition were written on twelve tablets.) Both of these numbers have symbolic value: the Hebrew alphabet has twenty-two letters and the Greek alphabet twenty-four.[57] Moreover, these statements need not reflect different contents. The book of Ruth, which is set "in the days when the judges judged" (1:1), could have been counted as part of Judges and Lamentations linked with Jeremiah, to whom it was often attributed.[58] More important is the belief that the number of sacred books was limited—in other words, that the canon was closed.

That is not to say that everyone agreed. The rabbinic warning that "Whoever brings more than 24 books into his house brings confusion into his home"[59] suggests that there were those who did precisely that. Even the rabbis disagreed about the sanctity of certain books. According to the Mishnah:

> The Song of Songs and Ecclesiastes defile the hands [i.e., are holy]. Rabbi Judah says that the Song of Songs defiles the hands but there is disagreement about Ecclesiastes. Rabbi Yossi says that Ecclesiastes does not defile the hands, but there is disagreement about the Song of Songs.[60]

Later rabbis noticed contradictions within Ecclesiastes and inconsistencies between Ezekiel and the Pentateuch.[61] Others claimed that the Song of Songs, Proverbs, and Ecclesiastes, which are traditionally attributed to Solomon, were purely human compositions,[62] and Esther was too nationalistic.[63] Similar concerns may explain why the story of Susanna, which describes a legal procedure that differs from rabbinic guidelines, is included in Greek translations of Daniel but not in Hebrew editions.[64] The books of Maccabees may also have been problematic, since they recount the achievements of a group vehemently opposed by the rabbis' forebears.[65] On the other hand, some rabbis quoted the Wisdom of Ben Sira (Ecclesiasticus) and *Megillat Ta'anit*, a first- or second-century list of dates on which fasting is prohibited, as scripture, despite others' insistence that the former, along with the works of Homer, gospels, and "outside books," was not sacred.[66] It is noteworthy that the Qumran community, which lived by the Judean desert site where the Dead Sea Scrolls were found, had copies of Ben Sira, the Psalms of Joshua, the Testament of Levi, and Jubilees, and may have considered some of their own texts, such as the Temple Scroll which presents itself as divine revelation, as authoritative, along with the book they called *Sefer Hagy*, though its identity is not clear.[67] Copies of some of these works were found there along with the books of Tobit and Enoch; the latter is also cited by the New Testament book of Jude (14–15) and recognized by the Orthodox and Ethiopian churches.[68] To this day, the Roman Catholic Old Testament includes several books that, though not recognized by Jews, are based on Jewish translations into Greek. (Protestant authorities removed these books during the Reformation, calling them "Apocrypha."[69])

Vowels and Punctuation

Although ancient Hebrew was written with spaces between words (unlike Greek), it had no vowels. Instead, certain consonants were used to mark long vowels that occurred at the end of words. Over time these *matres lectionis* (lit. "mothers of reading," i.e., reading aids) were included in the middle of words as well, albeit not consistently and with some representing several different vowels.[70]

There was also no system of punctuation, which made public recitation of the Bible difficult.[71] Although the Talmud takes the Bible's statement that the people who listened to Ezra's recitation of Scripture *yābînû* (lit., "understood," Neh 8:8) as a reference to accentuation, its warning that "one not wipe oneself with the right hand because one uses it for indicating Torah accents" suggests that the melody was indicated by hand motions.[72]

Medieval scholars, called "masoretes," undertook to ensure that the Bible was read in accordance with tradition (*masoret*), which Rabbi Akiva (second century) had thought of as protecting the Torah.[73] Their efforts may have been influenced by the Karaite movement, which emphasized the Bible, and Islamic treatment of the Qur'an; some masoretes may even have been Karaites.[74] After being prohibited from working in Jerusalem during the eighth century, the masoretes established a center in Tiberias; others lived in the Babylonian towns of Sura and Nehardea, where there were important rabbinic academies.[75]

The masoretes created symbols for vowels and punctuation, though it is not clear which came first or if they developed in tandem.[76] A comment by the Church father Jerome suggests that this happened sometime after the fifth century.[77] In fact, there were several different systems, as noted by the eleventh-century Maḥzor Vitry, which states that "the Tiberian vowels are not like our [Babylonian] vowels, nor are the two of them like the vowels in the land of Israel."[78] The Babylonian symbols were modeled on consonants and placed above the letters, whereas the Palestinian system used dots located above and to the left of the consonant with which they were pronounced.[79] Eventually, however, the Tiberian vowels prevailed, so much so that the other systems were not recovered until the early nineteenth century. Tiberian vowel marks also began with dots,[80] which were initially used with ambiguous symbols, such as the one which represents two different consonants that are pronounced *sh* and *s*, the letter *h*, which can indicate either a consonant or a vowel, and the letters *bet*, *gimel*, *dalet*, *peh*, and *tav*, which can be pronounced as either stops or spirants. Another symbol (*sh'va*) was used to indicate the absence of a vowel.

The masoretes also developed several systems of musical notation (*ṭeʿamim*), using "ecphonetic" symbols (neumes) to indicate phrases. Because these reflect syntax, they can be expressed with different melodies for different purposes or different occasions. The Tiberian symbols were most often placed over accented syllables, following a principle of "continuous dichotomy" in which each group of words is divided by a hierarchy of disjunctive marks, much like our period, semicolon, and comma. (A different system was used for the poetic books of Psalms, Proverbs, and Job.) Other marks indicate stress or separate names that are written twice, such as "Abraham" in Genesis 22:11, "Jacob" in Genesis 46:2, and "Samuel" in 1 Samuel 3:10.[81]

Producing manuscripts with all these features required several people. Scribes copied the consonants from existing scrolls, pronouncing each word as they wrote the consonants. A *naqdan* (vocalizer) then added vowels and accents, after which a masorete inserted marginal notes, placing more expansive ones at the top and bottom of each page. The finished product had to be perfect. Incorrect letters could be corrected, but sheets with four errors had to be rewritten entirely.[82]

The Dead Sea Scrolls and manuscripts of various Greek translations demonstrate that paragraphs were marked in antiquity. The masoretes distinguished those that began on a new line (*petuḥah*) from those that followed a space (*setumah*), the latter of which had to be at least nine letters long.[83] All of the Babylonian Sabbath *parashot* begin with one or the other of these.[84]

Other biblical books, except for the Song of Songs, Ruth, and Lamentations, are divided similarly; however, chapters were not indicated in Hebrew editions until the sixteenth century.[85] Although sentences, which the rabbis called *pesuqim* (lit. "breaks" or "interruptions"), were not marked in the oldest biblical manuscripts, the Bible's alphabetic acrostics (Lam. 1–4 and Pss. 9–10, 25, 34, 111, 112, 119, and 145) demonstrate that these were recognized in antiquity, though they too were not numbered until the Middle Ages.[86]

Even then, biblical manuscripts were not entirely uniform: Palestinian manuscripts differed from those in Babylonia, and Tiberian ones differed from those produced elsewhere. Within the Tiberian school, there were differences between copies produced by the families of Aaron ben Asher and Moshe ben David ben Naftali, and later between Ashkenazi and Sephardic editions.[87] One seventeenth-century masoretic scholar therefore lamented that "the Torah has become not two Torahs but numberless Torahs, owing to the great number of variations found in our local books—old and new alike—throughout the entire Bible. There is not a passage which is clear of confusion and error."[88]

Codices

Throughout this process, what we call "the Bible" was really a collection of sacred books. To be sure, the Pentateuch (Torah) had been understood as a single work since antiquity,[89] as had the twelve books of the so-called Minor Prophets ("the Book of the Twelve").[90] The rabbis also speculated about the possibility of including all the scriptural works on a single scroll, even mentioning a large volume (*kerekh*) in Rome,[91] but no scroll could accommodate the entire corpus of scriptural works. That wouldn't change until Jews adopted the codex format (a stack of pages held together at one edge), which originated in ancient Rome and China but didn't become popular in the West until the third century, and then only in Christian circles.[92] The earliest known single volume collections of scriptural works—Vaticanus, Sinaiticus, and Alexandrinus—were produced in the fourth and fifth centuries. All three are in Greek and include the New Testament as well as several works that were not part of the eventual Christian canon. Moreover, their purpose is not entirely clear. One-volume Bibles did not become common until the twelfth century.[93]

The oldest known Jewish biblical codex was completed by Aaron ben Asher's father in the year 856 CE and contains only the prophetic books.[94] It would be many years before the appearance of single-volume Jewish editions of the entire Hebrew Bible, most likely produced for the benefit of scribes and professional readers. The oldest complete volume is now in the Saint Petersburg (formerly Leningrad) public library. According to a notation at the end, it was written in Cairo in the year 1008–1009 by one Samuel ben Jacob, following the model of books that had been corrected by Aaron ben Asher.[95] As such it is the basis for the edition published by Stuttgart's Deutsche Bibelstiftung in 1977, which most biblical scholars use.[96] Its identification as a *maḥzor shel miqra'* (lit. "cycle of scripture") suggests that it, too, was understood as a collection of works that belong to a single genre.

Local tradition ascribed a volume called *Keter* ("the Crown" or *al-Taj* in Arabic) *Aram Ṣova*, which was kept in the Jewish synagogue in Aleppo, to Ezra the scribe.[97] According to its dedication, it had been copied around the year 930 by a scribe named Samuel ben Buya'a, with vowels added by Aaron ben Asher himself.[98] A Basran Karaite named Israel ben Saadia gave it to the Karaite community in Jerusalem. It was captured by Crusaders, but eventually came into the possession of the Jewish community in Cairo, where it was seen by Moses Maimonides. His description of it as "the well-known book in Egypt which contains twenty-four books, that was in Jerusalem for many years in order that books might be corrected from it and on which everyone relied because [Aaron] ben Asher had corrected it" established Ben Asher's as the most authoritative masoretic school.[99] From Cairo it was taken to Aleppo, where it remained until the synagogue there was burned down during a 1947 riot that grew out of events relating to the upcoming establishment of the State of Israel. Although initially thought to have been destroyed, it had actually been secretly transported to Israel; however, about one-third (including most of the Torah) disappeared along the way.[100]

With the production of these volumes, the Jewish Bible existed in two very different forms: scrolls, especially those containing Genesis through Deuteronomy with (almost) no marks; and codices of twenty-four books with vowels, accents, and masoretic annotations.[101] The fact that the latter are typically titled *Esrim ve-Arba* (lit. "twenty-four") suggests that they were still not perceived as single, unified works. That wouldn't change until the invention of movable type enabled Bibles to be mass produced, making them inexpensive enough to be "in every vulgar hand," as the poet John Dryden observed.[102]

Printing a Hebrew Bible couldn't have been easy. The Tiberian system, with vowels and accents above and below consonants, was particularly challenging, especially since Jews were excluded from Germany's printers' guild.[103] As the editor of the first printed edition of the Writings (Naples, 1486–87) explained, "We who are engaged in this art have only recently taken it up as beginners. . . . We have not yet had sufficient time to practice thoroughly as we ought in the matter of vowel points."[104] Nonetheless, an edition of Psalms with David Kimḥi's (twelfth to thirteenth century) commentary was produced in Bologna in 1477, just two decades after Gutenberg's Latin Vulgate, making it the first printed book in Hebrew. An edition of the Pentateuch with the Aramaic translation (targum) and Rashi's eleventh-century commentary followed five years later.[105] (It had extra *matres lectionis* but only sporadic vowels.[106]) Over the next fifty years printers produced twenty-two editions of Hebrew biblical texts, eight of which included the complete Bible.[107]

In 1483 a Jewish family from Speyer, Germany, set up a printing press in the north Italian town of Soncino, taking its name as their own. Five years after printing the talmudic tractate *Berakhot*, Joshua Soncino printed the first complete Hebrew Bible, leading some to proclaim, "Out of Zion comes forth the Torah and the word of the Lord from Soncino."[108] His brother Gershon moved to Naples, where he produced a smaller edition "in order that it be near all the people night and day to think on it and not go four cubits without the Torah . . . so he can read it when he lies down and stands up . . . just as he carries *tefillin* and not spend the night without it."[109] At last the Bible had become as portable as Judaism itself.

The Soncino press was soon eclipsed by one established in Venice by the non-Jewish merchant Daniel Bomberg. At first he hired Felix Pratensis (of Prato), an apostate Jew, to create an authoritative edition of the Bible. Following Christian practice, Pratensis divided the books of Samuel and Kings into two parts and included the Aramaic translation (targum) along with several commentaries. However, his religious status and the book's dedication to Pope Leo X doomed its acceptability to Jews, leading some to lament that "our inheritance has passed to the stranger" (Lam. 5:2).[110] Bomberg then hired the Tunisian-born Jacob ben Ḥayyim to produce a new edition.[111] Like Pratensius, he found the available manuscripts to be "utterly confused and corrupt."[112] His eventual edition included masoretic notes, not just in the margins but also in summary form at the end of each book, along with what he considered the most important available commentaries, all on the same page as the biblical texts to which they referred.[113] The resulting set, which came to be known as *Mikra'ot Gedolot* (on analogy with the Latin "Magna Biblia") appeared in the sixteenth century.[114] At last Jews had a definitive text of the Bible as well as easy access to their classic commentaries. What would come to be regarded as "the received edition" had been born.

A by-product of this process was the standardization of the sequence of biblical books. Although Melito and the Babylonian Talmud had specified their orders centuries earlier, it is not at all clear what that actually meant, since books (except for the Torah and the twelve Minor Prophets) were kept on separate scrolls. Some have thought that it referred to their placement in a list; others that it described their arrangement in a library or some other storage setting.[115] It might even have reflected the order of the periods they describe; the twelve Minor Prophets, the sequence of which appears to have been fairly standardized, do seem to be in roughly chronological order.

Jewish orders of the books

TALMUD	SPANISH MANUSCRIPTS	GERMAN & FRENCH MANUSCRIPTS	MASORETIC MANUSCRIPTS	PRINTED BIBLES
Genesis	Genesis	Genesis	Genesis	Genesis
Exodus	Exodus	Exodus	Exodus	Exodus
Leviticus	Leviticus	Leviticus	Leviticus	Leviticus
Numbers	Numbers	Numbers	Numbers	Numbers
Deuteronomy	Deuteronomy	Deuteronomy	Deuteronomy	Deuteronomy
Joshua	Joshua	Joshua	Joshua	Joshua

TALMUD	SPANISH MANUSCRIPTS	GERMAN & FRENCH MANUSCRIPTS	MASORETIC MANUSCRIPTS	PRINTED BIBLES
Judges	Judges	Judges	Judges	Judges
Samuel	Samuel	Samuel	Samuel	Samuel
Kings	Kings	Kings	Kings	Kings
Jeremiah	Isaiah	Jeremiah	Isaiah	Isaiah
Ezekiel	Jeremiah	Isaiah	Jeremiah	Jeremiah
Isaiah	Ezekiel	Ezekiel	Ezekiel	Ezekiel
XII prophets	XII prophets	XII prophets	XII prophets	XII prophets
Ruth	Chronicles	Psalms	Chronicles	Psalms
Psalms	Psalms	Proverbs	Psalms	Proverbs
Job	Job	Job	Job	Job
Proverbs	Proverbs	Song of Songs	Proverbs	Song of Songs
Ecclesiastes	Ruth	Ruth	Ruth	Ruth
Song of Songs	Song of Songs	Lamentations	Song of Songs	Lamentations
Lamentations	Ecclesiastes	Ecclesiastes	Ecclesiastes	Ecclesiastes
Daniel	Lamentations	Esther	Lamentations	Esther
Esther	Esther	Daniel	Esther	Daniel
Ezra & Nehemiah	Daniel	Ezra & Nehemiah	Daniel	Ezra & Nehemiah
Chronicles	Ezra & Nehemiah	Chronicles	Ezra & Nehemiah	Chronicles

Source: Adapted from Henry Barclay Swete, *An Introduction to the Old Testament in Greek,* 200, itself adapted from Herbert Ryle, *The Canon of the Old Testament,* 280; and Nahum M. Sarna, "Bible: Canon, Text," *EJ*, 4, 829–30.

In point of fact, the order of scriptural books had long varied, even after they were all included between two covers. Early Greek codices seem to have been arranged by genre, with the historical books (plus Ruth, which identifies its setting as the period of the

Judges) in chronological order, followed by groups of prophetic books (with Lamentations alongside Jeremiah, to whom it was attributed by the Septuagint and the Talmud), poetic writings, and finally didactic works. However, the Greek Sinaiticus and Alexandrinus codices place the prophetic books before the poetic and didactic books, while Codex Vaticanus puts them at the end of the Old Testament, with the Minor Prophets first. Jewish editions differ from both the Greek codices and the talmudic list, typically putting Chronicles at the beginning of the Writings and the Major Prophets (Isaiah, Jeremiah, and Ezekiel) in every possible order, with the Talmud listing Isaiah last, Ashkenazi manuscripts placing it in the middle and Sephardic manuscripts and masoretic editions placing it first. The Five Scrolls were not grouped together until the Middle Ages, presumably due to their use for major festivals. Even then, some manuscripts arrange them according to the order of their traditional authorship (Ruth, Song of Songs, Ecclesiastes, Lamentations, Esther), while others follow the order of the holidays on which they are read, beginning either in the fall (Ecclesiastes, Esther, Song of Songs, Ruth, Lamentations) or the spring (Song of Songs, Ruth, Lamentations, Ecclesiastes, Esther).[116]

The Five Scrolls

1	2	3	4	5
Song of Songs	Esther	Ruth	Ruth	Song of Songs
Ruth	Song of Songs	Song of Songs	Song of Songs	Ruth
Lamentations	Ruth	Ecclesiastes	Lamentations	Lamentations
Ecclesiastes	Lamentations	Lamentations	Ecclesiastes	Ecclesiastes
Esther	Ecclesiastes	Esther	Esther	Esther

Source: Adapted from N. M. Sarna, "Bible," *EJ*, 4, 830; and H. M. Orlinsky, "Prolegomenon" to Christian Ginsburg, *Introduction to the Masoretic-Critical Edition of the Hebrew Bible*, xviii–xix.

◆ ◆ ◆

THE BIBLE AS WE KNOW IT TODAY can, therefore, be said to have evolved over nearly three millennia. While its contents may have been composed and some of its books considered sacred during the biblical period itself, the final determination of which books to include, their texts and sequence, stretched over centuries. Some of these processes, such as the selection of books and the development of vowel and accent systems, happened within the Jewish community; others, such as the organization into sections, were influenced by both theological concerns, including Jewish-Christian debate and Protestantism's elevation of the Bible, and technological developments, such as the adoption of the codex and the invention of the printing press.

In that sense, the Bible as we understand it today is something of a latecomer to Jewish thought. It culminated in the adoption of the term "Tanakh," a Hebraized form of the Aramaic acronym *ʾ-N-Kh* which stands for *ʾOraita* (the Aramaic equivalent of the word *torah*), *Neviʾim* (prophets), and *Ketuvim* (writings), which the masoretes used to identify the parts of the Bible in which unusual features were found.[117] Not until two to three hundred years ago did it become a freestanding word. In that regard, it parallels the word "Bible," which originated as a Greek feminine plural (*ta biblia*, "the books") that only later came to be understood as a Latin singular ("the Bible"), thereby completing the process of turning the Bible into a single, unified work.[118]

THREE

Theologies of Scripture

AS WE HAVE SEEN, THE BIBLE'S CENTRALITY in Jewish life and practice is beyond dispute. Over one thousand years ago the Babylonian Talmud used it to support practices mandated by rabbinic tradition.[1] In our own time, Solomon Schechter, who is credited with having revived the Jewish Theological Seminary of America, spoke of it as Jews' "sole raison d'être," while Leo Baeck, leader of Berlin's Jewish community in the first half of the twentieth century, called it Judaism's "secure and immovable foundation, the permanent element amid changing phenomena."[2]

A significant factor contributing to that status was the Romans' destruction of the Jerusalem Temple in the first century which, as the German poet Heinrich Heine observed, made the Bible the Jews' spiritual and, fortunately, portable homeland.[3] It is no accident that medieval biblical manuscripts sometimes bear the title *mikdashyah* ("divine sanctuary").[4]

However, the authors of the biblical books made no such claim. Although various passages claim divine inspiration, only later did writers begin referring to scriptural works as collections of oracles and their authors as prophets.[5] That made it reasonable to infer that they convey a single, coherent message and for the twentieth-century philosopher Martin Buber to explain, "It is really one book."[6] The rabbis conveyed the same point when they chose prophetic selections that reflect the Torah's message to be read during worship, used passages from later books to introduce sermons on pentateuchal texts, and cited verses from each of the Bible's three sections as the basis for various teachings.[7]

Still, the Pentateuch was, and is, supreme in Jewish tradition. In Aaron ben Asher's comparison of the Bible's three-part structure to that of the Jerusalem Temple, the Torah emerges as the Holy of Holies.[8] And so it is cited far more often than other scriptural works by the sectarians who wrote the Dead Sea Scrolls, philosophers such as Philo, and, most obviously, the rabbis themselves.[9] As the sixteenth-century kabbalist Moses Cordovero explained, "There is nothing new that is not found in the Torah, neither the Prophets, nor the Hagiography, nor the sayings of the sages, nor what has been innovated and will be innovated from now forever."[10] No less an authority than Maimonides taught that all the non-pentateuchal books except for Esther would be revoked in the Messianic Age.[11]

Although the Bible credits Moses with having transcribed only certain legal provisions, that status was eventually extended to all the pentateuchal laws and, by the second century BCE, the book of Genesis as well.[12] Maimonides codified that position in his Principles of Faith: "We are to believe that the whole Torah that we now possess was given through Moses and that it is in its entirety from the mouth of God. . . . This Torah was precisely transcribed from God and no one else."[13] Over time, later works, such as Ruth, Song of Songs, and Esther, were also traced to Sinai; and, of course, the rabbis made similar claims for their own traditions and even those of later generations.[14]

However, Jewish thinkers have not been unanimous in their understanding of the Bible's role. While some emphasize its contents, others focus on its status, and still others on its function—in other words, what it says, what it is, and what it does. Even within these categories, one can find a variety of approaches.

The Bible's Contents

Easily the most pervasive attitude is that which sees the Bible as a conduit for revelation. As Rashi's grandson Samuel ben Meir

(Rashbam) wrote, "The Torah's main purpose is to teach us and inform us."[15] Centuries later, the Sephardic scholar Isaac Abarbanel explained that "the entire Torah and every single verse and letter in it is a principle and root which ought to be believed."[16] Joseph ibn Kaspi (fourteenth century), therefore, saw it as a vehicle for achieving intellectual perfection, while the Spanish community leader and philosopher Hasdai Crescas considered it an avenue to eternal happiness.[17]

These views take Scripture's content to be what matters. Hasidic tradition holds that even the white spaces convey meaning. As Levi Isaac of Berditchev (eighteenth century) explained, "The whiteness constitutes letters, but we do not know how to read them as [we know] the blackness of the letters. But in the future God, blessed be He, will reveal to us even the whiteness of the Torah."[18]

This idea—that the Bible is the repository of truth—has been understood in several different ways. Some have interpreted the Mishnah's statement that "everything is in it" (*m. Avot* 5:22) to mean that it contains all significant truths.[19] As the fifteenth-century Italian philosopher Judah Messer Leon put it, "Every science, every rationally apprehended truth that any treatise may contain, is present in our Holy Torah and in the book of those who speak by the Holy Spirit . . . all the sciences and truths of reason, including all that were humanly attained, for everything is either latent therein or plainly stated."[20] Thus, there are those who claim that it teaches science, while others more modestly suggest only that it is in accordance with science.[21]

A different view sees the Bible's message as theological. For example, Joseph Soloveitchik argued that "the Bible is not a book of stories, but a book of great spiritual message and way of life."[22] A dramatic version of this viewpoint is the kabbalistic belief that it contains hidden information about God. As Abraham bar Ḥiyya (twelfth-century Spain) put it, "Every letter and every word in every section [of the Torah] has a great, wise meaning with a secret and mystery from among the mysteries . . . of understanding which we do not have the strength to penetrate."[23] Judaism's classical mystical work, the Zohar, defends this position by pointing out the seeming triviality of much of the Bible's contents: "What difference does it make to us whether the ark rested in this or in the other place. . . . Perdition to anyone who maintains that any narrative in the Torah comes merely to teach us a piece of history and nothing more. If that were so, the Torah would not be what it actually is, to wit, the Supernal Law, the Law of Truth."[24]

Jews have most often located the Torah's essence in its commandments.[25] According to the ancient Alexandrian philosopher Philo, "The sacred scriptures are not monuments of knowledge and vision but are the divine commands and the divine words."[26] In keeping with that attitude, the ancient Greek translation of the Pentateuch rendered the Hebrew word *torah*, which has a broad range of meanings, with the Greek word *nomos* ("law"),[27] and the medieval *Tiqqunei Zohar* claimed that "without the commandments, the Torah is not God's Torah."[28] Thus the blessings recited in conjunction with various Jewish practices begin "Blessed are You, O Lord our God, King of the universe, who has sanctified us with His commandments *and commanded us to . . . ,*" thereby linking those acts to scriptural commands. This understanding also underlies Baruch Spinoza's depiction of the Torah as a national constitution, which Moses Mendelssohn regarded as binding only on Jews.[29]

Other thinkers, such as the medieval philosophers Maimonides and Joseph Albo, regarded ethics as Scripture's core message.[30] As the fourteenth-century French philosopher Gersonides explained, "The Torah guides us towards the [moral] perfection in many of the commandments."[31]

This emphasis on the Bible's commandments puts the role of its stories, especially those set prior to the revelation at Mount Sinai, into question. For Saadia Gaon, leader of the Babylonian rabbinical academy in Sura in the tenth century, they present model behavior, an attitude that has persisted to this day.[32] The midrash *Mekhilta d'Rabbi Ishmael* gave these stories a theological significance, for which it offered an analogy:

> What does this resemble? Someone who entered a country. He said to them, "Let me rule over you." They said to him, "What good have you done for us that you should rule over us?" What did he do? He built the wall for them, brought water in for them, [and] fought wars for them. Then he said to them, "Let me rule over you." They said to him, "Yes, yes." Thus, God brought Israel out of Egypt, split the sea for them, brought the manna down for them, brought up the well for them, brought the quail for them, made war with Amalek for them. Then He said to them, "Let me rule over you," and they said to Him, "Yes, yes."[33]

In other words, the stories that open the book of Exodus (and, more broadly, the entire Bible) are there to justify the laws that follow. As Saadia put it, "God has provided us with summary accounts of all that has transpired in order that we might thereby be put into a fit condition for obeying Him. These accounts were incorporated by Him into His Holy Book. He attached to them also His precepts and appended to the latter a statement of the rewards He would mete out for their observance."[34]

The Bible's Status

However important its content, this is not the only aspect of the Bible that Jews value. The Mishnah's warning that holy writings defile the hands demonstrates the ancient rabbis' belief in the sanctity of the physical Bible.[35] Some groups even conceived of the texts as alive.[36] However, the rabbis went further, as the Palestinian midrash *Genesis Rabbah* explains:

> The Torah said, "I was the craft tool of the Holy One, blessed be He." Normally, when a mortal king builds a palace, he does not build it by himself but with an architect, and the architect does not build it by himself but has plans and diagrams so that he knows how to arrange the rooms and how to arrange the wicket door. Thus, the Holy One, blessed be He, looked in the

> Torah and created the world. The Torah says, "In the beginning God created" (Gen 1:1); "beginning" (*reisheet*) refers to the Torah, as in the verse "the LORD made me as the beginning (*reisheet*) of His way." (Prov. 8:22)[37]

According to this midrash, the wisdom depicted in Proverbs 8:22 is the Torah, and therefore the Bible's statement that God made wisdom as "the beginning of His way" describes the Torah as the first of His creations.[38] From that the rabbis inferred that God used the Torah—which, after all, begins with a description of creation—as a kind of manual for making the world. They supported this conception by interpreting the word *b'reisheet* (lit. "in beginning"), with which the Bible begins, as meaning that God had created the world "*by means of* (*b-*) Torah (*reisheet*)."

For the Torah to have participated in creation it must have existed long before the exodus, which the Bible situates some twenty-six generations later.[39] As a result, what happened at Sinai was the transmission of the cosmic "Ur-Torah" (*torah kelulah*) from heaven to earth.[40]

If the Torah had existed since the beginning of time and assisted in creation, then it must be of universal importance, metaphysically vital and cosmically powerful. Such a Torah could hardly be a parochially Jewish possession. The rabbis, therefore, explained God's decision to reveal it in the desert as evidence that it does not belong to any one nation.[41] They even suggested that it had been proclaimed in four languages (or maybe seventy) in order to make it accessible to all humanity.[42] Only after Adam's sin did God decide to give it to the descendants of Abraham, who had observed the commandments even before they were revealed.[43] Others thought that God had offered it to all the other nations, which turned it down, leaving the Jews as the only ones to whom God could give it.[44] Even then God had to hold Mount Sinai over their heads, warning them that "if you accept the Torah, it will be well with you, but if not, you will find your grave there."[45] Meanwhile, the angels had wanted it kept in heaven, relenting only after God pointed out that its teachings did not pertain to them.[46] In fact, the Torah itself wanted to stay there, causing the heavens to weep as it descended and was accepted by Moses.[47]

It was important that this effort succeed. According to one rabbinic tradition, God did not create the world until He was sure that the Torah would be accepted; others believed that Israel's acceptance of the Torah held off the world's reversion to chaos.[48]

Jewish mystical tradition has sometimes equated Scripture with God, albeit most often with qualifications. According to the Zohar, "Whoever is occupied with the Torah, it is as if he is occupied with the Holy One, blessed be He,"[49] while the fourteenth-century kabbalist Joseph of Hamadan wrote, "The Torah is, as it were, the shadow of the Holy One, blessed be He . . . and inasmuch as the Torah is the form of God, He commanded us to study it so that we may know the pattern of the upper form."[50] Thus, a thirteenth-century Castilian treatise asserted that "All the letters of the Torah . . . are the shape of God."[51] Elsewhere it is described as God's cloak, which cannot be separated from divine substance, "like the grasshopper whose clothing is part of itself."[52]

The distinction between God and the Torah occasionally disappears altogether. The Zohar itself states that "the Holy One is called Torah,"[53] an idea that the thirteenth-century Italian kabbalist Menaḥem Recanati took to mean that "God is nothing outside of the Torah, neither is the Torah something outside of Him."[54] Although the modern philosopher Franz Rosenzweig warned against turning the book into an idol ("Buch Vergötzung"),[55] kabbalists identified the "real" Torah with one or another of the divine emanations (*sefirot*), describing the primordial Torah as the linguistic expression of the *Ein Sof*, the written Torah as the *sefirah Tiferet* (or *Ḥesed*, according to the *Sefer ha-Bahir)*, and the oral Torah as *Malkhut* (= *Shekhinah*).[56]

This idea is rooted in antiquity. As we have seen, the synagogue ark was originally a portable box that was brought into the sanctuary during worship and placed in a niche in the wall. The holy buildings of several religious traditions have such niches, which typically house the statues or objects that serve as the focal point of worship. Torah scrolls, therefore, occupy the architectural space usually reserved for idols. One ancient synagogue inscription even identifies the ark as "the receptacle of the Merciful (*taqah raḥamanah*),"[57] and 1 Maccabees observes that ancient Jews "opened the book of the law to inquire into those matters about which the gentiles consulted the images of their idols" (3:48). To this day, Torah scrolls are treated much like "idols"—adorned and paraded around in dramatic procession.[58] It is therefore noteworthy that their appearance during synagogue worship is accompanied by the recitation of verses such as Psalm 86:8 ("There is none like You among the gods, O Lord, and there are no deeds like Yours"), Psalm 145:13 ("Your kingship is an eternal kingship, and Your dominion is for all generations"), and Exodus 15:18 ("The Lord will reign forever and ever"), followed by Psalm 29:11, Deuteronomy 6:4, Psalm 34:4, and 1 Chronicles 29:11, all of which invoke God rather than the scroll.

Jewish thinkers have occasionally elevated the Bible above God.[59] Although most conspicuous in Elie Wiesel's accounts of rabbinic courts that indicted God for violating Scripture,[60] this concept has deep roots in Jewish tradition. A famous talmudic story tells of a discussion that took place after a session of the rabbinical court. Unhappy that his colleagues had rejected his position, Rabbi Eliezer ordered a carob tree to support his view, in response to which the tree moved from one place to another. When his colleagues remained unconvinced, Eliezer called on a river to demonstrate the validity of his position; however, the river's flowing upstream also failed to achieve the desired effect, as did the collapse of the study hall's walls Eliezer then called for. Finally Eliezer asked for heavenly confirmation. But when a voice was heard endorsing his position, Rabbi Joshua quoted the book of Deuteronomy: "It is not in heaven" (30:12). The talmudic narrator thus uses God's own words to prove that divine revelation is no longer determinative. What matters is Scripture's report of God's will, at least as interpreted by a rabbinic vote. This story even ends with God acknowledging the irrelevance of His own voice with laughter while saying, "My children have defeated Me; My children have defeated Me."[61]

The Bible's Function

Where the first two Jewish approaches to the Bible focus on its contents and its status, a third approach rests on the conviction that the Torah's value lies in what it represents. Thus Joseph Albo refers to the Torah as testimony (*'ēdût*), the vehicle for bringing God's presence into the world.[62]

It is this attitude that underlies the designation of the cabinet in which the Torah scroll is stored as an *'aron* ("ark"), an appellation denigrated by the Talmud, which prefers the term *teivah* (lit. "box").[63] The Bible uses the term *'aron* for the chest that held the tablets of the covenant while the Israelites wandered through the desert. They later took it with them when they went to battle and saw losing it as tantamount to losing God, while those who captured it suffered severe disruptions and its return occasioned great rejoicing.[64] This chest plainly signified God's presence, as is clear from biblical references to it as God's throne (1 Sam. 4:4) or footstool (1 Chron. 28:2), and statements about God's speaking from between or above the cherubs that were on top of it (Exod. 25:10–22, 37:1–9; Num. 7:89).[65] Speaking of the cabinet that houses the Torah as *'aron* thus links it to the desert chest, which symbolized God's presence. That connection is reinforced by the recitation of several biblical passages pertaining to that chest (Num. 10:35–36; Ps. 132:8) during the synagogue Torah service.

A similar view underlies the rabbis' comparison of the Torah to a marriage contract:

> It is like a king who married a woman and wrote her a large marriage contract: "I am making you so many state rooms, I am giving you so much jewelry, I am giving you so many treasures." He left her and went away to sea, staying there

> for many years. Her companions taunted her, saying to her, "How long will you sit? Take a husband while you are young and still have your strength." But she would go into her house, take her marriage contract and read it, and be comforted. After a long time the king came back. He said to her, "My daughter, I am surprised. How did you wait for me all these years?" She said to him, "My lord, O king, were it not for the large marriage contract that you wrote for me, my companions would have made me give up on you long ago." Similarly, in this world the nations taunt Israel, saying to them, "How long will you be killed for your God and give up your lives for Him and be murdered for Him? How much pain He causes you; how much contempt He brings over you, how much suffering He causes you. Come with us, and we will make you commanders and lieutenants and governors." But Israel goes into their synagogues and houses of study and takes the Torah and reads in it, "I will walk in your midst" (Lev. 26:10) and "I will make you fruitful and multiply you and establish My covenant with you" (Lev 26:9), and they are comforted. When the end comes, the Holy One, blessed be He, will say to Israel, "I am surprised; how did you wait for Me all these years?" And Israel will say before the Holy One, blessed be He, "Master of the universe, were it not for the Torah which You wrote for us, the nations of the world would have made us give up on You long ago." That is why it is said, "I call this [the Torah] to mind; therefore, I have hope" (Lam. 3:21), and thus David said, "Were not your Torah my delight, I would have perished in my affliction" (Ps. 119:92) and "I recall this [i.e. the Torah] to my mind; therefore, I have hope." (Lam. 3:21)[66]

This image implies that the Torah has no more intrinsic value than the parchment on which it is written. What matters is what it represents—God's commitment to the Jewish people which, the midrash suggests, can bring consolation even when events seem to contradict its assurances. As the modern philosopher Abraham

Joshua Heschel put it, "The Torah is not an end in itself"; what is "decisive is that which happened between God and the prophet rather than that which happened between the prophet and the parchment."[67]

Elsewhere, the Torah is described as God's daughter.[68] A memorable liturgical poem (*piyyuṭ*) tells how heaven and earth rejoiced when God arranged the Torah's marriage to Israel.[69] God is even compared to a committed (some might say overprotective) father, who follows His daughter after her marriage; in acquiring the Torah, Israel, therefore, acquired God.[70]

Because this approach does not require accepting the Bible literally or according it unique metaphysical stature, it has been especially attractive in our own time with its challenges to the Bible's authority. As Leo Baeck explained, "Mere scholarship, with all its ingenuity, only concerns itself with the outer shell; that which lives in the book is not yet revealed to it."[71] Instead, he believed that "the books of the Bible . . . are confessions of individual religious quests."[72] Likewise, Mordecai Kaplan, who founded Judaism's Reconstructionist movement, stressed the Bible's collective character as "the hypostasis of the civilization of the Jewish people."[73]

Noting that "revelation is not legislation," Martin Buber emphasized the Bible's power to provide a link to God.[74] In his words, the Bible is "the humanized voice of God, resounding in human idiom and captured in human letters"; as such it is neither purely divine nor wholly human, but the arena where the two meet—"the great document of the dialogical reciprocity between heaven and earth."[75] Or, as the twentieth-century rabbinic scholar Jakob Petuchowski later put it, "Jewish literature, beginning with the Bible itself, is full of love letters which the partners to this particular union have addressed to each other."[76]

Of course, dialogue was central to Buber's thought; that is why he insisted that the Bible not be read like any other book—not an "it," but as a vehicle for experiencing God as the eternal Thou. Using more traditional terminology, Abraham Joshua Heschel wrote that "as a report about revelation, the Bible itself is a *midrash* . . . [it]

is not a book to be read but a drama in which to participate; not a book about events but itself an event."[77]

This view is not a recent invention. Shneur Zalman of Lyadi, the eighteenth-century founder of Chabad Ḥasidism, explained that "the Bible is called *mikra*, for it summons (*kore*) and draws down revelation of the light of the '*Eiyn Sof* through the letters, although the reader may grasp nothing of their meaning."[78] Even earlier, the kabbalist Meir ibn Gabbay described the Bible as mediating the upper and lower realms, something to be experienced rather than explained.[79] Thus Heschel could speak of the Bible as "always being written, always disclosing and unfolding," an impression he found confirmed during the 1967 Middle East crisis, when "the Bible, we discovered, is not a book sealed and completed; the Bible lives on, always being written, continuously proclaimed."[80]

This understanding of the Bible as always being given has a long history in Jewish tradition. Deuteronomy asserts that it was "not with our fathers that the LORD made this covenant, but with us, the living, every one of us who is here today" (5:3) before quoting God as stating, "I am not making this covenant with its sanctions with you alone, but with those who are standing here with us this day before the LORD our God and with those who are not with us here this day" (29:13–14). In that spirit, the blessings that accompany the reading of Scripture during synagogue worship speak not only of God's past acts—having chosen Israel, given them the Torah, and laid the groundwork for immortality—but also God's present work: "Blessed is the LORD, who *gives* the Torah."[81] As the kabbalist Isaiah Horowitz explained, "The Holy One, blessed be He, gave the Torah, and He gives the Torah at every time and every hour,"[82] a message concretized in the widespread custom of having youngsters who are entering religious maturity stand before the ark while a scroll is removed and given to a grandparent to be handed to their offspring, who in turn gives it to their child who is becoming a bar or bat mitzvah, thereby transforming the covenant at Sinai from an ancient historical event to an ongoing experience.

◆ ◆ ◆

OVER THE CENTURIES JEWS HAVE DESCRIBED SCRIPTURE in a variety of ways—as the bearer of divine revelation, as an object of cosmic stature, and as a symbol of their relationship to God. They have disagreed as to whether it contains law or science, theology or ethics. Some have seen it as assisting God in the creation of the world; others allowed it to all but replace God in its governance; and still others understood it as a vehicle for experiencing God. Alongside those for whom it is of one piece have been those who insist on the primacy of the Pentateuch, all of which was given at Sinai, though the Bible itself describes later revelations.[83] It has been regarded as a gift from God, an expression of human striving, and even the mediator of Jews' complex relationship with God. At the same time, this diversity of views, which has existed in all periods of Jewish civilization, demonstrates the unyielding centrality of the Bible in Jewish life and thought, an anchor even when subjected to pressures from without or within.

FOUR

A Tale of Two Torahs

WHEN LEADERS OF JUDAISM'S NASCENT REFORM movement set out to modify the traditional prayerbook in the nineteenth century, several of their changes were more subtle than simply removing references to what they considered outmoded ideas, such as resurrection and the sacrificial cult. Among these was their moving the final phrase from the first blessing over the Hanukkah candles ("to kindle the Hanukkah lights") to the end of the third blessing ("Blessed are You, LORD our God, King of the Universe, who has kept us alive, sustained us, and brought us to this season").[1] This change was not a matter of style, but theology: since the events commemorated by Hanukkah took place after the biblical period, the first blessing's statement about God having "commanded us to kindle the Hanukkah lights" contradicted the Jewish teaching that all the commandments had been given at Mount Sinai.

That same issue had been raised a thousand years earlier, when the Karaite writer Jacob al-Qirqisani asked, "What is stranger than someone pronouncing a blessing over the Sabbath eve lamp and saying in the blessing that God commanded it? Likewise, over the Hanukkah lamp."[2]

In fact, the problem had already occurred to the ancient rabbis, who constructed much of Jewish liturgy. According to the Talmud,

> R. Ḥiyya b. Ashi said, "Whoever lights the Hanukkah lamp must pronounce a blessing." . . . What blessing does he say? This: ". . . who sanctified us with His commandments and

> commanded us to kindle the Hanukkah light." But where did He command us?[3]

As al-Qirqisani's reference to the Sabbath lamp demonstrates, Hanukkah is not the only Jewish practice not explicitly mandated by the Bible, nor is this problem limited to ritual practices. For example, the medieval philosopher Moses Maimonides recognized that the Bible's "eye for an eye" principle (Lev. 24:19–20; cf. Exod. 21:23–24) had been meant literally, even though the Talmud treats it as requiring financial compensation.[4]

Many Jewish practices actually originated with the rabbis, whose teachings are collected in the Talmud, and an assortment of other works written centuries after the biblical period. The rabbis were the intellectual heirs of the Pharisees, one of several competing Jewish groups that flourished in antiquity. As the first-century historian Flavius Josephus observed, the Pharisees had "passed on to the people certain regulations handed down by former generations and not recorded in the Laws of Moses."[5]

The Jewish community has been haunted by questions of the legitimacy of these nonscriptural traditions throughout its history. Early Christians, such as the Church father Jerome, charged that the Jews had abandoned God's word for human *deuterosis*, which the sixth-century emperor Justinian noted "is not part of the sacred books, nor was it handed down by divine inspiration through the prophets, but is the handiwork of men, speaking only of earthly things and having nothing of the divine in it."[6]

The rabbis acknowledged as much when they described some of their practices as "floating in the air with nothing to support them" and others as being "like mountains that hang by a hair with little scripture but many laws."[7] Nonetheless, they sought biblical warrants for these practices, as when the Babylonian Talmud reacts to mishnaic laws with the question, "What is the source of this rule?" to which it invariably responds, "As it is taught in Scripture."[8] On other occasions the rabbis simply acknowledged that "It is a rabbinical ordinance; the verse is just an *asmakhta* (lit. 'support')."[9]

Although the rabbis distinguished regulations based in the Bible (*d'oraita*) from those that are rabbinic (*d'rabbanan*), the distinction between these categories is not always clear. For example, they debated whether the marriage contract (*ketubah*) is rabbinic or biblical.[10] In the Middle Ages, Naḥmanides (Moses ben Naḥman) classified laws derived from the Bible by means of rabbinic interpretive principles as biblical, while Maimonides (Moses ben Maimon) considered them rabbinic.[11]

According to the ancient rabbis, some of the laws Moses received at Mount Sinai were not included in the Torah. An ancient rabbinic story reflects the paradoxical nature of that concept:

> When Moses went up to heaven, he found the Holy One, blessed be He, sitting and affixing crowns onto the letters [of the Torah]. [Moses] said to Him: "Lord of the universe, who is holding Your hand back?" He answered, "In several generations there will arise a man by the name of Akiva who will interpret piles and piles of laws based on each and every stroke." [Moses] said to Him, "Master of the universe, show him to me." [God] replied, "Turn around." [Moses] went and sat down at the back of eight rows but didn't understand what they were saying. His strength weakened. When they reached a certain matter, [Akiva's] students said, "Rabbi where did you get this?" He said, "It is a law of Moses from Sinai (*halakha l'Mosheh mi-Sinai*)," and [Moses] was comforted.[12]

In other words, Moses himself did not recognize all of the teachings he was said to have been given. In this, rabbinic tradition pays homage to the Bible by tracing its own distinctive ideas to Sinai and even calling Moses "our rabbi" (*rabbenu*).

This point came to be expressed in the assertion that Moses had been given two Torahs or, perhaps better, that separate parts of the Torah had been transmitted in two different ways—some sections written down in the Pentateuch and others passed on orally.[13] But both were considered Sinaitic. As the Sifre, a rabbinic commentary to Deuteronomy, explains, "The words of Torah are all one, and it includes Scripture (*miqra*) and Mishnah, Talmud, laws (*halakhot*), and stories (*aggadot*)."[14]

Other Jewish thinkers saw the Oral Torah as explaining the written one. According to the thirteenth-century rabbi Moses of Coucy, "the Torah was so very large that the text could not contain it. . . . Therefore, the Holy One, blessed be He, wrote a short precis of the commandments in the Written Torah and their explanation and details in the Oral Torah."[15] Still others regarded the Oral Torah as a fence (*s'yag*) that extends the Written Torah's regulations in order to protect Jews from violating its provisions.[16]

These two points of view—that the Oral Torah is either an expansion of the written Torah or a parallel set of regulations—have coexisted throughout Jewish history. The first underlies the ancient midrashim, many of which proceed sequentially through the biblical text in order to identify the various practices that are rooted in each passage, whereas the Mishnah's topical arrangement presents its contents as self-evident.[17] Sometimes the two perspectives appear side by side, as when the Babylonian Talmud classifies the practice of waving a willow branch on the holiday of Sukkot as non-biblical (*halakha l'Moshe mi-Sinai*) even though the second-century authority Abba Saul had rooted the ritual in Leviticus 23:40.[18]

Although the Written and the Oral Torahs were, in principle, equal in status, it was inevitable that one would come to be seen as more important than the other. The important one turned out to be the Oral Torah (which was eventually committed to writing). The Jerusalem Talmud explicitly states that "Mishnah takes precedence over Scripture,"[19] a position reflected in the Babylonian Talmud's teaching that "those who occupy themselves with Scripture are of indifferent merit; with Mishnah—some merit, for which they are rewarded; but nothing can be more meritorious than gemara."[20] This is also evident in the more stringent punishments assigned for violations of rabbinic laws than for violations of biblically based ones[21] and in the treatment of the biblical text during worship, where certain passages are read (*qĕrei*) differently from the way in which they are written (*kĕtîv*).[22] Although authorities generally decline to change the text in Torah scrolls that differs from the Talmud's citation of those passages, only the latter are regarded as binding for legal matters.[23] The early twentieth-century rabbi Abraham Karelitz (the Ḥazon Ish) even insisted that established Jewish law would prevail over any newly discovered text, even if such a text could be shown to have been approved by Moses or Rabbi Akiva.[24]

Although some authorities justified the Talmud's priority by noting its many biblical quotations, Natronai, who headed the rabbinic academy in Sura in the tenth century, pointed out that this attitude had led Ashkenazi Jews to abandon the Bible.[25] In the sixteenth century Rabbi Aaron Land asserted that "no Jew needs to study anything but Talmud; all other books are worthless, even the Bible" (lit. "the 24"); and the seventeenth-century German rabbi Joseph Hahn observed that "in our generation there are many rabbis who have never seen the Bible."[26] A widespread joke, therefore, told of East European yeshiva students who, when asked, "Where does it say 'In the beginning God created the heavens and the earth'?" were likely to respond, "In *Ḥagigah* and also in *Tamid*," the two talmudic tractates where that verse is cited.[27]

Christianity's adoption of the Hebrew Bible lowered it even further in Jewish eyes. While denying that the gospel message was present there, Jews could hardly ignore statements such as those of the second-century theologian Justin Martyr, who warned that the Scriptures are "not yours but ours. For we believe them, but you, though you read them, do not catch the spirit that is in them."[28] As a result, the modern Jewish theologian Leo Baeck observed that "the book which was a book of this people and a book for this people, now was to be a book against this people and was to belong to others."[29]

This attitude underlies a medieval midrash:

> Moses asked that the Mishnah be written down, but the Holy One, blessed be He, saw that the nations were going to translate the Torah in order to read it in Greek and say that they are Israel. So the Holy One, blessed be He, said to him, "Moses, the nations are going to say 'We are Israel, we are God's children,' and Israel will say, 'We are God's children,' and the scales will be evenly balanced." The Holy One, blessed be He, said to the nations, "How can you say that you are My children? I only recognize those who have My secret as My child." They said to Him, "What is Your secret?" He said to them, "It is the Mishnah."[30]

In other words, the reason the Mishnah had been transmitted orally was to keep it from being coopted by non-Jews in the way the Bible had been. That may also account for Rashi's explanation that the talmudic command to "keep your children from *higgayon*" means "Do not let them become too accustomed to Scripture."[31] Some yeshivas prohibited Bible study altogether, describing it as an "idol in the Temple."[32] It therefore came to be thought of as something for those who were not up to the Talmud, or even as a woman's book.[33] As the thirteenth-century *Sefer Ḥasidim* explained, "Study of the Bible is sometimes worthier than that of the Talmud—as with the unlearned or others who do not study Talmud but go and learn Bible, for if one did not teach them Bible they would not learn anything at all, neither Talmud nor Bible."[34]

Over time, Bible study came to be associated with heresy. As one rabbi put it, "Many biblicists whom we see nowadays are close to being heretics, since they do not know Talmud or the interpretation of the commandments."[35]

Back to the Bible

The idea that there are two Torahs was controversial from the start. Josephus tells of a first-century party called the Sadducees, who insisted that "only those regulations which were written down should be considered valid and those which had been handed down by former generations [lit. 'the fathers'] need not be observed."[36] Although often portrayed as heretics or sectarians, the Sadducees were not radicals; rather, the innovation was the Pharisees' adherence to non-biblical precepts.

This idea has been challenged several times over the course of Jewish history. The ninth-century Karaites took their very name (Hebrew *qārā'îm* or *ba'ăle miqrā'*, Arabic *qarā'iyyūn*) from the term for Scripture.[37] Although traditionally said to have originated when Anan ben David refused to accept his younger brother as the leader (exilarch) of Babylonian Jewry, the Karaites were more likely a coalition of several already-existing dissident groups that coalesced against those who had "abandoned Moses's Torah in order to go astray in the commandments of learned men."[38] As one tenth-century Karaite explained, "The rabbis' practice and their involvement in the gemara made them forget the LORD's Torah and the understanding of its truths."[39] Thus their slogan: "Search the Torah and don't rely on my opinion."[40]

Arguing that "every tradition which is not from the Bible is null," the Karaites rejected the holiday of Hanukkah, based their liturgy on the book of Psalms, and insisted that the holiday of Shavuot fall on a Sunday.[41] (The rabbis understood the Bible's command that it be celebrated forty-nine days after the *shabbat* in Passover [Lev 23:15–16] as counting from the holiday's first day of rest, which could theoretically fall on any day of the week.[42])

Christian authorities also challenged the idea of an Oral Torah, arguing that Jews had elevated human doctrine over that of God.[43] In 1240 Pope Gregory IX put the Talmud on trial and had it publicly burned.[44] Ironically, Protestant Reformers later leveled similar charges against Roman Catholic doctrine, using the Renaissance emphasis on classical sources to support their view that the Bible was the only legitimate basis for religious truth; they sometimes even identified themselves as Karaites.[45]

Sephardic Jews responded to the challenge of Karaism by developing a vibrant interest in the Bible, even borrowing from Islamic approaches to the Qur'an. A seventeenth-century Ashkenazi Jew therefore observed that "there is not one [Sephardic Jew] who isn't expert in the Bible, whereas among us Ashkenazim everything is the opposite."[46] This approach persisted among those who had experienced the Spanish Inquisition, among whom were the family of Baruch Spinoza, who was born to Portuguese Jewish emigres in Amsterdam. Despite having received a traditional education, Spinoza distanced himself from the local Jewish community, which excommunicated him for his "evil opinions . . . and abominable heresies" in 1656.[47] Spinoza devoted a major portion of his *Tractatus Theologico-Politicus* to the Bible, beginning with the premise, common in Protestantism, that "the knowledge . . . of nearly the whole contents of Scripture must be sought from Scripture alone."[48]

Spinoza's emphasis on reason, a central feature of the European Enlightenment, raised difficult questions about the Bible's authority, especially its miracle stories. Christian scholars responded by seeking the Bible's spiritual "core."[49] Some found that core in its moral teachings, which the British philosopher John Locke equated with natural law; others emphasized its literary merit, as when the German Johann Gottfried Herder spoke of it as incorporating "die ältesten, einfältigsten, vielleicht herzlichsten Poesie der Erde" (the most ancient, innocent and perhaps most heartfelt poetry on earth).[50]

Jews drew on Christians' growing appreciation of the Bible and the Enlightenment's emphasis on reason to elevate their social standing. Leading the way was Moses Mendelssohn, an observant Jew who became a model for Jewish integration into German society in the eighteenth century. He stressed the Bible's aesthetic virtues and oversaw the creation of a German translation that was intended to improve Jews' linguistic skills.

European Jewish writers continued to draw on biblical themes and characters, using a heavily biblical style that was built around a pastiche of quotes to ensure that "the tongue of the stammering might soon speak with elegance."[51] Journals of the eighteenth- and nineteenth-century Jewish Enlightenment (Haskalah), such as

Ha-Me'asef (a title taken from Joshua 6:9 and 13), also focused on the Bible. Echoing Christian caricatures, the movement contrasted the Bible, which the eighteenth-century maskil Isaac Euchel called "pure Judaism," to the Talmud's collection of "ridiculous traditions and far-fetched interpretation."[52] As the president of Vienna's Israelitische Allianz said, "We don't know it [the Talmud] and don't want it any more."[53] The Talmud was therefore removed from the curriculum of Jewish schools in Berlin and Bordeaux.[54] Thus, Heinrich Heine concluded: "As Luther had overthrown the Papacy, so Mendelssohn overthrew the Talmud; and he did so after the same fashion, namely by rejecting tradition, by declaring the Bible to be the source of religion, and by translating the most significant part of it. By these means he shattered Judaic, as Luther had shattered Christian, Catholicism."[55]

The Haskalah proved a passing phase, but it marked the Ashkenazi world's transition to modernity and laid the groundwork for much that would become characteristic of modern Jewish life, including Reform Judaism, Wissenschaft des Judentums (the academic study of Judaism), and Zionism.

Modern Biblicizing Movements

Efforts to reform Judaism began with sporadic changes to Jewish practice: recitation of the prayers in German rather than in Hebrew, reduction of holiday observance from two days to one, and occasional shifts of the major weekly gathering from Saturday to Sunday. To justify these decisions, leading reform-minded rabbis convened a series of conferences in the late nineteenth and early twentieth centuries, typically drawing on Haskalah ideas that emphasized Judaism's universal, moral, and aesthetic dimensions, which these rabbis anchored in the Bible. Thus, Frankfurt's (lay) Society of the Dawn (Lesegesellschaft zur aufgehenden Morgenröthe) proudly stated its intention of "not subscribing to Talmudical ceremonialism which segregated the Israelites from their fellow citizens. . . . How long," its leaders asked, "will the Talmud devotees confound the pure religion of an Isaiah, a Jeremiah, a Micah with the ceremonial religion of the Pharisees?"[56] And so, in 1842, that city's Jüdischen Reformfreunde (Jewish Friends of Reform) declared, "The collection called the Talmud, as well as all the rabbinic writings and statutes which rest upon it, possess no binding force for us either in dogma or in practice."[57] According to Baltimore's German-born rabbi David Einhorn, the Talmud's "morals are narrow; the exalted universal spirit of the Bible is strange to it; the letter into which [it] forces everything is its be-all and end-all."[58] These attitudes culminated in the Central Conference of American Rabbis' 1895 resolution that "our relations in all religious matters are in no way authoritatively and finally determined by any portion of our Post-Biblical and Patristic literature."[59]

As Isaac Harby, an early nineteenth-century Jewish community leader in Charleston, South Carolina, explained, the goal was "divesting it [Judaism] of rubbish and beautifying that simple Doric column, that primeval order of architecture."[60] To do that, the reformers emphasized the Bible's universalistic morality, which they found in what they perceived to be the prophets' ethical monotheism, a posture that persists to this day, as evidenced by the theme of the Central Conference of American Rabbis' 2011 convention: "Prophetic Voice in the Twenty-First Century."

At the same time, the Bible's credibility was being undermined by geological research into the earth's age, biological theories of evolution, and biblical scholars' literary and historical questions. As Ira Gershwin would later put it, "The things that you're liable to read in the Bible, it ain't necessarily so."

The most intense forms of academic research into the Bible took place in Germany, home of both the Protestant Reformation and Judaism's Reform movement. Scholars there found evidence that individual biblical books had been constructed out of separate literary strands, which they tried to disentangle in order to identify when each had been written. At the same time, archeologists were beginning to uncover evidence of the world in which the Bible had been created.

The significance of these efforts became evident in the work of two prominent German scholars. The first was Assyriologist Friedrich Delitzsch, who delivered a dramatic series of lectures in the early years of the twentieth century under the title "Babel und Bibel," in which he tried to demonstrate the ancient Near Eastern roots of biblical concepts such as the Sabbath and monotheism. As he explained, "Now that the pyramids have opened their depths and the Assyrian palaces their portals, the people of Israel, with its literature, appears as the youngest member only of a venerable and hoary group of nations."[61] Delitzsch saw the Bible's antiquity as evidence of its authenticity, but also its naïveté. In his view biblical religion reflected the "unsophisticated anthropomorphic conceptions that are characteristic of the childhood of the human race."[62] The implication was clear, even without the antisemitic tirades that emerged in the last of his talks: Israel's best teachings had been borrowed; what was unique was not good.[63]

Around the same time, the German biblical scholar Julius Wellhausen was drawing historical conclusions from the findings of literary analysis in a magnum opus that would dominate biblical studies for decades. Arguing that the legal sections of the Pentateuch had been written after the Babylonian exile, he distinguished post-exilic "Judaism" from the earlier prophetic teachings, which he called "Israelite religion."[64] In his mind Judaism was "a mere empty chasm over which one springs from the Old Testament to the New," a product of "the Pharisees [who] killed nature through statute . . . the 613 commandments of the written and the thousand other commandments of the unwritten law left no room for conscience."[65] He saw the Torah as having turned "the people of the word" into a "people of the book."[66]

For Jewish thinkers, these developments were deeply unsettling. Whereas Moses Mendelssohn and Heinrich Heine had expected Protestantism's elevation of the Bible to raise the stature of Judaism as its creator and transmitter,[67] some Jews considered biblical studies a Christian field.[68] The Central Conference of American Rabbis even described "the Bible [as] reflecting the primitive ideas of its own age."[69] One prominent Reform rabbi went so far as to remove both the Torah scroll and the ark from his Chicago synagogue.[70]

Several traditional rabbis retreated to the *derash*, which Meir Leibush ben Yeḥiel Michael (Malbim, 1809–79) called "the simple *peshat*."[71] Jacob Zvi Meklenburg (1785–1865), the chief rabbi of Königsburg, titled his commentary on the Bible *HaKetav vehaKabbalah* (*The Text and the Tradition*), describing the Written Torah (*ketav*) as the body and the Oral Torah (*kabbalah*) as the soul.[72]

Of particular concern to Jewish scholars were Protestant challenges to the reliability of the Hebrew text, the cohesion of biblical books, and their overall historicity. Thus, Sabato Morais, an early leader of New York's Jewish Theological Seminary, saw biblical scholarship as "insidious, aye, murderous to our creed," while Hebrew Union College president Isaac Mayer Wise called it "negative criticism," explaining that "Judaism . . . is Mosaic and Sinaitic or it is nothing." For his part, Joseph Hertz, chief rabbi of the United Kingdom during the first half of the twentieth century, described Christian treatment of the biblical text as the "barbarous vivisection of the Sacred Scripture."[73]

Equally concerning were the use of archeological discoveries to minimize Israelite creativity, the prioritization of ancient translations over the Hebrew text, and the portrayal of the Bible's legal component, which lies at the heart of rabbinic Judaism, as late and degenerate.[74] Solomon Schechter encapsulated Jewish objections to the entire project when he titled a speech he gave at the Hebrew Union College "Higher Criticism—Higher Anti-Semitism," noting how "every discovery of recent years is called to bear witness against us and to accuse us of spiritual larceny."[75] Clearly, many Jews felt that their Bible had been taken away. As the biblical scholar Benno Jacob put it, "Our Bible is no longer our Bible."[76]

Others pointed to Jewish scholarship's failure to address this new phenomenon. In part this was attributable to Jewish focus on the Oral Torah, but Jews' exclusion from the European theology faculties where biblical studies was centered had also contributed to a paucity of Jewish biblical scholars that JTS chancellor Cyrus Adler found embarrassing.[77] The editor of the *Jewish Encyclopedia* (1901–6) even explained the decision to assign most of the encyclopedia's articles on biblical subjects to non-Jews as being because "scarcely any Jewish writers have produced works of importance on this subject."[78]

In response, several early twentieth-century scholars sought to "repossess ourselves of our scripture."[79] Within the American Reform community, Kaufmann Kohler asked, "What but Jewish scholarship possesses the key to unlock the treasures of the Bible?"[80] Julian Morgenstern, Kohler's successor as president of the Hebrew Union College, argued that biblical scholarship requires "one who is not alien to this language from birth."[81]

Significantly, this was also the time at which Judaic scholarship was emerging under the rubric "Wissenschaft des Judentums" (lit. "the science of Judaism"). Although that movement is conventionally said to have left the Bible to Christian scholars, the reality is more complex. Leopold Zunz, who is usually considered the movement's founder, oversaw a German translation of the Bible,[82] while the great wissenschaftlich historian Heinrich Graetz wrote studies on Jeremiah, Ezekiel, Joel, Proverbs, Esther, and Ezra, as well as commentaries on Psalms, Song of Songs, and Ecclesiastes (though none on the Pentateuch or books devoted to Israel's pre-exilic history).

In fact, Jews had long paid attention to and even learned from Christian biblical interpreters, despite the theological tensions. Mendelssohn knew several Christian biblical scholars personally and did not hesitate to cite and sometimes emulate their work, as did Samuel David Luzzatto and David Zvi Hoffmann.[83] After citing several Jewish and Christian interpretations of a specific passage, Isaac Abarbanel even claimed to "find their [Christian] interpretations more satisfying than all the interpretations of the aforementioned Jewish scholars."[84]

Many of the Wissenschaft movement's leading figures had actually been trained in biblical studies, often under the supervision of prominent Christian scholars. For example, Leopold Zunz had studied with Wilhelm deWette, while Abraham Geiger, Solomon Mandelkern, and Jacob Lauterbach had worked with both Julius Wellhausen and Rudolf Smend.[85] Even Friedrich Delitzsch had Jewish students, including Richard Gottheil, Jacob Hoschander, Jakob Barth, Arnold Ehrlich, and Julian Morgenstern. Other Jews who had studied with Protestants included Esriel Hildesheimer at Halle and David Zvi Hoffmann at Tübingen.[86] That pattern would continue with American Jewish scholars such as Moses Buttenweiser, Kaufmann Kohler, Julius Lewy, Eugen Täubler, Bernard Drachman, Julian Morgenstern, Nelson Glueck, Sheldon Blank, Marcus Jastrow, Louis Ginzberg, and Israel Friedlander, as well as the Israelis Yeḥezkel Kaufmann, Martin Buber, Abraham Yahuda, Harry Torczyner (Tur-Sinai), Moses Zvi Segal, Umberto Cassuto, and Neḥama Leibowitz.

Nor did Jewish scholars reject modern methods or assumptions. As the Italian traditionalist Samuel David Luzzatto explained, "The Torah of God has no dread of light and is not afraid of true criticism."[87] Citing the talmudic interpretation of Noah's blessing, "Let Japheth's beauty dwell in Shem's tents" (Gen. 9:27 in *b. Megillah* 9b), David Zvi Hoffmann, rector of Berlin's Orthodox rabbinical seminary and author of an imposing refutation of Wellhausen that led one scholar to characterize him as "a Jewish St. George to Wellhausen's dragon," acknowledged similarities between the Bible and ancient Near Eastern cultures while advocating the inclusion of a "scientific approach" to the Bible in the seminary's curriculum.[88]

Other Jewish scholars used the same kinds of arguments as Christian scholars, albeit to reach quite different conclusions. For example, Nachman Krochmal (1785–1840), who was known as "the Socrates of Galicia," observed that late authors can be just as creative as early ones,[89] while Benno Jacob viewed compilation as a creative endeavor.[90] Franz Rosenzweig even suggested that the letter "R," which was widely used to indicate the compiler ("redactor") of the pentateuchal text, should be understood as *rabbenu* ("our rabbi").[91] Drawing on rabbinic tradition, the Italian-born Umberto Cassuto, who took a position at Jerusalem's Hebrew University in 1938, argued that the Torah's different terms for God reflected different aspects of God's personality rather than different sources,[92] while Martin Buber adopted a holistic approach that focused on the unifying nature of the book of Genesis.[93]

Still, those who accepted modern approaches were cautious. The prominent Bible teacher Neḥama Leibowitz warned that the *peshat* has the power to destroy the Bible's depth.[94] Zionist thinker Aḥad Haam refused to publish articles devoted to biblical criticism, which he regarded as assimilationist, in his journal *Ha-Shiloaḥ*.[95] Britain's *Jewish Quarterly Review* took a similar approach. These methods were also avoided to varying degrees at Zacharias Frankel's Breslau seminary, Cincinnati's Hebrew Union College, and New York's Jewish Theological Seminary, despite the latter's constitutional claim that "the Bible shall be impartially taught."[96] In Jerusalem, H. J. Chajes was rejected for the faculty of the newly founded Hebrew University's Institute for Jewish Studies due to his support for critical biblical scholarship; fourteen years would pass before the institute included a position in Bible, with the appointment of Umberto Cassuto to its faculty.[97]

Even such anchors of Jewish tradition as the masoretic text, which Solomon Rapaport had called "an iron wall," and the Pentateuch, which Alexander Kohut characterized as "Hands off!" were not exempt from Jewish critique.[98] The sixteenth-century Hebrew scholar Elijah Levita had rejected the antiquity of the vowel signs, a raging issue between Catholics and Protestants at the time, even as Italian scholar Azariah de' Rossi was accepting the possibility that ancient translations might rest on Hebrew readings (*Vorlagen*) that were more authentic than the accepted Jewish tradition.[99] By the nineteenth century, Isaac Reggio, Joshua Heschel Schorr, Samuel David Luzzatto, and Heinrich Graetz were all suggesting textual emendations.[100]

Although Alexander Kohut, an early faculty member at New York's Jewish Theological Seminary, dismissed source criticism as a "sharp knife which cuts the Bible" into a thousand pieces,[101]

Jewish scholars still accepted various elements of the documentary hypothesis, which, though taboo in Breslau, was taught at Berlin's Orthodox seminary.[102] Both Solomon Rapaport and Abraham Geiger divided the Pentateuch into sources, the latter relying on variations in divine names.[103] However, many Jewish scholars rejected the assumption that simpler religious practices are necessarily earlier than more complex ones, along with the corollary that the priestly source ("P"), with its extensive technical and ritual detail, was later than other pentateuchal components, which had led to the distinction between pre-exilic "Israelite religion" and post-exilic "Judaism." Nonetheless, Leopold Zunz regarded Leviticus, the most "priestly" of the pentateuchal books, as having originated after the Babylonian exile.[104]

The most prominent challenge to this idea was leveled by Yehezkel Kaufmann, who had been born in the Ukraine (1889) and earned a doctorate at the University of Berne (1923) before emigrating to Israel, where he taught at Haifa's Reali School and then the Hebrew University until his death in 1963.[105] Kaufmann's preeminent work of biblical studies, *The History of Israelite Religion,* followed the lead of scholars such as David Zvi Hoffmann, citing the priestly source's ignorance of Deuteronomy's hallmark teaching about cult centralization and its use by the prophet Ezekiel, who lived at the end of the pre-exilic period, as evidence that it had been composed before the Babylonian exile.[106] That position has since been supported by linguistic evidence and defended by an army of Jewish scholars. Kaufmann also traced monotheism back to the time of Moses and claimed that "the Bible is utterly unaware of the nature and meaning of pagan religion."[107]

Zionism

With Kaufmann we arrive at the most recent of Judaism's biblicizing movements: Zionism. Although fundamentally secular, its resonance rested on a centuries-old Jewish longing that had originated in the prophets' assurance that those in Babylonian exile would eventually return to the land God had promised, where their ancestors would dwell forever (e.g., Gen. 14:15). As the prophet now called Deutero-Isaiah put it, "The redeemed of the LORD shall return and come to Zion with singing" (51:11).[108] The power of these words became clear when the newborn Zionist movement rejected Britain's offer of territory in east Africa.[109] As Theodor Herzl observed, "If there is such a thing as a legitimate claim to a portion of the earth's surface, all people who read the Bible must recognize the rights of the Jews."[110]

At the time that Herzl made that statement in 1898, Jews were already establishing a presence in Palestine, often inspired by the biblical vision. For example, the young Russian Jews who had begun settling in Palestine a decade earlier called themselves *BILU-im*, an acronym based on the biblical phrase "House of Jacob, come, let us go" (*beit ya'aqov lekhu venelkha*, Isa. 2:5). Similarly, the first immigrant settlement in Palestine took its name, Rishon Le-Zion (1882), from Isaiah 41:27. Other creations of that generation—the town Petaḥ Tikvah (1878), the Mikveh Israel school (1870), and, most famously, the city of Tel Aviv (1909)—also drew their names from the Bible, just as contemporary Hebrew writers had based their coinages for modern terms such as "telegraph" and "telescope" on biblical phrases (e.g., Ps. 19:4–5; 1 Kings 5:13; Ps. 92:13).[111]

For Zionism, like other national movements, language was an important component of identity. The adoption of Hebrew as the primary language of the Jewish settlement (*yishuv*) strengthened its link to the Bible and thereby the historical basis for its claim to the land. Although never entirely dormant, the language had previously been confined to artistic and scholarly writing. Eliezer ben Yehuda (né Perelman), who is generally credited with its revival for daily communication, arrived in Palestine from Russia in 1881 vowing to speak only Hebrew, published a Hebrew newspaper and created a Hebrew dictionary. As he saw it, "Just as Jews cannot really become a living nation other than through their return to the land of the Fathers, so too, they are not able to become a living nation other than through the return to the language of the Fathers."[112] Although not all his proposals achieved acceptance, this approach endured, with the later Language Council giving preference to biblical Hebrew over rabbinic forms.[113] Of course, Israeli Hebrew inevitably evolved beyond biblical style, eventually leading the government to recommend that schools use a translation of the Bible into modern Hebrew.[114]

A second wave of immigration (Aliyah Bet) in the early years of the twentieth century brought many of those who would later become the state of Israel's leaders. They had rejected Eastern Europe's traditional (rabbinic) Jewish culture in a way reflected in the poet Saul Tchernichovsky's observation, "The mighty God who conquered Canaan with a whirlwind / now they have bound Him with tefillin straps."[115] Instead, they drew on the Bible, as described by the Labor Zionist Yitzchak Tabenkin, who explained that "the Tanakh is a spiritual reflection of an agricultural and military life, the image of a conquering people, a laboring people, a people of 'this world.'"[116]

This vision was embodied in the person of David Ben-Gurion who would become Israel's first prime minister. Born into a family of enlightened traditionalists, Ben-Gurion saw the Jewish religion as a diaspora phenomenon that was spiritually impoverished, "not because our creative power had atrophied . . . but because we had been torn from the source of our people's vitality, their independent homeland."[117] Ben-Gurion believed that the Jewish people had survived that trauma because "a secret resource safeguards our existence and uniqueness. . . . This is our Bible, which has given us the strength to remain steadfast in the face of hostile forces and influences that have threatened our national and spiritual integrity."[118]

Ben-Gurion saw the land of Israel and the Bible as interdependent: "When we went into exile, our people was uprooted from the soil in which the Book grew."[119] "Throughout the hundreds of years of wandering, scattered Jewry was accompanied by the Book of Books and by its promise of redemption and return to Zion; a promise of making desolation bloom and an ingathering of exiles."[120] "I believe that the inspiration of the Bible sustained us, returned us to the land, and created the state."[121] He therefore called on Jews to reject "narrow-minded" Yiddish in favor of "the continuation of the revolutionary thought of the Bible"[122] and, in 1937, testified to Great Britain's Peel Commission that "the Bible . . . is our mandate."[123] Ben-Gurion maintained his attachment to the Bible—"the greatest masterpiece of the Hebrew people to this very day"[124]—after becoming prime minister. He joined the World Jewish Bible Society, which still sponsors an international Bible contest on Israel's Independence Day, and hosted biweekly Bible study groups in his house.[125]

The military hero and later political leader Moshe Dayan also connected his endeavors (including his sometimes controversial activities) to the fact that his "parents who came from another country [during Aliyah Bet] sought to make the Israel of their imagination, drawn from descriptions in the Bible, their physical homeland. In somewhat the reverse way, I sought to give my real and tangible homeland the added dimension of historical depth, to bring to life the strata of the past which now lay beneath the desolate ruins and archaeological mounds—the Israel of our patriarchs, our judges, our kings, our prophets." "I was not content only with the Israel I could see and touch, I also longed for the Israel of antiquity, the Israel of the 'timeless verses' and the 'biblical names.'"[126] This attitude was concretized in the adoption of biblical names for new Jewish settlements, beginning with the state's own name ("Israel"), especially in the first generation after 1948, alongside its absorption of Jewish immigrants and sense of Zionism as a restoration.[127]

Israeli schools transmitted these attitudes, institutionalizing the recitation of a Bible verse every day already in the beginning of the *yishuv*. By the 1920s, 16 percent of each elementary school day was devoted to studying the Bible.[128] Following the Haskalah pattern, priority in biblical study was given the Prophets, with the Torah left to the Orthodox.[129] Already in 1892 required Bible study began with the book of Joshua and continued through Isaiah, emphasizing the monarchy period's military and political orientation along with the conquest-and-redemption pattern that was central to Israeli self-definition.[130] This approach also reflected the socialist values of the Second Aliyah (1904–14), particularly the new settlers' aim to make Israel "a light to the nations." That goal came to be enshrined in the 1948 Proclamation of Independence, which asserted: "The state of Israel . . . will be based on the principles of liberty, justice, and peace as conceived by the Prophets of Israel."[131]

Remarkably, the Bible became a tool for secularization, replacing traditional religious values with historical connections in a process that had begun already in Zionism's earliest stages. Although the BILU slogan "House of Jacob, come and let us go" was taken from the book of Isaiah (2:5), it leaves off the prophet's closing words: "To the house of the LORD." Similarly, Ben-Gurion proclaimed the Sabbath to be *labor*'s day of rest, the Israeli army was described as Israel's guardian (cf. Ps. 121:4), and Hebrew University's (secular) Institute of Jewish Studies inaugurated with the recitation of "for instruction (Torah) shall come forth from Zion" (Isa. 2:3).[132]

Ben-Gurion's right-wing rivals also appropriated the Bible. The Stern Gang (Leḥi) based its expansive vision of the nation as reaching from the Nile to the Euphrates on the Bible's patriarchal promise (Gen. 15:18). After Israel's dramatic victory in the 1967 Six-Day War, the Orthodox community revived this approach when Zvi Yehudah Kook, the son of Jewish Palestine's first Ashkenazi chief rabbi, linked the state to the Bible's prophetic vision, and Gush Emunim, a religious group committed to expanding the Jewish presence on the Jordan River's west bank, called the region by the biblical terms Judea and Samaria.[133] Orthodox settlers even chose biblical place names for settlements in occupied territories.[134] Other right-wing leaders applied the biblical mandate to "drive them out" (Exod. 23:30) to the region's Arab inhabitants, whom they identified with the biblical Amalekites.[135]

Relinking the Oral and Written Torahs

Throughout Jewish history traditional leaders have responded to biblicizing movements by emphasizing the connection between the written and the oral traditions. The medieval scholar Saadia Gaon challenged Karaite claims by insisting that the Bible could not be understood without the oral (rabbinic) tradition.[136] As we have seen, nineteenth-century traditionalists such as Jacob Zvi Meklenburg rejected Reform views by emphasizing the interdependence of Judaism's written and oral Torahs. As he put it, "the written and the oral Torah are twins."[137]

In the end several of the Jewish biblicizing movements changed course with regard to their emphasis on the Bible alone. According to one source, the Sadducees had a "Book of Decrees (*sefer gezerata*)."[138] Nor were the medieval Karaites the pure biblicists that their name and reputation suggest. A prominent opponent reports that Anan had beseeched his followers to "forsake the words of the Mishnah and the Talmud, and I will make you a Talmud of my own,"[139] hardly the cry of someone committed to the Bible alone. Over time they even accepted several rabbinic practices, such as a fixed calendar rather than actual observation of the moon, the Passover Haggadah, and lighting Sabbath candles, while employing characteristically rabbinic interpretive principles.[140]

Later still, Isaac Mayer Wise, the nineteenth-century founder of Reform Judaism's major American institutions, called himself "a Talmudical Jew" and insisted that "all Biblical law still in practice shall be practiced according to Talmudical interpretation."[141] In fact, that position had already been endorsed by the 1855 Cleveland Conference of rabbis when it approved Wise's statement that "the Talmud is . . . the legal and obligatory commentary of the Bible."[142] In 1937 the Reform movement's Central Conference of American Rabbis declared: "Revelation is a continuous process. . . . The Torah, both written and oral, enshrines Israel's ever-growing consciousness of God and the moral law . . . as a depository of permanent spiritual ideals."[143] Reform leaders even cited the Talmud as the prototype for their program of reform, inasmuch as it had "broken the inflexibility of the Biblical letter . . . [and] *reformed* the Mosaic law in its most vital aspect" (emphasis added).[144] In that spirit, Abraham Cronbach, longtime professor of Jewish social studies at the movement's Hebrew Union College, portrayed Jewish history as one long series of reform movements.[145]

The Oral Torah thus prevailed, even among those who rejected it in principle. To be sure, the rabbis did not understand themselves as advocating a second Torah; rather, they saw the Oral Torah as linked to the Written Torah, whether as a partner or an explanation. Maimonides even tied each of Judaism's 613 commandments to a biblical verse.[146] That, in the end, was the point of tracing all revelation to Sinai.

In other words, whatever the rhetoric, Judaism has fundamentally held that there is only one Torah with one revelation, though its contents may be divided into separate parts that have been transmitted in different ways. In doing this, proponents of the Oral Law acknowledge the written tradition as their model and concede its authority. The Bible—itself a product of rabbinic Judaism—thus serves as "a source of living waters, a wellspring of an everlasting flow,"[147] providing rabbinic Judaism with its legitimacy and the Jewish people with their memories and hopes. Still, normative Judaism sees the Oral Torah as providing the correct understanding of the written word. Thus, as one modern Jewish scholar has observed, "in many respects, the Torah, and indeed the whole Bible, has been marginalized in Judaism . . . placed on a pedestal . . . yoked to the rabbinic system that it serves . . . a king or queen in captivity."[148]

FIVE

The Bible's Many Meanings

JUDAISM'S GROUNDING IN SACRED WRITINGS CREATED several problems. As time passed, old texts could be difficult to understand while new practices emerged that were different from those mandated by Scripture. Jews therefore sought ways to clarify obscurities, harmonize contradictions, and apply the sacred text to the needs of later generations. As one rabbi explained, the Torah was given to be interpreted.[1]

That process was underway already toward the end of the biblical period. The book of Chronicles, which draws heavily on Samuel and Kings, reflects changes in the Hebrew language as its author replaced older words, such as *mamlakha* ("kingship") and *gufah* ("corpse"), with their later equivalents, *malkhut* and *geviyah*.[2] He also tried to resolve inconsistencies, such as 1 Samuel's attribution of Goliath's death to David (17:48–51) rather than to his soldier Elhanan as it appears in 2 Samuel (21:19), by crediting Elhanan with having killed Goliath's brother (1 Chron. 20:5). Similar concerns underlie 2 Chronicles' strange statement that the Passover sacrifice should be "boiled in fire" (35:13), which blends Deuteronomy's insistence that it be boiled (16:7) with Exodus's requirement that it be "roasted over fire" (12:9).

Elsewhere, Chronicles adds explanatory information that is not in its sources. For example, it specifies which of David's sons would succeed him (1 Chron. 28:3–6), a detail not mentioned in the book of Samuel (2 Sam. 7:12). It also tells that Judah's King Manasseh had repented while in Babylonian captivity (2 Chron.

33:12) in order to account for that evil king's long reign.[3] Conversely, it omits some of its heroes' problematic behavior, such as David's affair with Bathsheba and the various uprisings that took place during his reign, while "updating" its theology, as when it blames Satan for David's apparently sinful census (1 Chron. 21:1) rather than God, as in 2 Samuel (24:1).

Although Chronicles' reliance on Samuel and Kings provides a unique opportunity to see how later authors addressed problems in their sacred sources, the phrasing in other biblical books suggests efforts to explain earlier traditions. For example, the book of Esther follows references to "the first month" and "the twelfth month" with the words "that is, Nisan" (3:7) and "that is, Adar" (9:1), which may have been inserted to "update" these months' earlier designations with their later names.[4] That may also account for the comment "that is, *goral*" following the Assyrian word *pur*, both of which mean "lot" (3:7 and 9:24). Similar phrasing is found in the books of Genesis and Joshua, which follow their reference to "the Shaveh Valley" with the explanation "that is, the king's valley" (Gen. 14:17) and "Luz" with "that is, Bethel" (Josh. 18:13).

Alongside these scribal efforts to explain sacred traditions both linguistically and theologically, biblical authors also clarified practices they thought their audience might not understand. For example, the narrator of the tower of Babel story follows the statement about the tower being built out of brick with the explanation that "they used brick for stone and bitumen for mortar" (Gen. 11:3), presumably because he thought that his audience would be unfamiliar with the Mesopotamian use of brick and bitumen as building materials. So, too, the book of Samuel interrupts its account about Saul's seeking a seer's help in finding his father's donkeys with the comment, "Formerly in Israel when a man went to inquire of God he would say, 'Come, let us go to the seer,' for the prophet of today was formerly called a seer" (1 Sam. 9:9).

The book of Psalms demonstrates another way in which the Bible provides background information, with editors adding headings to identify the authors or historical circumstances under which these poems were thought to have been composed. For example, the introduction about Psalm 51 having been composed by David "when Nathan the prophet came to him after he had come to Bathsheba" may be due to the words "I have sinned" in verse 6, which also occur in 2 Samuel 12:13; similarly, Psalm 90 may have been attributed to Moses because of its reference to God's wrath (vv. 7, 9, and 11) and its plea, "How long" (v. 13), both of which echo Moses's statements in Exodus 32:10–13.[5]

Elsewhere, biblical authors present events in ways that evoke earlier incidents, an approach that medieval scholars called "typological." For example, the description of Joshua as having split the Jordan River (Josh. 3:4–17) and removed his shoes (5:15) calls to mind Moses's actions at the burning bush and the Red Sea (Exod. 3:5, 14:21). So, too, the book of Kings reports that Elijah spent forty days on Mount Horeb (1 Kings 19:8), which is another name for Sinai. Similarly, several prophets described their expectation that God would restore the Judeans from Babylonian exile in ways that recall the exodus from Egypt, as when Isaiah 43 reports, "Thus said the LORD who made a road through the sea and a path through mighty waters, who destroyed chariots and horses . . . 'I will make a road through the wilderness and rivers in the desert'" (vv. 16–19).

Post-Biblical Interpretation

Later generations continued these efforts to clarify and update biblical texts, harmonize apparent contradictions, and draw ethical and theological lessons from them as well as insights into what the future would be. Their interpretations can be found in several different genres, ranging from prayers and sermons to mystical texts and legal codes, as well as artistic compositions and philosophical and grammatical treatises. Literary, poetic, and musical retellings of biblical passages were prominent in both the Ashkenazi and Sephardic worlds.[6] Thus even though the medieval sage Moses Maimonides never fulfilled his plan to write a commentary on the Bible, much of his classic *Guide of the Perplexed* is really an exposition of Scripture.[7] Some of these works, such as the Babylonian Talmud and the New Testament, even came to be regarded as canonical by Jewish and Christian authorities.

Two formats that proved particularly popular were retellings and passage-by-passage explanations of biblical passages. The Bible itself contains examples of both. We have already seen explanatory glosses in the books of Genesis, Samuel, and Esther, while Chronicles recounts much of what is in Samuel and Kings, as does Deuteronomy for many of the laws found in earlier pentateuchal books. Retelling biblical accounts became popular during the last few pre-Christian centuries and the first centuries CE (the "intertestamental period"), when the book of Jubilees, Josephus's *Antiquities*, and the *Biblical Antiquities*, traditionally though incorrectly attributed to Philo (hence sometimes called "Pseudo-Philo"), were composed. The Dead Sea Scrolls include several similar works, such as the Genesis Apocryphon and the Temple Scroll. This format continued with later rabbinic texts such as the (eighth century) *Pirqei deRabbi Eliezer* and innumerable medieval and modern works, ranging from dramas to poems and musical compositions. It is still used in our own time, as in Anita Diamant's popular novel *The Red Tent*, Joseph Heller's *God Knows*, and Stefan Heym's *The King David Report*.[8]

The commentary format, in which each line of the biblical text ("lemma") is explained in sequence, resembles those biblical passages in which old place names are followed by the phrase "that is" and then a presumably more current term. Several of the Dead Sea Scrolls use a similar approach, proceeding through biblical texts (most often prophetic books) with each phrase followed by the term *pishro* ("its meaning is") and then an explanation of the passage.[9] Interestingly, the book of Daniel uses the Aramaic cognate of that very word to introduce its interpretation of visions, suggesting that later authors may have understood biblical passages as symbolic forms of divine communication, like dreams.[10]

This format has been popular throughout Jewish history. The first-century philosopher Philo used it for several of his works, as did later rabbinic midrashim, the medieval Zohar, and biblical scholars such as Rashi and Abraham ibn Ezra (twelfth century). The medieval masoretes put their textual notes in the margins of biblical manuscripts alongside the relevant passages. That pattern persists to this day in the Bibles intended for synagogue use. For the better part of the twentieth century American Jews followed Scripture reading with the commentary of Joseph Hertz, chief rabbi of the British Empire, although each of the major American movements and the Jewish Publication Society have now produced commentaries of their own, with several others underway in Israel.[11]

Gershom Scholem, the preeminent twentieth-century scholar of Jewish mysticism, described interpretation as "the characteristic expression of Jewish thinking about truth."[12] Interpretive works have sometimes even been granted the status of revelation, most obviously in the case of Deuteronomy and Chronicles, but also by the authors and readers of later works, such as Jubilees and the Temple Scroll. The Dead Sea Scrolls' commentary on the prophet Habakkuk even claims to contain the inspired message of that community's "Teacher of Righteousness, to whom God made known all the mysteries of the words of His servants the prophets,"[13] much as rabbinic Judaism teaches that the Oral Torah was revealed at Sinai. The sixteenth-century Galli Razaya considered Rashi's commentary to be inspired.[14]

Multiple Meanings (Polyvalence)

Thinkers throughout Jewish history have taught that biblical passages can have several different meanings. Already the Dead Sea Scrolls distinguished passages' revealed (*nigleh*) and hidden (*nistar*) meanings.[15] Moses Maimonides made a similar point using the Arabic terms *bâṭin* (inner) and *zâhir* (outer), while Moses Mendelssohn contrasted the "first" (*peshat*) and "second (*derash*) intention."[16]

Rabbinic and medieval interpreters concretized that view, providing biblical phrases with several different meanings, as when a midrash explains the word *hiqriv* in Numbers 7:18 to be simultaneously imperative ("Offer!"), causative (Moses "forced him to offer"), and past ("he offered").[17] The Talmud even honored those who could offer multiple interpretations, whether Manasseh's 55 or Moses's 2,401 (= 49x49).[18] The modern scholar Cyrus Gordon described what he called "Janus parallelism" in which a single word can simultaneously have two different meanings, one with respect to what precedes it and the other with regard to what follows.[19]

The rabbis rooted this approach in Jeremiah's comparison of God's word to a hammer that can shatter a rock into numerous pieces (23:29).[20] As one midrash explains, "If the contents of a dream, which neither raises nor lowers, can have many meanings, how much more should the Torah's important contents convey many interpretations in each verse."[21]

Authorities have disagreed about the number of meanings each passage can have. Where Philo and Maimonides distinguished two, the philosopher Joseph ibn Aqnin (twelfth- to thirteenth-century North Africa) identified three (the literal, the aggadic, and the philosophical-allegorical), while the Zohar listed seven ("the literal meaning, the homiletical meaning, the mystery of wisdom, numerical values, hidden mysteries, still deeper mysteries, and the laws of fit and unfit, forbidden and permitted, and clean and unclean"[22]). The sixteenth-century mystic Isaac Luria cited a view which held that there are six hundred thousand meanings—the same number as that of (adult male) Israelites who came out of Egypt—suggesting that each Jew can have his (or her) own interpretation.[23] However, the most prevalent tradition speaks of four, though the specific categories vary.[24] That number, which matches a long-standing Christian view, was formalized in the term *pardes*, an acronym for *peshat* (straightforward), *remez* (allegorical), *derash* (homiletical), and *sod* (mystical).[25]

It is important to understand that these are not alternative possibilities but rather multiple meanings, each with its own value and legitimacy. Philo compared the allegorical and historical meanings to the body and the soul, explaining that "exactly as we have to take thought for the body, because it is the abode of the soul, so must we pay heed to the letter of the laws. If we keep and observe these, we shall gain a clearer conception of those things of which these are the symbols."[26] Centuries later, Samuel ben Meir (Rashbam), who emphasized the *peshat* more strongly than any other medieval interpreter, insisted that the *derash* is more important.[27] Jewish mystics did not reject the *peshat* but, like the rationalist philosopher Maimonides, saw it as appropriate for the masses.[28] As the sixteenth-century kabbalist Moses Cordovero explained, the *peshat* was necessary so that the text could teach about "lower matters" while simultaneously alluding to celestial ones.[29] The *Mikra'ot Gedolot* ("Big Bibles") communicate this concept visually by printing several commentaries on the same page as the text they explain.

Interpretive Approaches

To avoid interpretive chaos, the ancient rabbis formulated lists of accepted techniques. The earliest of these, comprising seven principles, was attributed to the legendary first-century figure Hillel; a second, containing thirteen, was credited to the second-century rabbi Ishmael; and a third, with thirty-two (or thirty-six), to a Galilean rabbi named Eliezer.[30]

A famous passage in the Tosefta describes how Hillel used several of these techniques to justify allowing the Passover sacrifice to be offered on the Sabbath, even though that might appear to violate several prohibitions:

> Once the 14th [of Nisan, i.e., Passover] fell on the Sabbath. They asked Hillel the Elder, "Does the Passover sacrifice supersede the Sabbath?" He said to them, "Do we have only one Passover sacrifice that supersedes the Sabbath? Each year there are more than 300 Passover sacrifices that supersede the Sabbath." The entire community protested against him. He said to them, "Both the Passover and the daily offering are public sacrifices; just as the daily offering, which is a public sacrifice, supersedes the Sabbath [cf. Num. 28:10], so too the Passover sacrifice, which is a public sacrifice, supersedes

> the Sabbath. In addition, *bemo'ado* ("at its set time") is used regarding the Passover sacrifice [Num 9:2] and regarding the daily offering [Num 28:2]; just as the daily offering, regarding which *bemo'ado* is said, supersedes the Sabbath, so too the Passover sacrifice, regarding which *bemo'ado* is said, supersedes the Sabbath. Moreover, *a forteriori*: just as the daily offering which is not subject to divine punishment supersedes the Sabbath, should not the Passover sacrifice, which is subject to divine punishment, supersede the Sabbath? And what's more, I received a tradition from my teachers that the Passover sacrifice supersedes the Sabbath, and not only the first Passover, but also the second Passover [cf. Num 9:10–12], and not just the communal Passover offering, but also an individual Passover sacrifice."[31]

Hillel provided three separate reasons why the Passover offering can be sacrificed on the Sabbath, all based on comparison with the daily sacrifice, which the Bible explicitly states should be offered then (Num. 28:9). The first relies on the fact that both are public offerings; the second on the presence of a common term (the Hebrew word *bemo'ado,* which means "at its set time"); and the third that since rabbinic tradition considers a violation of the Passover sacrifice to be subject to divine punishment, it must be more important than the daily sacrifice, which is not subject to divine punishment but nonetheless supersedes the Sabbath. Significantly, these approaches resemble Greek interpretive techniques, such as dislegomenon (*gezerah shavah*), parathesis (*heqesh*), and a minori ad maius (*qal vaḥomer*).[32]

Another rabbinic principle links laws that appear in adjoining biblical passages. The rabbis used this to determine that the biblical prohibition of working on the Sabbath applies to those activities that were involved in building the tabernacle, since the book of Exodus describes the construction of the tabernacle (35:4–19) immediately after mandating Sabbath observance (35:1–3).[33] Elsewhere they tried to identify the general principles that underlie specific biblical regulations, as when they inferred that species of birds that lack a prolonged toe and a crop but have a gizzard that cannot be peeled and catch prey with their claws are prohibited on the basis of the Torah's list of forbidden birds (Lev. 11:13–19; Deut. 14:11–18).[34]

Several interpretive principles rely on biblical syntax, such as apparent redundancies in the use of general and specific terms. Thus specific instances that are mentioned before general categories were taken to be examples, as when the rabbis extended Exodus 22:9's assurance that one who takes care of someone else's "donkey or an ox or a lamb *or any animal*" is not liable for its loss to apply to any animal.[35] On the other hand, regulations in which general categories precede specific instances, such as Leviticus 18:6–17's prohibition of sexual relations with *any* relative followed by the enumeration of specific individuals (mother, sister, etc.), were limited to those cases alone.[36] Finally, passages where specifics are bracketed by general terms were understood to be setting forth criteria. Thus, Exodus 22:8 ("for every kind of transgression—whether ox, donkey, lamb, or cloak—for every loss . . .") was applied only to movable property with intrinsic value but not to real estate or currency.[37]

At the same time, the rabbis limited how these techniques could be used. For example, they prohibited analogies (*heqesh*) between civil and ritual laws and required that the common words used to link separate passages (*gezerah shavah*) be superfluous (*mufneh*).[38] They eventually banned the use of this latter technique to derive new regulations altogether, as well as the use of *a forteriori* (*qal vaḥomer*) for expanding laws.[39]

The rabbis justified their close attention to biblical vocabulary and phrasing by citing the Psalmist's statement that God's Torah is perfect (Ps. 19:8), from which they inferred that everything in it is there for a reason.[40] For them, Deuteronomy's statement "It is not empty for you" (32:47) means that "If it is empty, that is only because of you."[41] As Maimonides put it, the genealogical lists in Genesis 10 and 36 are as important as the *Shema* or the theological assertion that introduces the Ten Commandments.[42]

This attitude has led Jews to subject every idiosyncrasy in the Bible, whether spelling or style or letter shape or sound to close scrutiny; even the decorative crowns on top of various letters have been considered meaningful, whether for ritual or law, theology or ethics. Thus, Deuteronomy's use of the long form *levavekha* rather than the more common *libbĕkha* in its statement "You should love the LORD, your God, with all *your heart*" (6:5) was taken to mean that one should use both the good and the evil inclinations to show love for God,[43] whereas Exodus's description of the plague of frogs with a singular (collective) noun (*ṣefardea*, Exod. 8:2) demonstrated that Egypt had been afflicted with only one (very big) frog; and the (poetic) plural form in the Bible's statement about Sarah nursing sons (Gen. 21:7) was indicative of her having nursed several children.[44]

The rabbis attributed this approach to Akiva's teacher Naḥum of Gimzu, who was said to have found meaning even in grammatical particles. For example, he took the words *gam* ("also") and *'et* (which marks a definite direct object, but can also mean "with") as broadening the words they precede, whereas *'akh* and *raq* ("only") limit them.[45] Using this principle, the midrash *Genesis Rabbah* explained the Bible's opening sentence ("In the beginning God created *'et* the heaven and *'et* the earth") as indicating that the sun, moon, stars, and vegetation were created *alongside* (i.e., "with") heaven and earth, whereas the phrasing "You shall observe *raq* My sabbaths" in Exodus 31:13 signals that Sabbath restrictions should be ignored when lives are at stake.[46]

Given this attitude, it is not surprising that the rabbis found meaning in the repetition that is a common feature of biblical style. For example, they based the requirement that one eat three meals on the Sabbath on the threefold use of the word *hayyom* ("today") in Moses's statement about the manna ("Eat it *today*, for *today* is a Sabbath to the LORD; you will not find it on the plain *today*"—Exod. 16:25).[47] So, too, they considered biblical Hebrew's emphatic use of infinitives alongside regular verbs significant, as when Exodus 23:5 and Deuteronomy 22:1 require stipulated actions to be repeated multiple times.[48] Biblical poetry's parallelism, in which adjacent lines repeat the same idea in different words, was therefore frequently taken literally.[49]

Similarly, close scrutiny of biblical chronology led the rabbis to calculate that Methuselah would have known Adam, that Job (=Jobab in Gen. 36:33) had known Jethro, and that Moses's father, Amram, knew Jacob, who had studied with Noah's son Shem.[50] In doing this, they were not alone. The author of *Biblical Antiquities* concluded that Abraham had been present at the tower of Babel on the basis of careful reading of the biblical genealogies.[51]

Similar techniques were used to find ethical teachings in the Bible, which, as Philo explained, does not contain "anything base or unworthy of their dignity."[52] Thus, Gersonides opened each section of his Bible commentary with a list of that passage's moral lessons *to'aliyot* This attitude also originated with the ancient rabbis, who cited various stories as demonstrating proper behavior, pointing to Rebecca as illustrating how brides should be blessed and Job's friends for how to console those in pain.[53] Even God was considered a role model, whether for visiting the sick or donning *tefillin*.[54] The Bible itself had laid the groundwork for this approach, as when it described the events at the end of David's life as retribution for his earlier misdeeds (1 Sam. 15:33) and observed that Haman was hung on the very gallows he had built for Mordecai (Esther 7:10), an idea formalized in the rabbinic principle "measure for measure" (*middah keneged middah*).[55]

Of course, not all the behavior described in the Bible is edifying. Following the lead of Chronicles, Jubilees omits Abraham's presentation of Sarah as his sister (13:10–13), and Pseudo-Philo leaves out Moses's hitting the rock and Aaron's construction of the golden calf.[56] Similarly, Josephus doesn't mention Jacob's claim to be Esau nor his outwitting Laban (Gen. 30:37–43); Judah's relationship with Tamar (Gen. 38); Reuben's sexual encounter with Bilhah (Gen. 35:22); Moses's slaying of an Egyptian taskmaster (Exod. 2:11–12) and making a bronze serpent (Num. 21:8–9); the golden calf incident (Exod. 32); or Miriam's contracting leprosy

(Num. 12)—all despite Josephus's assurance of having included everything that is in the Bible.[57] He also qualified his report of Esau and Solomon's foreign wives as well as Ruth's Moabite heritage, an issue that had troubled the ancient writer Demetrius, who emphasized that Moses's "Cushite" wife (Num. 12:1) was not Ethiopian.[58]

Conversely, Josephus reports several things that are not in the Bible, describing Noah as having warned his neighbors of the impending flood and insisting that Ruth and Boaz had not engaged in sexual activity at the threshing floor.[59] The rabbis displayed similar moral concerns in their attribution of Hagar's expulsion to Ishmael's wrongdoing, as did Rashi when he claimed that the Israelites had received permission from the Egyptians before taking their property at the time of the exodus, and David Kimḥi, who suggested that Rachel took her father Laban's household idols to prevent him from being able to consult them.[60]

As much as these efforts to find religious and moral meaning in the Bible demonstrate its importance and authority, they also tend to transform complex biblical characters into one-dimensional "types" that reflect the values of the interpreters rather than those of the authors. Thus, Josephus portrays Nimrod, Zimri, Abimelech, and Eli's sons as villains, Moses as a legislator in the style of the Greeks Lycurgus and Solon, and Solomon's response to the two prostitutes in a way that resembles Sophocles's account of the riddle of the Sphinx.[61]

Facilitating these efforts was the Bible's laconic style, in which, as literary critic Erich Auerbach observes, "time and place are undefined . . . [and] thoughts and feelings remain unexpressed."[62] This characteristic left room for later readers to provide motives for actions that the Bible leaves unexplained, such as God's rejection of Cain's sacrifice.[63] Occasionally, these interpretations even differ from the biblical account, as when Josephus attributed the decision by Eglon's servants not to enter the king's chamber to their belief that he was asleep, even though the Bible explicitly says that they thought he was relieving himself (Judg. 3:24).[64]

A particularly notable example of later interpretation has to do with the fruit eaten by Adam and Eve, which has been variously identified as a fig, a grape, a citron, and even wheat.[65] Similarly, Genesis's introduction of Abraham at the age of seventy-five (12:4) sparked speculation about his childhood and God's reason for choosing him. A widespread tradition took the statement that he had come from the city of Ur (Gen. 11:31) as an allusion to his having survived being thrown into a fire (*'ur*) for believing in one god.[66] Not only did that fill in Abraham's early life and explain God's having chosen him, but it also transformed a figure whom Genesis presents as an obedient follower of God into a committed monotheist—an important idea in later times, even if not in the Bible.

Following the model of Roman historians, Jewish interpreters created speeches for biblical characters, including an elaborate dialogue between Cain and Abel, a lament by Jephtha's daughter, a prayer by Shadrach, Meshach, and Abed-nego while in the fiery furnace, and several deathbed testaments.[67] They also provided names for figures who are unnamed in the Bible, such as the daughters of Pharaoh and Jephtha, the Egyptian magicians who competed with Aaron, and the medium who communicated with the deceased Samuel on Saul's behalf.[68] Other anonymous characters were linked with more familiar figures, as when the author of the *Biblical Antiquities* identified Delilah as Samson's prostitute (Judg. 16:1–4) and the rabbis named Zelophehad as the Sabbath woodgatherer mentioned in Num. 15:32–36.[69] Elsewhere, they connected ostensibly separate characters that bear the same name. Thus, the Koraḥ mentioned in the headings of several psalms (42, 44–49, 84–85, 137–38) was identified with the Koraḥ who rebelled against Moses (Num. 16) and the Obadiah who saved prophets in the time of King Ahab (1 Kings 18:4) with the author of the book bearing that name.[70] This linkage was extended to characters with similar names, such as Job and Jobab (Gen. 36:33–34 and 10:29) or Boaz and Ibzan (Judg. 13:8–10), as well as figures with similar personalities, such as the religious zealots Phineas and Elijah, whom the Bible places centuries apart.[71] Nor was that approach restricted to people. The rabbis regarded the rod that Aaron turned into a serpent (Exod. 7:8–12) to be the same as the one that Jacob had taken with him when he fled from Esau (Gen. 32:11) and which Judah had given as a pledge to Tamar (Gen. 38:18) and David took with him to confront Goliath (1 Sam. 17:40).[72] So, too, the altar that Noah built after the flood (Gen. 8:20) was the same one earlier used by Cain and Abel (Gen. 4:3–4).[73] Such efforts illustrate the growing tendency to see separate parts of the Bible as belonging to a single, cohesive unit.

Hebrew's lack of capital letters made it possible to treat proper nouns as descriptions, thereby facilitating additional connections. For example, several ancient interpreters regarded the name Melchizedek (Gen. 14:18–20), which literally means "righteous king," as a title for Noah's brother Shem[74]; and the rabbis treated Malachi as a noun ("my messenger") that referred to Mordecai or Ezra.[75] Other names were thought to reflect their bearers' personalities. In that spirit Josephus connected Joseph's Egyptian name Tsafenat Paneakh (Gen. 41:45), to the Hebrew root *ṣ-f-n* ("hide") inferring that Joseph was someone who uncovered secrets,[76] while Philo linked Abraham's background in astrology to the patriarch's name, which he interpreted as meaning "lofty father" (*'ab ram*).[77] A similar approach enabled the rabbis to describe Delilah as having weakened (*dildel*) Samson and Ruth's sister-in-law Orpah as shameful (*ḥerpah*).[78]

Several Jewish interpreters followed the principle articulated by the medieval Spaniard Naḥmanides that "whatever happened to the patriarchs is a sign for their descendants."[79] According to one midrash, "Everything that David said in his book of Psalms applies to himself, to all Israel, and to all ages."[80] By tracing Goliath's ancestry to Orpah, *Biblical Antiquities* turned his battle with David into a reenactment of her (inferred) tension with her sister-in-law Ruth.[81] It also presented Moses's plea in a way that echoes Abraham's defense of Sodom and Gomorrah (Gen. 18:32).[82] Paul (who was, after all, a Jew) exploited this approach by using biblical figures as symbols of enduring dynamics, presenting stories such as the exodus and desert wandering as models of later Christian experiences.[83] So, too, his near-contemporary Philo described Enosh, Enoch, and Noah as men or types of soul,[84] and the modern rabbi Joseph Soloveitchik explained that the first man, whose creation is described in both Genesis 1 and Genesis 2, actually represents two different kinds of people.[85]

This typological approach has often been applied to the Bible's command that the memory of the tribe of Amalek, which had threatened the Israelites as they made their way to the Promised Land, should be blotted out (Deut. 25:18, cf. Exod. 17:14–16). Jewish tradition has sometimes understood this as requiring scribes to cross out the word "Amalek" or obligating Jews to drown out the name of Haman, who was descended from the Amalekite tribe, when the book of Esther is read on Purim or reflecting something God will do at the end of time.[86] However, it has most often been understood as requiring the extermination of those who threaten Jews, whether ancient Idumeans and Romans, medieval Christians, or modern Ukrainians, Nazis, Palestinians, or Iranians; even Jews, such as *maskilim* (enlightened ones), Zionists, ultra-Orthodox, non-observant, social oppressors, and various Israeli government officials, have been included in this category.[87] Christians have followed suit, applying this command to the Crusaders' Muslim enemies, Native Americans, and, ironically, Jews.[88]

Yet another approach treats the Bible as speaking about the distant future. An early example of this is the book of Daniel's explanation of Jeremiah's statement that the Babylonian oppression would last seventy years (25:11–12 and 29:10) as meaning that seventy "weeks" (units of seven) of years, that is, 490 (70x7) years (Dan 9:24). In that same spirit, one of the Dead Sea Scrolls reports, "God told Habakkuk to write down what would happen to the final generation," even though the biblical prophet seems to have had the immediate future in mind.[89] Similarly, Paul understood the "acceptable time" mentioned in Isaiah 49:8 as being "now" (i.e., the first century, more than 700 years after Isaiah),[90] while the rabbis took the Bible's statement that Moses had seen the "west sea" (*yam ha'aḥaron*, i.e., the Mediterranean) as referring to the "last day" (*yom ha'aḥaron*).[91]

At the root of these many and diverse approaches is the conviction in the Bible's lofty and enduring significance. As the Zohar explains, "Alas for the one who regards the Torah as a book of mere tales and everyday matters. Were that so, even we could compose a Torah dealing with everyday affairs and of even greater excellence. Nay, even the princes of the world possess books of greater worth which we could use as a model for composing some such Torah."[92] It therefore took Scripture's call for God to open our eyes (Ps. 119:18) as a request for the ability to see its essence and compared the Torah to

> a beautiful and attractive beloved woman, who is hidden in a secluded chamber of her palace, but has a lover of whom no one but she knows. Because of his love for her, that lover passes by her gate, turning his eyes to all sides. What does she do, knowing that the lover is routinely passing by the palace? She opens a little door where she is in that palace and shows her face to her lover, then quickly hides it. No one but the lover alone looks or sees her; but his heart and soul and all that is within him are drawn to her, knowing that she loves him, since she revealed herself to him for a moment. It is the same with the Torah, which reveals itself only to those who love it. The Torah knows that whoever is wise of heart passes by the gates of its house every day. What does it do? It reveals its face to him from its palace and makes a sign to him, then immediately returns to its hiding place. No one there knows or understands it except him alone, and he follows it with all his being, his heart, and his soul. Thus the Torah reveals itself and hides itself, following its lover in love in order to awaken love in him.
>
> Come and see, this is the way of the Torah: When it first begins to reveal itself to someone, it gives him hints. If he understands, good; but if he does not understand, it sends for

> him and calls him a fool. . . . When he approaches it, it begins to speak to him (with) words suitable to his understanding from behind the curtain that it spread out for him until he understands a little; this is called *derash*. Then it speaks riddles to him from behind a fine cloth; that is *aggadah*. After he is used to that, it reveals itself to him face to face and tells him all its hidden mysteries and all the hidden ways which have been secreted in its heart from time immemorial.[93]

Efforts to find hidden meanings in the Bible go back to antiquity, when Jewish writers borrowed the idea of allegory, which sophisticated Greeks had used to explain Homer's and Hesiod's accounts of their gods' embarrassing behavior as referring to something different from what they seem to say. Philo told of a Jewish group called the Therapeautae, who lived in Egypt in the first century CE and believed that the Bible is filled with "symbols of something whose hidden nature is revealed by studying the underlying meaning."[94] In a similar way, the pre-Christian Letter of Aristeas explains the Bible's dietary laws as symbolizing human behavior, with the prohibition of wild birds representing the sinfulness of relying on strength for domination (§§146–48) and the acceptability of animals with cloven hooves indicating the importance of righteous deeds (§§150–51). Centuries later, Paul understood Sarah and Hagar as symbolizing Jews and gentiles.[95] However, the best-known allegorizer was Philo himself, who explained the Bible's expectation that one honor one's father and mother as requiring us to honor both God and wisdom.[96]

Jews have continued to interpret the Bible allegorically ever since. A talmudic rabbi saw the book of Job as a parable,[97] while Abba Mari b. Moshe (XIII Provence) insisted that "everything from creation to the giving of the Torah is an allegory."[98] Thus Solomon Ibn Gabirol (XI Spain) took Jacob's ladder as signifying metaphysical reality, while Maimonides regarded it as symbolizing the ascent to knowledge of God.[99] Maimonides also suggested that the desert ark represents the heart, and its seven lamps the five senses and the two "powers of the soul," thought and imagination.[100] According to Solomon ibn Gabirol, the four streams flowing out of Eden (Gen. 4:10–14) symbolize the four elements and Adam and Eve represent the animal and rational souls,[101] whereas David Kimḥi considered the garden a symbol for the Active Intellect, the tree of knowledge, the Material Intellect, and the tree of life, Human Intellect.[102] Centuries later, Moses Isserles took the Persian king Ahasuerus as a symbol for form, Queen Vashti for matter, Haman for the evil inclination, and Haman's sons for the five senses or powers of life.[103]

The erotic tone of the Song of Songs has made it particularly susceptible to this approach. Rabbinic sources treated it as an allegory of Israel's history from the exodus to the final redemption, while Maimonides construed it as depicting the relationship between God and humanity and others interpreted it as portraying the relationship between the Active and the Human Intellects.[104]

One effect of dehistoricizing biblical narratives is to make them more universal. This is explicitly the case with Philo's etymological explanation of the term "Israel" as referring to anyone "who sees (*r'h*) God (*'el*)," which enabled him to look forward to a time when Scripture would be acknowledged as an account of "each man's personal experience and spiritual journey."[105]

Allegorical interpretations were especially appealing to medieval kabbalists. As the Zohar puts it, "Each story . . . does not come to convey only that story, but celestial matters and celestial mysteries."[106] Drawing on the rabbinic interpretation of the Bible's first word (*reisheet*, "beginning") as a reference to wisdom (*ḥokhma*) and the preceding preposition (*be-*, lit. "in") as meaning "by means of," the Zohar understands Genesis's opening sentence as asserting that "———— [i.e. the *'ein sof*] created *'elohim* [*binah*] with *reisheet* [*ḥokhma*]."[107] Other mystics split the Hebrew word in two (*bara' sheet*), which yields "He created six (sefirot)," using the light (*'or* = the sefirah *ḥesed*) that had been created before the sun, moon, and stars (cf. Gen. 1:3).[108] A similar approach led the Spanish kabbalist Moses de Leon to see Esther as representing the *Shekhinah* and Haman representing the *sitra' 'ahra'* (lit. "other side").[109]

Allegorical interpretation is not the only way in which meanings that differ from the surface intent have been found in the Bible. Several approaches read it as being written in various kinds of code:

- *Gematria*, a term with visibly Greek roots that goes back to Maccabean times, treats Hebrew letters as numbers, with *aleph* representing 1, *bet* 2, etc.[110] A famous example, which occasionally appears in modern scholarship, involves the Bible's surprising statement that the pastoralist Abraham took 318 servants into battle with him (Gen. 14:14). According to several ancients, the reference is to Abraham's servant Eliezer, since the numerical value of the letters in Eliezer's name is 318 (1+30+10+70+7+200).[111] The early Christian Letter of Barnabbas followed a similar line of reasoning when it inferred that the reference was to Jesus, since J (iota) can stand for 10, E (eta) for 8, and so on.[112] There are other, more complicated forms of gematria. For example, the rabbis justified their understanding of the word *maqom* ("place") as a designation for God by pointing out that its numerical value (40+100+6+40=186) equals the sum of the squares of the letters in the divine name YHWH ($10^2+5^2+6^2+5^2$).[113] Others increased the value of each letter in a word by a specific number or a whole word's value by the number of letters in it, assigned each letter the numerical value of its name (e.g., *b* = 412, since its name is spelled *b-y-t* = 2+10+400), or counted only a word's initial letters.
- *Atbash* replaces each letter in a word with the letter that is the same distance from the other end of the alphabet, changing the first letter of the Hebrew alphabet (') into the last (*t*), the second (*b*) to the next to the last (*sh*), and so on. There is an example of this in our texts of Jeremiah

25:26 and 51:41, where the strange term *Sheshakh* is an apparent substitute for *Bavel* (Babylon).[114]

- *Notarikon* treats biblical words as acronyms or abbreviations,[115] as when the Talmud explains *amen* as an acronym for *'el melekh ne'eman* ("God, faithful king")[116] and the description of Shimei as *nimreṣet* (1 Kings 2:8) as a reference to his being an adulterer (*n̲o'ef*), bastard (*m̲amzer*), murderer (*r̲oṣeaḥ*), rebel (*ṣ̲orer*), and abomination (*ṭ̲o'evah*).[117] Using this technique, the rabbis explained the first word in the Ten Commandments (*'anokhi* lit. "I") as an abbreviation for "I myself wrote and gave" (*'ana nafshi kitvet yehavet*).[118]
- Finally, Jewish tradition sometimes rejects the existing text altogether, rearranging letters, removing vowels, or combining words. According to one mystical tradition, a certain letter has been removed from throughout existing Torah scrolls, although authorities disagree as to which letter that is.[119] More prevalent is the kabbalistic view that "the Torah consists entirely of [God's] holy name; in fact, every word written therein consists of and contains that Holy Name."[120]

Mystics most often claim that the Torah's real meaning (*sod*) has been concealed. This idea is evident already in the Dead Sea Scroll which asserts that "God told [the prophet] Habakkuk to write down what would happen to the final generation, but did not inform him when time would come to an end."[121] Similarly, the Zohar observes that, "the Torah's stories are only its outer garment, and woe to whoever looks upon that garment as being the Torah itself—such a person will have no portion in the next world. . . . Observe this: the garments worn by a man are the most visible part of him, and senseless people looking at the man do not seem to see more in him than the garments. But in truth the pride of the garment(s) is the man's body, and the pride of the body is the soul. So, too, the Torah has a body made up of the precepts, called *gufê torah*, and that body is (dressed) in garments made up of worldly stories. Those who don't know better don't look at what is underneath. Those who do know better don't look at the garment but at the body which is under the garment. But the wise servants of the Most High King, those who stood at Mount Sinai, look only at the soul, the root of all, the real Torah."[122]

Straightforward Interpretation

This proliferation of explanations could easily have led to interpretive chaos. Already in the second century, Rabbi Ishmael is said to have mocked Rabbi Eliezer for telling the text, "Be quiet until I interpret you."[123] Seven centuries later, Saadia Gaon insisted on the priority of Scripture's straightforward meaning when it contradicts perception, reason, another biblical passage, or rabbinic tradition.[124] That meaning came to be called *peshat*, an ancient term, though it wasn't understood that way until the Middle Ages.[125] It was then that Naḥmanides warned that the talmudic principle *ʾeyn miqra yoṣēʾ miyĕdē peshuṭo*, which meant that the text never loses its plain sense, should not be understood as stipulating that the straightforward meaning is the only credible one.[126]

Determining the plain sense requires understanding biblical Hebrew, which the ancient rabbis had already recognized as different from their own usage, thereby opening the door to a certain level of linguistic awareness.[127] For example, they observed its use of the suffix *-ah* to indicate motion toward and four distinct meanings of the word *kî* ("if," "perhaps," "but," and "because").[128] The rabbis sometimes used this linguistic sensitivity for their own purposes, as when they cited the root *ʿnh's* appearance in settings that relate to hunger (e.g., Deut. 8:3 and Ps. 35:13) to justify their interpretation of Leviticus's requirement to "afflict (*teʿannu*) one's soul" (16:29) on the Day of Atonement (Yom Kippur) as a reference to fasting.[129] In a similar way, they based their interpretation of Deuteronomy's statement about loving God with all your soul (*b̲ekhol nafshekha*, Deut. 6:5) as meaning "even at the cost of your life" on the Bible's occasional use of the preposition *be-* to express cost.[130] In the tenth century Menaḥem ibn Saruq, the personal secretary to the prominent Spanish Jew Ḥasdai ibn Shaprut, compiled an entire dictionary of biblical Hebrew.[131]

The rabbis also drew on related languages, including Phoenician, Coptic, Syriac, and Arabic, to explain problematic passages.[132] Medieval Jews, who were familiar with Islam's tradition of "language worship" and knew Aramaic, Arabic, and sometimes even non-Semitic languages, expanded on that approach. Saadia Gaon, described by one contemporary as the "master of exegetes," played a major role in this enterprise, composing both a grammar and a dictionary of biblical Hebrew along with treatises on various aspects of the language, all while translating the Bible into Arabic and writing commentaries on several of its books.[133] Further progress was made possible by the tenth-century grammarian Judah Ḥayyuj's recognition that Hebrew words are based on three-letter roots and, in modern times, by archeological finds, including ancient documents written in Akkadian and Ugaritic, languages of ancient Mesopotamia and northern Canaan.

The Bible's geographical references provided an obvious focus for *peshat* interpretation. That effort had begun already in biblical times, as demonstrated by the book of Chronicles's identification of Moriah (Gen. 22:2) with Mount Zion (2 Chron. 3:1). Josephus later identified the Pishon River (Gen. 2:11) with the Ganges River.[134] In 1819, Solomon Loewisohn composed an entire geography of the Holy Land.[135] Additional resources for such endeavors were provided by European exploration of the Holy Land in the nineteenth century and the emergence of contemporary Israel in the twentieth.

Jewish scholars, for whom "biblical theology is not just story and prophecy, but also law and cult," have paid close attention to the Bible's ritual provisions.[136] Some of these have been attributed to practical concerns, such as health; others to the rejection of neighboring practices.[137] Philo explained the dietary laws as a moral discipline, and Maimonides saw circumcision as a way to reduce passion.[138]

Ancient Jews sometimes connected biblical references to non-Jewish traditions. As early as the second century BCE, Pseudo-Eupolemus identified Enoch with Atlas, while Cleodemus claimed that Abraham's daughter had married Heracles.[139] More recently, Moses Mendelssohn saw Tubal-Cain (Gen. 4:22) as a reflection of the Roman god Vulcan and Ecclesiastes 12:6 as anticipating William Harvey's theory of blood circulation.[140]

Ancient readers also credited biblical heroes with all manner of cultural innovations. For example, the second century BCE historians Eupolemus and Artapanus claimed that Abraham had invented astronomy, which he then shared with the Phoenicians and Egyptians.[141] Eupolemus also reported that Moses invented the alphabet, which later made its way to the Phoenicians and the Greeks, and Aristobulus believed that Pythagoras, Socrates, and Plato had learned about God's role in creation from Moses.[142] According to Philo, the Greek philosopher Heraclitus derived his philosophical ideas from Moses.[143] Modern archeological discoveries have greatly multiplied the possibility for such comparisons. Drawing on allusions scattered throughout the Bible that resemble themes in Ugaritic literature, Umberto Cassuto reconstructed an entire Israelite epic, leading one scholar to describe the Old Testament as "new wine in old bottles."[144]

Biblical style has been another area of continuing Jewish attention. Already in antiquity Rabbi Ishmael cautioned that the Bible "speaks in human language," suggesting that it need not always be taken literally.[145] To prove that point, the ancient rabbis cited the Bible's statement about leftover quail becoming infested with maggots and stinking (Exod. 16:20, cf. v. 24), noting that maggots grow only *after* meat has become rotten.[146] Using that kind of careful reading, they were able to identify numerous features of biblical style, including repetitions, interruptions, introductions, and conclusions.

Attention to the Bible's literary features grew dramatically during the Middle Ages. For example, Saadia Gaon pointed out the figurative nature of Deuteronomy's description of God as a fire (4:24) and Genesis's explanation of Eve's name as meaning that she was "the mother of all things" (3:20),[147] while Menaḥem ibn Saruq identified the poetic use of parallelism.[148] Drawing on his knowledge of Arabic poetics, Moses ibn Ezra (eleventh to twelfth century Spain) enumerated a variety of figures of speech, including metaphor, simile, and hyperbole.[149] Abraham ibn Ezra (no relation to Moses ibn Ezra) identified antithesis, paronomasia, parallelism, chiasm, and inclusio,[150] while Rashbam pointed out how seemingly unimportant details sometimes provide information that proves relevant later on.[151]

During the European Enlightenment, Moses Mendelssohn spoke of "the purity of [the Bible's] refined language"[152] and recognized that some passages are written in poetic style.[153] More recent scholars have identified literary features in biblical prose. For example, Benno Jacob (1862–1945) pointed out the Bible's proclivity for scenes with only two characters and its tendency to repeat certain words ("bezeichende Wörter," which Martin Buber later labeled "Leitwörter") as a way of drawing attention to important aspects of a passage.[154] Jacob also explored the relationship between ostensibly separate passages, a phenomenon that has become prominent in contemporary scholarship under the rubrics of "inner-biblical exegesis" and intertextuality.[155]

Interest in the Bible's straightforward meaning (*peshat*) drew attention to those places where the text diverges from later scientific and religious views. The most obvious of these were its many miracle stories. That may be why Josephus leaves out Rahab's reference to the wonders that accompanied Israel's departure from Egypt from his retelling of the Israelite conquest.[156] For their part, the ancient rabbis suggested that not all biblical accounts should be taken literally.[157] Moses Maimonides later attributed Joshua's report about the sun "standing still" (10:13) to the summer solstice and Balaam's talking donkey (Num 22:28–30) to a prophetic vision,[158] while the twelfth-century French scholar Joseph Bekhor Shor insisted that Lot's wife was actually covered with salt so she only appeared to become a pillar of salt.[159]

Another set of problems were created by biblical passages that seem to differ from later Jewish thinking. That may be why Josephus omitted the Bible's reference to human beings as having been created in God's image and denied that God had any assistants, despite God's having said "Let *us* make man in *our* image" (Gen 1:26).[160] Other ancient writers thought that God had been speaking to Wisdom, angels, or the heavens and the earth.[161]

On a more practical level, Rashbam noticed that the creation story's phrasing "there was evening and there was morning, one day" presumes that days begin at dawn rather than sunset, as in later Jewish law.[162] He also cited the similarity between Exodus 13:16 ("a sign on your hands and a reminder [*zikkaron*] between your eyes") and verse 9 ("a sign on your hands and *ṭoṭafot* between your eyes") as evidence that the word *ṭoṭafot* does not refer to physical objects (*tefillin*) as it has traditionally been understood.[163]

Jewish readers have long noticed contradictions between different parts of the Bible.[164] We have already seen how 2 Chroncles 35:18 blends the insistence in Exodus that the Passover sacrifice be roasted (12:8–9) with Deuteronomy's commandment that it be boiled (16:5–7). Later authors, such as Josephus, continued that approach.[165] Ḥiwi Ha-Balkhi, who lived in what is today Afghanistan during the ninth century, compiled a list of inconsistencies such as these in order to discredit the Bible[166]; a similar effort was undertaken by the seventeenth-century apostate Uriel da Costa.[167] Other readers attributed inconsistent sentences to different speakers or different situations.[168] Thus Philo took the statement that "God created the man in His image" (Gen. 1:27) as referring to the idea of man and the later statement that "the Lord God formed the man out of dust from the earth" (Gen. 2:7) as a reference to the man's physical being.[169]

The rabbis sometimes resolved inconsistencies by appealing to a third passage.[170] For example, they drew on Leviticus's distinction between old and new grain (23:14) to harmonize Exodus's mandate that unleavened bread be eaten for seven days during Passover (12:15) with Deuteronomy's requirement that it be eaten for only six (16:8), inferring that the requirement that unleavened bread be made from new grain applies only during the last six days of the holiday.[171]

Other rabbinic explanations were more dramatic, as when they cited the fact that God's speech in Numbers 9 is dated a month prior to the one in Numbers 1 as evidence that biblical accounts are not always arranged chronologically.[172] As we have seen, they also allowed for the possibility that our biblical texts are inaccurate, identifying places where individual letters had been left out (*'itturei soferim*) or should be read (*qĕrê*) differently from how they are written (*kĕtîv*), and even disparities between the Hebrew (masoretic) text and the ancient Greek translation.[173] The medieval scholar David Kimḥi explained these as the result of textual disruptions that arose during the Babylonian exile, leading names that appear in one passage with the Hebrew letter *resh* to occur elsewhere with the similarly shaped letter *dalet*.[174] More radically, the Spaniard Jonah ibn Janaḥ suggested that the Bible sometimes uses one word when it actually means another, as in the case of 2 Samuel 21:8, which he suggested meant Merab even though it reads Michal, or 1 Kings 2:28, which reads Absalom but means Solomon.[175]

Jews have long speculated about the date and authorship of biblical books. According to the Talmud:

> Moses wrote his book and the portion of Balaam (i.e. Numbers 23–24) and Job; Joshua wrote his book and eight verses in the Torah; Samuel wrote his book and Judges and Ruth; David wrote the book of Psalms through the agency of ten elders, the first man, Melchizedek, Abraham, Moses, Heman, Jeduthun, Asaph, and the three Korahites; Jeremiah wrote his book and the book of Kings and Lamentations; Hezekiah and his council wrote Isaiah, Proverbs, Song of Songs, and Ecclesiastes; the men of the great assembly wrote Ezekiel and the twelve (minor prophets), Daniel, and the book of Esther; Ezra wrote his book and the genealogies in Chronicles until his (own time).[176]

By the Middle Ages, Jewish scholars were raising questions about the authorship of Joshua and Samuel, as well as the last section of Isaiah and even several psalms.[177] However, it was Baruch Spinoza (1632–77) who became the pivotal figure in such thinking. Prioritizing reason over tradition, he followed the lead of Abraham ibn Ezra in concluding that Moses could not have written certain passages in the Pentateuch, which he saw as a compilation of ancient Hebrew writings that had been compiled by Ezra.[178]

A century later, Moses Mendelssohn recognized that David had not written all the psalms, followed by the Italian scholar Samuel David Luzzatto, who noted that their superscriptions were not part of the original works.[179] Several nineteenth-century scholars, including Isaac Samuel Reggio, Nachman Krochmal, Heinrich Graetz, and Zacharias Frankel, recognized that the last twenty-seven chapters of Isaiah were the work of another prophet. Krochmal also realized that Ecclesiastes had been composed after the Babylonian exile and therefore could not have been written by Solomon, while Leopold Zunz proposed that the books of Ezra, Nehemiah, and Chronicles had originally been one work, a view that persisted throughout the last century.[180]

A Case Study: The Binding of Isaac

Because the long history, vast quantity, and diverse settings of Jewish biblical interpretation makes it difficult to comprehend its impact and import, we will examine Jewish treatments of a single passage—the account of Abraham's near-sacrifice of his son Isaac (Genesis 22). Isaac Abarbanel described the story as "worthier of study and investigation than any other section" of the Bible.[181] The mass of interpretation of this one short passage is illustrative of the extent and nature of the Jewish interpretive enterprise.

Jews are not alone in venerating this passage. For Christians, it foreshadows Jesus's crucifixion,[182] while Muslims reenact it during the "Feast of the Sacrifice" (Eid al-Aḍḥa) with which the annual pilgrimage to Mecca ends, albeit with Abraham's son Ishmael as the victim rather than Isaac.[183] In order to illustrate the breadth of

Jewish interpretions, we will draw examples from various times and places without trying to track their development.

Although the story seems to stretch over an "interminable interval of time," it occupies only nineteen sentences in the book of Genesis.[184] After the narrator introduces what follows as God's effort to test Abraham, it reports that God commands Abraham to offer Isaac on a mountain in the land of Moriah. Abraham responds by setting out early in the morning with his son, two servants, and some wood. On the third day he leaves the servants and donkey behind, continuing on with the fire and a knife while Isaac carries the wood. When Isaac notices that there is no lamb for the sacrifice, his father assures him that God will provide one. Once they arrive at the place God had chosen, Abraham builds an altar, lays out the wood, and ties Isaac down. But, as Abraham raises the knife, an angel cries out for him to stop, explaining, "Now I know that you fear God." Abraham then sacrifices a ram caught in a thicket and names the place *YHWH Yir'eh* (lit. "YHWH sees"), after which an angel blesses him and promises that his numerous descendants will dominate their enemies. Abraham then returns to his servants and proceeds to Beer-sheba.

The account of this incident was being interpreted already in biblical times. Many scholars believe that the angel's second speech (verses 15–18) was inserted into an earlier version of the story, transforming what is elsewhere presented as God's promise to Abraham (e.g., Gen 12:2–3, 13:14–17, 15:7, 15:13, 17:1–8) into a reward for his obedience.[185] Elsewhere, the book of Chronicles connects what Genesis calls "the land of Moriah" with the city Jerusalem (2 Chron 3:1), thereby providing the Temple Mount with an ancient pedigree, an identification that persists to the present day. One reader even pointed out that the Hebrew phrase "to the land of Moriah" (v. 2) has the same numerical value as the Hebrew words "to Jerusalem," and the phrase "to the place" (v. 3) as "Jerusalem."[186]

Later generations connected this story with other biblical passages, identifying Psalm 121 (v. 1—"I lift my eyes to the mountains from where my help will come") as the prayer Abraham uttered before starting to slay Isaac and citing Abraham's obedience as the inspiration for the Israelite midwives in Egypt, as well as the reason God split the Red Sea, forgave Israel for worshipping the golden calf, and saved them from Haman's massacre.[187]

Throughout their history Jews have applied all four of the approaches described earlier to what came to be called the binding of Isaac (*'aqedat yiṣḥaq*).[188] *Peshat* interpreters have addressed matters of vocabulary, plot, and style. One obvious focus has been the story's rare and obscure terms, such as the word *sĕbak* (v. 13, usually translated as "thicket"), which occurs only a handful of times in the Bible.[189] The Septuagint simply transliterates it ("Sabec tree"), while Targum Onkelos renders it "tree." The term used for Abraham's knife (*ma'akhelet*) is also rare, leading some interpreters to infer that it must have been special, perhaps because of its size,[190] and they attribute its designation to the fact that it eats (*'okhel*) its sacrifice.[191] Noting that there are twelve consonants in the phrase describing Abraham's taking the knife (*vayiqaḥ et hama'akhelet*—v. 10), the rabbis suggested that it had been inspected twelve times.[192]

More common terms have also attracted attention. For example, although it might seem odd to say that the ram was offered *taḥat* Isaac (v. 13), since that word usually means "under," the ancient rabbis found several places in the Bible where it means "instead of."[193] Modern scholars have been struck by the statement that Abraham carried fire (*'aish*) Noting that the related Babylonian word *ishātu* is sometimes prefixed by the term *aban* ("stone," cf. Hebrew *'eben),* they have suggested that what Abraham carried was actually a firestone.[194]

Also problematic is verse 13's statement that Abraham saw a ram *'aḥar* (lit. "after") caught in the thicket. Traditional interpreters took that as alluding to an earlier incident, such as Abraham's interchange with Abimelech (Gen 21:22–34), or perhaps to the end (*'aḥarit*) of days.[195] Most scholars today regard *'aḥar* as a scribal error for the similarly shaped *'eḥad* ("one"), which actually appears in several medieval biblical manuscripts and was apparently in the Hebrew texts used by various ancient translators and teachers.[196]

Grammatical particles have also attracted attention. For example, David Kimḥi regarded the prefixed *vav*, which usually means "and," in the statement that Abraham "arose *and* went" (v. 3, *vayaqom vayelekh*) as a stylistic flourish;[197] modern scholars consider such verb chains a single unit (hendiadys) that means "he started out."[198] Interpreters have also paid attention to the definite article, explaining the reference to Abraham's bringing *the* wood (*ha'eiṣîm* in vv. 3, 6, 7, 9) as alluding to a specific species (possibly fig or palm[199]), and his building *the* altar (*hammizbeiaḥ*, v. 9) as indicating that it was the same altar that had been used by Adam, Cain and Abel, and Noah.[200]

In addition to scrutinizing what the text contains, Jewish interpreters have tried to fill in what is missing, such as the identity of the servants who accompanied Abraham (Ishmael and Eliezer)[201] and the angel who stopped him (Michael or Gabriel).[202] They also note Isaac's absence from the story's closing statement, that "Abraham returned (*vayashov*) to his servants" (v. 19). David Kimḥi dismissed this as a result of style—the fact that Isaac is not the narrative's main focus; however, midrashic tradition took it as evidence that he had been sent away earlier—whether to the Garden of Eden, to study, to recover from the trauma, or even to avoid the evil eye.[203] A more dramatic view inferred that Isaac had actually been killed, though he was later restored to life.[204]

Other plot details that attracted the attention of *peshat* interpreters include Abraham's saddling the donkey (v. 3), something not normally performed by men of his wealth and stature, which the ancient rabbis regarded as evidence of his commitment to God.[205] In a similar spirit, Naḥmanides took the statement that Abraham "split wood for an offering" (v. 3) before leaving as evidence that he was worried that he might not find suitable wood at the unidentified spot to which he was going.[206] For Josephus, the statement that Abraham "rose early in the morning" (v. 3) suggested an effort to hide his plan from Sarah.[207] The rabbis attributed the fact that her death is reported immediately after the *akedah* (Gen 23:1) to her finding out what Abraham had attempted, though others thought that she had helped Abraham build the altar and even let him use her hair to tie down their son.[208]

Through all of this, the text provides remarkably little information about Isaac, which has led some to infer that he was an infant (especially since the preceding chapter describes his birth), though he has also been pictured with a beard.[209] References to his fear—trembling and wondering "Who will save me from my father?"[210]—seem to presume that he was young. However, written sources offer a wide variety of ages, ranging from nine to thirty-seven.[211]

Despite the repeated statement that Abraham and Isaac walked together (vv. 6 and 8), readers have long wondered about their relationship, as in the midrash's observation, "one to slaughter and the other to be slaughtered."[212] A Spanish ballad inserts a dialogue between Abraham and Isaac.[213] The Israeli poet Ḥayim Ḥefer also constructed a dialogue, with Abraham telling his son, "Come, climb the mountain, boy, and we shall say farewell," to which Isaac replies, "Yes, here I come, Papa; the sticks have cut my back / the road is dust, Papa; my throat is parched and cracked / Give me your hand, Papa; don't let me fall below / Papa I'm scared, Papa; Papa, don't let me go."[214]

Although some medievals considered Abraham's reassurance that "God will provide the lamb for the burnt offering, my son" (v. 8) as a bare-faced lie that was intended to keep Isaac from knowing what was about to transpire,[215] ancient rabbis took Abraham at his word, citing the statement as evidence of his faith in God.[216] Still others read it as elliptical: "God will provide a lamb; [but if not, then] the offering [will be] my son,"[217] or took the words "my son" as an appostive—"God will provide the lamb for the offering: my son."[218] According to an alternative tradition, the ram was actually named "Isaac."[219]

Alongside these efforts to understand the story's literal meaning, Jews have seen it as symbolic. For example, Philo considered it an allegory (*remez*), illustrating that the wise person (*sophos*, i.e., Abraham) recognizes that joy ("Isaac," from the Hebrew root *ṣḥq*) belongs to God.[220] For Abraham Kook, Abraham examplifies the passion with which rationalists can serve God.[221] Seeking insights into heavenly mysteries (*sod*), kabbalists identified the patriarchs with the various divine emanations (*sefirot*), as when Dov Baer, the Magid of Mezeritch, questioned whether Abraham's behavior in this incident correlates with the *sefirah Din*, which is normally associated with Isaac.[222] According to Isaac Arama (sixteenth-century Spain), Abraham's saddling his donkey refers to his subduing the material component.[223]

Finally, generations of Jews have drawn lessons of many kinds from the story (*derash*). Thus, Rashi attributed the rhythmic structure of God's command, "Take (*kaḥ na*) your son (*binkha*), your only one (*yeḥidekha*), whom you love (*'asher 'ahavta*) Isaac (*yiṣḥaq*)." (v. 2) to God's desire to avoid overwhelming Abraham with the magnitude of His command,[224] An earlier midrash took it as the remnant of a dialogue in which Abraham replied to the command "Take your son" by pointing out, "I have two." When God explained, "your only son," Abraham countered by pointing out that each was the only child of his mother. God then added, "whom you love," to which Abraham responded that he loved them both, forcing God to specify: "Isaac."[225] Other authors, beginning already before the birth of Christianity, noted that this sentence echoes God's earlier command that Abraham "go forth (*lekh lekha*) from your land (*mei'arṣekha*) and from your birthplace (*umimoladetkha*) and from your father's house (*umibeit 'avikha*) to the land I will show you (*'ar'eka*)" (Gen 12:1), leading them to infer that Genesis's stories about Abraham are actually a series of trials through which the patriarch demonstrates his loyalty to God.[226]

Another stylistic feature that has attracted attention is the redundancy in the angel's command that Abraham "not lay a hand on the boy or do anything to him" (v. 12). Connecting the latter word (*me'umah*) to the term for "wound" (*mum*), some have suggested that Abraham was eager to sacrifice Isaac or at least to spill his blood.[227] The nineteenth-century talmudist Isaac of Volozhin even thought that Abraham wanted to offer to sacrifice *both* his sons;[228] however, others were sure that he was confident that God would stop him in time.[229]

Some, like Josephus, who argued that God has "no craving for human blood," have seen this story as a repudiation of human sacrifice.[239] Noting that the verb *h'lh* ("offer up," v. 2) literally means "bring up," a medieval midrash claims that Abraham had misunderstood God.[231] Another tradition suggests that God had intended for Abraham to offer the ram, which was also named Isaac and had been destined for its role since the time of creation.[232]

A midrashic tradition compares the word for "test" (*nsh*) with the verb "make great" (*ns'*) and the noun for "sign" (*nes*), suggesting that God planned to make an example out of Abraham.[233] According to *Genesis Rabbah*, God acted like a potter who examines only good vessels or a worker who beats his flax in order to improve it.[234] On the other hand, Elie Wiesel suggested that it was Abraham who was testing God, who had earlier been passive in the face of human death.[235]

Then there are those who deny that the command came from God at all. Israeli songwriter Naomi Shemer presents it as anonymous, while *Genesis Rabbah* understood the plural suffix on the word (*'elohim*) ("God") as evidence that it was from angels.[236] Several ancient sources attribute it to the devil, to whom an entire stream of rabbinic thought gives a prominent role in this drama.[237] For example, various traditions cite the introductory statement, "Now it came to pass after these words (*devarim*)" as referring to a conversation in which Satan warned Abraham that he would later be accused of murder, alerted him to the fact that Sarah would be upset, and finally pushed the knife out of his hand.[238] Following a similar line of thought, Martin Buber warned people who think they hear God speaking to ask themselves, "Are you really addressed by the Absolute or by one of his apes?"[239] As Woody Allen observed, "Some men will follow any order no matter how asinine as long as it comes from a resonant, well-modulated voice."[240]

Recent readers have often treated the story typologically. Psychologist Erich Neumann cites Isaac's passivity as the prototype for what he called Jews' "Isaac complex."[241] Taking a different point of view, the Israeli author Yizhar Smilansky (S. Yizhar) insists, "I hate Abraham, our father. Let him sacrifice himself."[242] Modern Israelis refer to those who fought in the 1967 Six-Day War as "the Isaac generation."[243] As the poet Eli Alon observed, "Isaac, who came down from the *akedah,* will never be the same, an innocent Isaac, who believes without asking."[244] A similar perspective emerged among American Jews during the Vietnam War, when the activist Danny Siegel wrote about "every Father Abraham before he ties the rope around his preboxed son at local maddened drooling draft boards."[245] And the sculptor George Segal chose this incident to symbolize the 1970 killing of protestors at Kent State University.[246]

Others have credited Isaac with a more active role—helping to construct the altar on which he threw himself and then stretching out his neck to make his father's task easier.[247] By the first century, Isaac was seen as the prototypical martyr; thus the Babylonian Talmud tells that Hannah contrasted her loss of seven sons to Abraham's risking just one.[248] He has sometimes been invoked as an intermediary who can defend his descendants before God.[249] During the Crusades, Jewish communities recited poems called *aqedot* on the High Holidays and fast days.[250] According to Ḥasdai Crescas, whose son was killed during the 1391 pogrom in Spain, "Every Jew . . . should be prepared to kill his child . . . as Abraham did."[251] That linkage to martyrdom persists in the work of modern writers who contrast its denoument to that of the Holocaust.[252] To this day a ram's horn is blown and this passage recited on the Jewish New Year, the date on which this event is traditionally said to have taken place.[253] References to it are also incorporated in the biblical verses that are part of that day's liturgy at the beginning of the Jewish penitential season.[254]

◆ ◆ ◆

THE WIDE-RANGING TREATMENT OF THIS ONE STORY illustrates the wealth of attention Jews have accorded the Bible from antiquity to the present, demonstrating both its centrality and the diverse uses to which it has been put. Theological, ritual, and moral meanings have been found in its individual words—both rare (*sĕbak, ma'akhelet*) and common (*taḥat, 'aish*)—as well as its particles (*ve-*, *ha-*), stylistic oddities (the singular verb describing Abraham's return), and textual peculiarities (*'aḥar*), not to mention broader issues of characterization (why Abraham rose early and what he meant by reassuring Isaac that God would provide a lamb) and theology (e.g., God's need for a test in the first place and what an omiscient God could have learned from it). The story has been connected to rituals (blowing a ram's horn), theology (martyrdom, resurrection), and social concerns (generational tension and human sacrifice), as well as Jewish history (military victory and persecution).

Most importantly, none of these approaches—literal, allegorical, mystical, or homiletical—has been allowed to drown out the others. Rather, they exist alongside one another, providing each passage and every word with multiple explanations and even layers of significance. As Abraham Joshua Heschel explained, the Bible contains "an ocean of meaning" that makes it relevant to history and ethics, law and theology, edification and entertainment.[255] Interpretation is sometimes even elevated to the status of revelation. As the Talmud proclaims, "What is Torah? The interpretation of Torah."[256]

SIX

Making the Bible Accessible

DESPITE THE CENTRALITY ACCORDED THE BIBLE'S Hebrew form, Jewish tradition requires that its recitation during worship be accompanied by a translation.[1] However, there are several restrictions on how this should be done. The translator (*meturgeman*) must stand alongside the reader and translate each verse as it is read (or after every third verse of the haftarah reading) without looking in the scroll or using a written text, presumably so that listeners do not confuse the translation with the original.[2] However, certain passages may not be translated at all, whether because they are especially sacred (e.g., the priestly blessing in Num. 6:24–26) or on account of their sensitive content (the story of Reuben's adultery in Gen. 35:22 and the second part of the golden calf story in Exod. 32:21–25).[3]

As a result, Jews have translated the Bible into a remarkable array of languages. The Talmud itself mentions Egyptian, Median, Aramaic, Elamite, and Iberian renderings.[4] There are also Jewish versions in Amharic, Arabic, Dutch, English, French, Geez, Georgian, German, Greek, Hungarian, Italian, Persian, Russian, Spanish, Tatar, Yiddish, and even modern (Israeli) Hebrew, with multiple versions in some of these, most notably Greek, Aramaic, Arabic, Yiddish/German, and English.[5]

Greek

Although Jewish tradition traces the Aramaic translation to the end of the biblical period,[6] the oldest surviving translation is in

Greek. According to a legend first mentioned in a letter attributed to one Aristeas, the Greek translation had been commissioned by the Seleucid king Ptolemy II Philadelphus (285–247 BCE), who brought seventy-two Jewish elders to Alexandria from Palestine in order to produce a version of the Pentateuch for his collection of world literature. Later tradition adjusted the number of translators to seventy, hence the name "Septuagint," a title extended to the entire Greek Bible.[7]

Modern scholars doubt the accuracy of this account, which was probably intended to glorify the Greek version; however, they do think that the Septuagint, which is actually a collection of several separate translations, began with a third-century rendering of the Pentateuch in Alexandria. Besides making this one of the oldest translations of any major literary work, it also means that the process of translating the Bible had begun before all of its contents were completed. (The book of Daniel, which is the latest of the biblical books, was not finished until the middle of the second century BCE.) The rabbis conceded as much when they ascribed the beginnings of Bible translation to the time of Joshua.[8] By the third century CE the Church father Origen knew of several other Greek translations, three of which were attributed to figures named Aquila, Symmachus, and Theodotion, all of whom various Christian thinkers believed had converted to Judaism.[9]

Aramaic

There are several ancient Jewish translations of the Bible into Aramaic and even some into modern Aramaic.[10] In fact, the idea of Bible translation is so closely associated with that language, that by the tannaitic period the noun *targum*, which literally means "translation," was largely restricted to Aramaic versions and biblical passages originally written in Aramaic.[11]

The Aramaic translations probably originated as the work of professional translators who accompanied the reading of Scripture during worship.[12] Although rabbinic tradition traces these to the tannaitic period in the first two centuries CE,[13] the Dead Sea

Scrolls include earlier renderings of Leviticus and Job and the gospels quote an Aramaic version of Psalm 22:2 that matches the existing targum of that book.[14]

There are several targumim to the Pentateuch. Two of these seem to have been composed in Palestine; one is attributed to the same Jonathan who was credited with the targum to the Prophets (hence "Pseudo-Jonathan").[15] The other, which may date from the second to the fourth centuries, was discovered in 1949 at the Vatican Library, where it had been miscataloged as a copy of Targum Onkelos; it is now called Targum Neofiti, after the Pia Domus Neophytorum from which it had been brought to the Vatican in 1891. There are also several versions of a so-called Fragment Targum, which includes 850 verses.[16] However, none of these ever achieved the official status attained by a targum that Babylonian Jews brought to Palestine after removing much of the non-biblical lore (aggadah) incorporated in it. This has come to be attributed to "Onkelos," most likely because of a misunderstanding of a talmudic passage that actually refers to Aquila's Greek rendering.[17]

By contrast, there is only one complete targum of the Prophets. Its attribution to Jonathan ben Uzziel, the most distinguished of Hillel's students,[18] has been questioned, since the name Jonathan ("gift of God") is the Hebrew equivalent of the Greek "Theodotion." Several rabbinic traditions connect this targum with Rabbi Joseph bar Ḥiyya, who led a Babylonian rabbinic academy in the early fourth century.[19] Like Targum Onkelos on which it depends, it may have grown out of synagogue use, as haftarah translations were expanded to include all the prophetic literature.

Although the Talmud reports a heavenly prohibition against translating the Writings into Aramaic ("because it contains the date of the messiah"[20]), there are targumim to all the books in the third section of the Jewish Bible except Daniel and Ezra-Nehemiah, substantial sections of which are already in Aramaic. There are even three targumim of the book of Esther and references to several for Job, not counting a rather literal rendering that was found among the Dead Sea Scrolls.[21] Various sources also mention targumim of Tobit and, perhaps, Ben Sira.[22]

Much like the Septuagint, which is really a collection of often unrelated translations, the various targumim date from the pre-Christian version of Job found at Qumran to the medieval translation of Chronicles and range in style from the literal Onkelos to the allegorical rendering of the Song of Songs. However, the Greek renderings were collected by the Christian Church, which used them as its Bible in a way that the targumim never were.

Arabic

Medieval Jews in Islamic countries translated the Bible into Arabic. According to one tradition, the earliest versions were actually intended for non-Jews.[23] The predominant Jewish rendering was that of Saadia ben Joseph (892–942), who led the rabbinical academy in Sura, Babylonia.[24] This was a remarkable undertaking for one man; to this day only a handful of translations have been produced by individuals, most conspicuously Ludwig Philippson in Germany, Isaac Leeser in nineteenth-century America, and Robert Alter in our own time.[25] (Moses Mendelssohn did not produce his translation alone.) Beginning in the fifteenth century, several more literal translations (*shurūḥ*) were produced as well as others by Karaites.[26] However, Saadia's version, which has been revised several times and translated into French and English, is still in use.

Spanish, French, and Italian

Jews also translated the Bible into several other languages. The most prominent Ladino (Judeo-Spanish) version was produced in the sixteenth century by Jews who had settled in Ferrara, Italy, after being expelled from Spain; it was dedicated to the prominent sixteenth-century Sephardic figure Doña Gracia Nasi.[27] There have also been Italian and French translations.[28]

German and Yiddish

German and Yiddish versions of individual books and groups of books—some in rhyme, others in the form of paraphrases and romances—began to appear in the thirteenth century.[29] Early oral renderings seem to have drawn on glossaries.[30] Three hundred years later Jacob ben Isaac, who lived in the eastern Polish town of Yarnow, prepared a version of the Pentateuch that has gone through hundreds of editions and even been translated into English and Hebrew.[31] Initially called the *Teytsh Ḥumesh*, it came to be thought of as "the women's Bible" and is therefore named *Tsena Ureena*, two feminine verbs from the Song of Songs (3:11) that were mistakenly applied to the whole.[32] It has been translated into Latin, French, German, and English.[33]

Although the sixteenth-century printer Isaac Prossnitz planned a Yiddish translation of the entire Bible ("all twenty-four"), his dream was not fulfilled until 1678–79, when Yekutiel ben Isaak Blitz and Joslen Witzenhausen produced two versions, both published in Amsterdam, the latter with the approval of Poland's Jewish Council of the Four Lands.[34]

Moses Mendelssohn's German rendering (1780–83) was produced in response to criticism of these. Although never completed, his version proved controversial; it was banned in several towns and possibly even burned.[35] Nonetheless, it went through twenty-seven editions and was approved by the Berlin rabbinate.[36] The eighteenth-century Lithuanian scholar Elijah ben Solomon (the Vilna Gaon) owned a copy of Mendelssohn's rendering of the book of Proverbs.[37] The project helped legitimize Bible translation among Jewish circles, as evidenced by its detractors' creation of an orthodoxe-israelitische Bibel-Anstalt, which commissioned a translation that would follow traditional Jewish interpretations.[38]

An especially successful Jewish translation of the Bible into German was initiated by Leopold Zunz in conjunction with Julius Fürst, Heymann Arnheim, and Michael Sachs. Intended "for home and school," it was reprinted many times over the century following its initial appearance in 1837 as well as alongside the Hebrew in a

1997 edition that was produced in Israel.[39] Yet another version was commissioned by Berlin's Jewish community in 1924 and edited by Harry Torczyner.[40]

In 1913 Martin Buber, along with Moritz Heimann and Efraim Frisch, undertook what they intended to be a fresh, interdenominational rendering. When publisher Lambert Schneider asked that it be based on Martin Luther's version, Buber approached Franz Rosenzweig, whose translation of the medieval Hebrew poet Judah Halevi's work had caught his attention. They collaborated on the books of Genesis through Isaiah, with Buber sending preliminary drafts to Rosenzweig for revision. After Rosenzweig's death in 1929, Buber completed the project alone.[41]

English

Jewish translations into English follow a similar pattern as those into German. In 1840, David A. de Sola, the hazzan of London's Sephardic community, proposed a Jewish translation of the complete Bible into English. His vision was fulfilled by Isaac Leeser of Philadelphia, who dominated American Jewish life during the middle of the nineteenth century.[42] Leeser's version of the Pentateuch and *haftarot* (*Torat Ha'elohim*) was followed by the entire Jewish Bible (*The Twenty-Four Books*) in 1853 and revised three years later.

Despite Leeser's acknowledged limitations as a scholar and a thinker,[43] his translation became *the* Jewish version. It was published in Great Britain (1865) as well as in the United States and was even translated into German, with some of his renderings retained in later Jewish translations. However, it was also widely criticized. The nineteenth-century scholar Marcus Kalisch described it as "antiquated" and full of errors.[44] However, its eventual decline was less the product of any inherent flaw than the appearance of the Christian Revised Version at the end of the nineteenth century.

Although Isaac Mayer Wise, the organizer of the Reform movement in America, had already proposed creating a new translation in 1876, it would be sixteen years before the recently formed Jewish

Publication Society of America (JPS) put forth a concrete plan for a revision of Leeser's version.[45] However, only the book of Psalms ever appeared.[46] The Reform movement's Central Conference of American Rabbis therefore set out to produce its own edition of the Christian Revised Version, but subsequently agreed to participate in the Jewish Publication Society version, which finally appeared in 1917 under the leadership of Max Margolis, a professor at Hebrew Union College who had also taught at Dropsie College and the University of California.[47]

After the Protestant Revised Standard Version of the Old Testament (1952) and, to a lesser extent, the Roman Catholic Confraternity version (1969) began to capture the attention of the Jewish world, the Jewish Publication Society undertook an updated version, this time under the leadership of Harry Orlinsky, a professor of Bible at New York's Jewish Institute of Religion.[48] The Torah translation appeared in 1962 (a revised edition was published in 1967 and a gender-sensitive "adaptation" in 2006), followed by the Prophets (*Nevi'im*) in 1978 and the Writings (*Kethubim*), which, except for the Five Scrolls, was produced by a second committee in 1982.

As with previous renderings, the Orthodox Jewish community expressed reservations even before the JPS translation was published.[49] Alongside doctrinal concerns, the involvement of non-Orthodox and even liberal Orthodox participants, not to mention non-Jewish sources, were of particular concern. They therefore began to produce translations of their own, including Aryeh Kaplan's *Living Torah*, which was later joined by the *Living N"K,* and the monumental ArtScroll project.[50] There have also been numerous scholarly renderings of individual books as well as several literary translations of individual and groups of books by Stephen Mitchell, David Rosenberg, Marcia Falk, Ariel and Chana Bloch, Everett Fox (whose rendering of the Pentateuch and Former Prophets follows the principles set by Rosenzweig and Buber), and, most recently, Robert Alter, who has rendered the entire Bible.[51]

Characteristic Features

The immense amount of energy Jews have invested in producing Bible translations is especially notable in light of Jewish ambivalence about translating the Bible. The medieval tractate *Soferim* insists that "the Torah cannot be translated adequately" and equates the translation of the Torah into Greek with the making of the golden calf.[52] As the grandson of Jesus ben Sira explained in his introduction to the Greek rendering of his grandfather's Hebrew book (Ecclesiasticus), "Words spoken originally in Hebrew are not as effective when they are translated into another language."[53] The ancient rabbis taught that translations do not enjoy the same level of sanctity as the original Hebrew.[54] A commentary to the *Megillat Ta'anit* even attributes the fast on the 8th of Tevet to the fact that it was on that day during the time of King Ptolemy that "the Torah was written in Greek [after which] darkness came to the world for three days,"[55] and the Zohar describes the Aramaic translation of the Bible as being written in the language of the "evil force" (*sitra' 'aḥra'*).[56] In more recent times, Franz Rosenzweig insisted that "The German . . . can and will read the Bible in German . . . the Jew can understand it only in Hebrew," while Moses Mendelssohn asked, "Why would anyone dig from broken cisterns when he can draw from a pool of living water?"[57]

This attitude helps explain why Jewish translations are frequently said to be intended for women, children, and the uneducated,[58] which may have contributed to the perception of the *Teytsh Ḥumesh* (*Tsena Ureena*) as a women's Bible, a description that plainly served the self-interests of a male population unwilling to admit its own limitations. It was also a factor in the production of "children's" and "family Bibles" in the German- and English-speaking worlds.[59]

Jewish translations are often seen as responses to assimilation, as is an Israeli version in modern Hebrew.[60] The third-century church father Origen explicitly described Aquila's Greek translation as being for non-Hebrew-speaking Jews,[61] much as the *Teytsh Ḥumesh* was intended "so that all the people of the land, both small and great, might themselves know and understand how to read all of the twenty-four books . . . so that a person will not have to seek an exposition or interpretation . . . and can study them himself."[62] Similar logic underlies Saadia's references to the Bible as "Qur'an" (at Ps. 80:14), his rendering of "God" as "Allah," "priest" as "imam," and "king" as "caliph," and his description of Moses as "the messenger" (*al-rasūl*), Islam's title for Mohammad.[63] Likewise, Judeo-German renderings translate the terms for altar and priest with words drawn from Catholicism.[64] Other translations "update" geographical references, as when the Septuagint renders "Arameans" and "Philistines" as "Syrians" and "Greeks," and the Targum translates "Ishmaelites" as "Arabs" and "Edom" as "Byzantium."[65]

At the same time, these versions cannot be explained by assimilation alone. Several Jewish translations, including Saadia's version, the sixteenth-century Ferrara Bible, and modern Persian Bibles use a Hebrew font, while others were produced in communities that did not need them. For example, the oldest known targumim as well as early translations into Greek were found at Qumran, a presumably Hebrew-speaking settlement in the heart of the Holy Land. Likewise, a statement at the end of the Septuagint rendering of Esther attributes it to a Jerusalemite (i.e., a Jew).[66] Solomon Bloomgarden, a poet better known by his pen name Yehoash, produced a Yiddish translation in America;[67] the German renderings of Harry Torczyner and Buber-Rosenzweig were completed in modern Israel more than a decade after the destruction of the German-speaking community for which they had been planned.[68] Georgian and Amharic renderings were also produced there,[69] as was an English translation by Harold Fisch. Indeed, Yemenite Jews in Israel recite the Aramaic Targum Onkelos to this day, even though Aramaic is no longer spoken there.[70] Such versions are plainly about more than making the Bible's meaning accessible.

Surprisingly, several translations claim to be vehicles for improving Jews' proficiency in their local languages. One sixteenth-century Pentateuch included the Hebrew along with Aramaic, Ladino, and

Greek translations, "so that it may be of use to the young Israelite, so they may learn to speak correctly."[71] In a similar way, Moses Mendelssohn hoped "to render a service to my children and perhaps to a considerable part of my nation, if I give into their hands a better translation and explanation of the holy books than what they have had until now. This is the first step towards culture (*Cultur*), from which my nation, alas, is being kept in such a great distance."[72] Max Margolis, the central figure in the 1917 American JPS translation, consciously emulated that goal, observing that "we Jews of America—and of England—must study the Bible [in] English, read it and re-read it, that we may possess ourselves of an English style that may pass scrutiny on the part of those who know."[73]

With that in mind, several Jewish translators emphasize the importance of fluency. As Maimonides observed, "The translator who proposes to render each word literally and adhere slavishly to the order of the words and sentences in the original will meet much difficulty and the result will be doubtful and corrupt. This is not the right method. The translator should first try to grasp the sense of the subject thoroughly, and then state the theme with perfect clarity in the other language. This, however, cannot be done without changing the order of words, putting many words for one word or *vice versa*, and adding or taking away words, so that the subject be perfectly intelligible in the language into which he translates."[74]

Although Saadia claimed to "reproduce the simple meaning of the words of Scripture without linguistic digression or polemics against heresy,"[75] he did not hesitate to expand the original, divide verses differently than the Hebrew, rearrange some sections, or vary the rendering of the same phrase, including the common Hebrew conjunction *ve*-(lit. "and"), so as to create complex sentences with a variety of tenses rather than replicating biblical Hebrew's tendency to string together simple declarations using its two basic verbal forms.[76] Saadia also gave each book a distinctive name, calling Proverbs "The Book of Striving for Life's Wisdom" and Job "The Book of the Recognition of Divine Justice."[77]

In light of these features, it is ironic that Jewish versions have often been criticized for their lack of fluency. Ancient Christians cited the Septuagint's "Hebraic character," while Origen described Aquila as being "enslaved to the Hebrew language."[78] Both the Ferrara Bible and Blitz's Yiddish translation were called "barbaric," Joslen Witzenhausen's German version "rough and unpolished (*horrido et inculto*)," Zunz's as "slavish, literal" (*sklavisch, wortgetreue*), and Buber/Rosenzweig's as more Hebraic than German.[79] That critique has continued, with the 1917 JPS version being criticized for its "queer-ities of English" and its 1985 successor called "dull, colorless and pedestrian." One reader noted that Everett Fox's "signal limitation is his monogamous attachment to the Hebrew, often at the cost of the English."[80]

Such comments draw from a long-standing critique of Judaism as clinging to the letter of the Bible rather than its spirit,[81] but not without validity. Jewish translations do often try to replicate the original Hebrew, an approach that is most obvious in their transliterations of Hebrew terms. The Septuagint's incorporation of the words *amen, camel, hallelulah, manna, sabbath, sack, sapphire,* and *Satan* have even made their way into popular usage.[82] Later Greek versions continued that practice, as did early Judeo-German translations, the Spanish Ferrara Bible, and Karaite translations into Arabic.[83] Elsewhere, Jewish translations try to reproduce the original Hebrew's sound. Although most famously associated with Aquila, Buber/Rosenzweig, and Everett Fox, this is also true of the early Yiddish renderings and even purportedly sometimes more fluent translations. Thus the Septuagint translates *raq* ("only") as *rachis* (1 Sam. 5:4), *darĕvan* (goad) as *drepanon* (1 Sam. 13:21), *tokh* ("oppress") as *tokou* ("usury," Ps. 55/54:12, 72/71:14), and *ṭeref* ("prey") as *trophē* (Ps. 110:5).[84]

Several translations also use language that is awkward in the new tongue in order to approximate the relationship of the original Hebrew sounds. Thus Aquila translates Hebrew words that come from a common root with words that are related in Greek, rendering the word *rēʾšit* (lit. "beginning"), which opens the Hebrew Bible, as *kephalaion* (lit. "chief things") rather than the more common *arkē,* because of the former's relationship to the Greek word *kephalē* ("head"), which corresponds to *rēʾšîtʾ*s root *rōʾš* ("head").[85] Etymological concerns also explain medieval Judeo-German versions' rendering of *shēn* as "sharp" (at Isa. 45:9) rather than as "ivory," and Mendelssohn's translation of the Hebrew idiom *kārat bĕrît* ("to make a covenant") as "einen Bund zerschneiden."[86] Samson Raphael Hirsch used this same approach as a way of preserving sound relationships, such as those among *rōʾš, rāʿaš,* and *rāḥaš.*[87]

This sensitivity to linguistic relations reached its peak in the Buber/Rosenzweig translation, which sought to preserve words' etymological origins in order to make wordplays perceptible to non-Hebrew speakers. Thus they rendered *mizbēaḥ* (altar) as *Schlachtstatt* (slaughter site), *tĕhillîm* (psalms) as "Preisungen" (praisings), and *qorban* (sacrifice), which comes from the root *qrb* ("bring near," e.g., Num. 16:5), as "Darnahung" (from the German root meaning "near") instead of the more conventional "Opfer" (offering).[88] They also identified theme words (Leitwörter) that run through particular passages, finding related words for the Hebrew *moʿed* ("assembly"), *ʿedah* ("group"), and *yaʿad* ("join together") in Numbers 6:2–11.[89] Centuries earlier, a similar concern had led the Neofiti targum and Saadia to use the same word for each Hebrew term throughout.[90]

In order to accomplish this, Buber/Rosenzweig had to push the German language to its limits, inventing words and using archaic terms and constructions. In the words of one scholar, they believed that "the Bible means something to Jews in its very Hebraic formulation. The Jew must hear the Bible in Hebrew and, if not Hebrew, then a German or English that is bent into a Hebraic shape."[91] In keeping with Rosenzweig's view that "everything in Scripture is pure spokenness," they divided the text into breathing units rather than verses so that readers would be forced to read it aloud.[92]

As a result of these attitudes, Jewish translations include a large number of Hebraisms. For example, both the Septuagint and the Karaite renderings in Arabic sometimes translate Hebrew's emphatic use of the infinitive alongside a regular verb literally, yielding sentences like "And do we shall do . . . and confirm you will confirm . . . and do you will do" (Jer. 44:25/Septuagint 51:25) or "with theft I stole" (Gen. 40:5) and "with witness he witnessed" (Gen. 43:3). A similar motivation led Aquila to translate Hebrew's first-person pronoun *'ani* (*egō*) differently than the synonymous *'anokhi* (*egō eimi*, lit. "I am"). He also uses two prepositions for "between" in the way that Hebrew does (lit. "between x and between y," e.g., Gen. 1:4), even though Greek, like English, requires only one and translates Hebrew's direct object marker *'et,* which is not necessary in Greek, with *syn* (lit. "with"), reflecting Hebrew's homonymous *'et,* which means "with." Since Hebrew does not use a verb "to be" in the present tense, early Judeo-German versions often omit present tense forms of the verb "to be," leading to sentences such as "du er mein König" (lit. "you he my king").[93] They also translate verbs' pronominal prefixes even in cases where the Hebrew has an actual noun subject, resulting in German sentences such as "un er sagt got" (lit. "and he said God") for the Hebrew *vayo'mer 'elohim* ("and God said").[94]

Attitudes toward Translations

Despite its high regard for the original Hebrew, Jewish tradition has granted translations significant authority. The Mishnah allows biblical books to be written and the scroll of Esther to be read in any language.[95] In the Middle Ages, Judah ibn Tibbon called for the Torah portion to be "read every week . . . in Arabic"[96] and the Talmud cites Targum Onkelos for halakhic purposes.[97] Britain's chief rabbi Joseph Hertz went so far as to claim that "translations of the Bible share in the sacredness of the original."[98]

As we have seen, the rabbis considered translations to be biblically mandated, with origins that go back to the generation following Sinai. An early midrash claims that the Torah had been given in Greek, Arabic, and Aramaic as well as in Hebrew[99] and the targum of the Prophets as composed by the divinely inspired prophets Haggai, Zechariah, and Malachi.[100] This attitude underlies Philo's identification of the seventy(-two) translators of the Septuagint as prophets who produced identical renderings and whose work was honored by Alexandrian Jews with an annual festival.[101] Other traditions describe Aquila as a student of Rabbi Akiva[102] and Targum Onkelos, which had a masorah of its own, as holy.[103] According to Rashi, the targumim restored "what had been forgotten since Sinai,"[104] and Franz Rosenzweig claimed that "the translator, the one who hears and transmits, knows himself equal to the One who first spoke and received the word."[105] Rosenzweig's partner, Martin Buber, described his decision to produce a translation in language reminiscent of the prophets' description of their divine call:

> Once with a light keel
> I shipped out to the land of legends
> Through the storm of deceit play,
> with my gaze fixed on the goal
> And in my blood
> beguiling poison–
> then one descended to me
> who seized me by the hair
> And spoke: Now render the Scriptures![106]

In order to make sense of this, it is helpful to note that translations present themselves as the very works they render.[107] After all, Bible translations are typically titled "The Bible" (or the like), even though they are obviously only renderings of the "original" Bible into different languages at different times and for different contexts. As such, they resemble works like Jubilees and the Biblical Antiquities or the Genesis Apocryphon and the Temple Scroll from Qumran, which present themselves as Scripture rather than quoting it, citing sources, or offering multiple interpretations.

Like these works, which scholars sometimes call "rewritten Bible,"[108] Jewish translations often incorporate traditional interpretations, a practice their creators occasionally acknowledge.[109] Thus, Pseudo-Jonathan translates the Hebrew *ṭoṭafot* as *tefillin*,[110] while other targumim render Deuteronomy's commandment not to cook a kid in its mother's milk (14:23 and Exod. 23:19) as "Don't eat milk with meat."[111] Targum Pseudo-Jonathan also translates the Hebrew phrase "an eye for an eye" (Exod. 21:24) as "the value of an eye for an eye,"[112] while Isaac Leeser translates *lĕʿôlām* ("forever") in Exodus 21:6 as "till the jubilee," bringing it into conformity with Leviticus 25:10.[113] Following Leeser's lead, the 1917 Jewish Publication Society version rendered the command that the holiday now known as Shavuot be observed fifty days following "the day after the *shabbat* in Passover" (Lev 23:15), as counting from "the morrow after the day of rest" in accordance with the Jewish tradition that the counting begin after the holiday's first sacred day (i.e., day of rest) rather than the first Sabbath, though it did put "Sabbath" in the notes.[114]

In keeping with this approach, Jewish translations sometimes incorporate midrashic traditions. For example, Pseudo-Jonathan includes references to the rock that followed the Israelites through the desert and to Balaam's servants Jannes and Jambres.[115] The Septuagint refers to the afterlife, and several targumim incorporate allusions to resurrection, the messiah, Torah study, and angels.[116] They also translate biblical references to "prophets" as "scribes," the Jerusalem Temple as a synagogue, and visions as school.[117] Targum Neofiti identifies the garden of Eden's tree of life with the Torah (Gen. 3:24).

In keeping with the Jewish interpretive tradition, Targum Onkelos provides names for several characters who are anonymous in the Hebrew, identifying Cain's father as the evil angel Samael (Gen. 4:1) and the man who spoke with Jacob as the angel Gabriel (Gen. 37:15). More broadly, the Palestinian targumim frequently replace pronouns with proper names.[118] Saadia Gaon identifies the figures mentioned in the superscriptions to various Psalms and sections of Proverbs, as when he implies that the Lemuel mentioned in Proverbs 31:1 is Solomon.[119] He also supplements the genealogies of Job's companions with information drawn from other biblical passages.[120]

More dramatic (and somewhat jarring to modern eyes) are the paraphrasing targumim to the Five Scrolls, especially the second targum (Targum Sheni) to Esther and the one to the Song of Songs, which treats that book as an allegory tracing God's love for Israel from the revelation at Sinai to the Babylonian exile and then beyond to the messianic redemption. It, therefore, renders several verses in the book's opening chapter as follows:

	HEBREW	TARGUM
1	Let him kiss me with the kisses of his mouth, for your love is better than wine.	Solomon, the prophet, said: Blessed be the name of YYY/Y who gave us the Torah through Moses, the great scribe, written on two tablets of stone, and six orders of the Mishna, and the Talmud for study, and has spoken with us face to face like a man who kisses his fellow out of great love which he loved us more than the seventy nations;
5	I am black and lovely, O daughters of Jerusalem, like the tents of Kedar, like the curtains of Solomon.	When the people of the household of Israel made the calf, their faces darkened like Ethiopians who dwell in the dwellings of Kedar; and when they repented and were forgiven, the radiant glory of their faces increased like angels. This happened when they made the curtains for the tabernacle, and the Presence of YYY/Y dwelt among them, and Moses, their teacher, went up to the firmament and made peace between them and the king;
6	Do not look at me for I am dark, for the sun has scorched me. My mother's sons were angry at me; they made me guard the vineyards, but I have not guarded my own vineyard.	The assembly of Israel said before the nations: Do not despise me because I am darker than you, because I have acted in accordance with your deeds and bowed down to the sun and to the moon, inasmuch as false prophets have brought the virulent anger of YYY/Y upon me and taught me to worship their errors and to follow their law, but I have not worshipped the master of the world, who is my God, nor followed His law, nor kept His regulation and his Torah.

Jewish translations' treatment of God is especially revealing. For example, the Septuagint changes Moses's description of God as a "man of war" (Exod. 15:3; Isa. 42:13) to "He destroys war" and adds several prayers to the book of Esther that are not found in the Hebrew, where God is famously absent. (These passages are included in Roman Catholic Old Testaments and editions of the Apocrypha.) The targumim also add prayers[121] and soften anthropomorphisms. Thus the statement about God's being seen on Mount Sinai (Exod. 24:10) is translated as referring to His glory,[122] references to God's going down as "He revealed,"[123] active verbs with God as the subject to passive,[124] and metaphors into similes.[125] However, the targumim were not entirely consistent about this, retaining references to God's hands, eyes, and finger alongside statements about God's seeing and laughing, while sometimes adding anthropomorphisms where the Hebrew has none and intensifying those it does have.[126] Observing that "wherever our sages . . . encountered any such comparisons of God to physical beings, they did not translate them in an anthropomorphic way,"[127] Saadia Gaon rendered Genesis's reference to God descending (11:5) as God "caused something hidden to descend" and Exodus's mention of His feet (24:18) as "His light." Saadia also translated *vayo'mer* (lit. "He said") as "He willed" and *vayar'* ("He saw") as "He knew" in the first chapter of Genesis. Still, he was criticized for not eliminating all such instances.[128]

Possibly the most distinctive feature of Jewish Bible translations is their treatment of God's name, which Jews have avoided pronouncing since antiquity.[129] Ancient Greek versions sometimes write it out in Hebrew characters, an approach adopted in the most recent Jewish Publication Society edition.[130] Several ancient witnesses report that Aquila used the Hebrew alphabet for this purpose, leading the unknowing to mistake those letters for Greek, which they read as PIPI (ΠΙΠΙ).[131] Surviving manuscripts of the Septuagint, which were intended for Christian audiences, render it with the words *kyrios* ("lord") or *theos* ("God"), corresponding to the long-standing Jewish tradition of substituting *'ădônay* (lit. "my lord"), a practice that survives in Hebrew biblical texts, where the consonants YHWH are accompanied by the vowels for *'ădônay* to reflect how the word is read publicly.[132] The targumim use a variety of substitutes, including *shekhinta'* (presence), *yeqara'* (glory), *memra'* (word), and *ruaḥ qudsha'* (holy spirit).[133] Where early German Jewish translations used *got*, Mendelssohn preferred "der Ewige" (lit. "the Eternal") for both the tetragrammaton (YHWH) and other designations of God.[134] However, most German and English versions follow the classic Martin Luther and King James translations by rendering it as LORD or *Herr*, though the ArtScroll version uses "Hashem" (lit. "the name"). Everett Fox prefers the vowel-free YHWH, which obviously cannot be pronounced, whereas Buber/Rosenzweig uses capitalized pronouns (Ich, Du, etc.).

Why Jewish Translations

In order to make sense of this, it is useful to juxtapose the words of two Jewish thinkers: Solomon Grayzel, editor of the Jewish Publication Society of America in the 1960s when it embarked on a translation of the Bible into English, who observed that "for us Jews the sacred text is the Hebrew. No translation can replace it," versus the thirteenth-century Italian talmudist Zedekiah ben Abraham, who said, "Those who read the Torah are obligated to station translators to translate what they read so that women and *'amei ha'areṣ* can hear."[135] Taken together these statements reflect the fact that Jewish tradition regards both reading and explaining the Bible as obligatory yet complementary activities. This attitude is rooted in the Jewish understanding of the Bible's account of the first public scripture reading, when Ezra stood before those who had returned from the Babylonian exile in Jerusalem and read "from the book of God's Torah clearly and gave the sense so that they understood the reading" (Neh. 8:8). Jewish tradition has taken this to mean that it was *both* read *and* explained—the clarity understood as a reference to the Aramaic translation that was later extended to allow for Arabic, French, Greek, and Italian versions.[136] The Talmud even reports Rabbi Joseph's claim that "if it weren't for the *targum* of that scripture we wouldn't know its meaning."[137] A similar attitude is evident in the title of Saadia's version—*tafsir* (lit. "explanation")—and the Shulḥan Arukh's authorization of substituting other modes of explanation for the translation.[138] It is therefore noteworthy that modern synagogue Bibles include a translation and commentary alongside the original Hebrew, thereby ensuring that the Torah reading is accompanied by both a vernacular rendering and an explanation.

It is striking that some Jewish Bible translations were produced in environments that already had vernacular versions. Besides the ancient Greek translations that followed the Septuagint, Christian versions in Arabic existed prior to Saadia's.[139] Mendelssohn's German translation and Isaac Leeser's English rendering were both created in spite of the Martin Luther and King James versions, just as the Buber/Rosenzweig translation came after that of Zunz and the various English translations were produced despite the availability of the Christian Revised and Revised Standard versions.

It is, therefore, reasonable to see these editions as responses to the perceived inadequacy of non-Jewish renderings. Mendelssohn explicitly stated that Christian translations ignored the Hebrew accents and vowels, while Isaac Leeser warned that although "those who assisted in furnishing the common [King James] version may have been as honest as men writing for their sect are ever likely to be . . . they could not well avoid falling into the common error . . . of giving a colouring to their work which would . . . confirm their peculiar views."[140] That attitude existed already in antiquity, when Jews challenged Christians' reliance on the Septuagint, most conspicuously for its rendering of Isaiah's statement about a child being born to an *almah* (7:14) with the Greek term *parthenos*, which the gospels understood to mean "virgin."[141] Aquila, therefore, translated *almah* as *neanis* (young woman), the same rendering he used for the Hebrew word *betulah* ("virgin," e.g., Deut. 22:28). Over a thousand years later Yekutiel ben Isaak Blitz provided a ten-page description of the ways this passage has been misunderstood before rendering it as "d'junge frau" (a young woman), as have modern Jewish translations without exception.[142] Various manuscripts of the 1547 Ladino Ferrara Bible provide several different renderings, including *virgen* ("virgin"), *moça* ("maiden"), and the transliteration *la alma*.[143] Aquila's translation of the Hebrew *mashiaḥ* as *ēleimmenos* ("anointed," Dan. 9:26) rather than *christos* is another effort to avoid Christian overtones.[144] Several passages in the targumim also appear to be directed against Christianity and even Islam.[145]

Because of these concerns, nineteenth-century Jews created lists of annotations to Christian editions. For example, Selig Newman compiled his 1839 *Emendations of the Authorised Version of the Old Testament* "to point out and correct the mistranslations which exist in the authorised version of the Old Testament . . . [and] to make known to Bible-readers generally, the opinion[s] of the learned Jewish commentators, both medieval and modern."[146] Besides explaining that Isaiah 7:14 refers to a young woman rather than a virgin, he observed that the word *torah* means "instruction" not "law" and, in accordance with rabbinic tradition, that the Hebrew word *elohim* does not always mean God.[147] Similar motivations lay behind Benjamin Marcus's *Mykur Hayim* (1846) as well as the Jewish Religious Education Board of London's 1896 "Appendix to the Revised Version."[148]

In fact, the first Jewish translations of the Pentateuch into English were largely "sanitized" versions of the King James translation, with David Levi (1787) eliminating its captions while adding Jewish annotations and Isaac Delgado (1789) inserting "correction[s] . . . Wherever it deviates from the genuine Sense of the Hebrew Expressions, or where it renders obscure the Meaning of the Text; or, lastly, when it occasions a seeming Contradiction."[149] As the editors of the 1917 JPS version explained, "Jews who are familiar with Hebrew from their childhood may be expected to have an intimate feeling for the niceties of Hebrew idiom—and are more apt for this reason to do justice to the genius of the Hebrew language."[150]

More than accuracy was at stake in these projects. As we have seen, the rabbis saw the Christian adoption of the Septuagint as depriving them of their possession; the second-century Church father Irenaeus even acknowledged that Jews would have burnt the Septuagint had they known how Christians would come to use it.[151] Although the midrash uses this to account for the Mishnah's importance, it also helps explain the subsequent Greek translations—those of Symmachus, Theodotion, and Aquila. As David A. de Sola observed nearly two millennia later, "Everywhere the Israelite feels the necessity to have the word of God interpreted for him by a brother in faith. In Germany, in France, in the Netherlands, we have translations of Scripture marked by faithfulness and beauty, the work of Jews."[152] The Berlin Bible echoed that sentiment in its stated intention to "replace Christian spirit with ancient Jewish values,"[153] as did Franz Rosenzweig in his goal of producing an "un-Christian Bible,"[154] which Buber attributed to the fact that "Luther had translated the Hebrew Bible into the German of his New Testament."[155] In short, Jews have wanted translations of their own, even when they largely imitate non-Jewish versions. As Ismar Elbogen put it, Moses Mendelssohn's translation "has given the Bible back to the Jews."[156] That motivation was on vivid display in a 1956 letter circulated by the Jewish Publication Society to raise funds for its projected Bible translation, which pointed out that "The Catholics have done it; the Protestants have done it; and now the Jews are going to do it."[157]

Jewish versions often assert the Bible's Jewishness by replacing conventional vernacular forms of Hebrew proper names with transliterations. Although particularly conspicuous in Orthodox translations, such as that of S. R. Hirsch (e.g., Jisroël, Mauscheh, Odom, and Chawo), this approach was already evident in Aquila (e.g., *Iōsoua* in place of the Septuagint's *Iēsous* and *Amari* for Amorite) and the Ferrara Bible, as well as in Mendelssohn (who referred to Egypt as Mitsrayim), Zunz (Chawah, Jisraël, Mosche, and Aharon, in place of Luther's Hava, Israel, and Mose), Torczyner (Par'o, Mizrain, Mauscheh, and Aharon), de Sola (Yaakob, Paroh), Buber/Rosenzweig (Chawwa, Kajin, Mosche), and Everett Fox (Hevel, Kayin, Avram).[158] As Cynthia Ozick explained "Remember that when a goy from Columbus, Ohio, says 'Elijah the Prophet' he's not talking about *Eliohu hanovi*. Eliohu is one of us. . . . The same biblical figure, with exactly the same history, once he puts on a name from King James, comes out a different person."[159]

Another way in which Jewish versions express their identity is by translating words differently when they refer to Jews than when they refer to non-Jews. For example, the Septuagint and the targum translate *mizbeaḥ* ("altar") as *thusiastērion* and *madbĕḥā* when it refers to Israelite altars, but *bōmos* and *ĕgôrâ* when they are pagan.[160] Targum Onkelos renders the verb *brḥ* as *'rq* ("flee") for non-Jews but *'zl* ("go") for Jews.[161] A similar motive may account for the targum's avoidance of the term "priests" for non-Israelites, such as Melchizedek (Gen. 14:10), Potiphera (Gen. 41:45), and Jethro (Exod. 3:1).[162]

More broadly, the targumim treat Israelite characters differently than non-Israelites, describing the patriarchs as righteous (*ṣadiqim*) or pious (*ḥasidim*) while calling Nimrod, Esau, Pharaoh, and Nebuchadnezzar evil.[163] Targum Jonathan brands non-Israelite prophets as false.[164] Other targumim minimize Jewish characters' misdeeds while adding pious acts for Jews. Thus, Onkelos renders Abraham's statement that his servants would take (*yiqĕḥu*) spoil as saying that they would receive (*yĕqabbĕlun*) it (Gen. 14:29) and Rachel's stealing (*gnb*) Laban's idols as "taking" them (*nsb*, Gen. 31:19). A similar motive may account for its rendering the Bible's description of Moses's wife as a *kushît* ("Ethiopian," Num. 12:1) with *shapirta* (beautiful); Jacob's "deceitful" (*bĕmirmah*) behavior (Gen. 27:35) as "with wisdom"; and Rahab's identification as a *zonah* ("prostitute," Josh. 2:1) as "innkeeper" (*'ittĕtā' pundĕqîtā'*). A similar motive may underlie the Septuagint's omission of David's affair with Bathsheba (2 Samuel 11).[165]

Paradoxically, Jewish translations sometimes imitate the very versions from which they seek differentiation. Moses Mendelssohn retained some of Martin Luther's language and even acknowledged his debt to the Protestants Johann Gottfried Eichhorn and Johann Gottfried Herder.[166] Isaac Leeser echoed the Authorized (King

James) Version,[167] and Abraham Benisch explicitly followed the Revised Version "where it could be done without doing violence to the principle of fidelity" to the original.[168] Most striking is the 1917 Jewish Publication Society's retention of many of the Christian version's Anglicisms, such as the British spelling for words like "honour" and "labour," and "corn" instead of the American "grain," even though the Revised Version had followed American norms.[169]

Bible translations are often presented as evidence of a community's maturity. David de Sola concluded his call for a Jewish translation of the Bible into English with this observation: "In the land where the knowledge of the Bible goes forth to every part of the globe, British Jews offer the world the striking anomaly that they alone in the whole of Europe possess no Bible translation in the vernacular, made by Jews for Jews."[170] A similar attitude underlay the Jewish Publication Society's 1892 resolution that "look[ed] forward to the time when the Society shall furnish a new and popular rendition of the book which the Jews have given to the world, the Bible, that shall be the work of *American* Jewish scholars" (emphasis added).[171] Kaufmann Kohler reiterated that sentiment at the 1917 gala dinner celebrating the translation's publication, when he "Blessed the eye that beheld the vision of the new glory of Israel on our beloved American soil, which witnesses a revival of the study of the Torah, a renaissance of the spirit of Jewish knowledge and wisdom as in the days of Spain and Babylon."[172] As the introduction to the 1917 translation noted, "Out of a handful of immigrants . . . we have grown under Providence in both numbers and importance, so that we constitute . . . the greatest sector of Israel living in a single country outside of Russia."[173]

THE PRODIGIOUS NUMBER OF BIBLE TRANSLATIONS produced by Jews, beginning already in biblical times, thus reflects both Jewish history and Jewish self-understanding. Though often attributed to linguistic ignorance, these works sometimes presume a level of familiarity with the original and have even, on occasion, been intended to facilitate acculturation. At the same time, some have been created in places where they could not be understood or where there already were other, typically non-Jewish versions that they imitated and from which they even borrowed. Jewish Bible translations are thus expressions of Jewish identity, hence their frequently Hebraic character and incorporation of Jewish features. Often their very titles and formats assert the Bible's Jewishness. Both Zunz (1838) and Leeser (1853) called their editions *The Twenty-Four Books of the Holy Scriptures* (Protestant Old Testaments count thirty-nine books), and the 1985 Jewish Publication Society translation was titled *Tanakh*. Even the earlier 1917 version, which bore the distinctly Christian-sounding name *Holy Scriptures*, was accompanied by the words *Torah Nevi'im Ketuvim* in Hebrew script, followed by a notation that the rendering followed the Masoretic Text, which had been described as "the only authorized Hebrew text of the Bible."[174] In keeping with ancient tradition, several of its contents are identified with their Hebrew names and the *parashiyot* marked both within the text and in an appended table of lections, reflecting Kaufmann Kohler's position that "it is a Jewish Bible only insofar as it takes cognizance of the Synagogue usage regarding the order of the books and the division of the Pentateuchal Sabbath portions and their Hebrew nomenclatures."[175]

At the same time, it is worth noting that Jewish translations are not necessarily intended for Jews alone. Mendelssohn described his version as being "Für bibel freunde allen konfessionen und zunächst für Israeliten" (For Bible followers of all creeds and above all for Israelites);[176] Salomon Herxheimer called his 1841–48 translation a "worttreur Übersetzung" (faithful translation) for Christians and Jews.[177] In that spirit, the preface to the 1917 JPS version expressed the view that "the non-Jewish world, it is hoped, will welcome a translation that presents many passages from the Jewish traditional point of view."[178]

Although the goal of enhancing Jewish legitimacy in the eyes of non-Jews is particularly modern, it has deep cultural roots. An ancient midrash explains Noah's blessing that "Japheth . . . will dwell in his brother's tents" (Gen. 9:27) as a reference to Jews' having made the Bible available to non-Jews, and Jewish versions have indeed often sought non-Jewish acknowledgment and even support.[179] European royalty backed the Ferrara Bible and Mendelssohn's German translation, while Christians funded both Blitz's and Witzenhausen's Yiddish editions and Delgado dedicated his 1789 English version to the Bishop of Salisbury.[180] Centuries earlier the Roman emperor Justinian authorized the Greek rendering for synagogue use, while Mendelssohn's version was approved by the Danish king and crown prince.[181] Christian circles praised Isaac Leeser's translation, and Martin Buber received the 1963 Erasmus Prize for his rendering, along with compliments from Pope John Paul II, who also acknowledged the 1985 one-volume edition of the JPS *Tanakh*, which was presented to President Ronald Reagan.[182] Jewish communities have clearly looked outside themselves for validation.

In all this, Jewish Bible translations exemplify the difference between Jewish culture and its two major scriptural counterparts. After all, Christianity was founded on one Bible translation (the Greek) and canonized another (the Latin Vulgate). To this day Christians read, revere, and distribute their Scripture in translation, whereas Jews continue to emphasize the original Hebrew, even in their translations. However, Judaism also requires that its Bible be translated immediately after it has been read and has even granted some translations a degree of sanctity, in contrast to Islam, which expressly prohibits translating the Qur'an, a project that remains controversial in Muslim countries.[183] In sum, Jewish Bible translations are often assertions of Jewish ownership of the Bible directed at both Jews and non-Jews alike.

Conclusion

AS SHOULD NOW BE CLEAR, THE BIBLE'S centrality within Jewish tradition is beyond dispute. It serves as the basis for Jewish doctrine and practice. Physically present in Jewish homes and synagogues, it provides the warp and woof of Jewish language and literature—the vocabulary by which Jews express their deepest feelings, whether recurrent experiences of martyrdom, aspirations for a nation-state, or commitments to social justice. It is their biography, recounting how God rescued them from slavery, gave them their land, and commanded them to place the sign of the covenant on their sons. It is the link that ties them to their past, their future, each other, and the larger world.

Jews are proud of what they understand to be their book. As Max Margolis, editor of the 1917 Jewish Publication Society translation of the Bible, insisted, "Only a Jew can say on approaching the Holy Writ: This is flesh of my flesh and bone of my bones."[1] At the same time, as the State of Israel's Declaration of Independence notes, Jews are proud that they "wrote and gave the Bible to the world" even as they resent the fact that translations of it enabled others to "say that they are Israel."[2] That resentment persists in our own time, as expressed by Benno Jacob, who lamented that "the most unique thing that Israel produced as an eternal, universal blessing, the basis of its faith, the source of its three thousand year existence, its highest possession, its most cherished sanctuary has been torn away from it. Our Bible is no longer our Bible."[3]

However, such rhetoric masks a more complex reality. Jews do not treat all parts of the Bible equally. The Pentateuch (Torah, or Five Books of Moses) is predominant in traditional Jewish liturgy and law, while classical Zionism emphasizes the historical books and modern Reform Judaism the pre-exilic prophets.

Complicating matters further, many Jewish practices and beliefs did not originate in Scripture. Hanukkah is not mentioned there (though the book of Maccabees, which describes the events on which Hanukkah is based, is included in the Roman Catholic Old Testament), while Passover, which does commemorate a biblically described event, is not observed in the way the Bible prescribes. Even Jewish beliefs about God and the afterlife, though possibly alluded to in some of the later biblical books, achieved their familiar form long after.

More confusing are the many paradoxes inherent in Jewish attitudes toward Scripture: the remarkable number of translations Jews have created despite the express emphasis on the original Hebrew; the conviction in the authenticity and uniformity of the biblical text in spite of the reality of significant textual variations,[4] some of which are actually embedded within the traditional text; the commitment to Scripture's literal meaning alongside the promulgation of interpretations that are not at all literal; and, most striking of all, the claim that the Bible is the foundation stone of Jewish tradition while sometimes rejecting it outright.[5]

In none of this does Jewish tradition stand alone. Although the Bible's status within Judaism is without parallel in earlier cultures, the Jewish emphasis on writing is far from unique. To be sure, some traditions have shared Plato's skepticism about writing; others, such as Hinduism, prefer that their scriptures be kept oral.[6] However, the ancient Egyptians viewed writing as a divinely given vehicle for transcending mortality, and Islam even saw it as a category for religion.[7] Nor has Judaism been entirely univocal in its commitment to the written word, as can be seen in its stipulation that the Oral Torah be kept oral,[8] though it was eventually committed to writing.

Judaism is not the only tradition to accord a text iconic status. Sikhs also decorate their holy book, the Adi Granth, which is regarded as the embodiment of the last guru, and carry it in celebratory procession much as Jews do with the Torah scroll. They even call it the Guru Granth Sahib because it is regarded as their teacher (guru). Indeed, it is the last in the line of founding authorities.[9] Buddhists also carry their sacred books in procession, as did early Christians; so, too, do Muslims accord the Qur'an special honors.[10]

According to Islam, the Qur'an has primordial origins, much as Judaism holds that the Torah was the first thing created and the guide with which God created the world.[11] (Christians ascribe that status to Christ, characterized as the word of God in the beginning of John's Gospel.) Like Jews, Muslims also recite their scripture in its original language, whether they understand it or not, and have often proscribed its translation.[12]

Inevitably, individual traditions stress some of their sacred writings over others, a doctrine Christian theologians call a "canon within the canon," which parallels the priority accorded the Pentateuch in Judaism. Conversely, the Oral Torah's status as a second scripture resembles that of the Christian New Testament and Islam's oral tradition (*ḥadith*).[13] By contrast, the Latter-day Saints' open canon calls to mind the rabbinic view that "whatever a distinguished student might teach was already told to Moses at Sinai."[14]

Finally, every tradition—sacred or secular—that has special writings necessarily develops a body of interpretation with which to apply its texts to unforeseen circumstances. As we have seen, that process, which is the inevitable by-product of the commitment to a closed, authoritative text, was evident already in biblical times. So, too, Judaism's long-standing endorsement of the possibility that its Scripture can contain multiple, even inconsistent meanings was an idea that began in antiquity with the inclusion of Deuteronomy and Chronicles in the same corpus as Exodus and Kings. It continues today with the printing of several, often conflicting commentaries on the same page of Jewish editions. However, this too is not unique. The ancient Greeks read Homer ethically, symbolically, and allegorically, while Christianity has long endorsed the possibility of multiple modes of interpretation.[15]

Still, Mohammad was right to label Jews as "people of the book," a characteristic that Sigmund Freud attributed to "the political misfortune of the nation [which] taught them to appreciate the only possession they had retained, their written records, at its true value. . . . From now on, it was the Holy Book, and the study of it, that kept the scattered people together."[16] That undoubtedly accounts for the possessiveness with which Jews view what Franz Rosenzweig described as "the only book of antiquity still in living use."[17]

As their contribution to Western civilization, the Bible signals Jews' centrality in a world where they would otherwise be dwarfed. That view underlies the statement on the relationship between Judaism and Christianity that was issued by a group of Jewish scholars in 2000, which asserted that "Jews and Christians seek authority from the same book—the Bible (what Jews call 'Tanakh' and Christians call the 'Old Testament')."[18] As several observers pointed out, this is not entirely accurate. Jewish and Christian Bibles are not exactly the same, nor are they used in the same way.[19] Still, as Martin Buber noted, "To you the book is a forecourt; to us it is the sanctuary. But in this place we can dwell together."[20]

Notes

PREFACE AND INTRODUCTION

1. Louis Finkelstein, *The Jews, Their History, Culture, and Religion* (Philadelphia: Jewish Publication Society, 1949) vol. 1, p. xxvi. So, too, Joseph Hertz, who called it "*terra incognita*" (*Sermons, Addresses and Studies*, vol. 2, p. 64).

2. W. Smith, "The True Meaning of Scripture," 499.

3. Qur'an 9:29, 29:46; cf. 2:21, 3:23, 4:44,51, 17:39, 18:27, and 35:31. Zoroastrians, Mandeans, and Hindus were later included. See Graham, *Beyond the Written Word*, 57.

4. J. Sarna, "When Jews Were Bible Experts," 55.

5. J. Harris, *How Do We Know This?*, 25–49.

6. Solomon Schechter, "Higher Criticism–Higher Anti-Semitism" in *Seminary Addresses & Other Papers*, 37; Leo Baeck, *The Essence of Judaism* (rev. ed., New York: Schocken Books, 1948), 22.

7. Auld, "Can a Biblical Theology also be Academic or Ecumenical?," 13.

8. Origen, "Homilae In Librum Jesu Nave," Homily 7 §5 (PG 12:860).

9. Seidman, *Faithful Renderings*, 33.

10. "Lewis Black: Red, White and Screwed," Warner Theater, Washington DC, April 21, 2006, broadcast by HBO on June 10, 2006.

11. Hareven, "Are the Israelis Still the People of the Book?" 9.

12. E.g., *b. Avodah Zarah* 18a, *b. Giṭṭin 58a*, and the medieval etching noted by M. Waldman, "Sacred Communication," 315.

13. Siker, *Liquid Scripture*. Thus Conservative rabbi Charles Simon's article, "Can the People of the Book Become the People of the iPad?" CJ (Winter 2012/2013): 10, 15.

14. "Le-Veirur *Ha'Inyan* in *Kol Kitvei Y.H. Brenner* (Tel Aviv: Dvir, 1960) as cited in Shavit and Eran, *The Hebrew Bible Reborn*, 477.

15. For the history, see Baruch M. Bokser, *The Origins of the Seder, The Passover Rite and Early Rabbinic Judaism* (Berkeley: University of California Press, 1984).

16. *The Bible Today* 29, no. 6 (November 1991).

17. Samuel C. Heilman, *The People of the Book, Drama, Fellowship, and Religion* (Chicago: University of Chicago Press, 1983); thus Talya Fishman's *Becoming the People of the Talmud* (Philadelphia: University of Pennsylvania Press, 2011).

18. Cf. Ruth Kartun-Blum's reference to Judaism's "ongoing duel with the Bible" (*Profane Scriptures*, 90).

1. SURROUNDED BY SCRIPTURE

1. *B. Megillah* 9a allows Greek.

2. *B. Yoma* 11a; cf. Louis Rabinowitz, "Mezuzah," *EJ* 11: 1477.

3. Yoffie, "Popular Beliefs and Customs," 376.

4. Cf. *m. Menaḥot* 4:1.

5. *B. Menaḥot* 43b.

6. Cf. Gutmann, *The Jewish Sanctuary*, 12; Hachlili, *Ancient Jewish Art and Archaeology*, 287–88.

7. Shinan, "Synagogues in the Land of Israel," 134; Fraade, "Rabbinic Views on the Practice of Targum," 279.

8. A. Ascher, M.A. Signer, M.N. Adler, eds., *The Itinerary of Benjamin of Tudela, Travels in the Middle Ages* (Malibu CA: Joseph Simon/Pangloss , 1987), 102.

9. P. Miller, "Psalms and Inscriptions," 312; cf. Pss 16 and 56–60.

10. Judah He-Ḥasid disapproved of this practice because of the fact that the inscribed objects were eventually excreted (Marcus, *Rituals of Childhood*, 1, 27–29, 114).

11. M. Grunwald and K. Kohler, "Bibliomancy," *JE* 3:202–3.

12. *Shulḥan Arukh, Yoreh Deah* 179:4; cf. *b. Ḥagigah* 15ab and *b. Ḥullin* 95b.

13. Jacobs, *The Jewish Religion*, 131–32; Moses Gaster, "Divination (Jewish)," *ERE* 4:812.

14. Cohn, *Tangled Up in Text;* and Jeffrey H. Tigay, "On the Term Phylacteries (Matt. 23:5)," *HTR* 71 (1978): 49–51. Cf. *m. Shabbat* 6:2; *j. Shabbat* 6:2 8b; *j. 'Eruvin* 10:11 26c; *b. 'Eruvin* 96b; *b. Shabbat* 115; *Sifra Shemini* 8:6; *Tefillin* 2; and Maimonides, *Laws of the Torah Scroll* 10:5. Cf. also Meir of Rothenberg's statement that "no demon can have power over a house in which the mezuzah is properly affixed" (Trachtenberg, *Jewish Magic and Superstition*, 146).

15. Charles D. Isbell, *Corpus of the Aramaic Incantation Bowls* (Missoula MT: Society of Biblical Literature, 1975), 34 #8, 40 #10; Joseph Naveh and Shaul Shaked, *Amulets and Magic Bowls, Aramaic Incantations of Late Antiquity* (Jerusalem: Magnes; and Leiden: E. J. Brill, 1985); Joseph Naveh and Shaul Shaked, *Magic Spells and Formulae, Aramaic Incantations of Late Antiquity* (Jerusalem: Magnes, 1993); Schrire, *Hebrew Amulets*, 73, 100, 114, 117; Bohak, *Ancient Jewish Magic*, 310–11; and Lawrence H. Schiffman and Michael D.

Swartz, *Hebrew and Aramaic Incantation Texts from the Cairo Genizah, Selected Texts from Taylor-Schechter Box K1* (Sheffield: Sheffield Academic, 1992), 37–44. Cf. *b. Berakhot* 20a, 51a, and 55b.

16. Barkay et al., "The Amulets from Ketef Hinnom," 41–71.

17. Naveh and Shaked, *Magic Spells and Formulae*, 27.

18. *B. Berakhot* 55b, 56b; Rashi at *b. Sanhedrin* 101a s.v. *uveroqeq*; Maimonides, *Mishneh Torah, Laws of Idolatry* 11:12; and *Shulḥan Arukh, Yoreh Deah* 179:8.

19. *B. Shabbat* 67a; cf. *Shulḥan Arukh, Yoreh Deah* 179:10.

20. Trachtenberg, *Jewish Magic and Superstition*, 107; cf. *b. Berakhot* 56b; and *b. Pesaḥim* 111a and 112a.

21. Reuven Margaliot, ed., *Sefer Ḥasidim* (Jerusalem: Mosad haRav Kook, 1956/57), 568.

22. Bohak, *Ancient Jewish Magic*, 270; cf. T. Schrire, *Hebrew Amulets*, 61–63.

23. Bill Rebiger, ed., *Sefer Shimmush Tehillim, Buch vom Magischen Gebrauch der Psalmen* (Tübingen: Mohr Siebeck, 2010), 5*.

24. Bill Rebiger, ed., *Sefer Shimmush Tehillim, Buch vom Magischen Gebrauch der Psalmen* (Tübingen: Mohr Siebeck, 2010), 5*, 11*, 12*, 21*, 35*, 45*.

25. Bill Rebiger, ed., *Sefer Shimmush Tehillim, Buch vom Magischen Gebrauch der Psalmen* (Tübingen: Mohr Siebeck, 2010), 17*, 31*.

26. E.g., *b. Pesaḥim* 112a; cf. 11Q5 27:9–10.

27. *J. Shabbat* 6:2 8b; *j. Eruvin* 10:12 26c; and *b. Shevuot* 15b. Cf. *Num. Rabbah* 12:3.

28. Trachtenberg, *Jewish Magic and Superstition*, 112; Schiffman and Swartz, *Hebrew and Aramaic Incantation Texts from the Cairo Genizah*, 78.

29. Schrire, *Hebrew Amulets*, 117; and Bohak, *Ancient Jewish Magic*, 310.

30. Alan Corre, https://pantherfile.uwm.edu/corre/www/jatexts/Text123.html (accessed February 24, 2016).

31. E.g., *m. Yadayim* 3:5 and 4:6; cf. Baumgarten, "Sacred Scriptures Defile the Hands," 46–67; Friedman, "The Holy Scriptures Defile the Hands," 116–32; and Goodman, "Sacred Scriptures and 'Defiling the Hands,'" 99–107.

32. *M. Yevamot* 16:7; *b. Yoma* 70a. Cf. Josephus, *Jewish War* 2.xiv:5 §291 (LCL 2.436–7); and *j. Berakhot* 3:5 6d.

33. *M. Sanhedrin* 2:4; *j. Ta'anit* 3:8 66d; *b. Sanhedrin* 21b; Howard Adelman, "Italian Jewish Women" in *Jewish Women in Historical Perspective*, ed. Judith R. Baskin (Detroit: Wayne State University Press, 1991), 146; *Shulḥan Arukh, Yoreh Deah* 179:9–12; S. D. Goitein, *A Mediterranean Society, The Jewish Communities of the Arab World as Portrayed in the Documents of the Cairo Geniza* (Berkeley: University of California Press, 1971) vol. 2, 181; and Lee I. Levine, *The Ancient Synagogue, The First Thousand Years* (New Haven: Yale University Press, 2000), 433.

34. Ben-Zvi, "The Codex of Ben Asher," 10.

35. Elbogen, *Jewish Liturgy*, 139; Al Vorspan, "JFK Forgot the Kipah, Nixon Bugged the Office, and Other Recollections of a Reform Jewish Actionik," *Reform Judaism* 29:2 (Winter 2000): 22; Gillman, *A History of German Jewish Bible Translation*, 158; and Porat, *The Blue and the Yellow Stars of David*, 51. Cf. *j. Yoma* 7:1 44a.

36. So already 1 Macc. 1:56, 2 Esdras 14:21, Josephus, *Jewish War* 2.xxi.2 §§229–30 (LCL 2:412–13), and *Antiquities* 20 v.4 §115–17 (LCL 13:60–63). Cf. Shlomo Eidelberg, ed., *The Jews and the Crusaders, The Hebrew Chronicles of the First and Second Crusades* (Madison WI: University of Wisconsin Press, 1977), 37, 130. This is presumably the reason the Jews of Caesarea moved their Torah scroll in 66 CE (cf. Josephus, *Jewish War* 2:xiv.5 §§289–92 [LCL 2.434–37]).

37. *T. Megillah* 3:20; *j. Berakhot* 3:5 6d; *b. Shabbat* 14a; and *Soferim* 3:13.

38. *B. Soṭah* 39b.

39. Cf. Feldman, "The Development of *Minhag* as a Reflection of Halakhic Attitude," 19–30; cf. *b. Berakhot* 8a.

40. Ruderman, *The World of a Renaissance Jew*, 102.

41. *B. Megillah* 26b; *j. Mo'ed Qatan* 3:7 83b; *Soferim* 5:14; and *Sefer Torah* 5:14.

42. Cf. *t. Megillah* 4(3):20; *b. Megillah* 26b; *b. Shabbat* 133b; and Fine, "From Meeting Place to Sacred Realm," 25.

43. Landsberger, "The Origin of European Torah Decorations," 133–51; cf. Exod. 28:13–39, 39:1–31.

44. Kirshenblatt-Gimblett, "The Cut That Binds," 137; and van der Zan, "Ornamentation on Eighteenth-Century Torah Binders," 65.

45. *B. Qiddushin* 33b; cf. *j. Megillah* 4:1 2a; and *b. Makkot* 22b.

46. Cf. *Soferim* 14:14.

47. *T. Megillah* 4(3):10; *j. Megillah* 4:1 75a; *b. Bava Qamma* 82a; and *b. Megillah* 31b.

48. *B. 'Avodah Zarah* 19a; but cf. *m. Sotah* 7:1–2.

49. Joshua Blau, ed., *Teshuvot Ha-Rambam* #263 (Jerusalem: Mekize Nirdamim, 1960), vol. 2, 495–98.

50. *M. Megillah* 4:4; and *t. Megillah* 4(3):18.

51. Petuchowski, *Prayerbook Reform in Europe*, 55.

52. David Lieber, ed., *Etz Hayim, Torah and Commentary* (New York: Rabbinical Assembly, United Syngogue of Conservative Judaism, 2001), 1483.

53. The blessings were originally recited by the actual reader at the beginning and end of the entire portion (cf. *m. Bikkurim* 3:7; *m. Megillah* 4:4; *j. Megillah* 4:5 75b; and *b. Megillah* 22a).

54. *M. Giṭṭin* 5:8.

55. This practice was first mentioned in 1570 (Landsberger, "The Origin of European Torah Decorations," 148), but cf. *b. Shabbat* 14a; and *b. Megillah* 32a.

56. *J. Megillah* 4:5 75b; cf. Maimonides *Mishneh Torah, Hilkhot Tefillah* 12:6; and *Shulḥan Arukh, Oraḥ Ḥayim* 142:1.

57. *B. Soṭah.* 39b; but cf. *m. Megillah* 4:4,10; *t. Megillah* 4(3):31–38; and *b. Megillah* 25ab.

58. *Soferim* 14:10, 14. Sephardic Jews do this before reading from the Torah.

59. *J. Megillah* 4:1 74d; cf. *Zohar, Vayaqhel* 206a.

60. Cf. Yehudah Ya'aleh, *Oraḥ Ḥayim* #3, as cited by Guttmann, *The Struggle over Reform*, 280.

61. E.g., *j. Ta'anit* 2:1 65a, despite the prohibition in *b. Shabbat* 32a. Similarly, various synagogue objects bear the same names as those which accompanied the desert shrine (e.g., *kapporet, parokhet,* and *ner tamid*, cf. Exod. 25:17, 26:31, 27:20).

62. Jewish communities in the Persian Gulf also read the haftarah on Sabbath afternoons (Mann, "Changes in the Divine Service of the Synagogue Due to Religious Persecutions," 282–86).

63. Mann, *The Bible as Read and Preached in the Old Synagogue*, vol. 1, 555–71.

64. *B. Megillah* 29b. Acts 13:15 mentions reading from the Torah and the Prophets.

65. *Sefer Abudraham* (Warsaw: n.p., 1877), 47a; cf. Elijah Levita, *Sefer ha-Tishbi* (Basel: Konrad Waldkirch, 1601), 71a *s.v. pṭr*.

66. Cf. Luke 4:16–20, which mentions only prophetic reading. *T. Megillah* 4(3):1–4 lists fixed *haftarot*.

67. *M. Shabbat* 16:1; *t. Shabbat* 13:1; *b. Shabbat* 116b; *j. Shabbat* 16:1 15c; and *Lam. Rabbah* proem 17. Cf. *m. Yoma* 1:6. The Reform movement experimented with selecting *haftarot* from the Writings (Elbogen, *Jewish Liturgy*, 151–52).

68. *M. Megillah* 1:1; and *j. Megillah* 2:3 73b. Cf. 3:5 74b. Song of Songs, Ruth, Lamentations, and Esther are mentioned in *Soferim* 14:3. For Ecclesiastes, see Beckwith, *The Old Testament Canon of the New Testament Church*, 202–3.

69. For a broad typology of the different ways in which Scripture is incorporated into liturgy, see Bradshaw, "The Use of the Bible in Liturgy," 35–52.

70. *M. Rosh Hashanah* 4:6; *t. Rosh Hashanah* 4(2):6; *j. Rosh Hashanah* 4:7 59c; and *b. Rosh Hashanah* 32ab.

71. *B. Berakhot* 4b and 9b.

72. Reif, "The Bible in the Liturgy," 1945. Jewish mystics originally understood Proverbs 31 as referring to the *Shekhinah*. Levine, "'The Woman of Valor' in Jewish Ritual (Proverbs 31:10–31)," 339–47 (Hebrew).

73. Reif, *Problems with Prayers*, 72. For a list, see Louis I. Rabinowitz, "Bible: Religious Impact," *EJ* vol. 4: 918.

74. Psalm 24 on Sunday, Psalm 48 on Monday, Psalm 82 on Tuesday, Psalms 94 and 95 on Wednesday, Psalm 81 on Thursday, Psalm 93 on Friday, and Psalm 92 on Sabbath (*m. Tamid* 7:4; and the Septuagint).

75. *T. Sukkah* 3:2; *b. Arakhin* 10a; and *b. Ta'anit* 28b. For Purim cf. *m. Megillah* 2:5.

76. See *m. Tamid* 4:3, 5:1, 7:4; *b. Berakhot* 12a; Josephus *Antiquities* xx:9.6 §218 (LCL 13.116–17); and Jerome, "In Amos" 5:23 (*PL* 25:1054). H. St. J. Thackeray notes liturgical glosses in the Greek translation of Psalm 76 and Zechariah 14 (Thackeray, "Psalm LXXVI and Other Psalms for the Feast of Tabernacles," 430; and Thackeray, "The Song of Hanukkah and Other Lessons and Psalms for the Jewish New Year's Day," 192).

77. Cf. *Soferim* 18:1–3 and 19:2.

78. *B. Megillah* 29a and *Tg. Ezek.* 11:16. Cf. *Sifra Beḥuqotay* 6:4.

79. *J. Berakhot* 1:8 3c; *b. Berakhot* 12a; Maimonides at *m. Tamid* 5:1; and *Midrash HaGadol* Exodus 26:7, ed. Mordecai Margulies (Jerusalem: Mosad Harav Kook, 1956), 590.

80. *Gen. Rabbah* 68:11 and 74:11; cf. Jerome, "In Amos" 5:23 (*PL* 25:1054).

81. Pollack, *Jewish Folkways in Germanic Lands*, 148.

82. *Der Tehillim Yid* (New York: S. Skarsky, 1952; originally Warsaw, 1934), 21, 59, 67, 75, 80, 317–19, 361–62, published in English under the title *Salvation* 2nd ed. (New York: Schocken, 1968).

83. *Shenei Lukhot HaBerit* (Amsterdam: n.p., 1698); and *Amud Ha-Teshuvah*, 229a. Cf. Pollack, *Jewish Folkways in Germanic Lands*, 172.

84. Cf. Wilhelm, "The Order of Tiqqunim," 126–29 (Hebrew). Morris M. Faierstein traces the practice to sixteenth-century Turkey (Faierstein, "Tikkun Leil Shavuot," 76–78).

85. Wilhelm, "The Order of Tiqqunim," 130; cf. Solomon Schechter, *Studies in Judaism* (Piscataway NJ: Gorgias Press, 2003) vol. 2, 295.

86. Newman, *Praying by the Book*; cf. Julia Kristeva's phrase "a mosaic of quotations." Kristeva, *Desire in Language* (New York: Columbia University Press, 1980), 66; and Pelikan, *Whose Bible Is It?*, 125.

87. E.g., 1 Kings 8:23–53 draws on Deuteronomy 3 and 28; 1 Chron. 16:8–36 on Pss. 96:1–3, 105:1–15, and 106:1,47–48; Neh. 9:6–17 on Gen. 2:1, Exod. 9:16, 13:21, 19:11b, 20:19b, 20a, 16:4, Num. 20:8, 14:4, Deut. 32:15, Zech. 7:11–12, Deut. 30:15–20, Lev. 18:5, and Exod. 20:11.

88. *J. Berakhot* 1:8 3d; cf. *j. Ta'anit* 2:3 65c.

89. *B. Berakhot* 33b; cf. *j. Berakhot* 7:4 11c; and *b. Megillah* 25a. Note also Neh. 9:32.

90. Elizur, "The Use of Biblical Verses in Hebrew Liturgical Poetry," 85.

91. Rabin, "The Linguistic Investigation of the Language of Jewish Prayer," 167; cf. Reif, *Judaism and Hebrew Prayer*, 175–77.

92. *M. Berakhot* 6:1.

93. Heinemann, *Prayer in the Talmud*, 234.

94. Segal, *Biblical Interpretation*, 7, 45 (Hebrew); Weinberger, *Jewish Hymnography*, 45.

95. Reif, *Shabbethai Sofer and His Prayer-Book*, 90n5.

96. Reif, *Judaism and Hebrew Prayer*, 262.

97. The most complete version is in Exod. 34:6–7; shorter versions appear in Num. 14:18; Deut. 4:31; Joel 2:12; Jon. 4:2; Mic. 7:18; Nah. 1:3; Ps. 86:15, 103:8, 111:4, 145:8; Neh. 9:17,31; and 2 Chron. 30:9.

98. The end of the formula is also left out in Ps. 103:7 and Neh. 9:17.

99. Cf. *b. Ḥullin* 91b. The *Kedushah* originated among Palestinian merkavah mystics (Petuchowski, "The Liturgy of the Synagogue," 39).

100. *M. Soṭah* 7:8; cf. Josephus *Antiquities* IV.8.12 §209–11 (LCL 6.100–101); *m. Yoma* 7:1; *m. Soṭah* 7:7–8; *m. Ta'anit* 4:2–3; *t. Ta'anit* 4(3):3; and *j. Ta'anit* 4:2 67d.

101. Verbin, "Dating Theodotus," 243–80.

102. *T. Bava Meṣi'a* 11:23.

103. E.g., Justin Martyr, "Dialogue with Trypho" 72 (*PG* 6:645) and "Cohortatio ad Graecos" 13 (*PG* 6:268).

104. John Chrysostom, "Adversos Judaeos" 1:5 (*PG* 48:850; cf. 6:7; *PG* 48:914).

105. Cf. *m. Ta'anit* 2:1; *t. Megillah* 4(3):21; and pictures at Dura and Capernaum which show the ark with wheels. Erwin R. Goodenough, "The Problem of Method, Symbols from Jewish Cult," vol. 4 of his *Jewish Symbols in the Greco-Roman Period* (New York: Bollingen Foundation, 1954), 115; and Asher Ovadiah, "Art of the Ancient Synagogues in Israel" in *Ancient Synagogues, Historical Analysis and Archaeological Discovery*, ed. Dan Urman and Paul V. M. Flesher (Leiden: Brill, 1998), 304.

106. Elkan Nathan Adler, *Jewish Travellers in the Middle Ages, 19 Firsthand Accounts* (New York: Dover, 1987), 211.

107. E.g., Kampf, *Contemporary Synagogue Art*, 8; and Sukenik, *Ancient Synagogues in Palestine and Greece*, 56. Cf. Hachlili, "The Niche and the Ark in Ancient Synagogues," 51.

108. *B. Megillah* 31b; *b. Ta'anit* 27b; *b. Menaḥot* 110a; *Pesiqta of Rab Kahana* §6:3 (ed. Mandelbaum, p. 118); *Soferim* 16:10, 18:1; and *Lev. Rabbah* 7:3.

109. Levine, *The Ancient Synagogue*, 136, 271–80, 331; and Hachlili, "The Niche and the Ark in Ancient Synagogues," 50.

110. Cf. Josephus, *Antiquities* 16:2.4 §43 (LCL 11:18–19) and *Against Apion* 2.17 §175 (LCL 1:362–3); Philo, *On the Life of Moses* 2:xxxix §216 (LCL 6:556–7); *On*

the Embassy to Gaius 156 (LCL 10:78–9); and *Hypothetica* 7:12 (LCL 9:430–33), as well as his description of Essene practice in *That Every Good Person Is Free* XII §81–82 (LCL 9:56–59).

111. *M. Megillah* 3:4–6; cf. *t. Megillah* 4:1–9.

112. *T. Megillah* 4[3]:10; cf. *j. Megillah* 4:5 75b.

113. Cf. *b. Megillah* 29b; *Lev. Rabbah* 3:6; and *Soferim* 16:10.

114. Margulies, *The Differences Between Babylonian and Palestinian Jews* #48, 88.

115. A. Ascher, M.A. Signer, Marcus Nathan Adler, eds., *The Itinerary of Benjamin of Tudela* (Malibu: Joseph Simon/Pangloss, 1987), 129; Büchler, "The Reading of the Law and Prophets in a Triennial Cycle," 420; Naeh, "The Torah Reading Cycle in Early Palestine," 167 (Hebrew); Mann, *The Jews in Egypt and in Palestine*, vol. 1, 221–22; and Mann, "Anan's Liturgy and His Half-Yearly Cycle of the Reading of the Law," 342.

116. Yaari, *The History of Simchat Torah*, passim (Hebrew).

117. Yaari, *The History of Simchat Torah*, 215 (Hebrew).

118. *M. Sukkah* 4:5.

119. Other Sabbaths are named after the content of the Torah portion (e.g., the Sabbath when the Song at the Sea in Exodus 15 is read is called Shabbat Shirah) or the haftarah (e.g., the Sabbath seven weeks before the New Year is called Shabbat Naḥamu because the haftarah that week, Isaiah 40:1–26, begins with the verb *naḥamu*, which means "comfort").

120. The opening verses of Joshua are the haftarah for the last portion of Deuteronomy.

121. Cf. Steven Schwarzschild, "On Jewish Eschatology" in *The Pursuit of the Ideal, Jewish Writings of Steven Schwarzschild*, ed. Menachem Kellner (Albany: State University of New York Press, 1990), 209.

122. Cf. Moshe Greenberg, *Biblical Prose Prayer as a Window to the Popular Religion of Ancient Israel* (Berkeley: University of California Press, 1983).

123. Kaufmann, *The Religion of Israel*, 302–4; cf. Knohl, "Between Voice and Silence," 17–21.

124. Sukenik, *Ancient Synagogues in Palestine and Greece*, 57; and Hachlili, "The Niche and the Ark in Ancient Synagogues," 47–49.

125. Cf. Hachlili, *Ancient Jewish Art and Archaeology in the Land of Israel*, 280; also cf. 1 Kings 8:29–30,44,48; Dan. 6:11; Josephus, *Against Apion* 2:2 §10 (LCL 1:294–7); *t. Berakhot* 3:16; and *Pesiqta Rabbati* 33.

126. Roth, "Jewish Antecedents of Christian Art," 25.

127. Levy, *The Synagogue*, 50; and Sabar, "Torah and Magic," 150 (Hebrew).

128. Exod. 24:12, 31:18, 32:15–16; and Deut. 4:13, 5:19, 9:9–17.

129. Ezek. 2:9–10; cf. *m. Megillah* 2:2; *m. Yadayim* 4:5; *j. Megillah* 1:9,11 71d; *Tg. Ps.-J* Deut. 31:24; and *Soferim* 1:1–4.

130. Cf. *b. Bava Batra* 13b–14b; and *Soferim* 2:5.

131. *M. Megillah* 2:2; and *b. Sanhedrin* 21b. According to one tradition, Ezra actually *restored* the original script (*t. Sanhedrin* 4:7; *j. Megillah* 1:11 71c; and *b. Sanhedrin* 22a).

132. But see Japhet, "The Ritual of Reading Scripture (Nehemiah 8:1–12)," 175–90.

133. Cf. Josephus, *Antiquities* 4:8.12 §209 (LCL 6:102–3); and *t. Sukkah* 4:6, though references to descending before the ark (*m. Soṭah* 7:8; cf. *j. Sukkah* 5:1 55b) suggest that the Torah was located lower than worshippers (Hoffman, "The Ancient Torah Service in Light of the Realia of the Talmudic Era," 42).

134. *M. Megillah* 4:10; but *b. Megillah* 31a. In addition, Ezekiel 16 is sometimes used for a haftarah.

135. Jacobson, *Chanting the Hebrew Bible*, 641.

136. Cf. *j. Yoma* 7:1 44a; and *Midrash Psalms* 4:12.

137. Ben Zion Wacholder, "Prolegomenon" to Jacob Mann, *The Bible as Read and Preached in the Old Synagogue*, xxxi–xxxiii.

2. CREATING THE BIBLE

1. Exod. 24:1–8; Lev. 8–9; and Num. 7:1–9:5. Cf. *b. Ḥagigah* 6b.

2. Jer. 26:18; cf. Mic. 3:12.

3. According to Wilfred Cantwell Smith (*What Is Scripture?*, 22), Mani, the third-century founder of Manicheanism, was the first person to have consciously composed a scripture.

4. Francois Thureau-Dangin, *Rituals accadiens* (Paris: Ernest Leroux, 1921), 126, ll. 279–84.

5. Joseph Albo, *Sefer ha-'Ikkarim* 3:22 (ed. Isaac Husik [Philadelphia: Jewish Publication Society, 1946]), vol. 3, 199.

6. *B. Nedarim* 37b. The antiquity of the vowels became a point of contention between Protestants and Catholics and was the thesis topic for Harvard University's first graduating class in 1642 (Pool, "Hebrew Learning Among the Puritans of New England Prior to 1700," 39).

7. Philo, *Hypothetica*; and Eusebius *PE* 8:6 (*PG* 21:601). Cf. 1 Enoch 99:2; Aristeas 310–11; and Josephus, *Against Apion* 1:1.8 §42 (LCL 1:178–81), though Josephus does admit that the order had been changed (*Antiquities* 4:8.4 §197 [LCL 6:94–97]); cf. *b. 'Eruvin* 13a; and *b. Soṭah* 20a.

8. Cf. Deut. 4:2; Prov. 30:6; Eccles. 3:14; Sir. 42:21; and Rev. 22:18–19. For ancient Near Eastern parallels, see Levinson, "Esarhaddon's Succession Treaty as the Source for the Canon Formula in Deuteronomy 13:1," 337–38.

9. *J. Megillah* 3:1 74a; cf. *m. Megillah* 2:2; *m. Yadayim* 4:5; *j. Megillah* 1:11 71d; *b. Giṭṭin* 60a; *b. B. Batra*; *b. Menaḥot* 13b–14a; and *Soferim* passim.

10. Israel Yeivin (*Introduction to the Tiberian Masorah*, 43) lists the exceptions as Gen. 1:1, 49:8, Exod. 14:28, 34:11, Num. 24:5, and Deut. 31:28.

11. E.g., *b. Menaḥot* 30a; and *Soferim* 2:2.

12. Modern texts mark these passages with what appear to be reversed *nuns*. The rabbis speak of them as misplaced books (*b. Shabbat* 115b–116a; and *'Avot of Rabbi Nathan* 34:4; cf. *m. Pesaḥim* 9:2; *b. Berakhot* 4a; *b. B. Meṣi'a* 87a; *b. Nazir* 23a; and *Soferim* 6:1).

13. *B. Megillah* 16b; *Soferim* 1:10; and Yeivin, *Introduction to the Tiberian Masorah*, 43.

14. *J. Megillah* 1:11 71d; and *b. Megillah* 2b.

15. Yeivin, "Masorah," *EM* 5:133; cf. his *Introduction to the Tiberian Masorah*, 48.

16. *B. Qiddushin* 30a; and *Songs Rabbah* 1:1.11. Cf. *Pesiqta of Rab Kahana, Para Aduma* 4:3 (ed. Mandelbaum 1:62); and *b. Shabbat* 49b.

17. Leibowitz, "An Interpretation of the Jewish Religion," 33.

18. Ezek. 43:11; Hab. 2:2; Dan. 7:1; 1 Chron. 29:29; and 2 Chron. 9:29, 12:15, 13:22, 21:12, 26:22, 32:32, 33:19, 35:25; cf. Isa. 30:8; and Jer. 25:13, 29:1, 30:1–2, 36:1–32, and 51:60–64.

19. 1 Kings 11:41, 14:19,29, 15:7,23,31, 16:5,14,20,27, 22:39,46; 2 Kings 1:18, 8:23, 10:34, 12:20, 13:8,12, 14:15,18,28, 15:6,11,15,21,26,31,36, 16:19, 20:20, 21:17,25, 23:28, 24:5; and 2 Chron. 17:9, 24:27, 35:27. Cf. 2 Kings 23:1–3.

20. Exod. 32:32; and Ps. 69:29, 139:16; also Isa. 4:3; Mal. 3:16; Ps. 149:9; Dan. 7:10, 12:1; Rev. 20:15; and 1 Enoch 103:2. Also Enuma Elish 1:157, 3:47, 105; 4:121 (*COS* 1.392, 395–6, 398); the Myth of Zu iii.90 and ii.6 (*ANET* 390 and 516); and Ovid, *Metamorphosis* 15:809–15 (LCL 4:422–23), Aeschylus, *Euripedes* fr 506N, and Pyramid text 1146e in R. O. Faulkner, *The Ancient Egyptian Pyramid Texts* (Oxford: Clarendon, 1969), 186. Cf. Leo Koep, *Das Himmlische Buch in Antike und Chistentum, Eine Religionsgeschichtliche Untersuchung zur Altchristlichen Bildersprache* (Bonn: Peter Hanstein Verlag, 1952), 32.

21. Isa. 4:3; Jer. 17:1; Ezek. 13:9; Ps. 56:9, 69:29, 87:6, 139:16; Dan. 12:1; Jub. 30:22; and Luke 10:20.

22. Exod. 17:14, 31:18, 32:16, 34:27–29; Deut. 4:13, 9:10, 10:1–4, 27:2–8, 31:9,19–24; and Josh. 8:32.

23. Deut. 28:58, 31:9,24. Contrast Leviticus, where the word *torah* refers to specific rituals (e.g., 6:2,7:18, and 14:2); cf. Jer. 2:8, 18:18; Ezek. 7:26; Hag. 2:11; and Mal. 2:7.

24. 2 Kings 22–23. According to 2 Chronicles 34, the book was discovered after the reform was underway.

25. 2 Kings 14:6; Neh. 8:1,18. Also Josh. 8:31; Ezra 3:2; Neh. 8:14–15; 1 Chron. 16:40; and 2 Chron. 23:18, 30:5,18, 31:3. Cf. 1 Kings 2:3; Dan. 9:13; Sir. 24:23; Bar. 2:2; Luke 24:44; and 1 Cor. 9:9. For the terms, see Ezra 6:18; Neh. 13:1f; 2 Chron. 25:4, 35:12; 1 Esdras 8:19, 9:45; 1 Macc. 3:48; and Josephus, *Antiquities* 20:2.4 §43 (LCL 13:24–25).

26. The reference is to Jer. 29:10; cf. Zech. 1:12 and 7:5.

27. Contrast Ezra 7:10 to 1 Kings 22:2–6ff; cf. 1 Sam. 9:9 and also Exod. 18:15; Isa. 2:3; Hosea 10:12; and Mic. 4:2, where *torah* is parallel to *dĕbar yhwh*; and Sir. 32:18, where it is parallel to *ʾēl.*

28. 1 Macc. 3:48; contrast 1 Kings 22:1–12.

29. According to Roger T. Beckwith ("Formation of the Hebrew Bible" in *Mikra, Text Translation and Interpretation of the Hebrew Bible in Ancient Judaism and Early Christianity*, ed. Martin Jan Mulder [Assen/Maastricht: Van Gorcum; Philadelphia: Fortress, 1988], 47–48), the Scrolls use formulae to quote citations from Sam., Isa., Ezek., Hosea, Amos, Nah., Mic., Zech., Mal., Prov., and Dan. Philo quotes Josh., Judg., Sam., Kings, Isa., Jer., Hosea, Zech., Ps., Prov., and Job. Jesus and Paul quote Isa., Hab., Zech., Mal., Ps., Prov., and Job, while other New Testament passages cite Kings, Isa., Jer., Hosea, Joel, Amos, Mic., Hab., Zech., and Ps.

30. Craig A. Evans (*Exploring the Origins of the Bible*, 21) includes Genesis (6Q19) in this group, as does Émile Puech, "Qumrân et le Texte de l'ancien Testament," 440.

31. Mroczek, "Thinking Digitally About the Dead Sea Scrolls," 250; cf. Mastnjak, "Jeremiah as Collection," 25–34.

32. Sarna, *Songs of the Heart*, 15; and Yarchin, "Were the Psalms Collections at Qumran True Psalters?," 775–89.

33. *J. Taʿanit* 1:1 64a; *Gen. Rabb.* 20:12 9:5; and *Gen. Rabbati* §44, ed. Albek, 209.

34. So noted by the Tosafot at *b. Shabbat* 55b s.v. *maʿavirim*; 128a s.v. *venatan*; *b. Megillah* 3a s.v. *vayalen*; and *b. Niddah* 33a s.v. *vehinasē*. Cf. 2 Sam. 6:3–4 in *b. Shabbat* 56a; Ps. 95:5 in *b. Ketubot* 5a; 2 Chron. 33:13 in *Pesiqta of Rab Kahana ulaqaḥtam* (ed. Mandelbaum, 408); and Num. 13:29 in *Mekilta Beshalaḥ, d'Amalek* (ed. Horowitz, 176).

35. *B. Nedarim* 37b.

36. Greenberg, "The Stabilization of the Text of the Hebrew Bible," 165.

37. Aristeas 46; cf. Philo, *On the Life of Moses* 2.6.31 (LCL 6:464–65).

38. *M. Moʿed Qaṭan* 3:4; *j. Taʿanit* 4:2 68a; *Soferim* 6:4. Cf. the Talmud's insistence that teaching be done from corrected biblical texts (*b. Ketubot* 19b). For scrolls stored in the Temple, see Josephus, *Antiquities* 5:1.17 §61 (LCL 6:188–89), 4:8.44 §§303–4 (LCL 6:146–49), 3:1.7 §38 (LCL 5:336–37), 10:4.2 §58 (LCL

8:188–89); *m. Kelim* 15:6; *j. Shekalim* 4:3 48a; *b. Qiddushin* 30a; *b. Sanhedrin* 106b; *b. Ḥagigah* 15b; and *Num. Rabbah* 14:18.

39. *Avot of Rabbi Nathan* B 46; and *Sifre* Deut. 356. There are also references to *kotevanim* (*j. Megillah* 1:11 71d) and *lavlarim* (*Tg.* 2 Chron. 20:34 and 24:11).

40. Honigman, *The Septuagint and Homeric Scholarship in Alexandria*, 130; Lieberman, *Hellenism in Jewish Palestine*, 47; and Wyrick, *The Ascension of Authorship*, 290, 346. Cf. LXX Isa. 33:18, where the term *sofer* is translated *grammatikoi*.

41. 4Q11 paleoGen-Exod[d] is the only Qumran scroll that includes a link between two books, though there are fragments of scrolls that seem to have included multiple books (4Q1 [4QGen-Ex[a]], 4Q17 [4QExod-Lev[f]], 4Q23 [4QLev-Num[a]], 1Q3 [1Qpaleo Lev-Num[a]], and Mur 1), all of which are Pentateuchal books. 4QXII[a-g], 8Ḥev XIIgr, and Mur 88 include several of the minor prophets, which were widely regarded as a single book ("The Twelve").

42. Van der Toorn, *Scribal Culture and the Making of the Hebrew Bible*, 234.

43. Eusebius, *HE* 4:26.14 (LCL 1:392–93).

44. E.g., Eusebius, *Life of Constantine* 4:36; *HE* 4:26.14 (LCL 1:392–93); and *b. Bava Batra* 14b.

45. Sawyer, *Sacred Languages and Sacred Texts*, 60; Carr, *Writing on the Tablet of the Heart*, 185; Wyrick, *The Ascension of Authorship*, 346–47; and Colpe, "Sakralisierung von Textun und Filiationen von Kanons," 86.

46. Hermann W. Beyer, "*kanon*," *TDNT* vol. 3, 601.

47. *J. Soṭah* 9:14 24b; *b. Soṭah* 48b; *b. Sanhedrin* 11a; *b. Yoma* 9b; and *Songs Rabbah* 8:9.3.

48. E.g., Philo, *On the Contemplative Life* III.25 (LCL 9:126–27); and the prologue to Sira, 4QMMT397 frag. 14–21 ll. 10–11. Cf. 4Q398 frag. 14–17 l. 2–3; Josephus, *Against Apion* 1:38–40 (LCL 1:178–79); and 4 Macc. 18:10. Cf. Jerome, "Preface to Daniel" (*PL* 28:1294).

49. Ryle, *The Canon of the Old Testament*.

50. Cf. Beckwith, *The Old Testament of the New Testament Church*, 3.

51. E.g., 2 Macc. 15:9; 4 Macc. 18:10; Matt. 5:17, 7:12, 11:13; Luke 16:16; Acts 13:15, 28:23. Cf. CD 7:15–17; 1QS 1:3, 8:15–16, 6:1; *m. Rosh Hashanah* 4:6; *t. Terumah* 1:10; *t. Bava Meṣia* 11:23; *t. Bava Batra* 8:14; *t. Niddah* 4:10; Melito (Eusebius, *Ecclesiastical History* 4:26.12 [LCL 1.392]); and Clement, "Stromata" 1:22 (*PG* 8:890–92).

52. E.g., 1 Cor. 14:21; John 10:34, 12:34, 15:25; *Mekhilta Ha-Shira* (ed. Horowitz, 118); *b. ʿAvodah Zarah* 52b; *b. Bekhorot* 50a; *b. Moʿed Qatan* 5a; *b. Sanhedrin* 91b; and *Tanḥuma* Buber *Re'eh* §1.

53. Cf. Josephus, *Antiquities* 5:8.4 §285, 10:11.4 §246 and 249, 12:7.6 §322

(LCL 7:166–67); Matt. 24:15; Jude 14; Wisdom of Solomon 7:27; and *Seder Olam Rabbah* 21 (ed. Ratner, 46ab).

54. Ulrich, *The Dead Sea Scrolls and the Origins of the Bible*, 19; cf. Muslim references to the Qur'an as "between the boards" (*mā bayn al-daffatayn* or *al-lawḥayn*), Graham, *Beyond the Written Word*, 87–89, 208n28.

55. Josephus, *Against Apion* 1:1.8 §38 (LCL 1:178–79); so, too, Cyril of Jerusalem ("Catechesis" 4:35, *PG* 33:497), Eusebius (*Ecclesiastical History* 6:25.1 [LCL 2:73]); and Athanasius (Festal Letter 39 [*PG* 26:1436]). Cf. Jerome (Epistle 53 to Paulinus and "Preface in Libros Samuel et Malachim" [*PL* 28:593]).

56. 4 Ezra 14:45; *b. Ta'anit* 8a, *Num. Rabbah* 13:16, 14:4,18, 18:21; *Songs Rabbah* 4:11§1; and *Eccles. Rabbah* 12.12 §1. Epiphanius lists twenty-seven books (*Adversos Haereses* 8:6 [PG 41:213]).

57. Cf. Eusebius, *Ecclesiastical History* 6:25.1f (LCL 2:72–73); cf. Jerome, Prologue to Samuel/Kings (*PL* 28:597); Epiphanius, *Mensuris et Ponderibus* 3 and 22 (*PG* 43:244 and 277).

58. E.g., *b. Bava Batra* 15a.

59. *Eccles. Rabbah* 12:12 §1.

60. *M. Yadayim* 3:5; and *t. Yadayim* 2:14.

61. *B. Shabbat* 13b and 30b; *b. Ḥagigah* 13a; and *b. Menaḥot* 45a.

62. *T. Sanhedrin* 12:10 and *b. Sanhedrin* 101a both describe the Song of Songs as sung secularly.

63. *B. Megillah* 7a. The book of Esther is conspicuously absent from Melito's list (Eusebius, *Ecclesiastical History* 4:26.14 [LCL 1:392–93]).

64. Cf. Origen's letter to Africanus 7 and 9 (*PG* 11:64–65); and Jerome, "Preface to Daniel" (*PL* 25:492).

65. Cf. Origen, "Introduction to Psalms" 1 (*PG* 12:1085); and Eusebius, *Ecclesiastical History* 6:25 (LCL 2.73–74).

66. Cf. *b. Shabbat* 13b; *b. Niddah* 16b; *b. Yevamot* 63b; *b. Bava Qamma* 92b; and *Kallah Rabbati* 3:4. The Jews of Kai-Feng include Ben Sira (White, *Chinese Jews*, vol. 1, 45).

67. CD 10:6, 13:2, 14:7–8; and 1QSa 1:7.

68. CD 16:3–4 and 4Q228 I.ll.1 and 9 cite Jubilees as authoritative. For a list, cf. Puech, "Qumrân et le Texte de l'ancien Testament," 437–38.

69. The term itself goes back to Jerome ("Preface to Samuel," *PL* 28:601); the books are Tobit, Judith, Wisdom of Solomon, Ben Sira, Baruch, Letter of Jeremiah, and 1 and 2 Maccabees; to which the Greek Orthodox Bible adds 1 Esdras, the Prayer of Manasseh, Psalm 151, 3 Maccabees, and the Slavonic Bible 2 Esdras and 4 Maccabees. In addition, their editions of Daniel and Esther are larger than those that became normative in Jewish tradition.

70. Zevit, Matres Lectionis *in Ancient Hebrew Epigraphs*, esp. 33–35.

71. Cf. the debate in *b. Yoma* 52ab.

72. *B. Nedarim* 37b; cf. *j. Megillah* 4:1 74d; *b. Megillah* 3a; *Gen. Rabbah* 36:8; and *b. Berakhot* 62a. Cf. Livy 7:2.7 (LCL 2:350–51).

73. *M. 'Avot* 3:13. For the term's history and etymology, see Ben-Hayim, "*Masorah uMasoret*," 283–92; R. Edelmann, "*Masoret* and Its Historical Background," 372; and Yona and Gruber, "The Meaning of *Masoret* in Ezek. 20:37 and Rabbinic Hebrew," 210–20.

74. Roberts, "The Emergence of the Tiberian Massoretic Text," 14; but cf. N. Allony, "Was Ben Asher a Karaite?," 61–82, and Dotan, *Ben Asher's Creed*.

75. Mann, *The Jews in Egypt and in Palestine under the Fatimid Caliphs*, vol. 1, 54–55 and vol. 2, 43–49.

76. Yeivin, *Introduction to the Tiberian Masorah*, 164; and Revell, "Biblical Punctuation and Chant in the Second Temple Period," 181. Cf. Dotan, "The Relative Chronology of Hebrew Vocalization and Accentuation," 87–99.

77. Jerome, Epistle 73 (*PL* 22:680–81); but cf. Clement's criticism of Jews for using tone and voice to change meaning through the "accents and dots which are widely used" (*Stromata* 3:4 end [*PG* 8:1144]).

78. *Machsor Vitry*, ed. A. Berliner (Berlin: Mekize Nirdamim, 1893), §424, 462.

79. *Machsor Vitry*, ed. A. Berliner (Berlin: Mekize Nirdamim, 1893), §424, 104; and Dotan, "Masorah," *EJ* 16, 1434–35.

80. The *qameṣ* only seems to deviate from this pattern; it was originally written as a line with a dot underneath (Harris, "The Rise and Development of the Massorah," 233f.). *Siddur Sim Shalom* (ed. Jules Harlow; New York: Rabbinical Assembly and United Synagogue of Conservative Judaism, 1985) prints it as a line with a dot, albeit for a specialized purpose.

81. Kennedy, *The Note-Line in the Hebrew Scriptures*.

82. *J. Shabbat* 16:1 15b. This standard applies to Torah scrolls; there are lesser standards for the Prophets and Writings.

83. *B. Shabbat* 103b; and Maimonides, *Mishneh Torah, Hilchot Sefer Torah* 8:1–2.

84. Cf. Perrot, "*Petuḥot et Setumot*," 74–75. The only exception is *Va-yeḥi*, which begins at Gen. 47:28.

85. Harry M. Orlinsky, "The Masoretic Text: A Critical Evaluation," Prolegomenon to Christian Ginsburg, *Introduction to the Massoretic-Critical Edition of the Hebrew Bible* (New York: Ktav, 1966), 107–26; cf. Penkower, "The Chapter Divisions in the 1525 Rabbinic Bible," 360.

86. *Pesuqim* are mentioned in *m. Megillah* 4:4. Archbishop of Canterbury Steven Langton introduced the current numbers into the Vulgate (Latin) version near the end of the twelfth century "for finding what you want and for

remembering" (Smalley, *The Study of the Bible in the Middle Ages*, 224); only slowly were they incorporated into Hebrew editions (Penkower, "The Chapter Divisions," 361).

87. Cf. Lipschütz, "Kitāb al-Khilaf, The Book of the Ḥillufim," 1; and Zimmels, *Ashkenazim and Sephardim*, 140–41.

88. Jedidiah Norzi, *Minḥat Shai*, 8–9, as quoted by Levy, *Fixing God's Torah*, 32; cf. Moses Isserles, *Shulḥan Arukh, Oraḥ Ḥayim* 143:4.

89. The term "Pentateuch" was first used by the gnostic Ptolemy, ca. 150 CE (Bickerman, "Some Notes on the Transmission of the Septuagint," 151).

90. So also Melito: "the twelve in a single book" (Eusebius, *Ecclesiastical History* 4:26 [LCL 1:392–93]); and thus several manuscripts from the Judean desert (4QXII[a-g], 8ḤeverXIIgr, and Mur 88). Cf. Lim, "The Alleged Reference to the Tripartite Division of the Hebrew Bible," 31. See also Sira 49:10.

91. *J. Ta'anit* 1:1 64a.

92. Roberts and Skeat, *The Birth of the Codex*, 75.

93. De Hamel, *Glossed Books of the Bible*, 85.

94. Yeivin, *Introduction to the Tiberian Masorah*, 20.

95. Roberts, "The Hebrew Bible Since 1937," 257; cf. Kahle, *The Cairo Geniza*, 110, 117.

96. *Biblia Hebraica Stuttgartensia*, ed. Karl Elliger and Wilhelm Rudolph. The Wurttembergische Bibelanstalt published an earlier edition in 1937, and a new edition (*Biblia Hebraica Quinta*) is currently in progress. The first two editions (1906 and 1913), published by J. C. Hinrichs in Leipzig under the editorship of Rudolf Kittel, were based on Daniel Bomberg's Rabbinic Bible.

97. Ben-Zvi, "The Codex of Ben Asher," 3.

98. Tawil and Schneider, *Crown of Aleppo*, xii, 25.

99. Moses Maimonides, *Mishneh Torah, Hilchot Sefer Torah* 8:4.

100. Friedman, *The Aleppo Codex*. The missing pages include the entire Pentateuch from Genesis to Deuteronomy 28:17, though one page (with Gen. 26:34–27:30) had been photographed. (Cf. Wickes, *A Treatise on the Accentuation of the Twenty-One So-Called Prose Books of the Old Testament*, ii, frontispiece), and another (with Deut. 4:38–6:3) by J. Segall (*Travels Through Northern Syria* [London: London Society for Promoting Christianity amongst the Jews, 1910], 99). Also missing are 2 Kings 14:21–18:13; Jer. 29:9–31:34; Amos 8:13–Micah 5:1; Zephaniah (end)–Zechariah 9:17; 2 Chron. 35:7, 26:19; Pss. 15:1–25:1; Song of Songs 3:11–8:14; Ecclesiastes, Lamentations, Esther, Daniel, and Ezra-Nehemiah.

101. David Stern points out that the Leningrad codex is laid out like a Torah scroll ("The First Jewish Books and the Early History of Jewish Reading," 188; and "The Hebrew Bible in Europe in the Middle Ages," 240). There are also

synagogue Pentateuchs, which include haftarot and sometimes the five scrolls (Stern, *The Jewish Bible*, 88, where he distinguishes masoretic, liturgical, and study Bibles).

102. "Religio Laici 400" in *The Writings of John Dryden* (Berkeley: University of California Press, 1972), vol. 2, 21.

103. Posner and Ta-Shema, eds., *The Hebrew Book*, 86.

104. Ginsburg, *Introduction to the Massoretic-Critical Edition of the Hebrew Bible*, 808.

105. Ginsburg, *Introduction to the Massoretic-Critical Edition of the Hebrew Bible*, 794–95, cf. 780f.

106. N. Snaith, "Bible: Printed Editions (Hebrew)," *EJ* 4:836.

107. Orlinsky, "The Masoretic Text: A Critical Evaluation," prolegomenon in Christian Ginsburg, *Introduction to the Massoretic-Critical Edition of the Hebrew Bible* (New York: Ktav, 1966), x.

108. Goldschmidt, *The Earliest Editions of the Hebrew Bible*, 16, 19; and Zinberg, *A History of Jewish Literature*, vol. 4, 50.

109. Habermann, *History of the Hebrew Book*, 88, 94–95.

110. Weil, *Élie Lévita, Humaniste et Massorète (1469–1549)*, 113; and Goldschmidt, *The Earliest Editions of the Hebrew Bible*, 31.

111. Ironically, ben Ḥayim later converted to Christianity and was replaced by Elijah Levita.

112. Ginsberg, *Introduction to the Massoretic-Critical Edition of the Hebrew Bible*, 78.

113. For a Christian model, see Lesley Smith, *The* Glossa Ordinaria; and Salomon, *An Introduction to the* Glossa Ordinaria *as Medieval Hypertext*.

114. The term *Mikra'ot Gedolot* was first used in nineteenth-century printed Bibles (Levy, *Fixing God's Torah*, 187n55).

115. Cf. Greenspahn, "Canon, Codex, and the Printing Press," 203–12.

116. Emanuel Tov (*Textual Criticism of the Hebrew Bible*, 4) notes that some editions of *Miqra'ot Gedolot* place the Five Scrolls after the individual books of Torah, presumably to correlate with the season/Torah portion when they are read.

117. Ilan, "The Term and Concept of TaNaKh," in *What Is Bible?*, ed. Karin Finsterbusch and Armin Lange (Leuven: Peeters, 2012), 219–34; for the roots of these terms, see *b. Qiddushin* 49a. An example of the Aramaic acronym can be seen in the masoretic annotation to the word *'olotekha* in S. Frensdorff, *The Masorah Magna* (New York: Ktav, 1968), 140. It also appears in the writings of nineteenth-century scholars such as E. Ehrenberg's letter to Leopold Zunz on January 17, 1835. See Nahum N. Glatzer, ed., *Leopold and Adelheid Zunz, An Account in Letters, 1815–1885* (London: East and West Library, 1958), 80.

118. Robert Kraft cites the Lindisfarne Latin library catalog (1095 CE), which reads: "unum bibliam in duobus voluminibus" ("What Is 'Bible'?—From the Perspective of 'Text': The Christian Connections," in *What Is Bible?*, ed. Karin Finsterbusch and Armin Lange [Leuven: Peeters, 2012], 110); cf. Hildebrand Höpfl, "Écriture Sainte" in *Dictionnaire de la Bible, Supplément*, vol. 2, 461.

3. THEOLOGIES OF SCRIPTURE

1. Harris, *How Do We know This?*, 25–49.

2. Schechter, *Seminary Addresses & Other Papers*, 37; Leo Baeck, *The Essence of Judaism*, rev. ed. (New York: Schocken, 1948), 22.

3. Heinrich Heine, "Gestandnisse," *Sämtliche Schriften*, ed. Klaus Briegleb (Munich: Carl Hanser Verlag, 1975) vol. 6:1, 483; cf. "Ludwig Börne, Eine Denkschrift," book 2 (*Sämtliche Schriften*, vol. 4, 40).

4. Cf. Stern, "The Hebrew Bible in Europe in the Middle Ages," 265; Eva Frojmovich, "Jewish Ways of Reading the Illuminated Bible," in *Jewish Ways of Reading the Bible*, ed. George J. Brooke (Clarendon: Oxford University Press, 2002), 240; Gottheil, "Some Hebrew Manuscripts in Cairo," 615, 649; and N. Wieder, "'Sanctuary' as a Metaphor for Scripture," 166.

5. Aristeas §177; 11QPs[a] 5.xxvii.11; and Philo, *On the Life of Moses* II:35 §188 (LCL vol. 6, pp. 542–43). Cf. *On the Posterity of Cain* 43:143 (LCL vol. 2, pp. 412–13); Josephus, *Against Apion* 1:38 §§7–8 (LCL 1:178–9); and Rom. 3:2 Heb. 5:12.

6. Buber, *On the Bible*, 1.

7. This latter practice originated in the tannatic period, but gained force in the amoraic period (Heinemann, "The Proem in the Aggadic Midrashim," 110–21).

8. Wieder, "'Sanctuary' as a Metaphor for Scripture," 167; cf. Profiat Duran, *Ma'aseh 'Efod* (Vienna: J. Holzwarth, 1865; repr. Jerusalem: Makor, 1970), 11.

9. Carr, *Writing on the Tablet of the Heart*, 230; and Hengel, *The Septuagint as Christian Scripture*, 78–79. By contrast, almost half the Hebrew Bible quotes in the New Testament are from Psalms and Isaiah (Hengel, *The Septuagint as Christian Scripture*, 106–7), and more than half of Jesus's Old Testament quotations come from the book of Isaiah (McDonald, *Forgotten Scriptures*, 65).

10. *Sefer Or Yaqar*, as cited by Idel, *Absorbing Perfections*, v.

11. Maimonides, *Mishneh Torah, Hilkhot Megillah* 2:18.

12. Aristobulus (2nd century BCE) and Alexander Polyhistor (1st century BCE). cf. Josephus, *Antiquities* 1:15.1 §240 (LCL 5:118–19); and *Against Apion* 1.8 §39 (LCL 1:178–79). *B. Bava Batra* 14b excepts the last eight verses of Deuteronomy, which describe his death.

13. Introduction to Maimonides's commentary to *m. Sanhedrin* 10 §8, as translated by Isadore Twersky: *Maimonides Reader* (New York: Behrman House, 1972), 417–21. According to Rabbi Benjamin Zeev (eighteenth–nineteenth

centuries), assertions that "Moses wrote the Torah" should be understood as analogous to those stating that "Solomon built the Temple" in 1 Kings 6:10 and 9:1 (Shapiro, *The Limits of Orthodox Theology*, 109).

14. *J. Peah* 2:6 10a; *j. Megillah* 4:1 74d; *j. Ḥagigah* 1:8 76d; and *Lev. Rabbah* 22:1. Cf. *Exod. Rabbah* 28:6; and *b. Megillah* 19b.

15. At Gen. 37:2.

16. Isaac Abarbanel, *Principles of Faith (Rosh Amanah)*, ed. Menahem Kellner (Rutherford NJ: Fairleigh Dickinson University Press, 1982), chap. 24, p. 205.

17. *Mishneh Kesef*, ed. Isaac Last (Pressberg: Abraham b. David Alcalay, 1905; repr. Jerusalem: Sifriyat Meqorot, 1970), 2; and Guttmann, *Philosophies of Judaism*, 235.

18. *Imrei Ṣadiqim* 5b, as cited in Idel, *Absorbing Perfections*, 60. According to *j. Shekalim* 6:1 49d, "The Torah which the Holy One blessed be He gave to Moses was given to him with white fire engraved on black fire."

19. According to Naḥmanides, "The text contains everything" (*Sefer Ha-Mitzvot Leha-Rambam 'al pi Defus Ri'shon Qushta 'im Hassagot Ha-Ramban*, ed. Chaim Dov Chavel [Jerusalem: Mossad HaRav Kook, 1981], *Ha-Shoresh Ha-Sheni*, 44); thus Gersonides: "Behold, the book that God wrote [Exod 32:32] is all of reality" (*Peirush 'al Ha-Torah 'al Derekh Biur* [New York: Rabbi Jacob M. Sirkin, 1958, from Venice, 1547], 113b), and M. Cordovero: "The entire world is Torah" (cited by Idel, *Absorbing Perfections*, 26).

20. *The Book of the Honeycomb's Flow, Sepher Nopheth Sophim* 1:13 §§12–13, ed. Isaac Rabinowitz (Ithaca NY: Cornell University Press, 1983), 142–43.

21. According to Menaḥem Recanati, "All the sciences altogether are hinted at in the Torah because there is nothing that is outside of Her" (Introduction to his commentary on Rationales of the Commandments as cited in Idel, *Absorbing Perfections*, 122); cf. Shatz, "Is There Science in the Bible? An Assessment of Biblical Concordism," 198–200.

22. Joseph Soloveitchik, *Abraham's Journey*, 17.

23. *Megillat ha-Megalleh*, ed. Adolf Z. Poznanski (Berlin: Meqitsei Nirdamim, H. Itzkowski, 1924), 75.

24. *Zohar Be-Ha'alotekha* 149b.

25. Cf. *Zohar Be-Ha'alotekha* 152a, which describes the commandments as the Torah's body.

26. "Questions and Answers on Genesis" 4:140 (LCL vol. 11, supplement 1, 421–22); thus 1 Macc. refers to it as "a book of law" (3:48) and Josephus as "decrees of God" (*Against Apion* 1:1.8 §42 [LCL 1:180–81]).

27. Westerholm, "Torah, *nomos*, and Law: A Question of 'Meaning,'" 327–36. For other Greek renderings of "Torah," see Rajak, *Translation and Survival*, 22n35.

28. *Tiqqunim* 94a, as cited by Steven T. Katz, "Mysticism and the Interpretation of Sacred Scripture," in *Mysticism and Sacred Scripture*, ed. Steven T. Katz (New York: Oxford University Press, 2000), 33.

29. Benedict de Spinoza, "Theological-Political Treatise," chapter 5 in *The Chief Works of Benedict de Spinoza* (New York: Dover, 1951), 69–76; Moses Mendelssohn, *Jerusalem, or On Religious Power and Judaism*, trans. Allan Arkush (Hanover: University Press of New England, 1983), 99.

30. Maimonides, *The Guide of the Perplexed* 3:50, trans. Shlomo Pines (Chicago: University of Chicago Press, 1963), 613; and Joseph Albo, *Sefer ha-'Ikkarim* III:25, ed. Isaac Husik (Philadelphia: Jewish Publication Society, 1946) vol. 3, 221. Cf. S. D. Luzzatto, "The Torah's aim is not to teach the people wisdom and knowledge, but to guide them in paths of righteousness" (*HaMishtadel* [Vienna: Francesco nobile di Schmid and Il. Buscella 1847] at Lev. 1:1).

31. Menahem Kellner, "Introduction to the Commentary on Song of Songs Composed by the Sage Levi ben Gershon: An Annotated Translation," in *From Ancient Israel to Modern Judaism: Intellect in Quest of Understanding—Essays in Honor of Marvin Fox*, ed. Jacob Neusner, Ernest S. Frerichs, and Nahum M. Sarna (BJS 159 Atlanta: Scholars Press 1989), vol. 2, 95.

32. Rosenthal, "Saadya Gaon," 177.

33. *Mekhilta Yitro* §5 (ed. H. S. Horowitz, 219); cf. Philo "On the Creation of the World" 1.1§1 (LCL vol. 1, pp. 6–7); "On the Life of Moses" 2:ix.51 (LCL vol. 6, pp. 472–75); and modern scholars' suggestion that the Bible (especially Deuteronomy) was influenced by neo-Assyrian vassal treaties, which introduce their stipulations by enumerating the suzerain's beneficent acts (McCarthy, *Treaty and Covenant*).

34. *The Book of Beliefs and Opinions*, trans. Samuel Rosenblatt (New Haven: Yale University Press, 1948) III.6, 154–55.

35. *M. Yadayim* 3:5, 4:6; and *t. Yadayim* 2:19. Cf. John Chrysostom on the gospels ("Homily on Matthew" 2:6, *PG* 57, 30).

36. Philo, *On the Contemplative Life* 10:78 (LCL 9:160–61); and *Sefer ha-Temunah*, according to which certain scriptural verses "are the limbs of the body, and the sefirot are in a human image" (p. 25a; as cited by Wolfson, *Through a Speculum That Shines*, 329).

37. *Gen. Rabbah* 1:1; *Frag. Tg.*; and *Tg. Neofiti* Gen 1:1. Cf. *m. 'Avot* 3:14. The introduction to the Gospel of John makes a similar claim regarding Christ (1:1–3,14), and Islamic tradition ascribes a similar role to the Qur'an (cf. Wilferd Madelung, "The Origins of the Controversy Concerning the Creation of the Koran," 504–25). Midrash *Tanḥuma* (ed. Buber); *Bereisheet* 5 p. 2b; and *Pirqe Rabbi Eliezer* §11 take the plural pronoun "we" in Gen 1:26 as a reference to God and Torah. Cf. Philo, "On the Creation of the World" 4 §§16–20 (LCL vol. 1, 14–17).

38. E.g., *b. Pesaḥim* 54a; cf. Baruch 3:24–4:1, Sira 24:1–12, 4Q525.2.ii.3–4; and *b. Nedarim* 39b.

39. According to one tradition, the Torah had been made two thousand years before creation (*b. Shabbat* 88b; *Gen. Rabbah* 8:2,; *Songs Rabbah* 5:11.1; and *Tg. Neof.* Gen 3:24).

40. E.g., *b. Zevaḥim* 116a; *Gen. Rabbah* 21:9; *Midrash Pss.* 93:3; and *'Avot Rabbi Natan* 31:3. Cf. Aristobulus (*PE* 13:12 [*PG* 21:1101]) and Philo (*On the Creation of the World* IV [§§16–19] LCL 1.14–15); *Midrash Hashem beḤokhmah Yasad 'Areṣ* (*Bet ha-Midrash*, ed. Adolph Jellinek [3rd ed., Jerusalem: Wahrmann, 1967] vol. 5, 68); *Midrash 'Aseret HaDibrot* (*Bet ha-Midrash* vol. 1, 67); *Seder Eliyahu Rabbah* 7; and *Sifre Deut.*, 37. Gershom Scholem, "The Meaning of the Torah in Jewish Mysticism" in his *On the Kabbalah and Its Symbolism* (New York: Schocken, 1969), 48–49, 66–67.

41. *Mekhilta Yitro* §§1, 5 (ed. H. S. Horowitz, 205, 222); cf. *Sifra Aḥarei Mot* 13:13, p. 86b.

42. *Sifre Deut.* 343; *b. Shabbat* 88b; *Tanḥuma Shemot* 25, p. 69b; *Yitro* 11, p. 96a; *Tanḥuma* (ed. Buber) *Shemot* 22 p. 7a; and *Exod. Rabbah* 28:6.

43. *M. Qiddushin* 4:14; *Gen. Rabbah* 24:5; *Tanḥuma* (ed. Buber) *Lekh Lekha* 1:1 and 14; *Toledot* 1; and *Behar* 1 and 3. Cf. *Sifre* 336 (ed. Finkelstein, 386); *b. Nedarim* 32a; *b. Yoma* 28b; *Gen. Rabbah* 64:4 and 95:3; *Lev. Rabbah* 2:10; *Tg. Neofiti* Gen. 3:22; and *Midrash Pss.* 112:1. Note also Gen. 26:5.

44. *Mekhilta Haḥodesh* §5 (ed. H. S. Horowitz, 221); and *Pesiqta deRab Kahana* 12 (ed. Mandelbaum, 449–50). Cf. Shafat, "The Legend About Offering the Torah to the Nations of the World and Its Alternative in the Tannaitic Midrashim and Amoraic Homilies from the Land of Israel," 1*–48*.

45. *B. 'Avodah Zarah* 2b; *b. Shabbat* 88a. Cf. *Lam. Rabbah* 3:1.1; *Sifre Deut.* 343; *Pirqe Rabbi Eliezer* §41; *Mekhilta Haḥodesh* §5 (ed. Horowitz, 221); *Num. Rabbah* 14:10; and *Tg. Ps.-J.* Exod 19:17.

46. *Songs Rabbah* 8:11.2; cf. *b. Shabbat* 88b–89a; *Deut. Rabbah* 8:2; and Joseph ibn Kaspi in Israel Abrahams, *Hebrew Ethical Wills* (Philadelphia: Jewish Publication Society, 1954), 134.

47. *Pesiqta Rabbati* §20 (ed. Meir Friedmann, 95a).

48. *B. Shabbat* 88a; *b. Avodah Zarah* 3a, 5a; *Gen. Rabbah* 8:2; *Exod. Rabbah* 40:1 and 47:4; *Midrash Tanḥuma* (ed. Buber) p. 5b; and *Deut. Rabbah* 8:5. Cf. *Sifra Beḥuqotay* 8:10 p. 112c; *Pesiqta Rabbati* §21 (ed. Meir Friedmann, 100a); *Songs Rabbah* 1:9.6, 7:1.1; Hasidic R. Hayim Tirer of Chernowitz, *Be'er Mayim Ḥayim* 1:8d, as cited in Idel, *Absorbing Perfections*, 133, 159, and 499n30.

49. *Zohar Vayikra* 9b; cf. R. Solomon Alkabeṣ as cited by Idel, *Kabbalah, New Perspectives*, 245.

50. *Sefer Ta'amei Ha-Mitzvot*, ed. Meir, 58, as translated by Wolfson, *Through*

a Speculum That Shines, 377; also R. Shemaiah b Isaac (XII) (*Ṣeror Ḥayim* 198a, as cited by Idel, *Kabbalah, New Perspectives*, 247). Cf. Edmond Jabès, *The Book of Yukel, Return to the Book* (Middletown CT: Wesleyan University Press, 1976), 231.

51. *Sefer HaYiḥud* 113b, as quoted by Idel, *Absorbing Perfections*, 70.

52. Scholem, *Kabbalah*, 132.

53. *Zohar Beshalaḥ* 60a; cf. *Yitro* 90b.

54. *Sefer Taamei Ha-Mitzvot* (Basel: n.p., 1580), 3a; cf. Moses Hayim Luzzatto: "The Holy One, blessed be He, and the Torah, and Israel are one" (Tishby, *Studies in Kabbalah and Its Branches*, 950 51).

55. *Kleinere Schriften* (Berlin: Schocken Verlag, Jüdischer Buchverlag, 1957), 150; cf. Baruch Spinoza's *Theologico-Political Treatise*, chapter. 12, ed. Elwes, 166.

56. Scholem, *Kabbalah*, 132; and *On the Kabbalah and Its Symbolism*, 49. For *Sefer Bahir* §136, see Wolfson, "Female Imaging of the Torah: From Literary Metaphor to Religious Symbol," 289.

57. Joseph Naveh, *On Stone and Mosaic* (Tel Aviv: Israel Exploration Society and Carta, 1978), 144.

58. Cf. Tigay, "The Torah Scroll and God's Presence," 325.

59. E.g., Levinas, "Loving the Torah More than God," 142–45; and Jacques Derrida, *Writing and Difference* (Chicago: University of Chicago Press, 1978), 102.

60. E.g., Elie Wiesel, *The Gates of the Forest* (New York: Schocken, 1982), 197.

61. *B. Bava Meṣ'ia* 59b.

62. Joseph Albo, *Sefer ha-'Ikkarim* 1:3, ed. Isaac Husik, vol. 1, 59.

63. According to *b. Shabbat* 32a it is a sin to call the synagogue ark *'arna*; cf. Rashi and Tosafot ad loc. John Chrysostom calls the synagogue chest *kibotos* (*Adversos Judaeos* 6:7 [PG 48:914]), the very word the Septuagint uses to translate biblical occurrences of *ārôn*.

64. Num. 10:33–35, 14:44; and 1 Sam. 4.

65. Cf. Judah HaḤasid: "The Torah is His footstool" (*Sefer Ḥasidim* [Berlin: H. Engel and Frankfurt: J. Kauffmann, 1891] §1585, p. 387).

66. *Pesiqta de Rab Kahana* 19:4 (ed. B. Mandelbaum, 305–6); cf. *Lam. Rabbah* 3:21 §7; and *Deut. Rabbah* 3:12.

67. Heschel, "God, Torah, and Israel," 76, and also *God in Search of Man* (New York: Farrar, Straus, Giroux, 1978), 257–58.

68. *Exod. Rabbah* 33:1,6–7; *Lev. Rabbah* 20:10, 25:1; *Num. Rabbah* 12:4; *Deut. Rabbah* 8:7; and *Songs Rabbah* 8:11.2. *B. Pesaḥim* 49b presents the Torah as God's bride.

69. Weinberger, "God as Matchmaker: A Rabbinic Legend Preserved in the Piyyut," 238–44; cf. *Sifre Deut.* 345 and *Pesiq. Rabbati* §20 (ed. Meir Fried-

mann [Vienna: Y. Kaiser, 1880; reprint, Tel Aviv, 1963]), 95a, where the Torah is betrothed to Israel.

70. *Exod. Rabbah* 33:1,6,7; and *Songs Rabbah* 8:11.2.

71. Leo Baeck, *This People Israel: The Meaning of Jewish Existence* (New York: Holt, Rinehart, and Winston, 1964), 57; cf. Franz Rosenzweig, *Briefe* (Berlin: Schocken Verlag, 1935), 520; and Isaac Breuer, *Der Neue Kusari, Ein Weg zum Judentum* (Frankfurt a.M.: Verlag der Rabbiner Hirsch Gesellschaft, 1934), 327, 331.

72. Leo Baeck, *The Essence of Judaism*, rev. ed. (New York: Schocken, 1948), 41.

73. Mordecai M. Kaplan, *Judaism as a Civilization: Toward a Reconstruction of American Jewish Life* (Philadelphia: Jewish Publication Society, 1981), 411. Thus Kaplan's view that "the Torah reveals God, not that God revealed the Torah" (Mordecai Kaplan, *The Future of the American Jew* [New York: Macmillan, 1949], 382); and Herman Cohen's description of the Torah as "national literature" (*Religion of Reason Out of the Sources of Judaism* [New York: Frederick Ungar, 1972], 73).

74. *The Letters of Martin Buber: A Life of Dialogue*, ed. N. N. Glatzer and Paul Mendes-Flohr (New York: Schocken, 1991), 315 and 327; cf. *Two Types of Faith* (New York: Harper & Bros., 1961), 57; and Rosenzweig, *Briefe* (Berlin: Schocken Verlag, 1935) 535.

75. Buber, *On the Bible*, 214–15 and 240.

76. Petuchowski, *Ever Since Sinai*, 27.

77. Heschel, *God in Search of Man*, 185, 254.

78. *Liqqutei Torah, Vayiqra* 5b, as cited in Hallamish, *An Introduction to the Kabbalah*, 213.

79. *Avodat Ha-Qodesh*, p. 36d, as cited in Idel, *Kabbalah, New Perspectives*, 177.

80. Abraham Joshua Heschel, *Israel: An Echo of Eternity* (New York: Farrar, Straus & Giroux, 1969), 46 and 49.

81. *Soferim* 13:8.

82. *Shenei Luḥot Ha-Berit, Beit Ḥokhmah*, 25b; cf. *Tanḥuma* Buber *Yitro* 7, p. 37a; *Zohar Koraḥ* 179b ("Whoever is involved with Torah, it is as if he stands each day on Mt. Sinai and receives the Torah"); R. Zev Wolf of Zhitomir ("The reason for our blessing of the Torah by [the formula] 'He gives the Torah' is to show that the Holy One, blessed be He, is still revealing the Torah as He did then, in antiquity, at the holy assembly, at Mt. Sinai" [*Or Ha-Meir* 215d as quoted in Idel, *Absorbing Perfections*, 426]); and Emil L. Fackenheim ("the Torah is given whenever Israel receives it" ["The State of Jewish Belief, A Symposium," ed. Milton Himmelfarb, *Commentary* (August 1966), 87]).

83. E.g., Lev. 24:12; Num. 9:1, 15:32–34, 27:1–11.

1. Petuchowski, "Reform Benedictions for Rabbinic Ordinances," 177, and "The Magnification of Chanukah," 41.

2. Nemoy, "Al-Qirqisānī's Account of the Jewish Sects and Christianity," 349.

3. *B. Shabbat* 23a, where the blessing is justified on the basis of Deut. 17:11, which stipulates, "You shall act in accordance with the instruction they teach you and the ruling which they say to you"; and Deut. 32:7, which advises, "Ask your father and he will tell you, your elders and they will say to you."

4. Maimonides, *Guide of the Perplexed* 3:41; cf. *Mekhilta Mishpatim* 8 (ed. Horowitz and Rabin, 276–77); *b. Sanhedrin* 87b; and *b. Bava Qamma* 83b–84a.

5. Josephus, *Antiquities* 13:297 §6 (LCL 9:376–77); cf. Mark 7:3; Matt. 15:2; also *Tg.* Job 15:18; and *j. Berakhot* 1:7 3b.

6. Justin, Novella 146/I.i (Amnon Linder, *The Jews in Roman Imperial Legislation* [Detroit: Wayne State University Press, 1987], 406); cf. Jerome at Isa. 8:11 (*PL* 24:111), 59:12 (*PL* 24:603); and Letter 121:10, where he criticizes the preference for "doctrinae hominum" over "doctrina Dei" (*PL* 22 p. 1034).

7. *M. Ḥagigah* 1:8; and *t. ʿEruvin* 11(8):23–24. Cf. *t. Ḥagigah* 1:9.

8. Harris, *How Do We Know This?*, 48.

9. E.g., *b. Yoma* 74a; cf. *b. Yevamot* 52b.

10. *J. Ketubot* 13:11 36b; and *b. Ketubot* 10a, 110b.

11. Maimonides, *Sefer Ha-Mitzvot Leha-Rambam . . . im Hasagot ha-Ramban*, ed., Chaim Chavel (Jerusalem: Mossad haRav Kook, 1981): introduction, 2nd principle, pp. 29ff.

12. *B. Menaḥot* 29b.

13. Cf. *Sifre* Deut §351 (ed. Finkelstein, p. 408); *b. Shabbat* 31a; *b. Giṭṭin* 60b; *ʾAvot deRabbi Natan* 15:3; *j. Peah* 2:6 17a; *j. Ḥagigah* 1:8 76d; and Maimonides's introduction to his *Mishneh Torah*. For the history of the concept, which appears to have first emerged in the latter half of the third century though it was not fully formulated until the amoraic period, see Kraemer, *The Mind of the Talmud*, 118; and Peter Schäfer, "Das Dogma von der mündlichen Torah im rabbinischen Judentum," in *Studien zur Geschichte und Theologie des rabbinischen Judentums*, 153–97.

14. *Sifre* Deut 306 (ed. Finkelstein, p. 339).

15. Introduction, *Sefer Mitzvot Gadol* (Jerusalem: 1990/91); cf. R. Shlomo b. Mordecai: "It is not possible to understand the foundations of our holy Torah, which is the written Torah, except by means of the Oral Torah, which is its interpretation" (*Sefer Mizbeaḥ HaZahav* [Basel: 1601] §5, p. 12a).

16. Cf. *m. ʾAvot* 1:1; *b. Sanhedrin* 46a.

17. Cf. Halivni, *Midrash, Mishnah, and Gemara*, 4; regarding the chronological relationship between these two approaches, see 18–19.

18. *B. Sukkah* 34a.

19. *J. Horayot* 3:7 48c; cf. *j. Peah* 2:6 17a; and Rashi at *b. Bava Meṣia'* 33a s.v. *v'einah middah.*

20. *B. Bava Meṣi'a* 33a; cf. *j. Shabbat* 16:1 15c; and Baḥya ibn Pakuda's view that knowledge of Scripture occupies a lower level than that of Talmud (*Sefer Ḥovot Levavot*, trans. J. ibn Tibbon, ed. A. Ṣifroni [Tel Aviv: Hotsaat Maḥabarot Le-Sifrut, 1949], 235–36).

21. *M. Sanhedrin* 11:3; *b. 'Eruvin* 77a; *b. Ketubot* 56a; and *b. Zevaḥim* 101a. But cf. *b. Shabbat* 128b and *Shulḥan Arukh, Oraḥ Ḥayim* 141:8–9.

22. Note the rabbinic debate in *b. Sukkah* 6b; *b. Keritot* 17b; *b. Pesaḥim* 86b; *b. Qiddushin* 18b; *b. Sanhedrin* 4a; *b. Makkot* 7b; and *b. Bekhorot* 34a. Cf. Abramson, "The Ambiguity of the Talmudic *yeš 'ēm lĕmiqra', lamasoret*," 31–34; B. Barry Levy, *Fixing God's Torah*, 4; and Aminoah, "*'Em LaMikra'* and *'Em LaMasoret'* as Normative Expressions," 51. The only tannaitic usage is in *b. Sanhedrin* 4a.

23. Leiman, "Masorah and Halakhah," 298.

24. Yehuda, "Hazon Ish on Textual Criticism and Halakhah," 175–76; but cf. Leiman, "Hazon Ish on Textual Criticism and Halakhah—A Rejoinder," 301–10.

25. *Teshuvot HaGeonim*, ed. Jacob Mussafia; Lyck #90 (Rudolf Siebert, 1864; repr. Jerusalem, 1967) p. 28b; Cf. *Machsor Vitry*, ed. Shimon Hurwitz (Berlin: H. Itzkowski, 1899) §47 p. 26; and Hiyyah Cohen de Lyra of Amsterdam as quoted in S. Assaf, *Sources for the History of Jewish Education* (Tel Aviv: Dvir, 1925–36) vol. 1, p. 191; and Isaac Abarbanel, *Naḥalat Avot* (New York: Feldheim, 2004), *'Avot* 5:19.

26. Elbaum, *Openness and Insularity*, 94, 160; and Rabbi Joseph Hahn of Frankfort (d. 1637) as quoted in S. Assaf, *Sources for the History of Jewish Education*, vol. 1, p. 80.

27. Lenowitz, "Shukr Kuhayl II Reads the Bible," 245; the references are to *b. Ḥagigah* 12a, and *b. Tamid* 32a.

28. "Dialogue with Trypho the Jew" 29 (*PG* 6:537).

29. Leo Baeck, *This People Israel: The Meaning of Jewish Existence* (New York: Holt, Rinehart, and Winston, 1965), 255–56.

30. *Pesiqta Rabbati* 5 (ed. M. Ish-Shalom, p. 14b); cf. *Tanḥuma Va-yera'* §5, *Kî Tissa'* §34; *Midrash Tanḥuma* (Buber) *Va-yera* 6; *Ki Tissa'* §17; and *Exod. Rabbah* 47:1.

31. At *b. Berakhot* 28b; for the dictum's original meaning, see Lieberman, *Hellenism in Jewish Palestine*, 103, and 109n62; Wieder, *The Judean Scrolls and*

Karaism, 224–29, 236–39; and Talmage, "Keep Your Sons from Scripture," 81–101.

32. Luz, *Parallels Meet*, 223; and Aran, "Return to the Scripture in Modern Israel," 130.

33. Cf. Moses ben Henoch Yerushalmi Altshuler's description of his book *Brantshpigl* (1596), as "written in Yiddish for women and for men who are like women in not being able to learn much" (Chava Weissler, *Voices of the Matriarchs* [Boston: Beacon, 1998], 54).

34. *Sefer Ḥasidim al pi Nusaḥ Ketav Yad Asher be-Parma*, ed. Judah haCohen Wistenitzki (Berlin: Zvi Hirsch b. R. Yitzhak Itzkowski, 1891) §765, p. 193.

35. Judah b. Barzilay, *Perush Sefer Yetsirah Lehanasi R. Yehudah bar Barzilay haBartseloni z"l*, ed. Solomon Halberstamm (Berlin: H. Itzkowski, 1885), 5; cf. Rabbi Joshua Joseph Preil (*Ketavim Nivḥarim* [New York: 1924] part 1, p. 42); Mendele Mokher Sefarim, *Bayamim Hahem* in *Kol Kitvei M.M. Sefarim* (Tel Aviv: Dvir, 1958), 267; Chaim Potok, *In the Beginning* (New York: Alfred Knopf, 1975), 444; H. Hazaz in *The Bible and Israeli Identity*, ed. Anita Shapira, 144; Samuel David Luzzatto as quoted in Vargon, "The Date of Composition of the Book of Job," 393; and Zemaḥ ben R. Paltoi, the ninth-century gaon of the rabbinical academy in Pumpeditha, as quoted by Abraham Zacuti in *Sefer Yuḥasin Hashalem* (London: H. Filipowski, 1857), 124b.

36. Josephus, *Antiquities* 13:297, §6 (LCL vol. 9, pp. 376–77).

37. The title was previously used for specialists in the Bible (e.g., *b. Berakhot* 30b; *b. Ta'anit* 27b; *b. Yevamot* 40a; *b. Pesaḥim* 117a; *b. Qiddushin* 49a; *b. 'Avodah Zarah* 40a; and *Pesiqta d'Rav Kahana* 24 [*Shuva*], ed. Mandelbaum, 376.

38. *Pitron Shneim 'Asar, Peirush le-Trei 'Asar*, ed. Isaac D. Markon (Jerusalem: Mekize Nirdamim, 1957), 9, at Hosea 6:1–2; the closing phrase comes from Isa. 29:13.

39. Salmon ben Yeruḥim, commentary to Ps. 69:1 in Pinsker, *Liqqutei Qadmoniot*, 21.

40. The second clause may be a later, possibly even anti-Ananite, addition (Ankori, *Karaites in Byzantium*, 216).

41. Elijah Bashyachi, *Aderet Eliahu §Qiddush HaQodesh* 15 [9d]) as cited by Ankori, *Karaites in Byzantium*, 233, cf. 63, 276, and 282; Baron, *A Social and Religious History of the Jews*, vol. 5, 215, 218, and 278f; Szyszman, *Le Karaïsme, Ses doctrines et son histoire*, 27; and Wilhelm Bacher, "Qirqisani, the Karaite, and His Work on Jewish Sects," in *Karaite Studies*, ed. Philip Birnbaum, 267.

42. *B. Menaḥot* 65ab; cf. *Sifra Emor* 12:1.

43. Jerome, Epistle 121 as cited in Funkenstein, *Perceptions of Jewish History*, 190. According to Pope Innocent IV, Jews "throw away and despise the Law

of Moses and the prophets, and follow some tradition of their elders . . . which traditions are called 'Talmud' in Hebrew. . . . In it are found blasphemies against God and His Christ, and obviously entangled fables about the Blessed Virgin, and abusive errors, and unheard of follies" (Grayzel, *The Church and the Jews in the XIIIth Century*, 240–41, 250–51).

44. Grayzel, *The Church and the Jews in the XIIIth Century*, 240–41; for other such burnings, see Merchavia, *The Church versus Talmudic and Midrashic Literature*, 93, 227, 245, 348.

45. Kaplan, "Karaites' in Early Eighteenth-Century Amsterdam," in *Sceptics, Millenarians and Jews*, ed. David S. Katz and Jonathan I. Israel, 221–28.

46. Yekutiel Blitz, "Introduction," in S. Assaf, *Sources for the History of Jewish Education*, vol. 1, 153.

47. Nadler, *Spinoza*, 120. Although he referred to Jews in the third person, Spinoza continued contact with Amsterdam Jews and was said to have observed the Mosaic law. Nadler, 292, cf. 42, 173, 183, 290, 302, 312, and 315; and Asa Kasher and Shlomo Biderman, "Why Was Baruch de Spinoza Excommunicated?" in *Sceptics, Millenarians and Jews*, ed. David S. Katz and Jonathan I. Israel, 103.

48. *Theologico-political Treatise* chap. 7, ed. Elwes, 100; cf. Martin Luther: scripture is "sui ipsius interpres" (*Werke* [Weimar: Hermann Böhlaus, 1897], vol. 7, p. 97); and the rabbinic *Torah mitokh Torah* (*j. Megillah* 1:13 72b). Alexandrian analogists explained Homer with Homer's help; cf. Nünlist, "What Does *Omēron ex Omerou saphēnisein* Actually Mean?" 385–403.

49. Smend, "Die Mitte des Alten Testaments," 7–17; cf. Gerhard von Rad's rejection of this idea (*Old Testament Theology* [London: SCM, 175], vol. 2, 362–63); and *Mitte der Schrift? Ein jüdisch-christiliches Gespräch*, ed. Martin Klopfenstein, Ulrich Luz, Shemaryahu Talmon, and Emanuel Tov.

50. John Locke, *The Reasonableness of Christianity as Delivered in the Scriptures*, ed. John C. Higgins-Biddle (Oxford: Clarendon, 1999), 19; and Johann Gottfried Herder, "Vom Geist der Ebräischen Poesie" in *Herders Sämmtliche Werke* (Berlin: Weidmannisch Buchhandlung, 1879), vol. 11, p. 221.

51. Solomon Dubno as cited by Altmann, *Moses Mendelssohn*, 85.

52. Cf. Baruch Schotlaender's characterization of the Talmud as "a difficult and strange book full of impractical and useless things and could hardly be of any use as a source of religion" in contrast to "the pure and clear source of the Bible" (Barzilay, "The Treatment of the Jewish Religion in the Literature of the Berlin Haskalah," 45); for Moses Mendelssohn's reference to the Talmud as containing "absurd things (abgeschmackte Dinge)," see his *Gesammelte Schriften Jubiläumsausgabe* (Stuttgart-Bad Cannstatt: Friedrich Frommann Verlag, Günther Holzboog, 1991), vol. 5:1, p. 49.

53. Josef von Wertheim as cited in Robert W. Wistrich, "The Modernization

of Viennese Jewry: The Impact of German Culture in a Multi-Ethnic State," in *Toward Modernity, The European Jewish Model*, ed. Jacob Katz, 61.

54. Jacob Katz, *Out of the Ghetto*, 126; and Petuchowski, "Manuals and Catechisms of the Jewish Religion in the Early Period of Emancipation," 50.

55. Heinrich Heine, *Religion and Philosophy in Germany, A Fragment*, trans. John Snodgrass (Albany: State University of New York Press, 1986), 94.

56. Philipson, *The Reform Movement in Judaism*, 115.

57. Meyer, "Alienated Intellectuals in the Camp of Religious Reform," 63.

58. Plaut, *The Growth of Reform Judaism*, 14–15.

59. *Central Conference of American Rabbis Yearbook* 6 (1895), 61–62.

60. Meyer, *Response to Modernity*, 230.

61. Delitzsch, *Babel and Bible*, 3.

62. Delitzsch, *Babel and Bible*, 65.

63. Cf. Arnold and Weisberg, "A Centennial Review of Friedrich Delitzsch's 'Babel und Bibel' Lectures," 441–57.

64. For the roots of this idea, see Pasto, "W. M. L. DeWette and the Invention of Post-Exilic Judaism," 34–43, and "When the End Is the Beginning?," 161–64.

65. Wellhausen, *Prolegomena to the History of Ancient Israel*, 1, and *The Pharisees and the Sadducees*, 14–15.

66. Wellhausen, *Prolegomena*, 409. Thus "The law . . . takes the soul out of religion and spoils morality" ("Israel" in *Prolegomena*, 509).

67. *The Poetry & Prose of Heinrich Heine*, ed. Frederick Ewen (New York: Citadel, 1948), 663–64.

68. Dienermann, "Unser Verhältnis zur Bibel," 289; cf. Max Margolis, according to Robert Gordis, "The Life of Max Leopold Margolis: An Appreciation," in *Max Leopold Margolis*, ed. Robert L. Gordis, 2.

69. Plaut, *The Growth of Reform Judaism*, 33.

70. Morris A. Gutstein, *Priceless Heritage, The Epic Growth of Nineteenth Century Chicago Jewry* (New York: Bloch, 1953), 162–63; and Tobias Brinkman, *Sundays at Sinai: A Jewish Congregation in Chicago* (Chicago: University of Chicago Press, 2012), 172. Similar steps were taken at Cleveland's Tifereth Israel, where in 1894, Rabbi Moses Grieve replaced the Torah scroll with an English Bible (Zvi Hirsch Masliansky, *Kitvei Masliansky, Neumim, Zikhronot u-Masaot* [New York: Hebrew Publishing, 1929], vol. 3, pp. 188–89; and Lloyd P. Gartner, *History of the Jews of Cleveland* [Cleveland: Western Reserve Society and the Jewish Theological Seminary of America, 1978], 155).

71. *Sefer Torat Elohim im Perush* (New York: Torat Israel, 1950), vol. 3, p. 1b.

72. See p. xiii. So too Naftali Zvi Berlin (the Netsiv) (Yehoshua Horowitz, "Jewish Interpretation in the Later Generations," in *Jewish Biblical Exegesis: An Introduction*, ed. Moshe Greenberg, 131).

73. Sabato Morais, *American Hebrew* 29 (January 7, 1887): 132, as cited by Meirovich, *A Vindication of Judaism*, 6; Sheldon H. Blank, "Bible," in *Hebrew Union College-Jewish Institute of Religion at One Hundred Years*, ed. Samuel E. Karff, 288; and Joseph Hertz, "On 'Renaissance' and 'Culture' and Their Jewish Applications" in his *Sermons, Addresses and Studies*, vol. 2, p. 65. Cf. Benno Jacob: "der ungemessenen quellenkritischen Zersplitterung," *Der Pentateuch, Exegetisch-kritische Forschungen* (Leipzig: Veitt & Comp, 1905), 126.

74. Cf. Benno Jacob's words: "Die Bibelkritik ist der verlorene Sohn der christlichen Theologie" (The Bible scholar is the forlorn son of Christian theology). "Unsere Bibel in Wissenschaft und Unterricht," 512.

75. Schechter, *Seminary Addresses & Other Papers*, 37.

76. Benno Jacob, "Unsere Bibel in Wissenschaft und Unterricht," 511.

77. Ira Robinson, "Cyrus Adler, President of the Jewish Theological Seminary, 1915–1940," in *Tradition Renewed: A History of the Jewish Theological Seminary*, ed. Jack Wertheimer, vol. 1, p. 128.

78. Joseph Jacobs, "Historiography," *JE* vol. 6, p. 425.

79. Schechter, *Studies in Judaism*, 2nd Series, 200, and *Seminary Addresses and Other Papers*, 3. Cf. Graetz, "Zur hebräischen Sprachkunde und Bibelexegese," 20–21; Joseph Hertz, as cited in Meirovich, *A Vindication of Judaism*, 8; Benno Jacob, "Unsere Bibel in Wissenschaft und Unterricht," 42ff and 525–26; and Schine, *Jewish Thought Adrift*, 15; Ludwig A. Rosenthal, *Zurück zur Bible!* (Berlin: M. Poppelauer, 1902). Trude Weis Rosmarin, as cited by J. Sarna, *JPS*, 233; Ludwig Philipson, *AZJ* 23:13 (March 21, 1859): 183–85; and Perles, "What Is Biblical Studies for Us?," 6, 12.

80. Kaufmann Kohler, *Hebrew Union College and Other Addresses* (Cincinnati: Ark, 1916), 9.

81. Weinfeld, "Biblical Interpretation in the Generation of the Revival in Israel," 9.

82. David Rosin, "Die Zunz'sche Bibel," 504–14.

83. Spalding, "Toward a Modern Torah," 77n141; Soloveitchik and Rubashov, *History of Biblical Criticism*, 147; Shelly, *Biblical Research in Haskalah Literature*, 84; Ellenson and Jacobs, "Scholarship and Faith," 32; and Breuer, *Modernity Within Tradition*, 207.

84. Cited by Leiman, "Abarbanel and the Censor," 49n4. For precedents, cf. Rashbam at Gen. 49:10 and Exod. 20:13; and David Kimḥi's frequent references to Christian interpretations of the Bible.

85. Bechtoldt, *Die jüdische Bibelkritik in 19. Jahrhundert*, 13, 67, 202, 441.

86. Federbush, *The Science of Judaism in Western Europe*, vol. 1, p. 4; cf. Bechtoldt, *Die jüdische Bibelkritik in 19. Jahrhundert*, 13, 67.

87. Zinberg, *A History of Jewish Literature*, vol. 10, p. 128; but cf. his May 6, 1860, letter to S. L. Rapoport (*Iggrot* 9 [Cracow: Josef Fischer, 1894], 1367).

88. D. Hoffman, *Die Wichtigsten Instanzen gegen die Graf-Wellhausensche Hypothese*; and M. Goshen-Gottstein, "Christianity, Judaism, and Modern Bible Study," 80.

89. J. Harris, *Nachman Krochmal*, 142, 257, 325.

90. Almuth Jürgensen, "The Fascination of Benno Jacob and His Critique of Christian Scholarship," in *Die Exegese hat das Erste Wort, Beiträge zu Leben und Werk Benno Jacobs*, ed. Walter Jacob and Almuth Jürgensen, 74.

91. Letter to Jakob Rosenheim (April 21, 1927) in Franz Rosenzweig, *Briefe* (Berlin: Schocken Verlag, 1935), 582. So, too, Samson Raphael Hirsch's great-grandson Mordecai Breuer, who suggested understanding "R" as *ribono shel olam* ("master of the world") (Moshe J. Bernstein, "The Orthodox Jewish Scholar and Jewish Scholarship: Duties and Dilemmas," *Torah u-Madda Journal* 3 [1991–92]: 23).

92. Umberto Cassuto, "Our Task in Biblical Studies," in his *Studies on the Bible and the Ancient Orient* (Jerusalem: Magnes, 1972), vol. 1, p. 7 (Hebrew); cf. *Gen. Rabbah* 33:3, 73:3.

93. Cf. Martin Buber, *The Prophetic Faith* (New York: Harper & Row, 1960), 87–88.

94. Touito, "Between 'Scripture's Straightforward Meaning' and 'the Torah's Spirit,'" 225–27.

95. Gottschalk, *Ahad Ha-Am*, 87–88.

96. Sperling, *Students of the Covenant*, 61n79. Thus, the Hebrew Union College's withdrawal of its offer for Louis Ginzberg to join the faculty, possibly due to his acceptance of biblical criticism (J. Sarna, *JPS*, 130).

97. Myers, *Re-Inventing the Jewish Past*, 102–5.

98. David Ellenson and Lee Bycel, "A Seminary of Sacred Learning: The JTS Rabbinical Curriculum in Historical Perspective," in *Tradition Renewed*, ed. Jack Wertheimer, vol. 2, p. 545; in the end the Pentateuch was simply not taught there until the 1950s and 1960s (Mel Scult, "Schechter's Seminary," in *Tradition Renewed*, vol. 1, p. 63).

99. Élie Lévita, *The Massoreth haMassoreth*, ed. Christian D. Ginsburg, 112–13, 127–29; cf. Azariah deRossi, *The Light of the Eyes* III.59, trans Joan Weinberg (New Haven: Yale University Press, 2001), 699–709.

100. Bamberger, "The Beginnings of Modern Jewish Scholarship," 226; Samuel David Luzzatto, *Iggrot Shadal* (Jerusalem: Makor, 1966), vol. 3 #144 (January 24, 1837), 367, though only Prophets and Writings; and Clements, "Heinrich Graetz as Biblical Historian and Religious Apologist," 44n26. For

early antecedents, see Joseph Kara at Josh. 9:4 and Jer. 25:13; and Abraham ibn Ezra at Exod. 25:29.

101. *The Menorah* (July 13, 1892), 49, as cited in Elton, *Britain's Chief Rabbis and the Religious Character of Anglo-Jewry*, 60; the phrase is from *b. Bava Batra* 111b.

102. Bechtoldt, *Die jüdische Bibelkritik in 19. Jahrhundert*, 3; Ellenson, *Rabbi Esriel Hildesheimer and the Creation of a Modern Jewish Orthodoxy*, 158; and Breuer, *Modernity Within Tradition*, 204.

103. Bechtoldt, *Die jüdische Bibelkritik in 19. Jahrhundert*, 275; and Shelly, *Biblical Research in Haskalah Literature*, 70–71.

104. Zunz, "Bibel kritische," 684.

105. Silberstein, *History and Ideology*, 88, 99, 116; Krapf, *Yehezkel Kaufmann*, 13. Cf. Jindo, Sommer, and Staubli, *Yehezkel Kaufmann and the Reinvention of Jewish Biblical Scholarship*.

106. Cf. Y. Kaufmann, *The Religion of Israel*, 175–200, 205–6, 345, 433–35, 439–40.

107. Y. Kaufmann, *The Religion of Israel*, 7.

108. Yael Feldman points out that European romanticism and nationalism often drew on ethnic myths (*Glory and Agony*, p. 17).

109. Cf. Rovner, *In the Shadow of Zion*, 45–77. However, some rabbis argued that Uganda was part of the Promised Land (Luz, "Zion and Judenstaat," 225).

110. Almog, *Zionism and History*, 251.

111. Fellman, *The Revival of a Classical Tongue*, 63; cf. Hosea 2:17; Jer. 14:8; and Ezek. 3:15.

112. Saulson, *Institutionalized Language Planning*, 16ff. In doing this Ben Yehuda did not limit himself to biblical Hebrew, unlike David Yellin and David Frishman (Fellman, *The Revival of a Classical Tongue*, 136; and Waxman, *A History of Jewish Literature*, vol. 4, p. 59).

113. Fellman, *The Revival of a Classical Tongue*, 88.

114. Tamar Rotem, "Education Ministry to Ban 'Bible Lite' Study Booklet," *Haaretz*, September 5, 2008.

115. "Lenokhaḥ Pesel Apollo," Shaul Tschernikovsky, *Shirim* (Tel Aviv: Dvir, 1966), vol. 1, p. 88 (Hebrew).

116. "The Sources" in Habas, *The Book of the Second Aliyah*.

117. Moshe Pearlman, *Ben Gurion Looks Back in Talks with Moshe Pearlman* (New York: Simon and Schuster, 1965), 198.

118. David Ben-Gurion, *Israel: A Personal History* (New York: Funk & Wagnalls, 1971), xviii.

119. David Ben-Gurion, *Ben-Gurion Looks at the Bible* (Middle Village NY: Jonathan David, 1972), 53.

120. David Ben-Gurion, *Ben-Gurion Looks at the Bible* (Middle Village NY: Jonathan David, 1972), 289.

121. Jerold S. Auerbach, "Assimilation in Zion," *Midstream* 41 (May 1995): 23.

122. David Ben-Gurion,*Recollections*, ed. Thomas R. Bransten (London: Macdonald Unit 75, 1970), 107.

123. Shapira, "Ben-Gurion and the Bible," 651.

124. David Ben-Gurion, *Ben-Gurion Looks at the Bible* (Middle Village NY: Jonathan David, 1972), 145–46.

125. Katzoff, "The World Jewish Bible Society," 14–15; and Keren, *Ben-Gurion and the Intellectuals*, 105.

126. Moshe Dayan, *Living with the Bible* (New York: William Morrow, 1978), 7 and 6; cf. Abu el-Haj, *Facts on the Ground.*

127. Mazor, "On Bible and Zionism," 107, 122; and Cohen and Kliot, "Israel's Place-Names as Reflection of Continuity and Change in Nation Building," 238.

128. Schoneveld, *The Bible in Israeli Education*, 1–2, 145–46.

129. S. D. Goitein, "The Theoretical Principles for Bible Instruction in the Hebrew School," in *The Bible and Israeli Identity*, ed. Anita Shapira, appendix 6, p. 84; and J. Schoneveld, *The Bible in Israeli Education*, 76–78.

130. J. Schoneveld, *The Bible in Israeli Education*, 24, 58.

131. Walter Lacquer, ed., *The Israel/Arab Reader* rev. ed. (Harmondsworth: Penguin, 1970), 161; cf. Isa. 42:6, 49:6, 51:4, 60:3.

132. Zivion, "Ben-Gurion's Attachment to the Bible," 8; and Myers, *Re-Inventing the Jewish Past*, 6.

133. Shavit and Eran, *The Hebrew Bible Reborn*, 517.

134. Cohen and Kliot, "Israel's Place-Names," 241; cf. Zerubavel, "Back to the Bible," 514–15.

135. Liebman and Don-Yehiya, *Civil Religion in Israel*, 198, 200ff; cf. Amnon Rubenstein, *The Zionist Dream Revisited*, 116, 123–25.

136. Saadia, *Sefer Bei'ur Tish'im Millot Bodedot BeTanakh*, ed. Solomon Wertheimer (Jerusalem, 1931).

137. Breuer, "Between Haskalah and Orthodoxy," 269.

138. Scholion to *Megillat Ta'anit*, Tammuz 4 (ed. Vered Noam, *Megillat Ta'anit, Versions, Interpretation, History* [Jerusalem: Yad Ben-Zvi, 2003], 77–78).

139. Natronai as quoted in *Siddur Tefillah ke-Minhag Ashkenaz im Seder Rav Amram ha-Shalem*, ed. Aryeh Leib Frumkin (Jerusalem: S. Zuckerman, 1911), vol. 2, p. 207.

140. Ankori, *Karaites in Byzantium*, 209, 235, 251, 307–8; Baron, *A Social and Religious History of the Jews*, vol. 5, 213–14; L. Nemoy, *Karaite Anthology*, 8, 52; and S. Poznanski, "Anan et ses Écrits," 180.

141. Heller, *Isaac M. Wise*, 542 (from *the American Israelite*, March 7, 1856); and *Central Conference of American Rabbis Yearbook* 1 [1890], 14. Cf. Aryeh Rubinstein, "Isaac Mayer Wise," 59.

142. Heller, *Isaac M. Wise*, 289.

143. Plaut, *The Growth of Reform Judaism*, 97; cf. the CCAR's 1976 "Centenary Perspective," which stated: "For millennia, the creation of Torah has not ceased" (*Central Conference of American Rabbis Yearbook* 86 [1976], 176); and its 1999 "Statement of Principles," which speaks of Torah as "God's ongoing revelation to our people" (*CCAR Journal* 47, no. 1 [Winter 2000]: 3).

144. Heller, *Isaac M. Wise*, 542. So, already, is Geiger's description of the Sadducees as having resisted "durchgreifende Reform" (*Urschrift und Uebersetzungen des Bibel*, 151).

145. Abraham Cronbach, *Reform Movements in Judaism* (New York: Bookman, 1963).

146. A. Levenson, *The Making of the Modern Jewish Bible*, 31.

147. J. L. Gordon, "A Vial of Perfume" (Hebrew), *HaMelitz* 18 (1887), 793, as quoted by Shavit and Eran, *The Hebrew Bible Reborn*, 156.

148. Tikva Frymer Kensky, "The Emergence of Biblical Theologies," in *Jews, Christians, and the Theology of the Hebrew Scriptures*, ed. A. O. Bellis and J. S. Kaminsky, 211.

5. MANY MEANINGS

1. *Seder Eliyahu Zuta* 2 (ed. M. Ish Shalom, p. 172).

2. E.g., 1 Sam. 31:12 = 1 Chron. 10:12; 2 Sam. 5:12 = 1 Chron. 14:2; 2 Sam. 7:12 = 1 Chron. 17:11; 2 Sam. 7:16 = 1 Chron. 17:14; 1 Kings 6:1 ≈ 2 Chron. 3:2; 1 Kings 9:5 = 2 Chron. 7:18; and 2 Kings 23:23 = 2 Chron. 35:19.

3. 2 Kings 21:2,17; cf. the Septuagint's Prayer of Manasseh.

4. Thus 2 Chron. 5:3 removed the old month name, "Etanim," from 1 Kings 8:2 and substituted "the second month" (2 Chron. 3:3) for Kings' reference to "the month of Ziv" (1 Kings 6:1).

5. Fishbane, *Biblical Interpretation in Ancient Israel*, 404–5; cf. F. F. Bruce, "The Earliest Old Testament Interpretation," 44.

6. Cf. Barugel, *The* Sacrifice of Isaac *in Spanish and Sephardic Balladry*, 7, and Shmeruk, *Yiddish Biblical Plays*, 31.

7. Paul B. Fenton, "The Post-Maimonidean Schools of Exegesis in the East: Abraham Maimonides, The Pietists, Tanḥûm ha-Yerushalmi and the Yemenite School," in *Hebrew Bible/Old Testament: The History of Its Interpretation*, ed. Magne Sæbø, vol. I/2 (The Middle Ages), 435.

8. Anita Diamant, *The Red Tent* (New York: St. Martin's, 1997); Joseph Heller, *God Knows* (New York: Alfred A. Knopf, 1984); and Stefan Heym, *The King David Report* (New York: Putnam, 1973).

9. The Dead Sea Scrolls include commentaries to Isaiah (3Q4, 4Q161–5), Micah (1Q14, 4Q 168), Nahum (4Q 169), Habakkuk (1QpHb), Zephaniah (1Q15, 4Q 170), and Psalms (1Q16, 4Q 171,173). For Mesopotamian precedents and possible models, see Frahm, *Babylonian and Assyrian Commentaries.*

10. Dan. 2:4–7,9,16,24–26,30,36, and 4:3–6,15–16,21, 7:15–16. cf. 5:7–8,12, 15–17,26, also *ptr* in 2:36 and 4:15 as well as Gen. 40:13,18. See also Oppenheimer, *The Interpretation of Dreams in the Ancient Near East*, 186–217.

11. Cf. Greenspahn, "Competing Commentaries," 461–80. The Israeli commentaries are *Miqra LeYisrael* (Magnes) and *Da'at Miqra* (Mosad haRav Kook).

12. Scholem, *The Messianic Idea in Judaism*, 290.

13. 1QpHab VII.1–5 at Hab. 2:1.

14. Idel, *Kabbalah*, 238–39, also some manuscripts of Rashi's commentary at Ezek. 42:3 (Heschel, *Prophetic Inspiration After the Prophets*, 38).

15. E.g., CD 3:13–14 and 1QS 5:9–11; the terms are juxtaposed in Deut. 29:28.

16. Moses Maimonides, *Guide of the Perplexed*, trans. Shlomo Pines (Chicago: University of Chicago Press, 1963), 12; and M. S. Segal, *Biblical Interpretation*, 117.

17. *Num. Rabbah Naso* 13:15.

18. *B. Sanhedrin* 103b.

19. Gordon, "New Directions," 59–60.

20. *B. Sanhedrin* 34a.

21. *Midrash HaGadol* Genesis, ed. Mordecai Margaliot (Jerusalem: Mosad HaRav Kook, 1947), 39.

22. *Zohar Balak* 202a.

23. Scholem, *On the Kabbalah and Its Symbolism*, 65.

24. According to Scholem, this was first expressed in *Midrash Ne'elam* to Ruth (*On the Kabbalah and Its Symbolism*, p. 54); cf. van der Heide, "PARDES," 151–53.

25. Bacher, "Das Merkwort *Pardes* in der jüdischen Bibelexegese," 294–305; and Alan Cooper, "The Four Senses of Scripture and Their Afterlife" (paper delivered at the 2017 meeting of the Society of Biblical Literature). Cf. de Lubac, *Medieval Exegesis: The Four Senses of Scripture.*

26. *On the Migration of Abraham* 16:93 (LCL 4:184–5).

27. Rashbam at Gen. 1:1 and 37:2; cf. at Exod. 21:1 and Lev. 13:2.

28. Cf. Idel, *Language, Torah, and Hermeneutics in Abraham Abulafia*, 83; cf. Zohar *Aḥarei Mot* 73a; and Mamonides, *The Guide of the Perplexed*, trans. Shlomo Pines (Chicago: University of Chicago Press, 1963), 10–11.

29. Elliot R. Wolfson, "Beautiful Maiden Without Eyes: *Peshat* and *Sod* in Zoharic Hermeneutics," in *The Midrashic Imagination: Jewish Exegesis, Thought,*

and History, ed. Michael Fishbane, 172. Thus Naḥmanides's comment that the cherubs on top of the ark point to a divine reality (at Exod. 25:21).

30. *T. Sanhedrin* 7:11 end; cf. *Avot deRabbi Natan* 37:10, *Sifra* introduction; cf. D. Cohen, "36 Interpretive Principles," 249.

31. *T. Pesaḥim* 4:1–2.

32. Daube, "Rabbinic Methods of Interpretation and Hellenistic Rhetoric," 251; Lieberman, *Hellenism in Jewish Palestine*, 57–60; and Kaminka, "Hillel's Life and Work," 121–22. See already Judah Hadassi, *Eshkol HaKofer* (Gozlo: Mordecai Tirishken, 1836), 124a.

33. *B. Shabbat* 49b.

34. *B. Ḥullin* 60b–61a.

35. *Mekhilta Mishpatim* 16 (ed. Horowitz, pp. 303–4).

36. *Sifra Aḥarei Mot* 13:15; cf. the treatment of Exod. 21:33 in *b. Bava Qamma* 54a.

37. *B. Bava Qamma* 54a and 62b.

38. *B. Ketubot* 38a; *b. Yoma* 81a. Cf. *b. Sanhedrin* 54a, 40b; *b. Bava Qamma* 25b; *b. Yevamot* 70a; *b. Niddah* 22b; and *b. Shabbat* 64a.

39. *B. Pesaḥim* 66a and *b. Niddah* 19b. Cf. *b. Makkot* 5b.

40. E.g., *Zohar Beha'alotekha* 149b.

41. *Gen. Rabbah* 1:14 and 22:2; cf. *j. Ketubot* 8:11 32c.

42. Maimonides's commentary on *m. Sanhedrin* chapter 10 #8 (Heschel, *Heavenly Torah*, 673); cf. *b. Sanhedrin* 99b.

43. *M. Berakhot* 9:5.

44. *B. Sanhedrin* 67b; and *Gen. Rabbah* 53:9. So too that Reuben's defiling his "father's beds" (*mishkevey 'avikha*-Gen 49:4) showed that he had slept with *both* Bilhah and Zilpah (*Gen. Rabbah* 98:4).

45. Cf. *b. Shevuot* 26a; *Gen. Rabbah* 1:14, 22:2.

46. *B. Yoma* 85b; and *Gen. Rabbah* 1:14.

47. *Mekhilta d'Rabbi Ishmael Beshalaḥ* 4 (ed. Horowitz, p. 168).

48. *M. Bava Meṣ'ia* 2:9–10; cf. *b. Sanhedrin* 64b re. Num. 15:31.

49. E.g., *Gen. Rabbah* 53:1 re Ezek. 17:24; but cf. *j. Shabbat* 19:1 17a; *j. Yevamot* 8:1 8d; *j. Nedarim* 1:1 36c; and *j. Soṭah* 7:5 21d.

50. *B. Bava Batra* 121b.

51. *L.A.B.* 6, albeit while denying the possibility that Abraham would have participated in such a sinful act; cf. *Pirqe Rabbi Eliezer* 24.

52. *That the Worse Attacks the Better* V:13 (LCL 2:210–11).

53. *Kallah Rabbati* 1:1; and *Avot d'Rabbi Nathan* 37:13.

54. *B. Berakhot* 6a; and *b. Sota* 14a.

55. *B. Shabbat* 105b; *b. Nedarim* 32a; and *b. Sanhedrin* 90a and 100a.

56. Cf. *L.A.B.* 12:3.

57. *Antiquities* 1:18.6 §270 (LCL 4:132–3), 1:19.8 §§310–21 (LCL 4:148–55), and 1:1.3 §17 (LCL 5:8–9), but note 4:8.4 §196–7 (LCL 4:568–69); cf. Inowlocki, "Neither Adding nor Omitting Anything," 48–65.

58. *Antiquities* 1.18.4 §§265–66 (LCL 5:130–1), 8:7,5 §191 (LCL 7:318–19), but cf. *L.A.B.*'s criticism of Samson's marriage to a non-Jew (Feldman, "Josephus' *Jewish Antiquities* and Pseudo-Philo's *Biblical Antiquities*," 74–75; and Gooding, *Relics of Ancient Exegesis*, 114).

59. *Antiquities* 1:3.1 §74, 5.ix.3 §§328–31 (LCL 5:34–35 and 6:306–9).

60. D. Kimḥi at Gen 31:19; cf. Wisdom of Solomon 10:207. In Josephus's retelling, Isaac speaks but doesn't lie (*Antiquities* 1:18.6 §271 [LCL 4:132–33]; cf. 2:7.3 §173 [LCL 4:238–39]).

61. *Antiquities* 1:4.2 §§113–14 (LCL 4:54–55), 4:vi.11 §§145–49 (LCL 4:546–90), 5.7.1 §§233–34, and 5.x.i §§338–40 (LCL 5:106–7, 150–53); *Against Apion* 2:15 §154 and 38 §279 (LCL 1:352–3 and 404–5). Cf. *Antiquities* 8:2.2 §30 (LCL 5:586–87) in contrast to 1 Kings 3:23–27. Thus his statement, "Our own famous men who are entitled to rank with the highest" (*Against Apion* 2:12 §136 [LCL 1:346–7]); cf. Sophocles, "Oedipus the King," 391–94.

62. Erich Auerbach, *Mimesis, The Representation of Reality in Western Literature* (Princeton: Princeton University Press, 2003), 11–12, though not every biblical account fits that description (e.g., Exod. 25–28, 30–31, 36:8–39:43).

63. *Gen. Rabbah* 22:5, LXX Gen 4:7; cf. Philo, *Questions and Answers on Genesis* 1:59 (LCL 11, Supplement 1, p. 36); and Josephus's *Antiquities* 1:2.1 §54 (LCL 4:24–27).

64. *Antiquities* 5:5.3§193 (LCL 6:248–49).

65. E.g., *Gen. Rabbah* 15:7; and *b. Berakhot* 40a.

66. *L.A.B.* 23:5; cf. *Gen. Rabbah* 38:13. Contrast *Apocalypse of Abraham* 8:1–6; and *Jubilees* 12:12–14.

67. See the works collected in *The Old Testament Pseudepigrapha*, ed. James H. Charlesworth, including the testaments of Abraham, Isaac, Jacob, the 3 Patriarchs, Job, Moses, and Solomon, as well as *L.A.B.* 40:5–7; the *Song of the Three Young Men*, *Gen. Rabbah* 22:7; and *Tg. Ps.-J.* Gen. 4:8.

68. E.g., Josephus, *Antiquities* 2:9.5 §224 (LCL 5:260–61); *Jubilees* 47:5; and *L.A.B.* 40:1 and 64:3. Cf. Adele Reinhartz, *"Why Ask My Name?": Anonymity and Identity in Biblical Narrative* (New York: Oxford University Press, 1998).

69. *L.A.B.* 43:5.

70. *B. Sanhedrin* 39b.

71. Cf. LXX Job 42:17; *b. B. Batra* 91a; and *Tg. Ps.-J* Exod 6:18. Cf. *Pirqe Rabbi Eiezer* 47 (Warsaw: n.p., 1851–52), p. 113.

72. *Yalkut Shimoni, Ḥuqat* 22 §763.

73. *Pirqe Rabbi Eliezer* 23, p. 55b.

74. Josephus, *Jewish War* 6:10.1 §438 (LCL 4.304–5); cf. *Antiquities* 1:20.2 §180 (LCL 4:88–9); and Heb. 7:2.

75. *B. Megillah* 15a. Most modern biblical scholars regard the word, which occurs in Mal. 3:1, as a title, not the prophet's name.

76. *Antiquities* 2:6.1§91 (LCL 5:206–7).

77. Sandmel, *Philo of Alexandria*, 27.

78. *B. Soṭah* 9b; *Ruth Rabbah* 2:9.

79. At Gen. 12:6; cf. at Exod. 1:1; *Tanḥuma Lekh Lekha* 9; and *Gen. Rabbah* 40:6.

80. *Midrash Pss.* 18:1.

81. *L.A.B.* 61:6; cf. *b. Soṭah* 42b; and *Tanḥuma* (ed. Buber) *Vayigash* 8, p. 104b. This dynamic is already present in the book of Esther, where the conflict between Haman (the Agagite) and Mordecai (the Kishite) replays the one between Saul (son of Kish) and the Amalekite king Agag (1 Sam. 15).

82. *L.A.B.* 19:14; cf. Gen. 18:32.

83. 1 Cor. 10:1–5.

84. *On the Life of Abraham* 9:47 (LCL 6:26–7).

85. J. Soloveitchik, "The Lonely Man of Faith," 10–18.

86. Mordecai Richler, *This Year in Jerusalem* (New York: A. A. Knopf, 1994), 203–4; cf. the picture in Paul Cowan, *A Torah Is Written* (Philadelphia: Jewish Publication Society, 1986); David Golinkiin, "Blotting Out Haman on Purim," *Responsa in a Moment* 5:5 (March, 2011), shechter.edu/blotting-out-haman-on-purim, accessed May 25, 2020; Maimonides, *Mishneh Torah* Kings 5:5 and Wars 5:59; *b. Sanhedrin* 96b; *b. Yoma* 54a; and Naḥmanides at Exod. 17:9,16. For a contrary view, see *b. Sanhedrin* 20b.

87. Horowitz, *Reckless Rites*, 1–4, 109, 112–13, 116, 140, 145–46; Jaffee, "The Return of Amalek," 61; Shochet, *Amalek*, 78, 106, 169; Jeffrey Goldberg, "Israel's Fears, Amalek's Arsenal," *New York Times*, May 17, 2009; Hertz, *Sermons, Addresses and Studies*, vol. 1, p. 13; R. Hershel Shacter, as quoted in, "Wright and Wrong," *Jewish Forward*, May 9, 2008; and Jewish Telegraphic Agency, "Modern Orthodox Are 'Amalek': Shas Rabbi," *Intermountain Jewish News*, July 19, 2013.

88. Horowitz, *Reckless Rites*, 1, 87, 109–46; Shochet, *Amalek*, 54; Jeffrey Goldberg, "Among the Settlers: Will They Destroy Israel?" *New Yorker*, May 31, 2004, 48ff; Roland Bainton, *Christian Attitudes Towards War and Peace, A Historical Survey* (New York: Abingdon, 1960), 168; Robert L. Wilken, *The Land Called Holy* (New Haven: Yale University Press, 1992), 235; and Theophanes, *The Chronicle of Theophanes*, §332, trans. Harry Turtledove (Philadelphia: University of Pennsylvania Press, 1982), 336.

89. 1QpHab VII.1–5 at Hab. 2:1.

90. 2 Cor. 6:2; cf. 1 Peter: "It was revealed to [the prophets] that they were serving not themselves but you . . . ," i.e., his first-century contemporaries (1:12).

91. *Sifre* Deut. 357 (at Deut 34:2, ed. Finkelstein, p. 426).

92. *Zohar BeHa'alotekha* 152a.

93. *Zohar Mishpaṭim* 99a.

94. Philo, *On the Contemplative Life* 3.2 (LCL 9:128–29).

95. Gal. 4:22–26.

96. *On Drunkenness* 9:30 (LCL 332–33).

97. *B. Bava Batra* 15a, *j. Soṭah* 5:8 20d.

98. Abba Mari Moshe, *Sefer Minḥat Qena'ot* (Pressburg: Anton Edlin v. Schmid, 1838), 153; cf. Joseph Kaspi in Israel Abrahams, *Hebrew Ethical Wills*, vol. 1 (Philadelphia: Jewish Publication Society, 1954), 155ff.

99. Abraham ibn Ezra at Gen 28:12 and Maimonides, *Guide of the Perplexed* 1:15.

100. Wilhelm Bacher, "The Treatise on Ethical Bliss Attributed to Moses Maimûni (*Pirqei HaHaṣlaḥah*)," JQR os 9 (1897): 274–75.

101. Talmage, "Apples of Gold," 330.

102. Talmage, "Apples of Gold," 326.

103. Ginzberg, *On Jewish Law and Lore*, 143.

104. *B. Shabbat* 88ab; cf. *b. Shabbat* 63a; Maimonides, *Guide of the Perplexed* 3:51; *Mishneh Torah Laws of Repentance* 10:3; and Joseph b. Yehudah b. Yaakov ibn Aknin, *Hitgalut haSodot veHofa'at HaMe'orot, Peirush Shir HaShirim*, ed. A. S. Halkin (Jerusalem: Mekize Nirdamim, 1964).

105. Sandmel, *Philo of Alexandria*, 59; and Birnbaum, *The Place of Judaism in Philo's Thought*, 30–43. Cf. *On the Embassy to Gaius* 1 §4 (LCL vol. 10, pp. 4–5); and *On Rewards and Punishments* VII §44 (LCL 8:336–39).

106. Zohar *BeHa'alotekha* 149b.

107. Zohar *Bereisheet* 15a; but see *b. Megillah* 9a; *Gen. Rabbah* 1:1, citing Prov. 8:22.

108. Zohar *Bereisheet* 15b.

109. Moses de Leon, *The Sheḳel Haḳ-ḳodesh of Moses de Leon*, ed. A. W. Greenup (London: n.p., 1911; rprt., Jerusalem: n.p., 1969), 91.

110. Also called *ḥushbana* (*Esther Rabbah* 7:21; cf. Arabic *ḥisāb*). Dornseiff, *Das Alphabet in Mystik und Magie*, 91; and S. A. Horodezky, "Gematria," *Encyclopaedia Judaica*, vol. 7 (Berlin: Eschkol, 1928–34), 171–74. For a survey of recent interpretations that perceive secret numerical meanings in the biblical text, see Bar-Ilan, "Back to the Middle Ages," 154–59.

111. *B. Nedarim* 32a; *Gen. Rabbah* 43:2.

112. *Barnabbas* 9:8 (LCL *The Apostolic Fathers*, vol. 2, pp. 44–45).

113. Stephen J. Lieberman, "A Mesopotamian Background for the So-Called Aggadic 'Measures' of Biblical Hermeneutics?," *HUCA* 58 (1987): 172–73.

114. So, too, the Septuagint's translation of *lēb qamay* in Jer. 51:1 (LXX 48:1) as referring to the Chaldeans (*kasdim*).

115. Cf. Christian interpretation of "fish" (*ichthys*) as *Iēsou christos theou yios sōter* (Dornseiff, *Das Alphabet*, 136).

116. *B. Shabbat* 119b.

117. Lieberman, *Hellenism in Jewish Palestine*, 69.

118. *B. Shabbat* 105a; *Pesiqta Rabbati* 21 (ed. Meir Ish Shalom, p. 105a); and *Pesiqta deRab Kahana* 12:24 (ed. Mandelbaum, p. 222).

119. Gershom G. Scholem, "The Meaning of the Torah in Jewish Mysticism," in his *On the Kabbalah and Its Symbolism*, 80ff.

120. *Zohar Yitro* 87a; cf. *Zohar Yitro* 90b, *Aḥarei Mot* 73a, and *Ha'azinu* 298b. In the introduction to his commentary on the Torah, Naḥmanides notes: "It would appear that the Torah . . . was written in this form that we have mentioned, with continuous writing, without a break between words, so that it was possible for it to be read as divine names or in our normal way with the Torah and the commandments. It was given to Moses our teacher divided so as to express the commandment, but transmitted to him orally in the rendition of Divine Names. Thus . . . the Great Name that I have mentioned is written continuously and then divided into words of 3 letters and other divisions, as is the practice among the masters of the Kabbalah."

121. 1QpHab 7:1–5 at Hab. 2:1.

122. Zohar *BeHa'alotekha* 152a.

123. *Sifra Tazria* 13:2 (ed. Weiss, p. 68b).

124. Saadia Gaon, *The Book of Beliefs and Opinions*, 7:2, trans. Samuel Rosenblatt (New Haven: Yale University Press, 1948), 265–66; and *Perushei Rabbenu Saadia Gaon al haTorah*, trans. Yosef David Qapaḥ (Jerusalem: Mosad HaRav Kook, 1984), 13.

125. Cf. W. Bacher, *Die exegetische Terminologie der jüdischen Traditionsliteratur*, vol. 1, p. 162; vol. 2 pp. 170–73.

126. E.g., *B. Shabbat* 63a; *b. Yevamot* 11b and 24a; and N. Sarna, "The Modern Study of the Bible in the Framework of Jewish Studies," 21. Although the terms *peshat* and *derash* originated in the amoraic period, Rashi understood them differently; cf. Kamin, "Rashi's Exegetical Categorization," 16–32; and Gelles, *Peshat and Derash in the Exegesis of Rashi.*

127. *B. 'Avodah Zarah* 58b; *b. Ḥullin* 137b. Cf. *b. Qiddushin* 2b.

128. Cf. *j. Yevamot* 1:6 3a; *b. Yevamot* 13b; *b. Giṭṭin* 90a; *b. Rosh Hashana* 3a; and *Gen. Rabbah* 50:3.

129. Cf. *b. Yoma* 74b (re Lev 8:3) and Num. Rabbah 19:28: "All the words of Torah need each other; whatever one closes, another opens."

130. Cf. *m. Berakhot* 9:5; cf. *j. Soṭah* 5:7 20c; *b. Yoma* 82a; and *b. Sanhedrin* 74a.

131. *Maḥberet Menaḥem*, ed. A. Filipowski (London: Filipowski, 1854).

132. E.g., *Sifre* 306; *Pesiqta deRab Kahana* 12:24 (ed. Mandelbaum, p. 223); and *b. Rosh Hashana* 26a. Cf. *b. Sanhedrin* 38b; *b. Pesaḥim* 41a and 61a; *Tanḥuma Tsav* 3 (p. 7a); *b. Menaḥot* 34b; *b. Sanhedrin* 8b and 76b; and *b. Shabbat* 3b.

133. M. Z. Cohen, *Opening the Gates of Interpretation*; and U. Simon, "The Contribution of R. Isaac b. Samuel al-Kanzi to the Spanish School of Biblical Interpretation," 174.

134. *Antiquities* 1:1.3§38 (LCL 5:18–19).

135. Solomon Loewisohn, *Land Researches: A Geographical Lexicon of the Holy Writings* (Vienna: Holzinger, 1819) (Hebrew).

136. N. M. Sarna, "The Bible and American Judaism," 14.

137. E.g., Maimonides, *Guide of the Perplexed* 3:37 and 48; Joseph Bekhor Shor at Exod. 15:26; and Bekhor Shor's and Joseph Qara's explanation of Lev. 19:19's prohibition on interbreeding as an effort to maintain the natural order.

138. Philo, *On the Special Laws* 4:xvii.100 (LCL 8:68–69); cf. Maimonides, *Guide of the Perplexed* 3:49 (ed. S. Pines, vol. 2, p. 609)

139. *PE* 9:17 and 20 (*PG* 21, pp. 709, 713); Josephus, *Antiquities* 1:15 §§240–1 (LCL 5:118–19); and Epiphanias, *Panarion* 55, no. 2 (*PG* 41:973).

140. Shelly, *Biblical Research in Haskalah Literature*, 14; Sorkin, *Moses Mendelssohn and the Religious Enlightenment*, 43.

141. Eusebius *PE* 9:17.3–4 and 18.1 (*PG* 21:708–9, 728); cf. Josephus, *Antiquities* 1:7.2 §158 (LCL 4:78–79) and 8:2 §166–68 (LCL 5:78–79, 82–83); *PE* 9:29.4, 9:23.1–4; and 1QapGen 19:24–5.

142. *PE* 9:26.1 13:12 (*PG* 21:728, 1097).

143. *Questions and Answers on Genesis* 3:5, 4:152 (LCL Suppl. 1 pp. 187–88 and 434); cf. *On the Special Laws* 4:10.61 (LCL 8:44–47).

144. H. L. Ginsberg, "A Phoenician Hymn in the Psalter," 472–76; cf. Umberto Cassuto, "The Israelite Epic," in *Biblical and Oriental Studies*, vol. 2, 69–109.

145. *B. Berakhot* 31b; *b. Nedarim* 3a; *b. Yevamot* 71a; *b. Bava Meṣʿia* 31b; *b. Zevaḥim* 108b; *b. Shabbat* 63a; *b. Ketubot* 67b; *b. Giṭṭin* 41b; *b. Qiddushin* 17b; *b. Tamid* 29a; and *b. Ḥullin* 90b. Cf. *m. Bava Qamma* 5:7 and *Mekhilta de-Rabbi Ishmael Mishpatim*, 20 (ed. Horowitz, p. 321): "The Bible speaks of what is normal." For Christian parallels, cf. Funkenstein, "Scripture Speaks in the Language of Man," 92.

146. *Mekhilta deRabbi Ishmael Beshalaḥ* 4 (ed. Horowitz, p. 167).

147. Saadia Gaon, *The Book of Beliefs and Opinions,* 7:2 (ed. Rosenblatt, pp. 265–66); cf. Joseph Kimḥi's observations about its frequent use of seven and ten as round numbers (*Sefer Zikkaron,* ed. W. Bacher [Berlin: M'kize Nirdamim, 1888; rprt. Jerusalem: n.p., 1968], 29).

148. E.g., *Maḥberet,* 70–71; cf. Abraham ibn Ezra at Deut. 32:2.

149. M. Z. Cohen, "A Poet's Biblical Exegesis," 533–56.

150. E.g., at Deut. 32:2, Joel 3:3, Zeph. 2:4, Ps. 1:2, 29:1, 56:9, 103:22, 118:5, 119:150, and his long comment on Exod. 17:7 and 25:22.

151. Cf. Rashbam at Gen. 1:5. See also Joseph Kara at Judg. 1:16, 4:11; 1 Sam. 1:3 and 13:22; and at Hos. 2:7 and Job 1:4.

152. Breuer, *The Limits of Enlightenment,* 148; cf. Moses Lilienblum: "The poetry of Israel is totally removed from the poetry of the Aryan. Its amazing effect did not stem from power nor from beauty, but from the sublime" (Shavit, *Athens in Jerusalem,* 241).

153. *Moses Mendelssohn's Gesammelte Schriften,* vol. 5 (Leipzig: F. A. Brockhaus, 1843–45), 505.

154. Benno Jacob, *Das Erste Buch der Tora* (Berlin: Schocken Verlag, 1934), 235, 577; and Martin Buber, "Leitwort Style in Pentateuch Narrative," in Martin Buber and Franz Rosenzweig, *Scripture and Translation,* 114–28.

155. Almuth Jürgensen, "The Fascination of Benno Jacob and His Critique of Christian Scholarship" and also "'Die Exegese hat das erste Wort'–Zu Benno Jacobs Bibelauslegung," in *Die Exegese hat das Erste Wort,* ed. Walter Jacob and Almuth Jürgensen, 73, 83, 141. For the term "inner-biblical exegesis," see N. M. Sarna, "Psalm 89: A Study in Inner Biblical Exegesis," 29–46; cf. Sandmel, "The Haggada Within Scripture," 105–22; and Rober Alter's description of repeated narrative patterns, which he calls "type scenes" (*The Art of Biblical Narrative,* 47–62).

156. *Antiquities* 5.1.2§9–12 (LCL 6:164–7); contrast Josh. 2:9–12.

157. Cf. *b. Sanhedrin* 92b and *b. Bava Batra* 15a.

158. Maimonides, *Guide* 2:36 and 42.

159. Joseph Bekhor Shor at Gen. 19:26.

160. *Against Apion* 2:22 §192 (LCL 1:370–71).

161. 2 Enoch 30:8; but *Gen. Rabbah* 8:3–4 and 8; and Apostolic Constitutionns 7:34 (*PG* 1:1028); denied by 4 Ezra 3:4.

162. Samuel ben Meir (Rashbam) at Gen 1:5.

163. At Exod. 13:9; thus his statement, "I have not come to explain halachot, even though they are primary . . . but to explain Scripture's *peshut*" (at Exod 21:1).

164. E.g., *b. Shabbat* 30b; *Sifre Num. Balak* §131; Mann, "Some Midrashic Geniza Fragments," 338–52; Ginzberg, *Genizah Studies in Memory of Dr. Sol-*

omon Schechter, vol. 1, 217–19; and A. Marmorstein, "Der Midrasch (*Sheney Ketuvim*) von den Widersprüchen in der Bibel," 281–92.

165. E.g., Josephus's harmonization of 2 Samuel's conflicting statements about the number of Absalom's sons—three, according to 2 Sam. 14:27, but none, according to 18:18 (*Antiquities* 7:x.3 §243 [LCL 7:132–5]; cf. *b. Sotah* 11a); and Rashi's explanation of 2 Samuel's reference to Michal's children (21:8), despite its earlier statement that she was barren (6:23), by suggesting that she raised the sons of her sister Merab (at 2 Sam. 21:8).

166. M. Soloveitchik and Z. Rubashov, *History of Biblical Criticism*, 26. See also Schechter, "The Oldest Collection of Bible Difficulties by a Jew," 345–74.

167. Richard H. Popkin, "Spinoza and Bible Scholarship," in *The Cambridge Companion to Spinoza*, ed. Don Garrett (Cambridge: Cambridge University Press, 1996), 384. Manasseh ben Israel's reconciled such contradictions in his *Conciliador* (1632–51).

168. E.g., *t. Soṭah* 9:2–9; cf. *j. Soṭah* 9:7 2d 24a.

169. *On the Creation of the World* 146 §134 (LCL 11:106–7).

170. *Sifra* introduction (Vienna: Schlosberg, 1862), 1a; cf. *Mekhilta Bo* 4; and *Yitro* 9 (ed. Horowitz and Rabin, pp. 13, 238).

171. *Mekhilta Bo'* 8 (ed. Horowitz, p. 27); and *b. Menaḥot* 66a.

172. *J. Sheqalim* 6:1 49d; *j. Megillah* 1:7 70d; *j. Soṭah* 8:3 22d; *b. Pesaḥim* 6b; *Eccles. Rabbah* 1:12. f. *b. Berakhot* 10a,; *Mekhilta Beshalaḥ* 7 (ed. Horowitz, p. 139); and *Sifre Num. Beha'alotekha* §64.

173. A. Eppstein, "Biblische Textkritik bei den Rabbinen," 46; and *b. Nedarim* 37b. Rabbinic tradition attributes differences between the Hebrew and Greek editions to divine guidance (cf. *Mekhilta deRabbi Ishmael Bo* 1:4; *j. Megillah* 1:11 71d; *b. Megillah* 9a; *Sefer Torah* 1:6; and *Soferim* 1:7), though questioned by Jerome (Preface to the Pentateuch, *PL* 28:150–51).

174. David Kimḥi at 1 Chron. 1:7; cf. Gen. 10:4 (Dodanim) and 1 Chron. 1:7 (Rodanim); Num. 1:14 (Deuel), 2:14 (Reuel), 7:42 (Deuel), 7:47 (Deuel), 10:29 (Reuel); and 2 Kings 25:21 (Riblah) and Ezek. 6:14 (Diblah). For an antecedent of this view, see Wollenberg, "The Book That Changed: Narratives," 143–60.

175. *Sefer ha-Riqmah*, ed. M. Wilensky (Jerusalem: Academy for Hebrew Language, 1963–64), chap. 28(27), pp. 307–33.

176. *B. Bava Batra* 14b–15a. The Septuagint had already attributed Lamentations to Jeremiah centuries earlier.

177. Samuel Poznanski, *Moses ben Samuel haKohen ibn Chiquitilla nebst den Fragmenten seiner Schriften* (Leipzig: J. C. Hinrichs'sche Buchhandlung, 1895), 100–101, 109, 113; Abraham ibn Ezra at Isa. 40:1, Ps. 51:20, and 106:47; and Isaac Abarbanel, *Perush al Nevi'im Rishonim* (Jerusalem: Hotsaat Sefarim Torah veDaat, 1954/55), Introduction, 7a–7b. Cf. Joseph Kara at 1 Sam 9:9 and Lev.

Rabbah 6:6 re Isa 8:19–20; Simon, *Four Approaches to the Book of Psalms*, 68–71, 76–79, 120–32, 179–81, 198; M. B. Shapiro, *The Limits of Orthodox Theology*, 10; and Aharon Maman, "The Linguistic School: Judah Hayyuj, Jonah ibn Janāḥ, Moses ibn Chiquitilla and Judah ibn Bal'am," in *Hebrew Bible/Old Testament, The History of its Interpretation*, vol. 1, part 2, ed. Magne Sæbø, 276–77.

178. Spinoza, *Theological-Political Treatise*, chap. 8 (ed. R. H. M. Elwes, 120–26); cf. Abraham ibn Ezra at Gen. 12:6, 36:31; Deut. 1:2; and Job 2:11.

179. Shelly, *Biblical Research in Haskalah Literature*, 22, 26, 54–55, 61, 67–69; and Margolies, *Samuel David Luzzatto*, 96.

180. Vargon, "The Identity and Dating of the Author of Ecclesiastes According to Shadal," 366–68, cf. 372; Nachman Krochmal, *Guide of the Perplexed of the Time* (Leopoli: J. Schnayder, 1851), 149; and Zunz, *Die Gottesdienstlichen Vorträge der Juden, historisch Entwickelt*, 13–36. This latter view has been challenged by Sara Japhet ("The Supposed Common Authorship of Chronicles and Ezra-Nehemiah Investigated Anew," *VT* 18 [1968]: 330–71), and H. G. M. Williamson (*Israel in the Book of Chronicles* [Cambridge: Cambridge University Press, 1977]).

181. W. Gunther Plaut, Bernard J. Bamberger, and William W. Hallo, *The Torah: A Modern Commentary* (New York: Union of American Hebrew Congregations, 1981), 145; cf. A. B. Yehoshua: "This powerful and awesome myth, which hovers over our history and culture with great strength like a black bird" ("*Ḥatimah: Levatel et ha-Akedah al-yedei Mimushah,*" in Nitza Ben-Dov, *Bekivun HaNegdi, Qoveṣ Meḥqarim al Mar Mani le-A.B. Yehoshua* [Tel Aviv: Hakibbutz HaMeuḥad, 1995], 396; and Elie Wiesel: "a story that contains Jewish destiny in its totality" [*Messengers of God, Biblical Portraits and Legends* (New York: Summit, 1976), 69, cf. 95]).

182. E.g., Barnabbas 7:3 (*Apostolic Fathers*, LCL 2:36–37); Tertullian, "Adversus Marcion" 3:18 (*PL* 2:239); and "Adversus Judaeos" 10:6 (*PL* 2:666). This linkage is anticipated already in the New Testament description of Jesus as "beloved" (Mark 1:11, Matt. 3:17, Luke 3:22, 2 Peter 1:17), which was also used for Isaac (Gen. 22:2), and its emphasis on his having carried the cross and being bound (John 19:17, 18:12, 24) just as Isaac had carried the wood on which he would be bound (Gen 22:1). Thus the Akedah's recitation as part of the Easter liturgy (Delaney, *Abraham on Trial*, 137).

183. The Qur'an (37:100–11) never names which of Abraham's sons was to be offered, leading to al-Tabari's observation: "The earliest sages of our Prophet's nation disagree about which of Abraham's two sons it was that he was commanded to sacrifice. Some say it was Isaac; while others say it was Ishmael" (*The History of al-Ṭabarī*, trans. William M. Brinner [Albany: State University of New York Press, 1987], vol. 2, p. 82).

184. E. A. Speiser, *Genesis* (Garden City: Doubleday, 1964), 164.

185. R. W. L. Moberly, "The Earliest Commentary on the Akedah," 302–23.

186. Jacob ben Asher (Baal HaTurim) at Gen 22:1 and 4 (in fact, *el 'ereṣ ham-oriah* in v. 2 = 582, whereas *biyrushalayim* = 598, and verse 3 = 592 rather than 596, the value of *yerushalayim*).

187. Ps. 8 (*t. Soṭah* 6:5); and Ps. 60:6. Cf. *Midrash Vayosha'* (*Bet haMidrash*, vol. 1, p. 38) *Exod. Rabbah* 1:15; *Mekhilta Beshalaḥ* 3, p. 100; *j. Ta'anit* 2:4 65d; *Exod. Rabbah* 21:8; *Tg. Songs* 1:13, 2:17, 3:6; *Tg. Esther* II 5:1; and *Gen. Rabbah* 56:1.

188. This title first appeared in *Mekhilta Bo'* 7 and 11 (ed. Horowitz, pp. 34, 39); cf. *t. Sotah* 6:5.

189. Isa. 9:17 and 10:34; there are related forms in Jer. 4:7 and Ps. 74:5.

190. Nahum M. Sarna, *The JPS Torah Commentary: Genesis* (Philadelphia: Jewish Publication Society, 1989), 152.

191. So already *Gen. Rabbah* 56:3; cf. Deut. 32:42; *Tanḥuma*, ed. Buber *Vayera* 46, p. 57b; and Rashi at v. 6.

192. *Tanḥuma Ṣav* 13 (p. 9ab).

193. *Pesiqta Rabbati* 40 (ed. M. Friedmann, p. 171b); cf. 1 Kings 3:7, 5:15, 8:20; and 2 Kings 14:21, 15:17, 23:30,34.

194. E.g., E. A. Speiser, *Genesis*, 163.

195. David Kimḥi at Gen. 22:1; and Spiegel, *The Last Trial*, 98.

196. Cf. the Septuagint, Samaritan Pentateuch, Peshitta, and *Tg. Ps.-J.*

197. David Kimḥi at Gen. 22:4–5.

198. E. A. Speiser, *Genesis*, 163.

199. *Tg. Ps.-J.* Gen. 22:3.

200. *Pirqe Rabbi Eliezer* 31, p. 70b; *Tg. Ps.-J* Gen. 22:9, and Naḥmanides at Gen. 22:2.

201. *Tg. Ps.-J.* Gen. 22:3.

202. Jacob ben Asher (Baal HaTurim) at v. 11, based on gematria (Michael); cf. M. Schapiro, "The Angel with the Ram in Abraham's Sacrifice," 139–40. Josephus ascribes this to God (*Antiquities* 1:13.4:§233 [LCL 4:114–15]).

203. David Kimḥi at v. 19; *Gen. Rabbah* 56:11; *Tg. Ps.-J.* Gen. 22:19; and *Midrash HaGadol*, ed. Margulies, 360. Cf. *Bet HaMidrash* vol. 5, p. 157; and Joseph ibn Kaspi and Joshua Shuaib, according to S. Spiegel, *The Last Trial*, 7.

204. As one exegete put it, "When Abraham bound his son Isaac on the altar and slew him and burned him, [the lad] was reduced to ashes and his ashes were cast on Mount Moriah" (Cambridge University, mss Or 1080, box 1:48, as cited by S. Spiegel, *The Last Trial*, 37n. For other references to Isaac's ashes, see *j. Ta'anit* 2:1 65a; *b. Berakhot* 62b; *b. Ta'anit* 16a; *b. Zevaḥim* 62a; *Gen. Rabbah* 94:5; *Lev. Rabbah* 36:5; and *Tanḥuma Vayera'* 23 p. 31a. Others refer

to Isaac's blood (*Mekhilta Shimon bar Yoḥai, Va'era* [ed. J. N. Epstein and E. Z. Melamed (Jerusalem: Hillel, 1955)], 4; and*Mekhilta deRabbi Ishmael, Bo'* 7 [ed. Horowitz, p. 24]). Cf. *L.A.B.* 18:5–6; and *t. Soṭah* 6:5. Following this line of reasoning, the Zohar describes Isaac's ascent to heaven (*Zohar Vayera'* 120b.)

205. *B. Sanhedrin* 105b; cf. *Gen. Rabbah* 55:8.

206. Naḥmanides at Gen. 22:3.

207. *Antiquities* 1:13.2 §225 (LCL 5:110–11); cf. Philo, *On the Life of Abraham* 32:170; and David Kimḥi at Gen. 22:3. Alicia Ostriker attributed this to God, who insisted, "THIS IS BETWEEN US MEN" (Delaney, *Abraham on Trial*, 132–33). Others have seen it as evidence of Abraham's eagerness to do God's will (*Mekhilta deRabbi Ishmael Beshalaḥ* 1 [ed. Horowitz, p. 88]; *b. Pesaḥim* 4a; and *b. Yoma* 28b. Cf. *Midrash Ps.* 112:2); or that the prayers of the righteous are heard in the morning (*Mekhilta deRabbi Ishmael Beshalaḥ* 5 [ed. Horowitz, p. 107]).

208. *Gen. Rabbah* 58:5; cf. Burton Visotzky, in Bill Moyers, *Genesis, A Living Conversation* (New York: Doubleday, 1996), 238. By contrast, Marc Chagall's *Sacrifice of Isaac* shows Sarah waiting from the background as Abraham prepares to sacrifice Isaac.

209. Milgrom, *The Binding of Isaac*, 116.

210. E.g., Berta Kuznetsova Goldburt, "Sacrifice of Issak" (http://alla-goldburt-7h8p.squarespace.com/c04-miniaturesonstones, accessed October 23, 2020); cf. *Tanḥuma* (ed. Buber) *Toledot* 22, p. 71a.

211. Various sources describe him as twenty-three (Jubilees 17:15–16), twenty-five (Josephus, *Antiquities* 1:13.2 §227 [LCL 5:112–13], cf. 20:12.1), and thirty-six (*Exod. Rabbah* 1:1, *Lam. Rabbah* proem 24; cf. *Gen. Rabbah* 56:8). Cf. *Tg. Ps.-J.* Gen. 22:1; and Leonard Cohen, "The Story of Isaac," in *Voices Within the Ark: The Modern Jewish Poets*, ed. Howard Schwartz and Anthony Rudolf (New York: Avon, 1980), 750.

212. *Gen. Rabbah* 56:3; cf. *Tg. Neofiti* Gen. 22:6–8.

213. Barugel, *The* Sacrifice of Isaac *in Spanish and Sephardic Balladry*, 66.

214. "Come Angel Come" ("The Sacrifice") in the 1971 musical "To Live Another Summer, To Pass Another Winter" (available at https://archive.org/details/toliveanothersum00selt/03_Introduction.mp3, accessed October 26, 2021).

215. J. Levenson, *The Death and Resurrection of the Beloved Son*, 131.

216. E.g., Elimelech of Lyzhansk, *No'am Elimelekh* (New York: Shulsinger Brothers, 1941–42), 18a; cf. Abraham's statement that "*we* will return" in v. 5 (*b. Mo'ed Qatan* 18a, emphasis added).

217. *Gen. Rabbah* 56:4; *Frag. Tg.* Gen. 22:8; *Pesiqta Rabbati* 40 (ed. Meir Friedmann, p. 170b); *Tg. Neofiti* v. 8; and *Midrash HaGadol* at Gen. 22:8 (ed. M. Margulies, p. 253). Cf. the Cairo Genizah fragment printed in Mann, *The*

Bible as Read and Preached in the Synagogue, 65–66, which reads: "You are the lamb for the burnt offering," apparently correlating the Hebrew word *seh* (lamb) with the Greek word for "you" (*sy*).

218. *Pirqe Rabbi Eliezer* 31.

219. *Midrash HaGadol* at Gen. 22:13 (ed. M. Margulies, 356).

220. Cf. Philo, *On the Life of Abraham* xxxvi §§ 200–202 (LCL 6.98–9); contrast *That God Is Unchangeable* 1 §4 (LCL 3.12–13).

221. R. Abraham Isaac Kook, *Igrot HaRe'ayah*, Rosh Ḥodesh Elul, 5671 (Jerusalem: Mosad ha-Rav Kook, 1985) vol. 2, p. 43.

222. Gellman, *Abraham! Abraham!*, 4.

223. Isaac Arama, *Akedat Yitsḥaq*, vol. 1 (Pressburg: Franz Edlen von Schmidt, 1849), 154a.

224. Rashi at Gen 22:2; cf. H. Leivick's Yiddish poem "Sacrifice," which ends each stanza with "and waits" (David Curzon, *Modern Poems on the Bible: An Anthology* [Philadelphia: Jewish Publication Society, 1994], 139).

225. *Gen. Rabbah* 55:7.

226. Cf. *Gen. Rabbah* 39:9; *Tanḥuma* (ed. Buber), *Lekh Lekha* 4 p. 30b, and *Vayera'* 46 p. 57a. Cf. Sira 44:19–20; 1 Macc. 2:52; 4 Macc. 13:12 and 16:20; Jubilees 17:17–18, 19:2–3,8–9; *Tg. Neofiti* Gen 22:1; *m. 'Avot* 5:3; and *'Avot of Rabbi Natan* 33:2.

227. *Gen. Rabbah* 56:7. Rabbi Jacob Isaac of Lublin declared that Abraham "was very happy to slay him" (*Divrei Emet* [Warsaw: n.p., 1882], 7b). David Kimḥi considered the repetition to be purely emphatic (at v. 12).

228. *Peh Qadosh* (Warsaw: Y. Kapelovitz, 1890), 7b.

229. *Sefer Josippon* (Warsaw: Zvi Yosef Bamberg, 1853) §97.

230. *Antiquities* 1.13.4 §233 (LCL 4:114–15); cf. J. H. Hertz, *The Pentateuch and Haftorahs* (London: Soncino, 2001), 201; M. Fox, "Kierkegaard and Rabbinic Judaism," 161; Gordis, "The Faith of Abraham," 417n14; J. Levenson, *The Death and Resurrection of the Beloved Son*, 112.

231. *Gen. Rabbah* 56:8; cf. *Tanḥuma* (ed. Buber) *Beḥuqotay* 7 p. 57b. Saadia Gaon (*Beliefs and Opinions* 3:9, ed. Rosenblatt, p. 169) argued that Abraham was to set Isaac aside.

232. *Midrash HaGadol* Gen 22:13 (ed. Margulies, p. 356); thus the Israeli poet Yehuda Amichai's reference to the ram as "the true hero of the Akedah" (Abramson, "The Reinterpretation of the Akedah in Modern Hebrew Poetry," 109).

233. *Tanḥuma* (ed. Buber) *Vayera'* 43; and *Gen. Rabbah* 55:1.

234. *Gen. Rabbah* 32:3, 34:2, 55:2.

235. Elie Wiesel, *Messengers of God, Biblical Portraits and Legends* (New York: Random House, 1976), 91.

236. *Gen. Rabbah* 55:4; cf. *The Second Book of Naomi Shemer* (Tel Aviv: Lulav, 1975) #4 (Hebrew). According to Benno Jacob, *ha'elohim* in Gen 22:1 does not mean "God" (*Das Erste Buch der Torah, Genesis*, p. 492).

237. 4Q225:2.9, *Jubilees* 17:15; cf. *Midrash Vayosha'* (*Beit Hamidrash* 3rd ed., ed. Adolph Jellinek [Jerusalem: Wahrmann, 1967] vol. 1, p. 36).

238. Cf. *Seder Eliyahu Rabbah* chap. (7)8 (ed. Meir Friedman, p. 45). According to *Gen. Rabbah* 55:4 and *Tanḥuma* (ed. Buber) *Vayera'* 42 (p. 55a), the reference is to a conversation between Isaac and Ishmael.

239. Martin Buber, *Eclipse of God: Studies in the Relation Between Religion and Philosophy* (New York: Harper & Row, 1952), 119; cf. Immanuel Kant, *Religion within the Limits of Reason Alone*, 2nd ed. (LaSalle: Open Court, 1960), 125.

240. Woody Allen, *Without Feathers* (New York: Random House, 1975), 24.

241. Erich Neumann, *The Origins and History of Consciousness* (Princeton NJ: Princeton University Press, 1970), 189. Thus the Israeli poet Yitzhak Laor's description of Isaac as an idiot (D. Jacobson, *Does David Still Play Before You?*, 95). For a different view, see Shoham, "The Isaac Syndrome," 329.

242. *Yemei Ziklag* (Tel Aviv: Am Oved, 1958), 804. That generational tension is best known in Wilfred Owen's World War I poem "Parable" (*The Collected Poems of Wilfred Owen*, ed. C. Day Lewis [London: Catto & Windus, 1974], 42).

243. Kartun-Blum, *Profane Scriptures*, 58; cf. Haim Gouri's suggestion that Isaac "lived long . . . but he bequeathed that hour to his descendants. They are born with a knife in their heart" ("Yerushah," *The Penguin Book of Hebrew Verse*, ed. T. Carmi [Harmondsworth: Penguin, 1981], 565).

244. Amitay, *Ḥad Gadya veGadyo*, 351.

245. Danny Siegel, "Father Abraham," *Response* 3:2 (1969): 22.

246. Delaney, *Abraham on Trial*, 91. After being rejected, it was moved to Princeton University.

247. Josephus, *Antiquities* 1:13.4 §227 (LCL 5:114–15); cf. *L.A.B.* 32:3; 4 Macc. 13:12; *Gen. Rabbah* 56:8; *Lev. Rabbah* 2:10; *Zohar Vayera'* 120b; *Pesiqta deRav Kahana Zo't Haberakhah* (ed. Mandelbaum, p. 451); *Pesiqta Rabbati* 40 (ed. Ish Shalom, p. 170b); Weinberger, *Jewish Hymnography*, 224; and Rashi at Exod. 32:13. Note the rabbinic tradition that takes the phrase "with all your soul" in Deut. 6:5 as referring to Isaac (*Sifre Deut.* 32, ed. Finkelstein, p. 58) or asking to be bound tightly (*Pirqe deRabbi Eliezer* 31; *Pesiqta Rabbati* 40, p. 171a; and *Tg. Neofiti* Gen. 22:10; cf. Qur'an 37:102).

248. *B. Giṭṭin* 57b. Pseudo-Philo describes Jephtha's daughter Seilah as doing likewise (*L.A.B.* 40:2).

249. *Lam. Rabbah* proem 24. Thus the phrase about God being seen on the mountain (v. 14) came to be a slogan for generations of Jews who found themselves in trouble (Venerable Bede, "Questions on Genesis" [*PL* 93:319];

Alcuin, "Questions and Answers in Genesis" #2107 [PL 100:545]; and Remigius, "Commentary to Genesis" [PL 131:96]).

250. Mintz, *Ḥurban*, 90–91; and Weinberger, *Jewish Hymnography*, 223.

251. M. Saperstein, *Jewish Preaching 1200–1800*, 83. Contrast Saadia's view that Jews blow the ram's horn on Rosh Hashanah "to remind us of the Binding of Isaac, who offered himself to heaven. So ought we to be ready at all times to offer our lives for the sanctification of his Name" (S. Y. Agnon, *Days of Awe* [New York: Schocken, 1965], 72).

252. Elie Wiesel, *Ani Maamin: A Song Lost and Found Again* (New York: Random House, 1973), 83; cf. Yehoshua Rabinov, *"Mul Har HaAkedah,"* in Mordecai Amitay, *Ḥad Gadya veGado*, 18–19; Aliza Shenhar, *Ede Ḥalom* (Tel Aviv: Alef, 1970), 12; and Zalman Schneor in Kartun-Blum, *Profane Scriptures*, 43.

253. *B. Tamid* 31b; and *b. Shabbat* 54a. Other sources connect it with Passover, perhaps because of Abraham's reference to a lamb (v. 8). Cf. Jubilees 17:15–16, 18:18–19; *Mekhilta Bo'* 7 (ed. Horowitz, pp. 24–25); and *Exod. Rabbah* 15:11. This may also have contributed to its connection to Jesus's crucifixion, which is traditionally linked to Passover.

254. *B. Megillah* 31a.

255. Abraham Joshua Heschel, *God in Search of Man* (New York: Farrar, Straus & Cudahy, 1955), 241; cf. Emil Fackenheim, *The Jewish Bible After the Holocaust: A Re-Reading* (Bloomington: Indiana University Press, 1990), x.

256. *B. Qiddushin* 49b.

6. MAKING ACCESSIBLE

1. *M. Megillah* 2:9; *b. Berakhot* 8a; cf. *Soferim* 18:4; and *b. Megillah* 2b.

2. *J. Megillah* 4:1 74d; *Tanḥuma Vayera* 5, p. 26a; *Tanḥuma* (ed. Buber) *Vayera* 6, p. 44ab; and *Pesiqta Rabbati* 5 (ed. Friedman 14ab). Cf. L. Ginzberg, *Ginze Schechter*, vol. 1, p. 459.

3. *M. Megillah* 4:10. See P. Alexander, "The Rabbinic Lists of Forbidden Targumim," 179, 190–91.

4. *B. Shabbat* 115a; *b. Megillah* 17a as understood by M. Friedmann, *Onkelos und Akylas*, 2n1, but emended to *'aravit* by W. Bacher and H. Strack (Ludwig Blau, "M. Friedmann's Onkelos and Akylas," 728).

5. For a thorough overview, see Greenspoon, *Jewish Biblical Translations*; and di-Giulo, "Resisting Modernity."

6. *B. Megillah* 3a.

7. Letter of Aristeas (*The Old Testament Pseudepigrapha*, ed. James H. Charlesworth, vol. 2, pp. 12–34); and the entire Bible, according to Justin (Eusebius, HE 5:8.10 [LCL 1:458–59]). An alterate tradition holds that there were only five translators (*Avot deRabbi Natan* B 37).

8. *M. Soṭah* 7:5; *t. Soṭah* 8:6; *j. Soṭah* 7:5 21d; and *b. Soṭah* 32a.

9. Salvesen, "A Convergence of the Ways?," 247. Three others are anonymous and therefore called Quinta, Sexta, and Septima, in accordance with the columns in which Origen placed them on the page.

10. See Yona Sabar, *The Book of Genesis in Neo-Aramaic* (Jerusalem: Magnes, 1983); *The Book of Exodus in Neo-Aramaic* (Jerusalem: Hebrew University, 1988); *The Book of Leviticus in Neo-Aramaic* (Jerusalem: Hebrew University, 1990); *The Book of Numbers in Neo-Aramaic* (Jerusalem: Hebrew University, 1993); *The Book of Deuteronomy in Neo-Aramaic* (Jerusalem: Hebrew University, 1994); *The Five Scrolls in Jewish Neo-Aramaic Translation* (Jerusalem: Hebrew University, 2006); *The Five Scrolls in Neo-Aramaic Translations* (Jerusalem: Center for the Study of the Traditions of Israeli Communities, 2006); *The Book of Daniel in a Neo-Aramaic Translation* (Jerusalem: Magnes, 2014); and also *Targum de-Targum: An Old Neo-Aramaic Version of the Targum of Song of Songs* (Wiesbaden: Harrasowitz, 1991) (all published in Hebrew).

11. Cf. *m. Yadayim* 4:5; and *b. Shabbat* 115b.

12. E.g., *Sifre* Deut. 161; but cf. *m. Megillah* 4:6.

13. *M. Shabbat* 16:1; cf. *b. Megillah* 3a.

14. Mark 15:34 and Matt. 27:46.

15. First by the fourteenth-century Italian kabbalist Menaḥem b. Benjamin Recanati (Flesher and Chilton, *The Targums*, 72). As late as the end of the eleventh century, Hai Gaon commented, "We do not know who composed it, nor do we even know this Targum, of which we have heard only a few passages" (Wilhelm Bacher, "Targum," *JE* vol. 12, p. 60). According to Bernard Grossfield, the attribution to Jonathan is probably based on a misinterpretation of the acronym T"Y, which actually stood for *targum yerushalmi* ("Jerusalem Targum") ("Aramaic: The Targumim," *EJ* vol. 4, p. 845).

16. M. L. Klein, *The Fragment-Targums of the Pentateuch According to Their Extant Sources*, 12.

17. Called "our targum" at *b. Qiddushin* 49a; cf. *b. Sanhedrin* 106b: "as *we* translate" (emphasis added).

18. *B. Megillah* 3a; cf. *b. Sukkot* 28a; *b. Bava Batra* 134a; and *Avot deRabbi Natan* A 14:1.

19. *B. Mo'ed Qatan* 26a, 28b; and *b. Megillah* 3a.

20. *B. Megillah* 3a.

21. Cf. *b. Megillah* 21b; *t. Shabbat* 13(14): 2; *j. Shabbat* 16:1 15c; and *b. Shabbat* 115a. Targumim to Job, Psalms, and Qohelet sometimes add additional renderings under the rubric "another translation" (Flesher and Chilton, *The Targums*, 232).

22. Wilhelm Bacher, "Targum," *JE* vol. 12, p. 62.

23. Abu Huraya, a contemporary of Mohammad, reported that "the people of the book used to read the Taurah in Hebrew and interpret it into Arabic to the followers of Islam" (Richard Gottheil, "Bible Translations," *JE* vol. 3, p. 188).

24. Existing copies include only Genesis (through *vayeṣe'*), Exodus, Leviticus, Isaiah, Psalms, Proverbs, Job, Song of Songs, and Daniel (A. S. Halkin, "Saadia's Exegesis and Polemics," 123).

25. *Die Israelitische Bibel*, trans. Ludwig Philippson (Leipzig: Baumgärtners Buchhandlung, 1839–49; rprt., Freiburg: Herder, 2016–18); *The Twenty-Four Books of the Holy Scriptures*, trans. Isaac Leeser (Philadelphia: L. Johnson, 1853); and *The Hebrew Bible: A Translation with Commentary*, trans. Robert Alter (New York: W. W. Norton, 2019).

26. Hary, "Jewish Languages," 235–36; cf. Polliack, *The Karaite Tradition of Arabic Bible Translation*, 18.

27. Lazar, preface to *The Ladino Bible of Ferrara* (1553), xxii.

28. M. Waxman, *A History of Jewish Literature*, vol. 3, p. 552; cf. Greenspoon, *Jewish Bible Translations*. Y. S. Reggio's Italian Pentateuch, *Torat Elohim*, was published in Vienna in 1821 (Shelly, *Biblical Research in Haskalah Literature*, 58).

29. Staerk and Leitzmann, *Die Jüdisch-Deutschen Bibelübersetzungen von den Anfäng des 18. Jahrhunderts*, passim.

30. N. Leibowitz, *Die Übersetzungs-technik der jüdischen Bibelübersetzungen des 15. Und 16. Jahrhunderts*, 12.

31. Ben-Chorin, "Jüdische Bibelübersetzungen in Deutschland," 311.

32. Richard Gottheil, "Bible Translations," *JE* vol. 3, 191.

33. *EJ*, "Bible," vol. 4, p. 867.

34. Zinberg, *A History of Jewish Literature*, vol. 7, pp. 137–39; N. Leibowitz, *Die Übersetzungs-technik der jüdischen Bibelübersetzungen des 15. und 16. Jahrhunderts*, 26; and Staerk and Leitzmann, *Die Jüdisch-Deutschen Bibelübersetzungen von den Anfäng des 18. Jahrhunderts*, 172. On the relationship between these two versions, see Gillman, *A History of German Jewish Bible Translation*, 24–25.

35. Richard Gottheil, "Bible Translations," *JE* 3 p. 192; and P. Sandler, *Mendelssohn's Edition of the Pentatuch*, 215–17.

36. Lowenstein, "The Readership of Mendelssohn's Bible Translation," 181–86.

37. Israel Abrahams, *Hebrew Ethical Wills* (Philadelphia: Jewish Publication Society, 1954), 322.

38. Billigheimer, "On Jewish Translations of the Bible in Germany," 6.

39. Gillman, *A History of German Jewish Bible Translation*, 124; and *Die Heilige Schrift, Hebraisch-Deutsch* (Tel Aviv: Sinai, 1997).

40. Other participants included Elias Auerbach, Emil Bernhard-Cohen, Benno Jacob, and Max Wiener (Billigheimer, "On Jewish Translations of the

Bible in Germany," 13). Torczyner, who settled in Palestine and became a professor at Hebrew University, changed his name to Naftali Herz Tur-Sinai.

41. A revised edition was published in 1954–62. N. Glatzer, "Buber as an Interpreter of the Bible," 361n2.

42. Cf. L. Sussman, *Isaac Leeser and the Making of American Judaism.*

43. Leeser himself observed, "Knowing my own want of proper qualifications, I would never have consented to serve, if others more fitting in point of standing information or other qualities had been there" (Joseph H. Hertz, "Jewish Translations of the Bible in English," in *Sermons, Addresses and Studies*, 2: 82).

44. J. Sarna, *JPS*, 96.

45. J. Sarna, *JPS*, 97.

46. Translated by Kaufmann Kohler (Philadelphia: Jewish Publication Society, 1903).

47. *Central Conference of American Rabbis Yearbook* 17 (1907): 35; Greenspoon, "A Book 'Without Blemish,'" 8.

48. Orlinsky himself had been the sole Jewish member of the RSV translation committee; for his perceptions of that experience, see Orlinsky, "A Jewish Scholar Looks at the Revised Standard Version and Its New Edition."

49. H. L. Ginsberg, "The New Translation of the Torah: In the Path of True Scholarship," *Midstream* 9:2 (June 1963): 78. Thus the head of Yeshiva University's rabbinical seminary's complaint: "In this translation [JPS 1917] is found material sufficient to construct a new sect and germs enough to breed many a change in the religious life of Israel" (Rabbi Samuel Gerstenfeld, *Jewish Forum*, September 1928, p. 439, as cited by Hoenig, "Notes on the New Translation of the Torah," 177).

50. Aryeh Kaplan, *The Living Torah* (New York: Moznayim, 1981); *The Living Nach*, ed. Yaakov Elman, M. H. Mykoff, Moshe Schapiro, and Gavriel Rubin (New York: Moznaim, 1994–98); and *Tanakh*, ed. Nosson Scherman (Brooklyn: Mesorah, 1996).

51. Stephen Mitchell, *Genesis: A New Translation of the Classic Biblical Stories* (New York: HarperCollins, 1996), *A Book of Psalms: Selected & Adapted from the Hebrew* (New York: HarperCollins, 1993), and *Into the Whirlwind: A Translation of the Book of Job* (Garden City NY: Doubleday, 1979; rev. ed., San Francisco: North Point, 1987); David Rosenberg, *Lightworks: Interpreted from the Original Hebrew Book of Isaiah* (San Francisco: Harper & Row, 1978), *Blues of the Sky: Interpreted from the Original Hebrew Book of Psalms* (New York: Harper & Row, 1976), *Job Speaks: Interpreted from the Original Hebrew Book of Job* (New York: Harper & Row, 1977), and *A Poet's Bible: Rediscovering the Voices of the Original Text* (New York: Hyperion, 1991); Marcia Falk, *The Song of Songs: A New Translation and Interpretation* (San Francisco: Harper Collins,

1990); Ariel and Chana Bloch, *The Song of Songs: The World's First Great Love Poem* (New York: Modern Library, 1998, 2006); Everett Fox, *The Five Books of Moses: Genesis, Exodus, Leviticus, Numbers, Deuteronomy; A New Translation With Introductions, Commentary, and Notes* (New York: Schocken, 1995), and *The Early Prophets: Joshua, Judges, Samuel, and Kings-the Schocken Bible* (New York: Schocken, 2014); and Robert Alter, *The Hebrew Bible: Translation with Commentary* (New York: W. W. Norton, 2019).

52. *Soferim* 1:7; cf. Naḥmanides: "Holy books may only be written in the holy language, not in any dialect or other language" (I. Zinberg, *Die Geschichte von der Literatur bei Yidden* [New York: Farlag Moshe Shmuel Sklovsky 1943], vol. 6, p. 30); and Peretz Smolenskin: "Holy Scriptures in translation are like a rose whose beauty has vanished and whose smell has changed" (N. Peniel, *HaḤinuch Ha-Ivri BeYetsirato shel Peretz Smolenskin* [Tel Aviv: Dvir, 1957], vol. 1, p. 160).

53. Contrast Philo's description of Greek and Hebrew as "sisters . . . one and the same, both in matter and words" (*On the Life of Moses* 2:40 [LCL 6:468–69]).

54. *B. Megillah* 8b–9a; cf. *m. Megillah* 2:9; and *b. Shabbat* 115a.

55. A. Neubauer, *Mediaeval Jewish Chronicles and Chronicological Notes* (Oxford: Clarendon, 1895) vol. 2, p. 24.

56. *Zohar Terumah* 129b.

57. Franz Rosenzweig, *On Jewish Learning* (New York: Schocken, 1955), 30; Moses Mendelssohn, "Or LaNetivah," *Gesammelte Schriften Jübiläumsausgabe* (Stuttgart–Bad Cannstatt: Friedrich Fromann Verlag Günther Holzboog, 1972), vol. 14, p. 232.

58. E.g., *Soferim* 18:4; Rashi at *b. Megillah* 21b s.v. *uvenavi*; Yosef Qafiḥ, *Saadia Gaon's Commentary on the Torah* (rev. ed., Jerusalem: Mossad ha-Rav Kook, 1984), 11; Perles, "Bibliographische Mittheilungen aus München," *MGWJ* 25 (1876): 352–53n2; Staerk and Leitzmann, *Die Jüdisch-Deutschen Bibelübersetzungen von den Anfäng des 18. Jahrhunderts*, 24, 126, 128, 155, 191; Billigheimer, "On Jewish Translations of the Bible in Germany," 3; Sandler, *Mendelssohn's Edition of the Pentatuch*, 38; Bottigheimer, "Moses Mordechai Büdinger's Kleine Bibel (1823) and Vernacular Children's Bibles," 84; and Philipson, *The Reform Movement in Judaism*, 173.

59. E.g., Julius Popper, *Israelitische Schulbibel* (Dessau: A. Reissner, 1873); Julius Fürst, *Illustrierte Prachtbibel für Israeliten* (Leipzig: A. H. Payne, 1874); Gotthold Salomon, *Deutsche Volks-und Schul Bibel* (Altona: J. F. Hammerich, 1837); Ludwig Philipson, *Die Israelitische Bibel* (Leipzig: Baumgärtner, 1839–53), with illustrations and commentary to make it "edel and volkstümlic" (Schalom Ben-Chorin, "Jüdische Bibelübertzungen in Deutschland," *Leo Baeck Institute Yearbook* 4 [1959]: 317; and Jakob Auerbach, *Kleine Schul-und Haus-Bibel* [Leipzig: Brockhaus, 1858]). Similar versions in English, all of which drew on

existing translations, include Abraham Benisch, *The Jewish School and Family Bible* (London: Jewish Chronicle, 1851); Michael Friedländer, *The Jewish Family Bible* (London: J. and W. Rider, 1881); C. G. Montefiore, *The Bible for Home Reading* (London: MacMillan, 1896); and Mortimer J. Cohen, *Pathways Through the Bible* (Philadelphia: Jewish Publication Society, 1946). Cf. Penny Schine Gold, *Making the Bible Modern: Children's Bibles and Jewish Education in Twentieth-Century America* (Ithaca NY: Cornell University Press, 2004).

60. Zuckermann, "Do Israelis Understand the Hebrew Bible?" 1–7.

61. Origen, Epistle to Africanus §2 (PG 11:52).

62. Zinberg, *A History of Jewish Literature*, vol. 7:130–31.

63. See Gen. 4:26, Exod. 6:3, Exod. 11:3, and comment to Ps 80:14; cf. Halkin, "Saadia's Exegesis and Polemics," 121. David Norval Wigtil notes that translations of Vergil and the Res Gestae often change the names of Greek gods to the Roman and Christian equivalents (*The Translation of Religious Texts in the Greco-Roman World*, pp. 69, 299, and 308).

64. Sandler, *Mendelssohn's Edition of the Pentatuch*, 61.

65. Bickerman, "The Septuagint as a Translation," 31; cf. Komlosh, *The Bible in the Light of the Aramaic Translations*, 223.

66. Bickerman, "The Colophon of the Greek Book of Esther," 339–62.

67. Orlinsky, "Yehoash's Yiddish Translation of the Bible," 175; cf. Shandler, "A Tale of Two Translations."

68. Thus Gershom Scholem's description of the Buber-Rosenzweig version as "a kind of *Gastgeschenk* which German Jewry gave to the German people, a symbolic act of gratitude upon departure . . . the tombstone of a relationship that was extinguished in unspeakable horror" ("At the Completion of Buber's Translation of the Bible" in his *The Messianic Idea in Judaism and Other Essays on Jewish Spirituality*, 318).

69. Ben-Oren, "Three Recent Bible Translaions to Georgian," 84.

70. Shinan, "Live Translation," 41. Whether this custom is a continuation or a revival has been questioned by Philip S. Alexander ("Jewish Aramaic Translation of Hebrew Scripture" in *Mikra, Text Translation and Interpretation of the Hebrew Bible in Ancient Judaism and Early Christianity*, ed. Martin J. Mulder, 250).

71. Natalio Fernández Marcos, "*Non placet Septuaginta*: Revisions and New Greek Versions of the Bible in Byzantium," in *Jewish Reception of Greek Bible Versions, Studies in Their Use in Late Antiquity and the Middle Ages*, ed. Nicholas deLange, Julia G. Krivoruchko, and Cameron Boyd-Taylor, 45. The sixteenth-century translator of the Pentateuch into modern Greek expressed a similar sentiment (L. Modona, "Un Mot sur Deux Versions du Pentateuch," 135).

72. Letter to August Hennings, June 29, 1779, in Moses Mendelssohn's *Gesammelte Schriften, Jubiläumausgabe* (Stuttgart-Bad Cannstatt: F. Frommann, 1976), vol. 12.2, p. 149; Kayserling, *Moses Mendelssohn, Sein Leben und Seine Werke,* 522 #30. Cf. *Sefer Or Netivah HaShalom* (Vienna: Franz von Schmid, 1846), xxv.

73. "The Tercentenary of the English Bible," *B'nai Brith News,* April 1911, p. 10, as quoted in Greenspoon, "A Book 'Without Blemish,'" 18–19.

74. Letter to Samuel ibn Tibbon in Leon D. Stitskin, in *Letters of Maimonides* (New York: Yeshiva University Press, 1977), 133.

75. Poznanski, "The Anti-Karaite Writings of Saadiah Gaon," 256; and Yosef Qafiḥ, *Saadia Gaon's Commentary on the Torah,* rev. ed. (Jerusalem: Mossad ha-Rav Kook, 1984), 11.

76. This may have been in response to criticism from Arabs (R. C. Steiner, *A Biblical Translation in the Making,* 12, 14, 34f, 104, 149–50); A. S. Halkin, "Saadia's Exegesis and Polemics," 126; Yosef Qafiḥ, *Saadia Gaon's Commentary on the Torah* rev. ed. (Jerusalem: Mossad ha-Rav Kook, 1984), 11; and Harry M. Orlinsky, "Versions, Jewish," *The Anchor Bible Dictionary,* ed. David Noel Freedman (New York: Doubleday, 1992) vol. 6, p. 839.

77. Eppenstein, *Beiträge zur Geschichte und Literatur im Geonäischen Zeitalter,* 80.

78. Bickermann, "The Septuagint as a Translation," 11–12; and Origen, *Epistle Ad Africanum* 2 (*PG* 11.52). Jerome complained that Aquila translated "not words but etymologies" (Epistle 57, "Ad Pammachium" [*PL* 22:577–78]).

79. Wiener, "The Ferrara Bible," 82; Johann G. Carpzov, *Critica Sacra Veteris Testamenti,* as quoted by Staerk and Leitzmann, *Die Jüdisch-Deutschen Bibelübersetzungen von den Anfäng des 18. Jahrhunderts,* 162; Simon Bernfield, according to Plaut, "German-Jewish Bible Translations," 12; Witton-Davies, "Martin Buber's Contribution to Biblical Studies," 262–63.

80. Henry Pereira Mendez, as quoted in J. Sarna, *JPS,* 234; Mendell Lewittes, according to Borowitz, "Theological Issues in the New Torah Translation," 343; and Robert Alter, "It's Not Always English, But It Captures the Hebrew," *New York Times Magazine,* October 22, 1995, p. 66.

81. Cf. 2 Cor. 3:6.

82. See already the New Testament's incorporation of the terms *amen, hallelujah, hosanna, abba, rabbi, maranatha* (at Matt. 12:9,13; Mark 14:36; 1 Cor. 16:22; Rom. 8:15; Gal. 4:6; and Rev. 19:1–6).

83. Reider, *Prolegomena to a Greek-Hebrew and Hebrew-Greek Index to Aquila,* 26; Barthélemy, *Les Devanciers d'Aquila,* 86; Brock, "Aspects of Translation Technique in Antiquity," 84; Swete, *An Introduction to the Old Testament in Greek,* 39; Wiener, "The Ferrara Bible," 10 (1895): 81–85, and 11 (1896): 26;

Sandler, *Mendelssohn's Edition of the Pentatuch*, 61; and Polliack, *The Karaite Tradition of Arabic Bible Translation*, 170.

84. Cf. Caird, "Homeophony in the Septuagint," 24–25.

85. Barr, *The Typology of Literalism in Ancient Bible Translations*, 312; cf. Jerome's observation in his letter to Pammachius §11 (PL 22:577).

86. N. Leibowitz, *Die Übersetzungs-technik der jüdischen Bibelübersetzungen des 15. und 16. Jahrhunderts*, 75; and Sandler, *Mendelssohn's Edition of the Pentatuch*, 56.

87. Billigheimer, "On Jewish Translations of the Bible in Germany," 8.

88. Cf. Franz Rosenzweig's June 9, 1927, letter to Martin Buber (*Briefe* #501 [Berlin: Schocken, 1935], 598). In this, they had been anticipated by S. H. Hirsch, who rendered *hiqriv* as "nahe bringen" rather than the usual "darbringen" (Billigheimer, "On Jewish Translations of the Bible in Germany," 9).

89. Cf. Buber, *The Bible and Its Styles, Studies in a Pattern* (Jerusalem: Mossad Bialik, 1977–78), 287–88 (Hebrew); cf. the Septuagint, which translates *'ohel mo'ed* as *skēnēn toy martyrioy*, connecting *mo'ed* to the Hebrew *'ēd*, which means "witness."

90. McNamara, *The New Testament and the Palestinian Targum to the Pentateuch*, 63; and S. H. Margulies, *Saadia Al-Fajûmî's arabische Psalmenübersetzung*, part 1 (Breslau: Grass, Barth und Camp, 1884), 191.

91. Greenstein, *Essays on Biblical Method and Translation*, 138; cf. his "What Might Make a Bible Translation Jewish," in *Translation of Scripture*, ed. David M. Goldenberg, 87. For Protestant parallels, see J. Sheehan, *The Enlightenment Bible*, 64–73.

92. Kingsley, "The Buber-Rosenzweig Translation of the Bible," 17.

93. N. Leibowitz, *Die Übersetzungs-technik der jüdischen Bibelübersetzungen des 15. und 16. Jahrhunderts*, 43, 46; something similar is found in the Italian Ferrara translation, which appears to have drawn on earlier versions (Wiener, "The Ferrara Bible," 82).

94. Sandler, *Mendelssohn's Edition of the Pentatuch*, 77; cf. N. Leibowitz, *Die Übersetzungs-technik der jüdischen Bibelübersetzungen des 15. und 16. Jahrhunderts*, 25–26.

95. *M. Megillah* 1:8 and 2:1; *b. Shabbat* 115b; and *b. Soṭah* 33a. An alternative view limits this leniency to Greek (*b. Megillah* 9b; cf. *t. Megillah* 2:6; and *b. Megillah* 17a–b).

96. Israel Abrahams, *Hebrew Ethical Wills* (Philadelphia: Jewish Publication Society, 1954), 65–66.

97. *B. Nazir* 39a; cf. *b. Sanhedrin* 106b.

98. Hertz, "Jewish Translations of the Bible in English," in *Sermons, Addresses and Studies*, vol. 2, p. 71.

99. *Sifre* Deut. 343; cf. *Exod. Rabbah* 5:9 and 28:6.

100. *B. Megillah* 3a; cf. R. Hai Gaon and R. Sherira Gaon's responsum: "Our targum . . . heard from the prophets" (*Otzar HaGaonim: Thesaurus of the Gaonic Responsa and Commentaries following the Order of the Talmudic Tractates*, ed. Benjamim M. Lewin [Jerusalem: Hebrew University, 1939], vol. 9, pp. 130–31 [Hebrew]).

101. Philo, *On the Life of Moses*, 2:5–7.25–44 (LCL 6:460–71). According to one tradition, the translators had worked in separate cells, with the results of their individual efforts only later found to be identical (Pseudo-Justin, "Cohortatio ad Graecos" 13 [*PG* 6:265], *b. Megillah* 9a), a position that was rejected by Jerome (Preface to the Pentateuch, *PL* 28:149–52). Rabbinic tradition attributes differences between the Hebrew and Greek editions to divine guidance (*j. Megillah* 1:11 71d; and *Soferim* 1:8).

102. Jerome at Isa. 8:14 (*PL* 24:122).

103. The ninth-century Gaon Sar Shalom in *Otzar HaGeonim*, ed. B.M. Lewin, vol. 5, *Megillah* p. 29.

104. At *b. Qiddushin* 49a.

105. Franz Rosenzweig, *The Star of Redemption* (New York: Holt, Rinehart and Winston, 1971), 366.

106. "Confessions of the Author" in Martin Buber, *A Believing Humanism: My Testaments, 1902–1965* (trans. M. Friedman: New York: Simon & Schuster, 1967), 32–33.

107. Venuti, *The Translator's Invisibility*.

108. Vermes, *Scripture and Tradition*, 2nd ed., 67; cf. Zsengeller, *Rewritten Bible After Fifty Years*.

109. Cf. Leonard J. Greenspoon: "There is universal agreement that any Jewish translation must reflect in a distinctive manner the richness of the Jewish exegetical tradition" ("From the Septuagint to the New Revised Standard Version," 37–38).

110. *Tg. Ps-J.* Deut. 6:8 and 11:18.

111. *Tg. Onq.* and *Tg. Ps.J.* Deut. 14:21. So too Saadia (at Exod. 23:19, Polliack, *The Karaite Tradition of Arabic Bible Translation*, 19).

112. Also at Deut. 19:21, though *Tg. Onq.* renders the passage literally at Exod. 21:24 and Lev. 24:19.

113. Cf. *b. Qiddushin* 15a and 21b.

114. Cf. *b. Menaḥot* 65a; *Sifra Emor* 12; and *Tg. Onq.* Lev. 23:11 and 15, where it is translated *mibatar yama tava*. So too Saadia and Mendelssohn. Cf. the Conservative movement's *Siddur Sim Shalom* (ed. Jules Harlow [New York: Rabbinical Assembly and United Synagogue of Conservative Judaism, 1985], 237), where *mimŏḥŏrat hashabbat* is rendered "from the eve of the second day of Pesaḥ."

115. *Tg. Ps.-J.* and *Tg. Onq.* Num. 21:16–18 and 22:22; cf. 1 Cor. 10:4 and 2 Tim. 3:8.

116. LXX Job 14:14; *Tg. Onq.* Gen. 3:6, 49:10; Exod. 32:1; Lev. 9:2; Num. 24:17; *Tg.Ps.-J.* Gen. 49:1; *Tg. Isa.* 38:16; Tg. Ps. 50:4; *Tg. Songs* 1:8,15, 2:3, 4:5,9,15, 5:12, 6:2, 7:3,4,14, 8:1,2,13; and *Tg. Eccles.* 5:5, 10:20, 12:5.

117. *Tg. Neb.* 1 Sam. 10:5; Isa. 3:2; Jer. 8:10, 26:7; Ezek. 7:26, 11:16; and Zech. 7:3. Cf. *Tg. Neofiti* Gen. 30:13 and throughout Songs. Note the targum's rendering of *'eṣ* ("tree") at Isa. 65:22 as "the tree of life."

118. Michael L. Klein, *Genizah Manuscripts of Palestinian Targum to the Pentateuch* (Cincinnati: Hebrew Union College Press, 1986), vol. 1, p. xxx.

119. Halkin, "Saadia's Exegesis and Polemics," 132.

120. Lenn E. Goodman, "Saadia Gaon's Interpretive Technique in Translating the Book of Job," in *Translation of Scripture*, ed. David M. Goldenberg, 62.

121. E.g., *Tg. Neofiti* Gen. 23:17, 30:17,22; and Deut. 3:26, 9:19, 10:10, 26:7 (cf. 4:7). A. Shinan, "Live Translation," 46.

122. *Tg. Onq.* Exod. 24:10; cf. Isa. 38:11, where the Septuagint translates the Hebrew "I shall not see YH" as "see God's salvation," while the targum renders it as "be seen before the fear of God."

123. Cf. Maimonides, *Guide of the Perplexed* 1:27.

124. E.g., *Tg. Onq.* Gen. 22:8; cf. *Tg. Neofiti* Gen 3:5.

125. E.g., *Tg. Onq.* Gen. 4:14, Exod. 4:24, and *Tg. Ps.-J.* Exod. 15:8.

126. E.g., *Tg. Onq.* Exod. 31:18; *Tg. Ps.-J.* Exod. 15:8; *Tg. Onq.* and *Tg.Ps.-J.* Deut. 9:10; *Tg. Neofiti* Exod. 15:17 and Deut. 32:41; and Tg. Ps. 2:4, 11:4, 33:13 and 18, 37:13, and 119:73.

127. Saadia Gaon, *The Book of Beliefs and Opinions* 2:19, trans. Samuel Rosenblatt (New Haven: Yale Univerwsity Press, 1948), 115–16.

128. Abraham b. David HaLevi, *Das Buch Emunah Ramah* (Frankfurt a.M.: n.p., 1852), 89.

129. Cf. *m. Sanhedrin* 7:5 and 10:1; and *j. Sanhedrin* 10:1 28b. It is also avoided in Psalms 43–83 and at Qumran.

130. Origen, Comment on Ps 2:2 (*PG* 12:1104); and Jerome, "Preface to Samuel and Kings" (*PL* 28:594–95). Cf. *The Contemporary Torah: A Gender Sensitive Adaptation of the JPS Translation*, ed. David E. S. Stein (Philadelphia: Jewish Publication Society, 2006).

131. Jerome, Epistle 25 to Marcella (*PL* 22:429); confirmed by manuscripts from Geza (Swete, *An Introduction to the Old Testament in Greek*, 34) and a Greek translation of the Minor Prophets found among the Dead Sea Scrolls (Barthélemy, *Les Devanciers d'Aquila*, 168 and plate 2).

132. For the Septuagint, see W. G. Waddell, "The Tetragrammaton in the LXX," 158; *Tg. Neofiti* uses a triple *yod*, while the Ferrara Bible translates it "*adonay*" (Moshe Lazar, preface to *The Ladino Bible of Ferrara* [1553], p. xvii).

133. E.g., *Tg. Onq*. Gen. 28:13; *Tg. Neofiti* Gen. 11:5; Exod. 3:7; and *Tg. Neb.* Amos 9:1. Cf. *Tg. Neb.* Isa. 45:22. So already in the Hebrew Bible. Also cf. S. Dean McBride, "The Deuteronomic Name Theology" (Ph.D. diss., Harvard University, 1969). But *yhwh* is kept in *Tg. Neb.* Isa. 6:1, Zeph. 1:3, 3:15, and *Tg. Ket.* Ps. 33:6.

134. Staerk and Leitzmann, *Die Jüdisch-Deutschen Bibelübersetzungen von den Anfäng des 18. Jahrhunderts*, 96. Mendelssohn explained his approach, which was anticipated by Baruch 4:10, 5:2, and Jean Calvin's "l'Eternel," in his comment to Exod. 3:14 (*Jubiläumsausgabe* 16 [ed. W. Weinberg (Stuttgart: Friedrich Frommann, 1990)], 26–27).

135. Grayzel, "The Bible and I," 19; and Zedekiah ben Abraham, *Shibbolei he-Leket* (ed. S. Buber [Vilna: Romm Brothers, 1886/87], #78 p. 56).

136. Cf. *b. Megillah* 3a; and *b. Nedarim* 37b. Also Maimonides, *Mishneh Torah, Laws of Prayer* 12:10. Natronai Gaon and Judah ibn Quraish opposed using Arabic rather than Aramaic during worship (Polliack, *The Karaite Tradition of Arabic Bible Translation*, xiii). According to the Italian rabbi Judah ben Benjamin, "Our present-day vernacular occupies the same place as the Targum once held" (Zinberg, *A History of Jewish Literature*, vol. 7, p. 21).

137. *B. Sanhedrin* 94b; *b. Mo'ed Qatan* 28b; and *b. Megillah* 3a.

138. *Shulḥan Arukh Oraḥ Ḥayim,* 285; Natronai Gaon allowed someone other than the meturgeman to explain the reading in the colloquial (Jacob Mann, *The Jews in Egypt*, vol. 1, p. 34n3).

139. Griffith, *The Bible in Arabic*, 106–22.

140. Moses Mendelssohn, *Or Lanetivah* (Vienna: Franz von Schmidt, 1846), xxv; and Isaac Leeser, *The Twenty-Four Books of the Holy Scriptures* (Cincinnati: Bloch, 1853), iii.

141. Cf. already Trypho (Justin Martyr, *Dialogue with Tripho* 67:1 and 71:1 [PG 6:629 and 644]); and Irenaeus in *The Ante-Nicene Fathers*, ed. Alexander Roberts and James Donaldson (Grand Rapids: William B. Eerdmans, 1950–51) ,vol. 1, pp. 231, 234.

142. So Staerk and Leitzmann, *Die Jüdisch-Deutschen Bibelübersetzungen von den Anfäng des 18. Jahrhunderts*, 169–70.

143. Roth, "The Marrano Press at Ferrara," 310.

144. Reider, *Prolegomena to a Greek-Hebrew and Hebrew-Greek Index to Aquila*, 60.

145. Cf. *Tg. Ps.-J.* Gen 21:13.

146. Selig Newman, *Emendations of the Authorised Version of the Old Testament* (London: B. Wertheim, Paternoster Row, 1839), iii.

147. Selig Newman, *Emendations of the Authorised Version of the Old Testament* (London: B. Wertheim, Paternoster Row, 1839), vii, citing Gen 6:2 and 1 Sam. 28:13; cf. *b. Sanhedrin* 3b.

148. Richard Gottheil, "Bible Translations," *JE* vol. 3, p. 194. The Central Conference of American Rabbis had originally planned a Jewish edition of the Revised Version with an appendix listing the necessary changes (*CCAR Yearbook* 18 [1908]: 149).

149. Raphael Loewe, "Bible–Translation," *EJ* vol. 4, p.871; Hertz, "Jewish Translations of the Bible in English" in *Sermons, Addresses and Studies*, vol. 2, p. 75; Isaac Delgado, *A New Translation of the Pentateuch* (London: W. Richardson, 1789), title page.

150. Adler, "The Bible Translation," 117; thus Emil G. Hirsch's reference to Jews' "sprachgefühl" ("In the Field of Semitic Scholarship," 197). As Umberto Cassuto noted, "The language in which the biblical books are written is not a foreign language for us" (*Studies on the Bible and the Ancient Orient* [Jerusalem: Magnes, 1972], vol. 1, p. 5; Hebrew), while Solomon Schechter is reported to have told William Robertson Smith, "You Christians know Hebrew grammar. We know Hebrew" (Norman Bentwich, *Solomon Schechter, A Biography* [Philadelphia: Jewish Publication Society, 1938], 85).

151. *Adversus Haereses* 3:21.1 (*PG* 7:946).

152. Hertz, "Jewish Translations of the Bible in English," in *Sermons, Addresses and Studies*, vol. 2, p. 78; cf. Isaac Leeser, "Preface," *The Twenty-Four Books of the Holy Scriptures* (Philadelphia: C. Sherman, 1856), iv–vi; Solomon Schechter, *American Jewish Yearbook* 15 (1913/14): 173; Grayzel, "The Bible and I," 17; and *The Holy Scriptures According to the Masoretic Text* (Philadelphia: Jewish Publication Society, 1917), vii–viii.

153. Ben-Chorin, "Jüdische Bibelübersetzungen in Deutschland," 324–25.

154. Franz Rosenzweig, *Briefe* (Berlin: Schocken Verlag, 1935), 552.

155. Martin Buber, "The How and Why of Our Bible Translation," in Buber and Rosenzweig, *Scripture and Translation*, 209.

156. A. Levenson, *The Making of the Modern Jewish Bible*, 44.

157. J. Sarna, *JPS*, 240.

158. Reider, *Prolegomena to a Greek-Hebrew and Hebrew-Greek Index to Aquila*, 15, 20; Sandler, *Mendelssohn's Edition of the Pentatuch*, 67; Plaut, "German-Jewish Bible Translations," 12–13; Hertz, "Jewish Translations of the Bible in English," in *Sermons, Addresses and Studies*, vol. 2 p. 78; E. Fox, *The Five Books of Moses, The Schocken Bible* (New York: Schocken, 1995), though he retains

"Egypt," "Israel," and "Jordan" (Naudé, "A Descriptive Translation Analysis of the Schocken Bible," 86).

159. Cynthia Ozick, "Envy; or, Yiddish in America" in *The Pagan Rabbi and Other Stories* (New York: Alfred A. Knopf, 1971), 82.

160. Emanuel Tov, "Theologically Motivated Exegesis Embedded in the Septuagint," in *Translation of Scripture*, ed. D. Goldenberg, 225.

161. Churgin, "The Targum and the Septuagint," 56.

162. The Bible provides precedent for this when it differentiates idolatrous priests (*komer*) from non-idolotrous priests (*kohen*); cf. 2 Kings 3:4–5.

163. Tg. Ps.-J. Gen. 28:12, 29:17; and Deut. 10:6.

164. *Tg. Neb.* Jer. 2:8 and 5:31; cf. at 1 Kings 22:10.

165. A similar motive may account for Chronicles' leaving out David's rivalry with Saul (1 Sam. 19–31), the conflict with Jonathan's son Mephiboshet (2 Sam. 9), the war with Ishbaal (2 Sam. 2–4), and revolts by Absalom (2 Sam. 13–19) and Sheba (2 Sam. 20).

166. Cf. Rawidowicz, "Mendelssohn's Translation of Psalms," 293; cf. the excerpt from his preface to Psalms as cited by Billigheimer, "On Jewish Translations of the Bible in Germany," 4.

167. Hertz, "Jewish Translations of the Bible in English," in *Sermons, Addresses and Studies*, 84; cf. Leeser's comment in *The Occident* 9:9 (December 1851): 480.

168. Hertz, "Jewish Translations of the Bible in English," in *Sermons, Addresses and Studies*, 81. Noting that "Leeser's diction was hardly equal to that of the Authorized Revised Version" (Orlinsky, *Notes on the New Translation of the Torah*, 15), the introduction to the 1917 JPS translation acknowledges the Authorized Version's "admirable diction, which can never be surpassed" (viii).

169. Bamberger, "American Jewish Translations of the Bible," 36.

170Hertz, "Jewish Translations of the Bible in English," 78.

171. Adler, "The Bible Translation," 101.

172. J. Sarna, *JPS*, 14–15.

173. *The Holy Scriptures According to the Masoretic Text, A New Translation* (Philadelphia: Jewish Publication Society, 1945 [1917]), iv.

174. Adler, "The Bible Translation," 117.

175. Kaufmann Kohler, *Hebrew Union College and Other Addresses* (Cincinnati: Ark, 1916), 271.

176. Sandler, *Mendelssohn's Edition of the Pentatuch*, 186–87.

177. *Torah Neviim Khetuvim* (Berlin: Lewent's Verlagsbuchhandlung).

178. *The Holy Scriptures According to the Masoretic Text* (Philadelphia: Jewish Publication Society, 1917), vii.

179. *Gen. Rabbah* 36:8; cf. *b. Megillah* 9b.

180. Lazar, preface to *The Ladino Bible of Ferrara* (1553), xxii; S. Lowenstein, "The Readership of Mendelssohn's Bible Translation," 183; Staerk and Leitzmann, *Die Jüdisch-Deutschen Bibelübersetzungen von den Anfäng des 18. Jahrhunderts*, 161; Hertz, "Jewish Translations of the Bible in English," 75.

181. Novella 146, in Amnon Linder, *The Jews in Roman Imperial Legislation* (Detroit: Wayne State University Press/Jerusalem: Israel Academy of Sciences and Humanities, 1987), 406, 408.

182. Sarna and Sarna, "Jewish Bible Scholarship and Translations in the United States," 89; Sussman, "Another Look at Isaac Leeser," 179; Billigheimer, "On Jewish Translations of the Bible in Germany," 191; "Pope Meets with West German Jews and Protestants on Better Ties," *New York Times*, November 18, 1980; Muriel M. Berman, "Annual Report of JPS President at 96th Annual Meeting," in *American Jewish Yearbook* 85 (1985): 460.

183. Cf. Jansen, *The Interpretation of the Koran in Modern Egypt*, 10–11.

7. CONCLUSION

1. Margolis, "The Scope and Methodology of Biblical Philology," 32.

2. Walter Laquer, *The Israel-Arab Reader, A Documentary History of the Middle East Conflict* (New York: Citadel, 1969), 159.

3. B. Jacob, "Unsere Bibel in Wissenschaft und Unterricht," 511.

4. Cf. B. Levy, *Fixing God's Torah*.

5. Cf. Greenspahn, "Jewish Ambivalence Towards the Bible," 7–21.

6. Plato, *Phaedrus* (274DC) 275A; cf. Choctaw Chief Samuel Cobb: "Writing is the invention of the pale faces. It gives birth to trouble and fighting. The Great Spirit talks. We hear him in the thunder, in the sound of the wind, and in the water. He never writes" (Pattison, *On Literacy*, 37); and Pierre Abelard's reference to "the disease of writing" (Henige, "The Disease of Writing," 257).

7. Cf. New Kingdom papyrus: "A human being perishes, and his body becomes dirt; all his fellows dissolve to dust. But writings let him live on in the mouth of the reader. They have gone, their names have been forgotten, but writings keep their memory alive" (Chester Beatty Papyrus IV RS 3.5 as cited in W. Graham, *Beyond the Written Word*, 32); and the Latin proverb "Verba volent, scripta manent" (Words fly, writing remains) as cited by Jean-Louis Ska, "From History Writing to Library Building: The End of History and the Birth of the Book," in *The Pentateuch as Torah, New Models for Understanding Its Promulgation and Acceptance*, ed. Gary N. Knoppers and Bernard M. Levinson, 145–69. For Islam, see Hans-Michael Haussig, "Heilige Texte und Heilige Schriften, Einige Bemerkungen zu religiösen Überlieferungen," in *Schriftauslegung im antiken Judentum und im Urchristentum*, ed. Martin Hengel and Hermut Löhr (Tübingen: J. C. B. Mohr [Paul Siebeck] 1994), 73.

8. *J. Megillah* 4:1 743; *b. Giṭṭin* 60b; and *b. Temurah* 14b.

9. Singh, *The Guru Granth Sahib*, 278; cf. McCleod, "The Sikh Scriptures: Some Issues," 99.

10. Miriam Levering, "Scripture and Its Reception: A Buddhist Case," in *Rethinking Scripture, Essays from a Comparative Perspective*, ed. Levering, 62; Lanczkowski, *Sacred Writings*, 94; Leipoldt and Morenz, *Heilige Schriften*, 169n41; William A. Graham, "Scripture," *Encyclopedia of Religion*, vol. 13, p. 137; and Parmenter, "The Iconic Book," 69–71.

11. Geo Widengren, "Holy Book and Holy Tradition in Islam," in F. F. Bruce and E. G. Rupp, eds., *Holy Book and Holy Tradition*, 214.

12. Graham, *Beyond the Written Word*, 104, 85; Ismail K. Poonawala, "Translatability of the Qurān: Theological and Literary Considerations," in *Translation of Scripture*, ed. D. M. Goldenberg, 162–64.

13. Horovitz, "Alter und Ursprung des Isnād," 44; cf. G. Scholer, "Mündliche Thora und Ḥadīṯ," 213–51.

14. *J. Megillah* 4:1 74d; cf. Kent P. Jackson, "Latter-Day Saints: A Dynamic Scriptural Process," in *The Holy Book in Comparative Perspective*, ed. Frederick M. Denny and Rodney L. Taylor, 63.

15. Steven T. Katz, "Mysticism and the Interpretation of Sacred Scripture," in S. Katz, *Mysticism and Sacred Scripture*, 25; cf. de Lubac, *Medieval Exegesis*.

16. Sigmund Freud, *Moses & Monotheism* (New York: Vintage, 1939), 147.

17. Emil L. Fackenheim, *The Jewish Bible After the Holocaust, A Re-Reading* (Bloomington: Indiana University Press, 1990), 77.

18. "Dabru Emet," *New York Times*, September 10, 2000.

19. Cf. Jon D. Levenson, "How Not to Conduct Jewish-Christian Dialogue," *Commentary* 112:5 (December 2001): 34–35.

20. Martin Buber, *Israel and the World: Essays in a Time of Crisis* (New York: Schocken, 1948), 39.

Selected Bibliography

Abramson, Glenda. "Israeli Drama and the Bible: Kings on the Stage." AJS *Review* 28 (2004): 63–82.

———. "The Reinterpretation of the Akedah in Modern Hebrew Poetry." *JJS* 41 (1990): 101–14.

Abramson, Shraga. "The Ambiguity of the Talmudic *yeš 'ēm lĕmiqra, lamasoret.*" [In Hebrew.] *Leš* 50 (1985–86): 31–36.

Abu El-Haj, Nadia. *Facts on the Ground: Archaeological Practice and Territorial Self-Fashioning in Israeli Society*. Chicago: University of Chicago Press, 2001.

Ackroyd, Peter R. "The Chronicler as Exegete." *JSOT* 2 (1977): 2–32.

Adler, Cyrus. "The Bible Translation." *American Jewish Yearbook* 15 (1913–14): 101–21.

Albrektson, Bertil. "Reflections on the Emergence of a Standard Text of the Hebrew Bible." *Congress Volume Göttingen 1977* (VTSup 29). Leiden: E. J. Brill, 1977, 49–65.

Alexander, Philip S. "The Rabbinic Lists of Forbidden Targumim." *JJS* 27 (1976): 177–91.

———. "The Targumim and the Rabbinic Rules for the Delivery of the Targum." *Congress Volume Salmanaca 1983* (VTSup 36). Leiden: E. J. Brill, 1985.

Alexander, Philip S., and Jean-Daniel Kaestli, eds. *The Canon and Scripture in Jewish and Christian Tradition.* Lausanne: Éditions du Zébre, 2007.

Allony, Nehemiah. "Was Ben Asher a Karaite?" [In Hebrew.] *Tarbiz* 27 (1958): 61–82.

Almog, Shmuel. *Zionism and History: The Rise of a New Jewish Consciousness.* New York: St. Martin's; Jerusalem: Magnes, 1987.

Alter, Robert. *The Art of Biblical Narrative.* New York: Basic, 1981.

Altmann, Alexander. *Moses Mendelssohn: A Biographical Study.* Tuscaloosa: University of Alabama Press, 1973.

Aminoah, Noah. "*'Em LaMikra'* and *'Em LaMasoret* as Normative Expressions." [In Hebrew.] *Teudah* 2 (1982): 43–56.

Amir, Yehoshua. "From the Biblical Inquiring of God to the Rabbinic Interpretation of the Torah." [In Hebrew.] *Beth Mikra* 41 (1995–96): 128–34.
Amitay, Mordecai. *Ḥad-Gadya ve-Gado: Literary Motifs*. [In Hebrew.] Tel Aviv: HaMenorah, 1974.
Ankori, Zvi. *Karaites in Byzantium: The Formative Years, 970–1100*. New York: Columbia University Press, 1959.
Aptroot, Marion Jennifer. "Bible Translation as Cultural Reform: The Amsterdam Yiddish Bibles (1678–1679)." PhD dissertation, Oxford University, 1989.
Aran, Gideon. "Return to the Scripture in Modern Israel." In *Les Retours aux Écritures: Fondamentalismes Présents et Passés*, edited by Évelyne Patlagean and Alain leBoulluec, 101–31. Louvain: Peeters, 1993.
Arnold, Bill T., and David B. Weisberg. "A Centennial Review of Friedrich Delitzsch's 'Babel und Bible' Lectures." *JBL* 121 (2002): 442–57.
Attias, Jean Christophe. *The Jews and the Bible*. Stanford CA: Stanford University Press, 2014.
Auerbach, Jerold S. "Assimilation in Zion." *Midstream* 41 (May 1995): 22–26.
Auld, A. Graeme. "Can a Biblical Theology Also Be Academic or Ecumenical?." In *Text as Pretext: Essays in Honour of Robert Davidson*, edited by Robert P. Carroll, 3–27. Sheffield: Sheffield Academic Press, 1992.
Auwers, Jean-Marie, and Henk Jan DeJonge. *The Biblical Canons*. Leuven: Leuven University Press and Uitgeverig Peeters, 2003.
Bacher, Wilhelm. "A Contribution to the History of the Term 'Massorah.'" *JQR* os 3 (1891): 785–90.
———. *Die exegetische Terminologie der jüdischen Traditionsliteratur*. Leipzig: J. C. Hinrichs, 1905.
———. "Das Merkwert *pardes* in der jüdischen Bibelexegese." *ZAW* 13 (1893): 294–305.
Baltzer, Klaus. "Schriftauslegung bei Deuterojesaja?-Jes 43,22–28 als Beispiel." In *Die Väter Israels: Beiträge zur Theologie der Patriarchen-überlieferungen im Alten Testament*, edited by Manfred Görg, 11–16. Stuttgart: Verlag Katholisches Bibelwerk, 1989.
Bamberger, Bernard J. "American Jewish Translations of the Bible." *Jewish Book Annual* 15 (1957–58): 33–40.
———. "The Beginnings of Modern Jewish Scholarship." *CCAR Yearbook* 42 (1932): 209–35.
Bannitt, Menahem. *Rashi: Interpreter of the Biblical Letter*. Tel Aviv: Chaim Rosenberg School of Jewish Studies at Tel Aviv University, 1985.
Bar-Ilan, Meir. "Back to the Middle Ages: The Secret Numbers of the Bible." [In Hebrew.] *Beth Mikra* 58, no. 1 (2013): 153–66.

Barkay, Gabriel, Marilyn J. Lundberg, Andrew G. Vaughn, and Bruce Zuckerman. "The Amulets from Ketef Hinnom: A New Edition and Evaluation." *BASOR* 334 (2004): 41–71.

Barnes, W. E. "The Midrashic Element in Chronicles." *Expositor* 5, no. 4 (1896): 426–39.

Baron, Salo W. *A Social and Religious History of the Jews*. Philadelphia: Jewish Publication Society, 1960.

Barr, James. *Holy Scripture, Canon, Authority, Criticism*. Philadelphia: Westminster, 1983.

———. *The Typology of Literalism in Ancient Bible Translations* (Mitteilungen des Septuaginta-Unternehmens). Göttingen: Vandenhoeck & Ruprecht, 1979.

Barthélemy, Dominique. *Les Devanciers d'Aquila*, VT Sup 10. Leiden: E. J. Brill, 1963.

———. "Qui est Symmaque?" *CBQ* 36 (1974): 451–65.

Barugel, Alberto. *The Sacrifice of Isaac in Spanish and Sephardic Balladry*. New York: Peter Lang, 1990.

Barzilay, Isaac Eisenstein. "The Ideology of the Berlin Haskalah." *PAAJR* 25 (1956): 1–37.

———. "The Treatment of the Jewish Religion in the Literature of the Berlin Haskalah." *PAAJR* 24 (1955): 39–68.

Basser, H. W. "Josephus as Exegete." *JAOS* 107 (1987): 21–30.

Baumgarten, Albert I. "Sacred Scriptures Defile the Hands." *JJS* 67 (2016): 46–67.

Baumgarten, Jean. "Le Traductions de la Bible en Yidich (XVIe–XVIIe Siécles) et le *Zeenah Ureenah* (Bâle, 1622) de Yaakov Iṣhaq Achkenazi de Janow." *REJ* 144 (1985): 305–10.

Bechtoldt, Hans-Joachim. *Die jüdische Bibelkritik in 19. Jahrhundert*. Stuttgart: Verlag W. Kohlhammer, 1995.

Beckwith, Roger. *The Old Testament of the New Testament Church and its Background in Early Judaism*. Grand Rapids MI: William B. Eerdmans, 1985.

Bell, Catherine. *Ritual Theory, Ritual Practice*. New York: Oxford University Press, 1992.

Bellis, Alice Ogden, and Joel S. Kaminsky. *Jews, Christians, and the Theology of the Hebrew Scriptures*. Atlanta: Society of Biblical Literature, 2000.

Ben-Chorin, Schalom. "Jüdische Bibelübersetzungen in Deutschland." *Leo Baeck Institute Yearbook* 4 (1959): 311–31.

Ben-Hayim, Zev. "Masorah and Masoret (An Analysis of Meaning)." [In Hebrew.] *Leš* 2 (1956–57): 283–92.

Benjamin, Mara H. *Rosenzweig's Bible: Reinventing Scripture for Jewish Modernity*. Cambridge: Cambridge University Press, 2009.

Ben-Oren, Gershon. "Three Recent Bible Translations to Georgian." [In Hebrew.] *Pe'amim* 84 (Summer 2000): 77–87.

Ben-Zvi, Izhak. "The Codex of Ben Asher." *Textus* 1 (1960): 1–16.

Berenblut, Max. "A Comparative Study of Judaeo-Italian Translations of Isaiah." PhD dissertation, Columbia University, 1949.

Bernstein, Moshe J. "Angels at the Aqedah: A Study in the Development of a Midrashic Motif." *DSD* 7 (2000): 263–91.

———. "The Orthodox Jewish Scholar and Jewish Scholarship: Duties and Dilemmas." *Torah u-Madda Journal* 3 (1991–92): 8–36.

Bickerman, Elias J. "The Colophon of the Greek Book of Esther." *JBL* 63 (1944): 339–62.

———. "The Septuagint as a Translation." *PAAJR* 28 (1959): 1–39.

———. "Some Notes on the Transmission of the Septuagint." In *Alexander Marx: Jubilee Volume on the Occasion of His Seventieth Birthday*, English section, 149–78. New York: Jewish Theological Society of America, 1950.

Billigheimer, S. "On Jewish Translations of the Bible in Germany." *Abr-Nahrain* 7 (1967–68): 1–34.

Birnbaum, Ellen. *The Place of Judaism in Philo's Thought*. Atlanta: Scholars Press, 1996.

Birnbaum, Philip, ed. *Karaite Studies*. New York: Hermon, 1971.

Blake, Frank R. "The Development of Symbols for the Vowels in the Alphabets Derived from the Phoenician." *JAOS* 60 (1940): 391–413.

Bland, Kalman P. "Issues in Sixteenth-Century Jewish Exegesis." In *The Bible in the Sixteenth Century*, edited by David C. Steinmetz, 50–67. Durham NC: Duke University Press, 1990.

Blau, Joshua. "On Karaite Translations of the Bible into Arabic from the Tenth and Eleventh Centuries." [In Hebrew.] *Tarbiz* 67 (1997–8): 417–30.

Blau, Ludwig. "M. Friedmann's 'Onkelos and Akylas.'" *JQR* os 9 (1897): 727–40.

Bloom, Cecil. "The Hebrew Bible (Tanakh) in Music." *Midstream* 53, no. 1 (January-February 2007): 41–45.

Bohak, Gideon. *Ancient Jewish Magic: A History*. Cambridge: Cambridge University Press, 2008.

Bonfil, Robert, Isaac Gottlieb, and Hannah Kasher, eds. *Samuel David Luzzatto: The Bi-Centennial of His Birth*. Jerusalem: Magnes, 2004.

Borchardt, Francis. "The LXX Myth and the Rise of Textual Fixity." *JSJ* 43 (2012): 1–21.

Borowitz, Eugene B. "Theological Issues in the New Torah Translation." *Judaism* 13 (1964): 335–45.

Bottigheimer, Ruth B. "Moses Mordechai Büdinger's Kleine Bibel (1823) and Vernacular Jewish Children's Bibles." *Jewish Social Studies* ns 1, no. 3 (Spring 1995): 83–98.

Bowker, John. *The Targums and Rabbinic Literature: An Introduction to Jewish Interpretations of Scripture.* Cambridge: Cambridge University Press, 1969.

Bowley, James E., and John C. Reeves. "Rethinking the Concept of 'Bible': Some Theses and Proposals." *Henoch* 25 (2003): 3–18.

Bradshaw, Paul F. "The Use of the Bible in Liturgy: Some Historical Perspectives." *Studia Liturgica* 22 (1992): 35–52.

Brandt, Peter. *Endgestalten des Kanons: Das Arrangement der Schriften Israels in der jüdischen und christlichen Bibel.* Berlin: Philo Verlagsgesellschaft, 2001.

Bregman, Marc. "The Depiction of the Ram in the *Aqedah* Mosaic at Beit Alpha." [In Hebrew.] *Tarbiz* 51 (1981–82): 306–9.

Brettler, Marc Zvi. "Judaism in the Hebrew Bible? The Transition from Ancient Israelite Religion to Judaism." *CBQ* 61 (1999): 429–47.

Breuer, Edward. "Between Haskalah and Orthodoxy: The Writings of R. Jacob Zvi Meklenburg." *HUCA* 66 (1995): 259–87.

———. *The Limits of Enlightenment: Jews, Germans, and the Eighteenth-Century Study of Scripture.* Cambridge: Harvard University Press, 1996.

Breuer, Mordecai. *The Aleppo Codex and the Accepted Text of the Bible.* [In Hebrew.] Jerusalem: Mosad HaRav Kook, 1976.

———. "Das Studium der Tora nach der Bibelkritik." *Judaica* 58 (2002): 154–71.

———. "Keep Your Children from the Higgayon." In *Michtam Le-David: Rabbi David Ochs Memorial Volume (1905–1975)*, edited by Yitzchak Gilat and Eliezer Stein, 242–61. [In Hebrew.] Ramat Gan: Bar-Ilan University, 1978.

———. "Über die Bibelkritik." Introduction by Matthias Morgenstern. *Judaica* 58 (2002): 18–29.

Breuer, Mordechai. *Modernity Within Tradition: The Social History of Orthodox Jewry in Imperial Germany.* New York: Columbia University Press, 1992.

Brock, Sebastian. "Aspects of Translation Technique in Antiquity." *Greek, Roman and Byzantine Studies* 20 (1979): 69–87.

Bronznick, Norman M. "Qabbalah as a Metonym for the Prophets and Hagiographa." *HUCA* 38 (1967): 285–95.

Brooke, George J., ed. *Jewish Ways of Reading the Bible.* Oxford: Oxford University Press, 2002.

Brooks, Roger, and John J. Collins. *Hebrew Bible or Old Testament? Studying the Bible in Judaism and Christianity.* Notre Dame IN: University of Notre Dame Press, 1990.

Brown, C. Mackenzie. "Purāṇa as Scripture: From Sound to Image of the Holy Word in the Hindu Tradition." *History of Religions* 26 (1986): 68–86.

Brown, Michael. "Biblical Myth and Contemporary Experience: The *Akedah* in Modern Jewish Literature." *Judaism* 31 (1982): 99–111.

Broyde, Michael J. "Defilement of the Hands, Canonization of the Bible, and the Special Status of Esther, Ecclesiastes, and Song of Songs." *Judaism* 44 (1995): 65–79.

Bruce, F. F. "The Earliest Old Testament Interpretation." *OTS* 17 (1972): 37–52.

Bruce, F. F., and E. G. Rupp, eds. *Holy Book and Holy Tradition.* Manchester: Manchester University Press, 1968.

Buber, Martin. *On the Bible: Eighteen Studies by Martin Buber.* Edited by Nahum M. Glatzer. New York: Schocken, 1968.

Buber, Martin, and Franz Rosenzweig. *Scripture and Translation.* Bloomington: Indiana University Press, 1994.

Büchler, Adolf. "The Reading of the Law and Prophets in a Triennial Cycle." *JQR* OS 5 (1893): 420–68, and 56 (1894): 1–73.

Burkitt, F. C. "Aquila." *JQR* OS 10 (1898): 207–16.

Caird, G. B. "Homeophony in the Septuagint." In *Jews, Greeks and Christians: Religious Cultures in Late Antiquity; Essays in Honor of William David Davies,* edited by Robert Hamerton-Kelly and Robin Scroggs, 74–88. Leiden: E. J. Brill, 1976.

Calder, Norman. "From Midrash to Scripture: The Sacrifice of Abraham in Early Islamic Tradition." *Le Museon* 101 (1988): 375–402.

Campbell, Jonathan G. "4QMMT^{d} and the Tripartite Canon." *JJS* 51 (2000): 181–90.

Campenhausen, Hans F., von. *The Form of the Christian Canon.* Translated by J. A. Baker. Philadelphia: Fortress, 1972.

Caplan, Harry. "The Four Senses of Scriptural Interpretation and the Mediaeval Theory of Preaching." *Speculum* 4 (1929): 282–90.

Carr, David M. *Writing on the Tablet of the Heart: Origins of Scripture and Literature.* New York: Oxford University Press, 2005.

Cassuto, Umberto. *Biblical and Oriental Studies.* Jerusalem: Magnes, 1973–75.

Cavallo, Guglielmo, and Roger Chartier, eds. *A History of Reading in the West.* Amherst: University of Massachusetts Press, 1999.

Chapman, Stephen B. *The Law and the Prophets: A Study in Old Testament Canon Formation.* Tübingen: J. C. B. Mohr (Paul Siebeck), 2000.

Charlesworth, James H. "In the Crucible: The Pseudepigrapha as Biblical Interpretation." In *The Pseudepigrapha and Early Biblical Interpretation,* edited by James H. Charlesworth and Craig A. Evans, 20–43. Sheffield: Sheffield Academic Press, 1993.

———, ed. *The Old Testament Pseudepigrapha.* Garden City NY: Doubleday, 1985.

Chartier, Roger. "Languages, Books, and Reading from the Printed Word to the Digital Text." *Critical Inquiry* 31 (2004): 133–52.

Chiesa, Bruno. *The Emergence of Hebrew Biblical Pointing: The Indirect Sources.* Frankfurt a.M.: Peter D. Lang, 1979.

Childs, Brevard S. "Psalm Titles and Midrashic Exegesis." *JSS* 16 (1971): 137–50.

Chomsky, William. "The History of Our Vowel-System in Hebrew." *JQR* 32 (1941–42): 27–49.

Churgin, Pinkhos. "The Targum and the Septuagint." *AJSL* 50 (1933–34): 41–65.

Clements, R. E. "Heinrich Graetz as Biblical Historian and Religious Apologist." In *Interpreting the Hebrew Bible: Essays in Honour of E. I. J. Rosenthal,* edited by J. A. Emerton and Stefan Reif, 31–55. Cambridge: Cambridge University Press, 1982.

Cohen, Arthur A., and Paul Mendes-Flohr, eds. *Contemporary Jewish Religious Thought.* New York: Charles Scribner's Sons, 1987.

Cohen, Chaim. "Elements of *Peshat* in Traditional Jewish Bible Exegesis." *Immanuel* 21 (1987): 30–42.

Cohen, D. "36 Interpretive Principles." [In Hebrew.] *Tarbiz* 2 (1930–31): 249.

Cohen, Jeremy. "Philosophical Exegesis in Historical Perspective: The Case of the Binding of Isaac." In *Divine Omniscience and Omnipotence in Medieval Philosophy: Islamic, Jewish, and Christian Perspectives,* edited by Tamar Rudavsky, 135–42. Dordrecht: D. Reidel, 1985.

Cohen, Miles B. "Masoretic Accents as a Biblical Commentary." *JANESCU* 4 (1972): 2–11.

Cohen, Mordechai Z. "'The Best of Poetry': Literary Approaches to the Bible in the Spanish *Peshat* Tradition." *Torah u-Madda Journal* 6 (1995–96): 15–57.

———. *Opening the Gates of Interpretation: Maimonides' Biblical Hermeneutics in Light of His Geonic-Andalusian Heritage and Muslim Milieu.* Leiden: Brill, 2011.

———. "A Poet's Biblical Exegesis." *JQR* 93 (2003): 533–56.

Cohen, Naomi G. "Earliest Evidence of the Haftarah Cycle for the Sabbaths Between the 17th of Tammuz and Sukkot in Philo." *JJS* 48 (1997): 225–49.

Cohen, Naomi W. "The Challenges of Darwinism and Biblical Criticism to American Judaism." *Modern Judaism* 4 (1984): 121–57.

Cohen, Saul B., and Nurit Kliot. "Israel's Place-Names as Reflection of Continuity and Change in Nation-Building." *Names* 29 (1981): 227–48.

Cohn, Yehudah B. *Tangled Up in Text:* Tefillin *and the Ancient World.* Providence RI: Brown Judaic Studies, 2008.

Colpe, Carsten. "Sakralisierung von Texten und Filiationen von Kanons." In *Beiträge zur Archäologie der Literariswche Kommunikation, vol. 2, Kanon und Zensur,* edited by Aleida and Jan Assmann, 80–92. Munich: Wilhelm Fink Verlag, 1987.

Cook, Johann. "Towards the Dating of the Tradition 'The Torah as Surrounding Fence.'" *JNSL* 24, no. 2 (1998): 25–34.

Cooper, Alan. "On Reading the Bible Critically and Otherwise." In *The Future of Biblical Studies: The Hebrew Scriptures,* edited by Richard Elliott Friedman and H. G. M. Williamson, 61–79. Atlanta: Scholars Press, 1987.

Craigie, P. C. "The Influence of Spinoza in the Higher Criticism of the Old Testament." *Evangelical Quarterly* 50 (1978): 23–32.

Crockett, Larrimore. "Luke iv.16–30 and the Jewish Lectionary Cycle: A Word of Caution." *JJS* 17 (1966): 13–46.

Daniélou, Jean. "La Typologie d'Isaac dans le Christianisme Primitif." *Biblica* 28 (1947): 363–93.

Daube, David. "Rabbinic Methods of Interpretation and Hellenistic Rhetoric." *HUCA* 22 (1949): 239–64.

———. "Typology in Josephus." *JJS* 31 (1980): 18–36.

Davies, Philip R. "Passover and the Dating of the Aqedah." *JJS* 30 (1979): 59–67.

Delaney, Carol. *Abraham on Trial: The Social Legacy of Biblical Myth.* Princeton NJ: Princeton University Press, 1998.

deLange, Nicholas. *Japheth in the Tents of Shem: Greek Bible Translations in Byzantine Judaism.* Tübingen: Mohr Siebeck, 2015.

deLange, Nicholas, Julia G. Krivoruchko, and Cameron Boyd-Taylor. *Jewish Reception of Greek Bible Versions: Studies in Their Use in Late Antiquity and the Middle Ages.* Tübingen: Mohr Siebeck, 2009.

Delitzsch, Friedrich. *Babel and Bible.* Chicago: Open Court, 1903.

Denny, Frederick M., and Rodney L. Taylor. *The Holy Book in Comparative Perspective.* Columbia: University of South Carolina Press, 1985.

Dienermann, Max. "Unser Verhältnis zur Bibel." *AZJ* 81, no. 25 (June 22, 1917).

Dienstag, Jacob I. "Biblical Exegesis of Maimonides in Jewish Scholarship." In *Samuel K. Mirsky Memorial Volume: Studies in Jewish Law, Philosophy, and Literature,* edited by Gerson Appel, 151–90. New York: Yeshiva University, 1970.

Diez Macho, Alejandro. "The Recently Discovered Palestinian Targum: Its Antiquity and Relationship to the Other Targums." *Congress Volume Oxford 1959* (VTSup 7). Leiden: Brill, 1960, 222–45.

Di Giulio, Marco. "Resisting Modernity: Jewish Translations of Scripture and Rabbinic Literature in Mid-Nineteenth Century Italy." *Modern Judaism* 35 (2015): 203–32.

Dobschütz, Ernst, von. "Vom vierfachen Schriftsinn, Die Geschichte einer Theorie." In *Harnack-Ehrung: Beiträge zur Kirchengeschichte ihrem Lehrer*

Adolf von Harnack zu seinem Siebstigsten Geburtstage, 1–13. Leipzig: J. C. Hinrichts'sche Buchhandlung, 1921.

Dornseiff, Franz, *Das Alphabet in Mystik und Magie*. STOICHEIA (Studien zur Geschichte des Antiken Weltbildes und den Griechischen Wissenschaft) 7. Leipzig: B. G. Teubner, 1922

Dotan, Aron. "The Beginnings of Masoretic Vowel Notation." In *Proceedings IOMS* Masoretic Studies no. 1, edited by Harry M. Orlinsky, 21–34. New York: Ktav, 1974.

———. *Ben Asher's Creed: A Short History of the Controversy*. Missoula MT: Scholars Press, 1977.

———. "The Relative Chronology of Hebrew Vocalization and Accentuation." *PAAJR* 48 (1981): 87–99.

———. "Was Ben-Asher Indeed a Karaite?" [In Hebrew.] *Sinai* (1957): 28–312, 350–62.

Ecker, Roman. *Die arabische Job-übersetzung des Gaon Saadja ben Josef al-Fajjûmî: ein Beitrag zur Geschichte der Übersetzung des alten Testaments*. Munich: Kössel-Verlag, 1962.

Edelmann, R. "*Masoret* and Its Historical Background." In *Salo Wittmayer Baron Jubilee Volume*, 369–82. Jerusalem: American Academy for Jewish Research, 1974.

———. "Soferim-Masoretes, Masoretes-Nakdamim." *BZAW* 103 (1968): 116–23.

Eisen, Robert. "Reason, Revelation and the Fundamental Principles of the Torah in Gersonides' Thought." *PAAJR* 57 (1990–91): 11–34.

Eisenstein, Elizabeth L. *The Printing Press as an Agent of Change*. Cambridge: Cambridge University Press, 1979.

Ekstein, Meir. "Rabbi Mordechai Breuer and Modern Orthodox Biblical Commentary." *Tradition* 33, no. 3 (Spring 1999): 6–23.

Elbaum, Jacob. "From Sermon to Story: The Transformation of the Akedah." *Prooftexts* 6 (1986): 97–116.

———. *Openness and Insularity: Late Sixteenth Century Jewish Literature in Poland and Ashkenaz*. [In Hebrew.] Jerusalem: Magnes, 1990.

Elbogen, Ismar. *Jewish Liturgy: A Comprehensive History*. Philadelphia: Jewish Publication Society; and New York: Jewish Theological Seminary of America, 1993.

Ellenson, David. *Rabbi Esriel Hildesheimer and the Creation of a Modern Jewish Orthodoxy*. Tuscaloosa: University of Alabama Press, 1990.

Ellenson, David, and Richard Jacobs. "Scholarship and Faith: David Hoffman and His Relationship to *Wissenschaft des Judentums*." *Modern Judaism* 8 (1988): 27–40.

Elliott, J. K. "Manuscripts, the Codex and the Canon." *JSNT* 63 (1996): 105–23.

Elman, Yaakov. "'It Is No Empty Thing': Nahmanides and the Search for Omnisignificance." *Torah u-Madda Journal* 4 (1993): 1–83.

Elton, Benjamin J. *Britain's Chief Rabbis and the Religious Character of Anglo-Jewry, 1880–1970*. Manchester: Manchester University Press, 2009.

Englander, Henry. "Grammatical Elements and Terminology in Rashi's Biblical Commentaries." *HUCA* 11 (1936): 367–89,12–13 (1937–38): 505–21, and 14 (1939): 387–429.

———. "Mendelssohn as Translator and Exegete." *HUCA* 6 (1929): 327–48.

Eppenstein, Simon. *Beiträge zur Geschichte und Literatur im Geonäischen Zeitalter*. Berlin: Louis Lamm, 1913.

Epstein, Abraham. "Biblische Textkritik bei den Rabbinen." In *Recueil des Travaux Rédigés en Mémoire du Jubilé Scientifique de M. Daniel Chwolson*, edited by David Günzburg, 42–56. Berlin: S. Calvary, 1899.

Eshel, Esther, Hanan Eshel, and Armin Lange. "'Hear O Israel' in Gold: An Ancient Amulet from Halbturn in Austria." *JAJ* 1 (2010): 43–64.

Eslinger, Lyle. "Inner-Biblical Exegesis and Inner-Biblical Allusion: The Question of Category." *VT* 42 (1992): 47–58.

Evans, Craig A., and Emanuel Tov. *Exploring the Origins of the Bible*. Grand Rapids MI: Baker Academic, 2008.

Faierstein, Morris M. "Tikkun Leil Shavuot." *Conservative Judaism* 61, no. 3 (Spring 2009): 76–69.

Fantalkin, Alexander, and Oren Tal. "The Canonization of the Pentateuch: When and Why?" *ZAW* 124 (2012): 1–18, 201–12.

Faur, José. *Golden Doves with Silver Dots: Semiotics and Textuality in Rabbinic Tradition*. Bloomington: Indiana University Press, 1986.

———. "The Targumim and Halakha." *JQR* 66 (1975–76): 19–26.

Febvre, Lucien, and Henri-Jean Martin. *The Coming of the Book: The Impact of Printing, 1450–1800*. London: Verso, 1984.

Federbush, Simon. *The Science of Judaism in Western Europe*. [In Hebrew.] New York: Ogen, 1958–65.

Feiner, Shmuel. *Haskalah and History: The Emergence of a Modern Jewish Historical Consciousness*. Oxford: Littmann Library of Jewish Civilization, 2002.

Feldman, Daniel Z. "The Development of *Minhag* as a Reflection of Halakhic Attitude: Fasting for a Fallen *Sefer Torah*." *Tradition* 33, no. 2 (Winter 1999): 19–30.

Feldman, Louis H. "Josephus as a Biblical Interpreter: The Akedah." *JQR* 75 (1984–85): 212–52.

———. "Josephus' *Jewish Antiquities* and Pseudo-Philo's *Biblical Antiquities*." In *Josephus, The Bible, and History*, edited by Louis H. Feldman and Gohei Hata, 59–80. Detroit: Wayne State University Press, 1989.

———. *Josephus's Interpretation of the Bible.* Berkeley: University of California Press, 1998.
———. *Studies in Josephus' Rewritten Bible.* Leiden: Brill, 1998.
Feldman, Seymour. "The Binding of Isaac: A Test-Case of Divine Foreknowledge." In *Divine Omniscience and Omnipotence in Medieval Philosophy: Islamic, Jewish and Christian Perspectives,* edited by Tamar Rudavsky, 105–33. Dordrecht, Netherlands: D. Reidel, 1985.
Feldman, Yael. *Glory and Agony: Isaac's Sacrifice and National Narrative.* Stanford CA: Stanford University Press, 2010.
———. "Isaac or Oedipus? Jewish Tradition and the Israeli Aqedah." In *Biblical Studies/Cultural Studies: The Third Sheffield Colloquium,* edited by J. Cheryl Exum and Stephen D. Moore, 159–89. Sheffield: Sheffield Academic Press, 1998.
Fellman, Jack. *The Revival of a Classical Tongue: Eliezer Ben Yehuda and the Modern Hebrew Language.* The Hague/Paris: Mouton, 1973.
Ferziger, Adam S. "Fluidity and Bifurcation: Critical Biblical Scholarship and Orthodox Judaism in Israel and North America." *Modern Judaism* 39 (2019): 233–70.
Fierstien, Robert E. *A Different Spirit: The Jewish Theological Seminary of America, 1886–1902.* New York: Jewish Theological Seminary of America, 1990.
Fine, Lawrence. "The Study of Torah as a Rite of Theological Contemplation in Lurianic Kabbalah." In *Approaches to Judaism in Medieval Times,* vol. 3, edited by David R. Blumenthal, 29–40. Atlanta: Scholars Press, 1988.
Fine, Steven. "From Meeting Place to Sacred Realm: Holiness and the Ancient Synagogue." In *Sacred Realm: The Emergence of the Synagogue in the Ancient World,* edited by Steven Fine, 21–47. New York: Yeshiva University Museum and Oxford University Press, 1996.
Finsterbusch, Karin, and Armin Lange, eds. *What Is Bible?* Leuven: Peeters, 2012.
Firestone, Reuven. "Abraham's Son as the Intended Sacrifice (*al-dhabīḥ,* Qur'ān 37:99–113): Issues in Qur'ānic Exegesis." *JSS* 34 (1989): 95–131.
Fischel, Walter J. "The Bible in Persian Translation." *HTR* 45 (1952): 3–45.
Fishbane, Michael. *Biblical Interpretation in Ancient Israel.* Oxford: Clarendon, 1985.
———. *The Exegetical Imagination: On Jewish Thought and Theology.* Cambridge MA: Harvard University Press, 1998.
———. *The Garments of Torah: Essays in Biblical Hermeneutics.* Bloomington: Indiana University Press, 1989.
———. "Martin Buber as an Interpreter of the Bible." *Judaism* 27 (1978): 184–95.

———, ed. *The Midrashic Imagination: Jewish Exegesis, Thought, and History.* Albany: State University of New York Press, 1993.

Fitzmyer, Joseph A. "The Sacrifice of Isaac in Qumran Literature." *Bib* 83 (2002): 211–29.

Fleischer, Ezra. "Annual and Triennial Reading of the Bible in the Old Synagogue." [In Hebrew.] *Tarbiz* 61 (1991–92): 25–43.

Flesher, Paul V. M., and Bruce Chilton. *The Targums: A Critical Introduction.* Waco TX: Baylor University Press, 2011.

Fox, Everett. "Franz Rosenzweig as Translator." *Leo Baeck Institute Yearbook* 34 (1989): 371–84.

———. "Robert Alter's Bible Translations." *Expositions: Interdisciplinary Studies in the Humanities* 2, no. 2 (2008): 231–37.

———. "Technical Aspects of the Translation of Genesis of Martin Buber and Franz Rosenzweig." PhD dissertation, Brandeis University, 1974.

Fox, Marvin. "Kierkegaard and Rabbinic Judaism." *Judaism* 2 (1953): 160–69.

Fox, Tzvi. "Judaic Doctrine of Scripture." In *Holy Scriptures in Judaism: Christianity and Islam*, edited by Hendrik M. Vroom and Jerald D. Gort, 43–56. Amsterdam: Editions Rodopi B.V., 1997.

Fraade, Steven D. "Rabbinic Views on the Practice of Targum, and Multilingualism in the Jewish Galilee of the Third-Sixth Centuries." In *The Galilee in Late Antiquity*, edited by Lee I. Levine, 253–86. New York: Jewish Theological Seminary of America, 1992.

Frahm, Eckart. *Babylonian and Assyrian Text Commentaries: Origins of Interpretation.* Münster: Ugarit-Verlag, 2011.

Frampton, Travis L. *Spinoza and the Rise of Historical Criticism of the Bible.* New York: T&T Clark, 2006.

Frankel, Israel. *Peshaṭ (Plain Exegesis) in Talmudic and Midrashic Literature.* Toronto: LaSalle, 1956.

Freedman, David B., and Miles B. Cohen. "The Masoretes as Exegetes: Selected Examples." In *1972 and 1973 Proceedings: IOMS*, edited by Harry M. Orlinsky, 35–46. New York: Ktav, 1974.

Freedman, R. David. "The Father of Modern Biblical Scholarship." *JANESCU* 19 (1989): 31–38.

Friedman, Matti. *The Aleppo Codex: A True Story of Obsession, Faith, and the Pursuit of an Ancient Bible.* Chapel Hill NC: Algonquin Books, 2012.

Friedman, Shamma. "The Holy Scriptures Defile the Hands: The Transformation of a Biblical Concept in Rabbinic Theology." In *Minḥah le-Naḥum: Biblical and Other Studies Presented to Nahum M. Sarna in Honour of His 70th Birthday*, edited by Marc Brettler and Michael Fishbane, 116–32. Sheffield: Sheffield Academic Press, 1993.

Friedmann, Meir. *Onkelos und Akylas*. Vienna: Ch. D. Lippe, 1896.
Funkenstein, Amos. "Nachmanides' Typological Reading of History." [In Hebrew.] *Zion* (1980): 35–59.
———. *Perceptions of Jewish History*. Berkeley: University of California Press, 1993.
———. "'Scripture Speaks the Language of Man': The Uses and Abuses of the Medieval Principle of Accommodation." In *L'homme et son Univers au Moyen Âge*, vol. 1, edited by Christian Wenin, 92–101. Louvain-La-Neuve: Éditions de l'Institut Supéerieur de Philosophie, 1986.
———. *Theology and the Scientific Imagination from the Middle Ages to the Seventeenth Century*. Princeton NJ: Princeton University Press, 1986.
Gabbay, Uri. "Akkadian Commentaries from Ancient Mesopotamia and their Relation to Early Hebrew Exegesis." *DSD* 19 (2012): 267–312.
Gallagher, Edmon. "The Religious Provenance of the Aquila Manuscripts from the Cairo Genizah." *JJS* 64 (2013): 283–305.
Galli, Barbara E. "Rosenzweig and the Name for God." *Modern Judaism* 14 (1994): 63–86.
Garfinkel, Steven. "Applied *Peshat*: Historical-Critical Method and Religious Meaning." *JANESCU* 22 (1993): 19–28.
Gehman, Henry S. "The Hebraic Character of Septuagint Greek." *VT* 1 (1951): 81–90.
Geiger, Abraham. *Urschrift und Uebersetzungen des Bibel*. Breslau: J. Hainauer, 1857.
Geller, Stephen A. "Wellhausen and Kaufmann." *Midstream* 31 (December 1985): 39–48.
Gelles, Benjamin J. *Peshat and Derash in the Exegesis of Rashi*. Leiden: E. J. Brill, 1981.
Gellman, Jerome. *Abraham! Abraham! Kierkegaard and the Hasidim on the Binding of Isaac*. Burlington VT: Ashgate, 2003.
Gerhards, Albert, and Clemens Leonhard. *Jewish and Christian Liturgy and Worship: New Insights into Its History and Interaction*. Leiden: Brill, 2007.
Gesundheit, Shimon. "Gibt es eine jüdische Theologie der Hebräischen Bibel?" In *Theologie und Exegese des Alten Testaments/der Hebräischen Bibel: Zwischen Bilanz und Zukunftsperspektiven*, edited by Bernd Janowski, 73–86. Stuttgart: Verlag Katholisches Bibelwerk GmbH, 2005.
Geva, Shulamit. "Israeli Biblical Archeology—The First Years." [In Hebrew.] *Z'manim* 42 (1992): 92–102.
Gillman, Abigail. *A History of German Jewish Bible Translation*. Chicago: University of Chicago Press, 2018.

Ginsberg, H. L. "The New Jewish Publication Society Translation of the Torah." *JBR* 31 (1963): 187–92.
———. "The New Translation of the Torah: In the Path of True Scholarship." *Midstream* 9, no. 2 (June 1963): 75–83.
———. "A Phoenician Hymn in the Psalter." *Atti del XIX Congresso Internazionale degli Orientalisti*, 472–76. Rome: G. Bardi, 1938.
Ginsburg, Christian. *Introduction to the Massoretic-Critical Edition of the Hebrew Bible*. New York: Ktav, 1966.
———. *Jacob ben Chajim ibn Adonijah's Introduction to the Rabbinic Bible and the Massoreth ha-Massoreth of Elias Levita*. New York: Ktav, 1968.
Ginzberg, Louis. *Ginzei Schechter: Genizah Studies in Memory of Dr. Solomon Schechter*. New York: Jewish Theological Seminary, 1928.
———. *On Jewish Law and Lore*. Philadelphia: Jewish Publication Society of America, 1955.
Glatzer, Nahum. "Buber as an Interpreter of the Bible." In *The Philosophy of Martin Buber*, edited by Paul Arthur Schilpp and Maurice Friedman, 361–80. LaSalle IL: Open Court, 1967.
Gold, Leonard Singer, ed. *A Sign and a Witness: 2,000 Years of Hebrew Books and Illuminated Manuscripts*. New York: New York Public Library and Oxford University Press, 1988.
Gold, Penny Schine. *Making the Bible Modern: Children's Bibles and Jewish Education in Twentieth-Century America*. Ithaca NY: Cornell University Press, 2004.
Goldberg, Arnold. "The Rabbinic View of Scripture." In *A Tribute to Geza Vermes: Essays on Jewish and Christian Literature and History*, edited by Philip R. Davies and Richard T. White, 153–66. Sheffield: Sheffield Academic Press, 1990.
Goldenberg, David M., ed. *Translation of Scripture: Proceedings of a Conference at the Annenberg Research Institute, May 15, 1989* (*JQR* Supplement). Philadelphia: Annenberg Research Institute, 1990.
Goldman, Bernard. *The Sacred Portal: A Primary Symbol of Ancient Judaic Art*. Detroit: Wayne State University Press, 1966.
Goldschmidt, Lazarus. *The Earliest Editions of the Hebrew Bible*. New York: Aldus, 1950.
Golinkin, David. "Blotting Out Haman on Purim," "Responsa in a Moment" 5, no. 5 (March 2011). schechter.edu/blotting-out-haman-on-purim.
Goodenough, Erwin R. *By Light, Light: The Mystic Gospel of Hellenistic Judaism*. New Haven: Yale University Press, 1935.
Gooding, D. W. "Aristeas and Septuagint Origins: A Review of Recent Studies." *VT* 13 (1963): 357–79.

———. *Relics of Ancient Exegesis: A Study of the Miscellaneis in 3 Reigns 2*. Cambridge: Cambridge University Press, 1976.

Goodman, Martin. "Sacred Scripture and 'Defiling the Hands.'" *JTS* 41 (1990): 99–107.

Gordis, Robert. *The Biblical Text in the Making: A Study of the Kethib-Qere* (augmented edition). New York: Ktav, 1971.

———. "The Faith of Abraham: A Note on Kierkegaard's 'Teleological Suspension of the Ethical.'" *Judaism* 25 (1975): 414–19.

———, ed. *Max Leopold Margolis, Scholar and Teacher*. Philadelphia: Dropsie College for Hebrew and Cognate Learning, 1952.

Gordon, Cyrus H. "New Directions." Studies Presented to Naphtali Lewis. *Bulletin of the American Society of Papyrologists* 15, no. 1–2 (1978): 59–66.

Goshen-Gottstein, Moshe H. "The Authenticity of the Aleppo Codex." *Textus* 1 (1960): 17–58.

———. "Christianity, Judaism, and Modern Bible Study." *Congress Volume, Edinburgh, 1974*, (VTSup 28). Leiden: E. J. Brill, 1974, 69–88.

———. "Foundations of Biblical Philology in the Seventeenth Century: Christian and Jewish Dimensions." In *Jewish Thought in the Seventeenth Century*, edited by Isadore Twersky and Bernard Septimus, 77–94. Cambridge: Harvard University Press, 1987.

———. "Jewish Studies, Biblical Studies, and Jewish Biblical Theology." In *Studies in Bible and Exegesis 1: In Memoriam Arie Toeg*, edited by Uriel Simon and Moshe H. Goshen-Gottstein, 243–55. [In Hebrew.] Ramat Gan: Bar Ilan University, 1980.

———. "The Rise of the Tiberian Bible Text." In *Biblical and Other Studies*, edited by Alexander Altmann, 79–122. Cambridge: Harvard University Press, 1963.

Gottheil, Richard. "Some Hebrew Manuscripts in Cairo." *JQR* OS 17 (1905): 609–55.

Gottlieb, Isaac B. "Midrash as Biblical Philology." *JQR* 75 (1984–85): 134–61.

Gottschalk, Alfred. "Ahad Ha-Am, the Bible, and the Bible Tradition." PhD dissertation, University of Southern California, 1965.

Grabbe, Lester L. "Aquila's Translation and Rabbinic Exegesis." *JJS* 33 (1982): 527–36.

Graetz, Heinrich. "Zur hebräischen Sprachkunde und Bibelexegese." *MGWJ* 10 (1861): 20–28.

Graham, William A. *Beyond the Written Word: Oral Aspects of Scripture in the History of Religion*. Cambridge: Cambridge University Press, 1987.

Grayzel, Solomon. "The Bible and I: A Translator Reflects." *Sh'ma* 7, no. 123 (December 10, 1976): 19.

———. *The Church and the Jews in the XIIIth Century*. Philadelphia: Dropsie College for Hebrew and Cognate Learning, 1933.
Greenberg, Moshe. "Can Modern Critical Bible Scholarship Have a Jewish Character?" *Immanuel* 15 (1982–83): 7–12.
———. *Jewish Bible Exegesis: An Introduction*. [In Hebrew.] Jerusalem: Mosad Bialik, 1983.
———. "Kaufmann on the Bible: An Appreciation." *Judaism* 13 (1964): 77–89.
———. "On the Political Use of the Bible in Modern Israel: An Engaged Critique." In *Pomegranates and Golden Bells: Studies in Bible, Jewish and Near Eastern Ritual, Law and Literature in Honor of Jacob Milgrom*, edited by David P. Wright, David Noel Freedman, and Avi Hurwitz, 461–71. Winona Lake IN: Eisenbrauns, 1995.
———. "The Stabilization of the Text of the Hebrew Bible, Reviewed in the Light of the Biblical Materials from the Judean Desert." *JAOS* 76 (1956): 157–67.
Greenspahn, Frederick E. "Biblical Scholars, Medieval and Modern." In *Judaic Perspectives on Ancient Israel*, edited by Jacob Neusner, Ernest Frerichs, and Baruch Levine, 245–58. Philadelphia: Fortress, 1987.
———. "Canon, Codex, and the Printing Press." In *Le-ma'an Ziony: Essays in Honor of Ziony Zevit*, edited by Frederick E. Greenspahn and Gary A. Rendsburg, 203–12. Eugene OR: Cascade, 2017.
———. "Competing Commentaries." In *Seeking Out the Wisdom of the Ancients: Essays Offered to Honor Michael V. Fox*, edited by R. L. Troxel, K. G. Friebel, and D. R. Mangery, 461–80. Winona Lake IN: Eisenbrauns, 2005.
———. "Jewish Ambivalence Towards the Bible." *HS* 48 (2007): 7–21.
Greenspoon, Leonard. "A Book 'Without Blemish': The Jewish Publication Society's Bible Translation of 1917." *JQR* 79 (1988): 1–21.
———. "From the Septuagint to the New Revised Standard Version: A Brief Account of Jewish Involvement in Bible Translating and Translations." In *The Solomon Goldman Lectures*, vol. 6, edited by Mayer I. Gruber, 19–50. Chicago: Spertus College of Judaica Press, 1993.
———. "Jewish Bible Translation." In *The Biblical World*, vol. 2, edited by John Barton, 397–412. New York: Routledge, 2002.
———. *Jewish Bible Translations: Personalities, Passions, Politics, Progress*. Philadelphia: Jewish Publication Society, 2020.
———. *Jews and Christians as Bible Translators: A Heritage of Cooperation*. New York: Laymen's National Bible Association, 1992.
———. "On the Jewishness of Modern Jewish Biblical Scholarship: The Case of Max L. Margolis." *Judaism* 39 (1990): 82–92.

Greenstein, Edward L. *Essays on Biblical Method and Translation.* Atlanta: Scholars Press, 1989.

Griffith, Sidney H. *The Bible in Arabic: The Scriptures of the 'People of the Book' in the Language of Islam.* Princeton NJ: Princeton University Press, 2013.

Gumbert, J. P. "The Layout of the Bible Gloss in Manuscript and Early Print." In *The Bible as Book: The First Printed Editions*, edited by Paul Saenger and Kimberly van Kampen, 7–13. London: British Library and Oak Knoll, 1999.

Gurewicz, S. B. "The Mediaeval Jewish Exegetes of the Old Testament." *Australian Biblical Review* 1 (1951): 24–53.

Gutmann, Joseph. *Beauty in Holiness: Studies in Jewish Customs and Ceremonial Art.* New York: Ktav, 1970.

———. "The History of the Ark." ZAW 83 (1971): 22–30.

———. *The Jewish Sanctuary.* Leiden: E. J. Brill, 1983.

———. "The Sacrifice of Isaac: Variations on a Theme in Early Jewish and Christian Art." In *Thiasos tōn Mousōn, Studien zu Antike und Christentum: Festschrift für Josef Fink zum 70. Geburtstag*, edited by Dieter Ahrens, 115–22. Köln: Böhlau Verlag, 1984.

Guttmann, Alexander. *The Struggle over Reform in Rabbinic Literature During the Last Century and a Half.* New York: World Union for Progressive Judaism, 1977.

Guttmann, Julius. *Philosophies of Judaism: The History of Jewish Philosophy from Biblical Times to Franz Rosenzweig.* New York: Holt, Rinehart & Winston, 1964.

Habas, Bracha, ed. *The Book of the Second Aliyah.* [In Hebrew.] Tel Aviv: Am Oved, 1947.

Habermann, A. M. *The History of the Hebrew Book: From Marks to Letters, From Scroll to Book.* [In Hebrew.] Jerusalem: Rubin Mass, 1968.

Hachlili, Rachel. *Ancient Jewish Art and Archaeology in the Diaspora.* Leiden: E. J. Brill, 1988.

———. "The Niche and the Ark in Ancient Synagogues." *BASOR* 223 (1976): 43–53.

HaCohen, Ran. *Reclaiming the Hebrew Bible: German-Jewish Reception of Biblical Criticism.* Berlin: Walter de Gruyter, 2010.

Halbertal, Moshe. *People of the Book: Canon, Meaning, and Authority.* Cambridge: Harvard University Press, 1997.

Halivni, David Weiss. *Midrash, Mishnah, and Gemara: The Jewish Predilection for Justified Law.* Cambridge: Harvard University Press, 1986.

———. *Peshat and Derash: Plain and Applied Meaning in Rabbinic Exegesis.* New York: Oxford University Press, 1991.

———. *Revelation Restored: Divine Writ and Critical Responses*. Boulder CO: Westview, 1997.

Halkin, A. S. "Saadia's Exegesis and Polemics." In *Rab Saadia Gaon: Studies in His Honor*, edited by Louis Finkelstein, 117–41. New York: Jewish Theological Seminary of America, 1944.

Hallamish, Moshe. *An Introduction to the Kabbalah*. Albany: State University of New York Press, 1999.

Hallo, William W. "Assyriology and the Canon." *The American Scholar* 59 (1990): 105–8.

———. *The Book of the People*. Atlanta: Scholars Press, 1991.

———. "The Concept of Canonicity in Cuneiform and Biblical Literature: A Comparative Approach." In *The Biblical Canon in Comparative Perspective*, edited by K. Lawson Younger Jr., William W. Hallo, and Bernard F. Batto, 1–19. Lewiston NY: Edwin Mellen, 1991.

———. "Notes on Translation." *ErIsr* 16 (1982): 99*–105*.

Halperin, Dalia-Ruth. "Decorated Masorah on the Openings Between Quires in Masoretic Bible Manuscripts." *JJS* 65 (2014): 323–48.

Hamel, C. F. R. de. *Glossed Books of the Bible and the Origins of the Paris Booktrade*. Dover NH and Woodbridge, England: D. S. Brewer; 1984.

Handelman, Susan A. *The Slayers of Moses: The Emergence of Rabbinic Interpretation in Modern Literary Theory*. Albany: State University of New York Press, 1982.

Haran, Menahem. "Archives, Libraries, and the Order of the Biblical Books." *JANESCU* 22 (1993): 51–61.

———. "Bible Scrolls from Qumran to the Middle Ages." [In Hebrew.] *Tarbiz* 51 (1981–82): 347–82.

———. "Bible Scrolls in the Early Second Temple Period—The Transition from Papyrus to Skins." [In Hebrew.] *ErIsr* 15 (1982): 86–92.

———. *Biblical Research in Hebrew: A Discussion of Its Character and Trends*. Jerusalem: Magnes, 1970.

———. "Book-Scrolls at the Beginning of the Second Temple Period: The Transition from Papyrus to Skins." *HUCA* 54 (1983): 111–22.

———. "Book Scrolls in Israel in Pre-Exilic Times." *JJS* 33 (1982): 161–73.

———. "Book-Size and the Device of Catch-Lines in the Biblical Canon." *JJS* 36 (1985): 1–11.

———. "The Codex, The *Pinax* and the Wooden Slats." [In Hebrew.] *Tarbiz* 57 (1987–88): 151–64.

———. "Hebrew Biblical Research from the Beginning of the Nationalist Period." [In Hebrew.] *Bitzaron* 21 (1949): 110–14, and (1950): 174–78.

———. "Literacy and Schools in Ancient Israel." *Congress Volume Jerusalem 1986* (VTSup 40). Leiden: E. J. Brill, 1986, 81–95.
———. "Midrashic and Literal Exegesis and The Critical Method in Biblical Research." In *Studies in Bible*, ScrH 31, edited by Sara Japhet, 19–48. Jerusalem: Magnes, 1986.
———. "More Concerning Book-Scrolls in Biblical Times: The Fifth Proof." [In Hebrew.] *Tarbiz* 52 (1982–83): 643–44.
———. "More Concerning Book-Scrolls in Pre-Exilic Times." *JJS* 35 (1984): 84–85.
———. "Problems of the Canonization of Scripture." [In Hebrew.] *Tarbiz* (1956): 245–71.
———. "Scribal Workmanship in Biblical Times: The Scrolls and the Writing Implements." [In Hebrew.] *Tarbiz* 50 (1981): 65–87.
———. "The Size of Books in the Bible and the Division of the Pentateuch and the Deuteronomistic Work." [In Hebrew.] *Tarbiz* 53 (1983–84): 329–52.
Hareven, Alouph. "Are the Israelis Still the People of the Book?" *Jerusalem Quarterly* 30 (Winter 1984): 3–16.
Harris, Isidore. "The Rise and Development of the Massorah." *JQR* os 1 (1889): 128–42, 223–57.
Harris, Jay M. *How Do We Know This? Midrash and the Fragmentation of Modern Judaism*. Albany: State University of New York Press, 1995.
———. *Nachman Krochmal: Guiding the Perplexed of the Modern Age*. New York: New York University Press, 1991.
Hartman, Geoffrey H. and Sanford Budick. *Midrash and Literature*. New Haven: Yale University Press, 1986.
Hary, Benjamin. "Jewish Languages: Are They Sacred?" In *Lenguas en Contacto: El Testimonio Escrito*, edited by Pedro Bádenas de la Peña, Sofía Torallas Tovar, Eugenio R. Luján, and Maria Ángeles Gallego, 225–44. Madrid: Consejo Superior de Investigaciones Cientificas, 2004.
Hauptman, Judith. "Rabbinic Interpretation of Scripture." In *A Feminist Companion to Reading the Bible: Approaches, Methods and Strategies*, edited by Athalya Brenner and Carole Fontaine, 472–86. Sheffield: Sheffield Academic Press, 1997.
Hayward, C. T. R. "The Sacrifice of Isaac and Jewish Polemic Against Christianity." *CBQ* 52 (1990): 292–306.
Heide, A. van der. "PARDES: Methodological Reflections on the Theory of the Four Senses." *JJS* 34 (1983): 147–59.
Heinemann, Isaak. "Die Wissenschaftliche Allegoristik des jüdischen Mittelalters." *HUCA* 23, no. 1 (1950–51): 611–43.

———. "Scientific Allegorization during the Jewish Middle Ages." In *Studies in Jewish Thought: An Anthology of German Jewish Scholarship*, edited by Alfred Jospe, 247–69. Detroit: Wayne State University Press, 1981

Heinemann, Joseph. *Prayer in the Talmud: Forms and Patterns*. Berlin: Walter de Gruyter, 1977.

———. "The Proem in the Aggadic Midrashim: A Form-Critical Study." *Scripta Hierosolymitana. Studies in Aggadah and Folk-Literature* 22 (1972): 101–22.

———. "The Triennial Lectionary Cycle." *JJS* 19 (1968): 41–48.

Heller, James G. *Isaac M. Wise: His Life, Work and Thought*. New York: Union of American Hebrew Congregations, 1965.

Hendel, Ronald, Aviya Kushner, Shai Held, David Bentley Hart, Adele Berlin, and Adam Kirsch. "Robert Alter's Bible: A Symposium." *Jewish Review of Books* 9, no. 4 (Winter 2019): 5–12.

Hengel, Martin, with Roland Deines. *The Septuagint as Christian Scripture: Its Prehistory and the Problem of Its Canon*. Edinburgh: T&T Clark, 2002.

Henige, David. "'The Disease of Writing': Ganda and Nyoro Kinglists in a Newly Literate World." In *The African Past Speaks: Essays on Oral Tradition and History*, edited by Joseph C. Miller, 240–61. Folkestone, England: William Dawson & Sons, 1980.

Herr, Moshe David. "Actualisation des Écritures et Intolérance dans la Judée du 1er Siècle." In *Les Retours aux Écritures: Fondamentalismes présents et Passés*, edited by Évelynne Patlagean and Alain le Boulleuc, 383–99. Louvain, Belgium: Peeters, 1993.

Herrmann, Siegfried. "Kultreligion und Buchreligion: Kultische Funktionen in Israel und in Ägypten." *BZAW* 105 (1967): 95–105.

Hertz, Joseph H. *Early and Late Addresses, Messages, and Papers*. Hindhead, Surrey: Soncino, 1943.

———. *Sermons, Addresses and Studies*. London: Soncino, 1936.

Heschel, Abraham Joshua. "God, Torah, and Israel." In *Theology and Church in Times of Change: Essays in Honor of John Coleman Bennett*, edited by Edward LeRoy Long Jr. and Robert T. Handy, 71–90. Philadelphia: Westminster, 1970.

———. *Heavenly Torah as Refracted through the Generations*. New York: Continuum, 2006.

———. *Prophetic Inspiration After the Prophets*. Hoboken NJ: Ktav, 1996.

Himmelfarb, Milton, ed. "The State of Jewish Belief: A Symposium." *Commentary*, August, 1966, 71–160.

Hirsch, Emil G. "In the Field of Semitic Scholarship." *Biblical World* 27 (1906): 196–99.

Hoberman, Barry. "Translating the Bible." *Atlantic Monthly* 255, no. 2 (February 1985): 43–58.

Hoenig, Sidney. "Notes on the New Translation of the Torah—A Preliminary Inquiry." *Tradition* 5 (1963): 172–205.

Hoffman, Jeffrey. "The Ancient Torah Service in Light of the Realia of the Talmudic Era." *Conservative Judaism* 42, no. 2 (Winter 1989–90): 41–49.

Hoffman, Lawrence A. *The Canonization of the Synagogue Service*. Notre Dame IN: University of Notre Dame Press, 1979.

Hoffmann, David Ẓevi. *Die Wichtigsten Instanzen gegen die Graf-Wellhausensche Hypothese*. Berlin: H. Itzkowski, 1904.

Holdrege, Barbara A. *Veda and Torah: Transcending the Textuality of Scripture*. Albany: State University of New York Press, 1996.

Honigman, Sylvie. *The Septuagint and Homeric Scholarship in Alexandria:A Study in the Narrative of the Letter of Aristeas*. London: Routledge, 2003.

Höpfl, Hildebrand. "Écriture Sainte." In *Dictionnaire de la Bible, Supplément*, vol. 2, edited by Louis Pinot et al., 457–87. Paris: Letouzey et Ané, 1934.

Horovitz, Josef. "Alter und Ursprung des Isnād." *Der Islam* 8 (1918): 39.

Horowitz, Elliott. *Reckless Rites: Purim and the Legacy of Jewish Violence*. Princeton NJ: Princeton University Press, 2006.

Huffmon, Herbert B. "Babel und Bibel: The Encounter Between Babylon and the Bible." *Michigan Quarterly Review* 22 (1983): 309–20.

Hummel, Horace D. "The Old Testament Basis of Typological Interpretation." *Biblical Research* 9 (1964): 38–50.

Husik, Isaac. "Maimonides and Spinoza on the Interpretation of the Bible." In *Philosophical Essays: Ancient, Mediaeval and Modern*, edited by Milton C. Nahm and Leo Strauss, 141–59. Oxford: Basil Blackwell, 1952.

Hyvärinen, Kyösti. *Die Übersetzung von Aquila*. Uppsala: C. W. K. Gleerup, 1977.

Idel, Moshe. *Absorbing Perfections: Kabbalah and Interpretation*. New Haven: Yale University Press, 2002.

———. "The Conception of the Torah in Heikhalot Literature and Its Transformations in Kabbalah." [In Hebrew.] *Jerusalem Studies in Jewish Thought* 1 (1981): 23–84.

———. *Kabbalah: New Perspectives*. New Haven: Yale University Press, 1988.

———. *Language, Torah, and Hermeneutics in Abraham Abulafia*. Albany: State University of New York Press, 1989.

Inowlocki, Sabrina. "Neither Adding nor Omitting Anything: Josephus' Promise Not to Modify the Scripture in Greek and Latin Context." *JJS* 56 (2005): 48–65.

Jacob, Benno. "Unsere Bibel in Wissenschaft und Unterricht." *AZJ* 62 (October 28, November 4, and November 11, 1898): 511–13, 525–26, 534–36.

Jacob, Walter, and Almuth Jürgensen. *Die Exegese hat das Erste Wort: Beiträge zu Leben und Werk Benno Jacobs*. Stuttgart: Calwer Verlag, 2002.

Jacobs, Louis. *The Jewish Religion: A Companion*. Oxford: Oxford University Press, 1995.

———. "The Problem of the Akedah in Jewish Thought." In *Kierkegaard: Fear and Trembling: Critical Appraisals*, edited by Robert L. Perkins, 1–9. Tuscaloosa: University of Alabama Press, 1981.

Jacobson, David C. *Does David Still Play Before You? Israeli Poetry and the Bible*. Detroit: Wayne State University Press, 1997.

———. *Modern Midrash: The Retelling of Traditional Jewish Narratives by Twentieth-Century Hebrew Writers*. Albany: State University of New York Press, 1987.

Jacobson, Joshua R. *Chanting the Hebrew Bible: The Art of Cantillation*. Philadelphia: Jewish Publication Society, 2002.

Jaffee, Martin. "The Return of Amalek: The Politics of Apocalypse and Contemporary Orthodox Jewry." *Conservative Judaism* 63, no. 1 (Fall 2011): 43–68.

Jansen, J. J. G. *The Interpretation of the Koran in Modern Egypt*. Leiden: E. J. Brill, 1974.

Japhet, Sara. "The Ritual of Reading Scripture (Nehemiah 8:1–12)." In *New Perspectives on Old Testament Prophecy and History: Essays in Honor of Hans M. Barstad* (VTSup 168), edited by Rannfrid I. Thelle, Terje Stordalen, and Mervyn E. I. J. Richardson, 175–90. Leiden: Brill, 2015.

Jensen, Robin M. "The Offering of Isaac in Jewish and Christian Tradition, Image and Text." *Biblical Interpretation* 2 (1994): 85–110.

Jindo, Job, Benjamin D. Sommer, and Thomas Staubli, eds. *Yehezkel Kaufmann and the Reinvention of Jewish Biblical Scholarship*. Göttingen: Vandenhoeck & Ruprecht, 2017.

Kabakoff, Jacob. "New Light on Arnold Bogomil Ehrlich." *American Jewish Archives* 36 (1984): 202–24.

Kahle, Paul. *Arabischen Bibelübersetzungen: Texte mit Glossar und Literaturübersicht*. Lepizig; J. C. Hinrichs'sche Buchhuandlung, 1904.

———. "Beiträge zur Geschichte der hebräischen Punktuation." *ZAW* 21 (1901): 273–317.

———. *The Cairo Geniza*. 2nd ed. New York: Frederick E. Praeger, 1959.

Kalimi, Isaac. "Die Bibel und die klassisch-jüdische Bibelauslegung: Eine Interpretations- und religionsgeschichtliche Studie." *ZAW* 114 (2002): 594–610.

Kalin, Everett R. "How Did the Canon Come to Us? A Response to the Leiman Hypothesis." *Currents in Theology and Mission* 4 (February 1, 1977): 47–52.

Kamin, Sarah. "Rashi's Exegetical Categorization with Respect to the Distinction Between Peshat and Derash: According to His Commentary to the

Book of Genesis and Selected Passages from His Commentaries to Other Books of the Bible." *Immanuel* 11 (1980): 16–32.

Kaminka, Armand. "Hillel's Life and Work." *JQR* 30 (1939): 107–22.

Kampf, Avram. *Contemporary Synagogue Art: Developments in the United States, 1945–1965*. Philadelphia: Jewish Publication Society of America, 1966.

Kanarfogel, Ephraim. "On the Role of Bible Study in Medieval Ashkenaz." In *The Frank Talmage Memorial Volume*, vol. 1, edited by Barry Walfish, 151–66. Haifa: Haifa University Press, 1993.

Kaplan, Lawrence. "Samuel David Luzzatto and the Unity of the Book of Isaiah: A Postscript." *Conservative Judaism* 38, no. 2 (Winter 1985–86): 77–81.

Kaplan, Steve, and Meley Mulugetta. "Bible Translations into Ge'ez–Jewish and Christian Contexts." *Pe'amim* 83 (2000): 118–31.

Karff, Samuel E. *Hebrew Union College-Jewish Institute of Religion at One Hundred Years*. Cincinnati: Hebrew Union College Press, 1976.

Kartun-Blum, Ruth. *Profane Scriptures: Reflections on the Dialogue with the Bible in Modern Hebrew Poetry*. Cincinnati: Hebrew Union College Press, 1999.

Kasher, Rimon. "Aramaic Bible Translations." [In Hebrew.] *Pe'amim* 83 (2000): 70–107.

Katz, David S., and Jonathan I. Israel, eds. *Sceptics, Millenarians and Jews*. Leiden: E. J. Brill, 1990.

Katz, Jacob. *Out of the Ghetto: The Social Background of Jewish Emancipation, 1770–1870*. Cambridge: Harvard University Press, 1973.

———. *Toward Modernity: The European Jewish Model*. New Brunswick NJ: Transaction, 1987.

Katz, Peter. "The Early Christians' Use of Codices Instead of Rolls." *JTS* 46 (1945): 63–65.

———. "The Old Testament Canon in Palestine and Alexandria." *ZNW* 47 (1956): 191–217, and 49 (1958): 223.

Katz, Steven T. *Mysticism and Sacred Scripture*. New York: Oxford University Press, 2000.

Katzoff, Louis. "The World Jewish Bible Society." *Immanuel* 20 (1986): 14–17.

Kaufmann, Yehezkel. *The History of Israelite Religion*. [In Hebrew.] Jerusalem: Mosad Bialik; Tel Aviv: Dvir, 1937–56. Translated and abridged by Moshe Greenberg as *The Religion of Israel: From Its Beginnings to the Bablonian Exile*. Chicago: University of Chicago Press, 1960.

Kayserling, M. *Moses Mendelssohn, Sein Leben und Seine Werke*. Leipzig: Hermann Mendelssohn, 1862.

Kemper, Wilhelm Engel. "Die Vorrede Saadja Gaons zu seiner arabischen Übersetzung des Pentateuchs." *Theologische Quartelschrift* 83 (1901): 529–54.

Kena'ani, David. *The Working Aliyah and Its Relationship to Religion and Tradition.* [In Hebrew.]Tel Aviv: Sifriyat ha-Poalim, 1976.

Kennedy, James. *The Note-Line in the Hebrew Scriptures.* Edinburgh: T&T Clark, 1903.

Keren, Michael. *Ben-Gurion and the Intellectuals: Power, Knowledge, and Charisma.* DeKalb IL: Northern Illinois University Press, 1983.

Kessler, Edward. *Bound by the Bible: Jews, Christians and the Sacrifice of Isaac.* Cambridge: Cambridge University Press, 2004.

———. "The Sacrifice of Isaac (the *Akedah*) in Christian and Jewish Tradition: Artistic Representations." In *Borders, Boundaries and the Bible,* edited by Martin O'Kane, 74–98. London: Sheffield Academic Press, 2002.

Kingsley, Ralph P. "The Buber-Rosenzweig Translation of the Bible." *CCAR Journal* 11, no. 4 (January 1964): 17–22.

Kirshenblatt-Gimblett, Barbara. "The Cut that Binds: The Western Ashkenazic Torah Binders as Nexus Between Circumcision and Torah." In *Celebration: Studies in Festivity and Ritual,* edited by Victor Turner, 136–46. Washington DC: Smithsonian Institution Press, 1982.

Klar, Benjamin. "Ben-Asher." *Tarbiz* 14 (1942–43): 156–74; and 15 (1943–44): 36–49.

Klein, Michael L. *The Fragment-Targums of the Pentateuch According to their Extant Sources.* Rome: Biblical Institute Press, 1980.

———. "The Translation of Anthropomorphisms and Anthropopathisms in the Targumim." *Congress Volume Vienne 1980* (VTSup 32). Leiden: E. J. Brill, 1981, 162–77.

Klopfenstein, Martin, Ulrich Luz, Shemaryahu Talmon, and Emanuel Tov. *Mitte der Schrift? Ein jüdisch-christliches Gespräch.* Bern: Peter Lang, 1987.

Knohl, Israel. "Between Voice and Silence: The Relationship Between Prayer and Temple Cult." *JBL* 115 (1996): 17–30.

Knoppers, Gary N., and Bernard M. Levinson. *The Pentateuch as Torah: New Models for Understanding Its Promulgation and Acceptance.* Winona Lake IN: Eisenbrauns, 2007.

Koep, Leo. *Das Himmlische Buch in Antike und Chistentum: Eine Religionsgeschichtliche Untersuchung zur Altchristlichen Bildersprache.* Bonn: Peter Hanstein Verlag, 1952.

Komlosh, Yehuda. *The Bible in the Light of the Aramaic Translations.* [In Hebrew.] Tel Aviv: Dvir, 1973.

Kooij, A. van der, and K. van der Toorn, eds. *Canonization and Decanonization.* Leiden: E. J. Brill, 1998.

Kraemer, David. "The Formation of Rabbinic Canon: Authority and Boundaries." *JBL* 110 (1991): 613–30.

———. *The Mind of the Talmud: An Intellectual History of the Bavli*. New York: Oxford University Press, 1990.
Krapf, Thomas. *Yehezkel Kaufmann, Ein Lebens-und Erkenntnisweg zur Theologie der Hebräischen Bibel*. Berlin: Institut Kirche und Judentum, 1990.
Kugel, James L., ed. *Prayers that Cite Scripture*. Cambridge: Harvard University Press, 2006.
Kugel, James L., and Rowan A. Greer. *Early Biblical Interpretation*. Philadelphia: Westminster, 1986.
Lambert, W. G. "Ancestors, Authors, and Canonicity." *JCS* 11 (1957): 1–14.
Lanczkowski, Günter. *Sacred Writings: A Guide to the Literature of Religions*. New York: Harper & Row, 1961.
Landsberger, Franz. "The Origin of European Torah Decorations." *HUCA* 24 (1952–53): 133–51.
Lang, Bernhard. "Buchreligion." In *Handbuch religionwissenschaftlichter Grundbegriffe*, vol. 2, edited by Hubert Cancik, Burkhard Gladigow, and Matthias Laubscher, 143–65. Stuttgart: Verlag W. Kohlhammer, 1990.
Langer, Ruth. "From Study of Scripture to a Reenactment of Sinai: The Emergence of the Synagogue Torah Service." *Worship* 72 (1998): 43–67.
Lauterbach, Jacob Z. "The Ancient Jewish Allegorists in Talmud and Midrash." *JQR* ns 1 (1911): 291–333, 503–31.
———. *Rabbinic Essays*. Cincinnati: Hebrew Union College Press, 1951.
Lazar, Moshe, ed. *The Ladino Bible of Ferrara, 1553*. Culver City CA: Labyrinthos, 1992.
Le Déaut, Roger. "La Presentation targumique du sacrifice d'Isaac et la Soteriologie Paulienne." In *Studiorum Paulinorum Congressus Internationalis Catholicus 1961*, Vol. 2, 563–74. Rome: Pontifical Biblical Institute, 1963.
Leibowitz, Nechama. *Die Übersetzungs-technik der jüdischen Bibelübersetzungen des 15. Und 16. Jahrhunderts*. Marburg/Halle (Saale): Max Niemeyer, 1931.
Leibowitz, Yeshayahu. "An Interpretation of the Jewish Religion." In *Judaism Crisis Survival: An Anthology of Lectures*, edited by Ann Rose, 30–50. Paris: World Union of Jewish Studies, 1966.
Leiman, Sid (Shnayer) Z. "Abarbanel and the Censor." *JJS* 19 (1968): 49–61.
———. *The Canonization of Hebrew Scripture: The Talmudic and Midrashic Evidence* (Transactions of the Connecticut Academy of Arts and Sciences 47 [Feburary, 1976] 1–234; Hamden CT: Archon, 1976).
———. "Hazon Ish on Textual Criticism and Halakhah–A Rejoinder." *Tradition* 19 (1981): 301–10.
———. "Masorah and Halakhah: A Study in Conflict." In *Tehillah le-Moshe: Biblical and Judaic Studies in Honor of Moshe Greenberg*, edited by Morde-

chai Cogan, Barry L. Eichler, and Jeffrey H. Tigay, 291–306. Winona Lake IN: Eisenbrauns, 1997.

Leipoldt, Johannes, and Siegfried Morenz. *Heilige Schriften: Betrachtungen zur Religionsgeschichte der Antiken Mittelmeerwelt*. Leipzig: Otto Harrassowitz, 1953.

Lenowitz, Harris. "Shukr Kuhayl II Reads the Bible." In *Sacred Text, Secular Times: The Hebrew Bible in the Modern World*, edited by Leonard Jay Greenspoon and Bryan F. LeBeau, 245–66. Omaha: Creighton University Press, 2000.

Levenson, Alan T. *The Making of the Modern Jewish Bible: How Scholars in Germany, Israel and America Transformed an Ancient Text*. Lanham: Rowman & Littlefield, 2011.

———. "The Rise of Modern Jewish Bible Studies: Preliminary Reflections." In *Biblical Interpretation in Judaism and Christianity*, edited by Isaac Kalimi and Peter J. Haas, 163–78. New York: T&T Clark, 2006.

Levenson, Jon D. *The Death and Resurrection of the Beloved Son: The Transformation of Child Sacrifice in Judaism and Christianity*. New Haven: Yale University Press, 1993.

———. "The Eighth Principle of Judaism and the Literary Simultaneity of Scripture." *JR* 68 (1988): 205–25.

———. *Inheriting Abraham: The Legacy of the Patriarch in Judaism, Christianity, and Islam*. Princeton NJ: Princeton University Press, 2012.

———. "Religious Affirmation and Historical Criticism in Heschel's Biblical Interpretation." *AJS Review* 25 (2000–2001): 25–44.

———. "Theological Consensus or Historicist Evasion? Jews and Christians in Biblical Studies." In *Hebrew Bible or Old Testament? Studying the Bible in Judaism and Christianity*, edited by Roger Brooks and John J. Collins, 109–45. Notre Dame IN: University of Notre Dame, 1990.

Levering, Miriam, ed. *Rethinking Scripture: Essays from a Comparative Perspective*. Albany: State University of New York Press, 1989.

Lévi, Israel. "Le Sacrifice d'Isaac et la Mort de Jésus." *REJ* 64 (1912): 161–84.

Levin, Saul. "From Scrolls to Codex: The Ancient and the Medieval Book." *Mediaevalia* 12 (1989–86): 1–12.

Levinas, Emmanuel. "The Jewish Understanding of Scripture." *Cross Currents* 44 (1995): 488–504.

———. "Loving the Torah More than God." Translated by Sean Hand. In *Difficult Freedom: Essays on Judaism*, 142–45. Baltimore: Johns Hopkins University Press, 1990.

Levine, Baruch A. "A Decade of Jewish Bible Scholarship in North America." *Jewish Book Annual* 39 (1981–82): 19–29.

Levine, Etan. *The Aramaic Version of the Bible: Contents and Context* (Bzaw 174). Berlin: Walter de Gruyter, 1988.
Levine, Lee I. *The Ancient Synagogue: The First Thousand Years*. New Haven: Yale University Press, 2000.
Levine, Yael. "'The Woman of Valor' in Jewish Ritual (Proverbs 31:1–31)." [In Hebrew.] *Beth Mikra* 31 (1985–86): 339–47.
Levinson, Bernard M. "Esarhaddon's Succession Treaty as the Source for the Canon Formula in Deuteronomy 13:1." *JAOS* 130 (2010): 337–47.
Levy, B. Barry. *Fixing God's Torah: The Accuracy of the Hebrew Bible Text in Jewish Law*. New York: Oxford University Press, 2001.
———. "Rabbinic Bibles, Mikra'ot Gedolot, and Other Great Books." *Tradition* 25, no. 4 (Summer 1991): 65–81.
Levy, Isaac. *The Synagogue: Its History and Function*. London: Vallentine, Mitchell, 1963.
Lewis, Jack P. "What Do We Mean by Jabneh?" *JBR* 32 (1964): 125–32.
Lieberman, Saul. *Hellenism in Jewish Palestine*. New York: Jewish Theological Seminary of America, 1950.
Lieberman, Stephen J. "A Mesopotamian Background for the So-Called Aggadic 'Measures' of Biblical Hermeneutics?" *HUCA* 58 (1987): 157–225.
Liebman, Charles S., and Eliezer Don-Yehiya. *Civil Religion in Israel: Traditional Judaism and Political Culture in the Jewish State*. Berkeley: University of California Press, 1983.
Leibowitz, Nechama. *Die Übersetzungs-technik der jüdischen Bibelübersetzungen des 15. Und 16. Jahrhunderts*. Marburg/Halle [Saale]: Max Niemeyer, 1931.
Lightstone, Jack N. "The Formation of the Biblical Canon in Judaism of Late Antiquity: Prolegomenon to a General Reassessment." *Studies in Religion* 8 (1979): 135–42.
Lim, Timothy H. "The Alleged Reference to the Tripartite Division of the Hebrew Bible." *RQ* 20 (2001): 23–37.
———. *The Formation of the Jewish Canon*. New Haven: Yale University Press, 2013.
Lipschütz, Lazar. "Kitāb al-Khilaf, The Book of the Ḥillufim: Mishael ben Uzziel's Treatise on the Differences between Ben Asher and Ben Naphtali." *Textus* 4 (1964): 1–29.
Lockshin, Martin. "Moses Wrote the Torah: Rashbam's Perspective." *HUCA* 84–85 (2015): 109–25.
———. "Tradition in Context: Two Exegetes Struggle with Peshat." In *From Ancient Israel to Modern Judaism: Intellect in Quest of Understanding*, vol. 2, edited by Jacob Neusner, Ernest S. Frerichs, and Nahum M. Sarna, 173–86. Atlanta: Scholars Press, 1989.

Loewe, Raphael J. "The Bible in Medieval Poetry." In *Interpreting the Hebrew Bible: Essays in Honour of E.I.J. Rosenthal*, edited by J. A. Emerton and Stefan C. Reif, 133–55. Cambridge: Cambridge University Press, 1982.

———. "The 'Plain' Meaning of Scripture in Early Jewish Exegesis." *Papers of the Institute of Jewish Studies* (University College, London) 1 (1964): 140–85.

Loewinger, D. S. "The Aleppo Codex and the Ben Asher Tradition." *Textus* 1 (1960): 59–111.

Lowenstein, Steven M. "The Readership of Mendelssohn's Bible Translation." *HUCA* 53 (1982): 179–213.

Lubac, Henri de. *Medieval Exegesis: The Four Senses of Scripture*. Grand Rapids: William B. Eerdmans, 1998–2000.

Luz, Ehud. "How to Read the Bible According to Leo Strauss." *Modern Judaism* 25 (2005): 264–84.

———. *Parallels Meet: Religion and Nationalism in the Early Zionist Movement, 1882–1904*. Philadelphia: Jewish Publication Society, 1988.

———. "Zion and Judenstaat: The Significance of the 'Uganda' Controversy." In *Essays in Modern Jewish History: A Tribute to Ben Halpern*, edited by Frances Malino and Phillis Cohen Albert, 217–39. Rutherford NJ: Farleigh Dickinson University Press, 1982.

Mach, Dafna. "Martin Buber und die jüdische Bibel." In *Martin Buber (1878–1965) internationales Symposium zum 20. Todestag*, vol. 1, edited by Werner Licharz and Heinz Schmidt, 198–210. Frankfort am Main: Haag und Herchen, 1989.

Madelung, Wilferd. "The Origins of the Controversy Concerning the Creation of the Koran." In *Orientalia Hispanica, sive Studia F.M. Pareja octogenaria dicata*, vol. 1, edited by J. M. Barral, 504–25. Leiden: Brill, 1974.

Magonet, Jonathan. "How Do Jews Interpret the Bible Today?" *JSOT* 66 (1995): 3–27.

Malachi, A. R. "Yiddish Translation of the Bible." *Jewish Book Annual* 21 (1963–64): 22–40. (Yiddish).

Maman, Aharon. "The Maghrebi Sharḥ of the Bible." *Pe'amim* 83 (2000): 48–56.

Mann, Jacob. "Anan's Liturgy and His Half-Yearly Cycle of the Reading of the Law." *Journal of Jewish Lore and Philosophy* 1 (1919): 329–53.

———. *The Bible as Read and Preached in the Old Synagogue*. New York: Ktav, 1971.

———. "Changes in the Divine Service of the Synagogue due to Religious Persecutions." *HUCA* 4 (1927): 241–310.

———. *The Jews in Egypt and in Palestine under the Fatimid Caliphs*. London: Oxford University Press, 1920; repr.: New York: Ktav, 1970.

———. "A New Midrash on the Torah to Genesis and Exodus." [In Hebrew.]

In *The Bible as Read and Preached in the Old Synagogue*, vol. 1, 44–68. New York: Ktav, 1971.
———. "Some Midrashic Genizah Fragments." *HUCA* 14 (1939): 303–58.
Manns, Frédéric. *The Sacrifice of Isaac in the Three Monotheistic Religions*. Jerusalem: Franciscan, 1995.
Manor, Dalia. "Biblical Zionism in Bezalel Art." *Israel Studies* 6 (2001): 55–75.
Manuel, Frank E. *The Broken Staff: Judaism through Christian Eyes*. Cambridge: Harvard University Press, 1992.
Maori, Yeshayahu. "The Approach of Classical Jewish Exegetes to Peshat and Derash and its Implications for the Teaching of Bible Today." *Tradition* 21, no. 3 (Fall 1984): 40–53.
Marcus, Ivan G. *Rituals of Childhood: Jewish Acculturation in Medieval Europe*. New Haven: Yale University Press, 1996.
Margolies, Morris B. *Samuel David Luzzatto, Traditionalist Scholar*. New York: Ktav, 1979.
Margolis, Max L. "The Scope and Methodology of Biblical Philology." *JQR* ns 1 (1910): 5–41.
———. *The Story of Bible Translations*. Philadelphia: Jewish Publication Society of America, 1943.
Margulies, Mordecai. *The Differences Between Babylonian and Palestinian Jews*. Jerusalem: Reuven Mass, 1938.
Marmorstein, A. "Der Midrasch (*Shney Ketuvim*) von den Widersprüchen in der Bibel." *MGWJ* 73 (1929): 281–92.
Marx, Moses. "Gershom (Hieronymus) Soncino's Wander Years in Italy, 1498–1527: Exempla Judaicae Vitae." *HUCA* 11 (1936): 427–501.
Masalha, Nur. *The Bible and Zionism, Invented Traditions: Archaeology and Post-Colonialism in Palestine-Israel*. New York: Zed, 2007.
Mastnjak, Nathan. "Jeremiah as Collection: Scrolls, Sheets, and the Problems of Textual Arrangement." *CBQ* 80 (2018): 25–44.
Mazor, Leah. "On Bible and Zionism: The Tribal Conception of Territory as Reflected in Israeli Place Names During the First Years of Statehood." [In Hebrew.] *Cathedra* 110 (2003–2004): 101–22.
———. "Translation of the Bible into Hebrew: The RAM Bible by Avraham Ahuvia." [In Hebrew.] *Beth Mikra* (2009): 126–66.
McCarthy, Dennis J. *Treaty and Covenant*. Rome: Pontifical Biblical Institute, 1981.
McCleod, W. H. "The Sikh Scriptures: Some Issues." In *Sikh Studies: Comparative Perspectives on a Changing Tradition*, edited by Mark Juergensmeyer and N. Gerald Barnes, 97–111. Berkeley CA: Graduate Theological Union, 1979.

McDannell, Colleen. *Material Christianity: Religion and Popular Culture in America*. New Haven: Yale University Press, 1995.
McDonald, Lee Martin. *Forgotten Scriptures: The Selection and Rejection of Early Religious Writings*. Louisville: Westminster John Knox, 2009.
McDonald, Lee Martin, and James A. Sanders, eds. *The Canon Debate*. Peabody MA: Hendrickson, 2002.
McLuhan, Marshall. *The Gutenberg Galaxy: The Making of Typographic Man*. Toronto: University of Toronto Press, 1962.
McNamara, Martin. *The New Testament and the Palestinian Targum to the Pentateuch*. 2nd printing. Rome: Biblical Institute Press, 1978.
Meirovich, Harvey. "Reclaiming Chief Rabbi Hertz as a Conservative Jew." *Conservative Judaism* 46, no. 4 (Summer 1994): 3–23.
———. *A Vindication of Judaism: The Polemics of the Hertz Pentateuch*. New York: Jewish Theological Seminary of America, 1998.
Melamed, Ezra-Zion. *Biblical Commentators*. [In Hebrew.] Jerusalem: Magnes, 1978.
Merchavia, Chenmelech. *The Church Versus Talmudic and Midrashic Literature (500–1248)*. [In Hebrew.] Jerusalem: Bialik Institute, 1970.
Meshel, Naftali. "Translating the Hebrew Bible from Hebrew into Hebrew." *HS* 57 (2016): 39–50.
Meyer, Michael A. "Alienated Intellectuals in the Camp of Religious Reform: The Frankfurt Reformfreunde, 1842–1845." *AJS Review* 6 (1981): 61–86.
———. *Response to Modernity: A History of the Reform Movement in Judaism*. New York: Oxford University Press, 1988.
Meyers, Eric. "The Torah Shrine in the Ancient Synagogue: Another Look at the Evidence." In *Jews, Christians, and Polytheists in the Ancient Synagogue*, edited by Steven Fine, 201–23. London: Routledge, 1999.
Mielziener, Moses. *Introduction to the Talmud*. 3rd ed. New York: Bloch, 1925.
Milgrom, Josephine Berman. *The Binding of Isaac: The Akedah, A Primary Symbol in Jewish Thought and Art*. Berkeley: Bibal, 1988.
Millard., A. R. "'Scriptio Continua' in Early Hebrew: Ancient Practice or Modern Surmise?" *JSS* 15 (1970): 2–15.
Miller, Patrick D., Jr. "Psalms and Inscriptions." *Congress Volume Vienne 1980* (VTSup 32). Leiden: E. J. Brill, 1981, 311–32.
Milson, David. *Art and Architecture of the Synagogue in Late Antique Palestine: In the Shadow of the Church*. Leiden: Brill, 2007.
Mintz, Alan. *Ḥurban: Responses to Catastrophe in Hebrew Literature*. New York: Columbia University Press, 1984.
Mirsky, Aaron. "The Power of the Bible in Sephardic Poetry." [In Hebrew.] *Sinai* 73 (1973): 19–23.

Moberly, R. W. L. "The Earliest Commentary on the Akedah." *VT* 38 (1988): 302–23.
Modona, Leonello. "Un Mot sur Deux Versions du Pentateuque." *REJ* 23 (1891): 134–36.
Montefiore, C. G. "Some Notes on the Effect of Biblical Criticism upon the Jewish Religion." *JQR* OS 4 (1892): 293–306.
Moore, George Foot. "The Vulgate Chapters and Numbered Verses in the Hebrew Bible." *JBL* 12 (1893): 73–78.
Mordell, Phineas. "The Beginning and Development of Hebrew Punctuation." *JQR* 24 (1933): 137–49.
Morenz, Siegfried. "Entstehung und Wesen der Buchreligion." *TLZ* 75 (1950): 709–16.
Morgenstern, Matthias. "Jüdisch-orthodoxie Wege zur Bibelkritik." *Judaica* 56 (2000): 178–92, 234–50.
Mroczek, Eva. "Thinking Digitally About the Dead Sea Scrolls: Book History Before and Beyond the Book." *Book History* 14 (2011): 241–69.
Muilenberg, James. "Buber as an Interpreter of the Bible." In *The Philosophy of Martin Buber*, edited by Paul Arthur Schilpp and Maurice Friedman, 381–402. LaSalle IL: Open Court, 1967.
Mulder, Martin Jan, ed. *Mikra: Text, Translation, Reading, and Interpretation of the Hebrew Bible in Ancient Judaism and Early Christianity*. Assen/Maastricht: Van Gorcum and Philadelphia: Fortress, 1988.
Myers, David N. *Re-Inventing the Jewish Past: European Jewish Intellectuals and the Zionist Return to History*. New York: Oxford University Press, 1995.
Nadler, Steven. *Spinoza: A Life*. Cambridge: Cambridge University Press, 1999.
Naeh, Shlomo. "The Torah Reading Cycle in Early Palestine: A Re-Examination." [In Hebrew.] *Tarbiz* 67 (1997–98): 167–87.
Najman, Hindy. *Seconding Sinai: The Development of Mosaic Discourse in Second Temple Judaism*. Leiden: Brill, 2003.
Narkiss, Bezalel. "The Heikhal, Bimah, and Teivah in Sephardi Synagogues." *Jewish Art* 18 (1992): 30–47.
Naudé, J. A. "A Descriptive Translation Analysis of the Schocken Bible." *OTE* 12 (1999): 73–93.
Naveh, Joseph. "Word Division in West Semitic Writing." *IEJ* 23 (1973): 206–8.
Nemoy, Leon. "Al-Qirqisānī's Account of the Jewish Sects and Christianity." *HUCA* 7 (1930): 317–97.
———. *Karaite Anthology: Excerpts from the Early Literature*. New Haven: Yale University Press, 1952.
Nestle, Eb. "Wie alt war Isaak bei der Opferung?" *ZAW* 26 (1906): 281–82.

Neubauer, Adolf. "The Hebrew Bible in Shorthand Writing." *JQR* os 7 (1895): 361–64.

Neusner, Jacob. *Torah From Scroll to Symbol in Formative Judaism*. Philadelphia: Fortress, 1985.

Neusner, Jacob, with William Scott Green. *Writing with Scripture: The Authority and Uses of the Hebrew Bible in the Torah of Formative Judaism*. Minneapolis: Fortress, 1989.

Newman, Judith H. *Praying By the Book: The Scripturalization of Prayer in Second Temple Judaism*. Atlanta: Scholars Press, 1999.

Nickelsburg, George W. E. "The Bible Rewritten and Expanded." In *Jewish Writings of the Second Temple Period*, edited by Micheel Stone, 89–156. Philadelphia: Fortress; Assen: Van Gorcus, 1984.

Nida, Eugene A. *Toward a Science of Translating, With Special Reference to Principles and Procedures Involved in Bible Translating*. Leiden: E. J. Brill, 1964.

Niehoff, Maren R. *Jewish Exegesis and Homeric Scholarship in Alexandria*. New York: Cambridge University Press, 2011.

Nielsen, Bruce. "Daniel van Bombergen, A Bookman of Two Worlds." In *The Hebrew Book in Early Modern Italy*, edited by Joseph R. Hacker and Adam Shear, 56–75. Philadelphia: University of Pennsylvania Press, 2011.

Nikiprowetzky, V. "L'exégèse de Philon d'Alexandrie." *Revue d'Histoire et de Philosophie Religieuses* 53 (1973): 309–29.

Nikolasch, Franz. "Zur Ikonographie des Widders von Gen 22." *VigChr* 23 (1969): 197–223.

Noort, Ed, and Eibert Tigchelaar, eds. *The Sacrifice of Isaac: The Aqedah (Genesis 22) and Its Interpretations*. Leiden: E. J. Brill, 2002.

Novak, David. "Jews, Christians, and Biblical Authority." In *Contesting Texts: Jews and Christians in Conversation about the Bible*, edited by Melody D. Knowles, Esther Menn, John Pawlikowski OSM, and Timothy J. Sandoval, 29–45. Minneapolis: Fortress, 2007.

Nünlist, René. "What Does *Omēron ex Omerou saphēnisein* Actually Mean?" *Hermes* 143 (2015): 385–403.

Offenberg, Adrian K. "Hebrew Printing of the Bible in the XVth Century." In *The Bible as Book: The First Printed Editions*, edited by Paul Saenger and Kimberly van Kampen, 71–77. London: British Library and Oak Knoll, 1999.

O'Flaherty, Wendy Doniger. *The Critical Study of Sacred Texts*. Berkeley: Graduate Theological Union, 1979.

Ofrat, Gideon. *The Binding of Isaac in Israeli Art*. [In Hebrew.] Ramat-Gan: Museum of Israeli Art, n.d., catalog #6.

Ong, Walter. *Orality and Literacy: The Technologizing of the Word*. London: Routledge, 1991.

Oppenheimer, A. Leo. *The Interpretation of Dreams in the Ancient Near East with a Translation of an Assyrian Dream Book.* Philadelphia: American Philosophical Society, 1956.

Orlinsky, Harry M. "Jewish Biblical Scholarship in America." *JQR* 45 (1954–55): 374–412.

———. "A Jewish Scholar Looks at the Revised Standard Version and Its New Edition." *Religious Education* 85 (1990): 211–21.

———. *Notes on the New Translation of the Torah.* Philadelphia: Jewish Publication Society of America, 1970.

———. "Yehoash's Yiddish Translation of the Bible." *JBL* 60 (1941): 173–77.

Orlinsky, Harry M., and Robert G. Bratcher. *A History of Bible Translation and the North American Contribution.* Atlanta: Scholars Press, 1991.

Parker, Simon. "Pushing the Limits: Issues in Jewish Bible Translation." In *Ḥesed ve-Emet: Studies in Honor of Ernest S. Frerichs,* edited by Jodi Magness and Seymour Gitin, 73–79. Atlanta: Scholars Press, 1998.

Parmenter, Donna Miller. "The Iconic Book: The Image of the Bible in Early Christian Rituals." In *Iconic Books and Texts,* edited by James W. Watts, 63–92. Sheffield: Equinox, 2013.

Pasto, James. "When the End Is the Beginning? Or When the Biblical Past Is the Political Present: Some Thoughts on Ancient Israel, Post-Exilic Judaism and the Politics of Biblical Scholarship." *SJOT* 12 (1998): 161–64.

———. "W. M. L. DeWette and the Invention of Post-Exilic Judaism: Political Historiography and Christian Allegory in Nineteenth-Century German Biblical Scholarship." In *Jews, Antiquity, and the Nineteenth-Century Imagination,* edited by Hayim Lapin and Dale B. Martin, 34–43. Bethesda: University Press of Maryland, 2003.

Pattison, Robert. *On Literacy: The Politics of the Word from Homer to the Age of Rock.* New York: Oxford University Press, 1982.

Pelikan, Jaroslav. *Whose Bible Is It? A History of the Scriptures Through the Ages.* New York: Viking, 2005.

Penkower, Jordan S. "The Chapter Divisions in the 1525 Rabbinic Bible." *VT* 48 (1998): 350–74.

———. "Jacob ben Hayyim and the Rise of the Biblia Rabbinica." [In Hebrew.] PhD diss., Hebrew University, 1982.

———. "Verse Divisions in the Hebrew Bible." *VT* 50 (2000): 379–93.

Perles, Felix. "What Is Biblical Studies for Us?" [In Hebrew.] Jerusalem: n.p., 1927.

Perlman, Lawrence. "As a Report About Revelation, the Bible Itself Is a Midrash." *Conservative Judaism* 55, no. 1 (Fall 2002): 30–37.

Perrot, Charles. "*Petuḥot et Setumot*: Ètude sur les alinéas du Pentateuque." *RB* 76 (1969): 50–91.

Petroski, Henry. *The Book on the Bookshelf*. New York: Alfred A. Knopf, 1999.

Petuchowski, Jakob J. "The Bible of the Synagogue: The Continuing Revelation." *Commentary* 27 (February 1959): 142–50.

———. *Ever Since Sinai: A Modern View of Torah*. New York: Scribe, 1961.

———. "Karaite Tendencies in an Early Reform Haggadah: A Study in Comparative Liturgy." *HUCA* 31 (1960): 223–49.

———. "The Liturgy of the Synagogue: History, Structure, and Contents." In *Approaches to Ancient Judaism IV*, edited by W. S. Green, 1–64. Chico: Scholars Press, 1983.

———. "The Magnification of Chanukah: Afterthoughts on a Festival." *Commentary* 29, no. 1 (January 1960): 38–43.

———. "Manuals and Catechisms of the Jewish Religion in the Early Period of Emancipation." In *Studies in Nineteenth-Century Jewish Intellectual History*, edited by Alexander Altmann, 47–64. Cambridge MA: Harvard University Press, 1964.

———. *Prayerbook Reform in Europe: The Liturgy of European Liberal and Reform Judaism*. New York: World Union for Progressive Judaism, 1968.

———. "Reform Benedictions for Rabbinic Ordinances: A Chapter in the History of European Liberal and Reform Liturgy." *HUCA* 37 (1966): 175–89.

Philipson, David. *The Reform Movement in Judaism*. New and rev. ed. New York: Macmillan, 1931.

Pick, B. "The Vowel-Points Controversy in the XVI and XVII Centuries." *Hebraica* 8 (1891–92): 150–73.

Pinsker, Simcha. *Liqqutei Qadmoniot: Zur Geschichte des Karaismus und der karäischen Literatur*. [In Hebrew.] Vienna: Adalbert della Torre, 1860.

Plaut, W. Gunther. "German-Jewish Bible Translations: Linguistic Theology as a Political Phenomenon." The Leo Baeck Memorial Lecture 36. New York: Leo Baeck Institute, 1992.

———. *The Growth of Reform Judaism: American and European Sources Until 1948*. New York: World Union for Progressive Judaism, 1965.

Pollack, Herman. *Jewish Folkways in Germanic Lands (1648–1800): Studies in Aspects of Daily Life*. Cambridge: MIT Press, 1971.

Polliack, Meira. "Alternate Renderings and Additions in Yeshu'ah ben Yehudah's Arabic Translation of the Pentateuch." *JQR* 84 (1993–94): 209–25.

———. *The Karaite Tradition of Arabic Bible Translation: A Linguistic and Exegetical Study of Karaite Translations of the Pentateuch from the Tenth and Eleventh Centuries C.E.* Leiden: E. J. Brill, 1997.

———. "Medieval Karaite Methods of Translating Biblical Narrative into Arabic." *VT* 48 (1998): 375–98.
———. "Medieval Karaite Views on Translating the Hebrew Bible into Arabic." *JJS* 47 (1996): 64–84.
Polzin, Robert M., and Eugene Rothman, eds. *The Biblical Mosaic: Changing Perspectives*. Philadelphia: Fortress; Chico CA: Scholars Press, 1982.
Pool, David de Sola. "Hebrew Learning Among the Puritans of New England Prior to 1700." *Publications of the American Jewish Historical Society* 20 (1911): 31–83.
Popkin, Richard H. *The History of Scepticism From Erasmus to Spinoza*. Berkeley: University of California Press, 1979.
———. "Newton and Spinoza and the Bible Scholarship of the Day." In *Rethinking the Scientific Revolution*, edited by Margaret J. Osler, 297–311. Cambridge: Cambridge University Press, 2000.
———. "Spinoza and Bible Scholarship." In *The Books of Nature and Scripture: Recent Essays on Natural Philosophy, Theology, and Biblical Criticism in the Netherlands of Spinoza's Time and the British Isles of Newton's Time*, edited by James E. Force and Richard H. Popkin, 1–20. Dordrecht: Kluwer Academic, 1994.
Porat, Dina. *The Blue and the Yellow Stars of David: The Zionist Leadership in Palestine and the Holocaust, 1939–1945*. Cambridge MA: Harvard University Press, 1990.
Posner, Raphel, and Israel Ta-Shema, eds. *The Hebrew Book: An Historical Survey*. Jerusalem: Keter, 1975.
Poznanski, Samuel. "Anan et ses Écrits." *REJ* 44 (1902): 161–87, and 45 (1902): 50–69, 176–203.
———. "The Anti-Karaite Writings of Saadiah Gaon." *JQR* OS 10 (1898): 238–76.
Preus, J. Samuel. *Spinoza and the Irrelevance of Biblical Authority*. Cambridge: Cambridge University Press, 2001.
Provoyeur, Pierre. *Marc Chagall: Biblical Interpretations*. New York: Alpine Fine Arts Collection, 1983.
Puech, Émile. "Qumrân et le Texte de l'ancien Testament." *Congress Volume Oslo 1998* (VTSup 80). Leiden: E. J. Brill, 2000, 437–64.
Rabin, Haim. "The Linguistic Investigation of the Language of Jewish Prayer." [In Hebrew.] In *Studies in Aggadah, Targum and Jewish Liturgy*, edited by Jakob J. Petuchowski and Ezra Fleischer, 163–71. Jerusalem: Magnes and Hebrew Union College Press, 1981.
Rabinowitz, Louis I. "Abravanel as Exegete." In *Isaac Abravanel: Six Lectures*, edited by J. B. Trend and H. Loewe, 75–92. Cambridge: Cambridge University Press, 1937.

———. "The Psalms in Jewish Liturgy." *Historia Judaica* 6 (1944): 109–22.

Rajak, Tessa. *Translation and Survival: The Greek Bible of the Ancient Jewish Diaspora*. Oxford: Oxford University Press, 2009.

Rawidowicz, Simon. "Mendelssohn's Translation of Psalms." [In Hebrew.] In *Sefer Klausner*, edited by N. H. Torczyner, A. Albek, A. Tcherikover, and B. Schachter, 203–301. Tel Aviv: Vaad HaYovel, 1933–34.

———. *Studies in Jewish Thought*. Philadelphia: Jewish Publication Society, 1974.

Reeves, John C. "Problematizing the Bible . . . Then and Now." *JQR* 100 (2010): 139–52.

Reider, Joseph. *Prolegomena to a Greek-Hebrew and Hebrew-Greek Index to Aquila*. Philadelphia: Dropsie College, 1916.

Reif, Stefan C. "The Bible in the Liturgy." In *The Jewish Study Bible*, edited by Adele Berlin and Marc Zvi Brettler, 1937–48. New York: Oxford University Press, 2004.

———. *Judaism and Hebrew Prayer: New Perspectives on Jewish Liturgical History*. Cambridge: Cambridge University Press, 1993.

———. *Problems with Prayers: Studies in the Textual History of Early Rabbinic Liturgy*. Berlin: Walter de Gruyter, 2006.

———. *Shabbethai Sofer and His Prayer-Book*. Cambridge: Cambridge University Press, 1979.

Resnick, Irven M. "The Codex in Early Jewish and Christian Communities." *Journal of Religious History* 17 (1992): 1–17.

Revell, E. J. "Biblical Punctuation and Chant in the Second Temple Period." *JSJ* 7 (1976): 181–98.

———. "The Oldest Evidence for the Hebrew Accent System." *BJRL* 54 (1971–72): 214–22.

———. "Pausal Forms in Biblical Hebrew: Their Function, Origin and Significance." *JSS* 25 (1980): 165–79.

Rippin, Andrew. "Sa'adya Gaon and Genesis 22: Aspects of Jewish-Muslim Interaction and Polemics." *Studies in Islamic and Judaic Traditions*, edited by William M. Brinner and Stephen D. Ricks, 33–47. Atlanta: Scholars Press, 1986.

Rivlin, Joseph Joel."Saadya's Commentary to the Torah Deduced from His Translation."[In Hebrew.] *Tarbiz* 20 (1949): 133–60.

Roberts, Bleddyn J. "The Emergence of the Tiberian Massoretic Text." *JTS* 49 (1948): 8–16.

———. "The Hebrew Bible Since 1937." *JTS* 15 (1964): 233–64.

Roberts, Colin H., and T. C. Skeat. *The Birth of the Codex*. London: British Academy, 1983.

Rojtman, Betty. *Black Fire on White Fire: An Essay on Jewish Hermeneutics from Midrash to Kabbalah*. Berkeley: University of California Press, 1998.
Rosenbloom, Noah. *Malbim, Interpretation, Phlosophy, Science and Mystery in the Writings of Rabbi Meir Leibush Malbim*. [In Hebrew.] Jerusalem: Mosad Harav Kook, 1988.
Rosensaft, Jean Bloch. *Chagall and the Bible*. New York: Universe, 1987.
Rosenthal, Erwin I. J. "Anti-Christian Polemic in Medieval Bible Commentaries." *JJS* 11 (1960): 115–35.
———. "Medieval Jewish Exegesis: Its Character and Significance." *JSS* 9 (1964): 265–81.
———. "Saadya Gaon: An Appreciation of His Biblical Exegesis." *BJRL* 27 (1942–43): 168–78.
Rosenthal, Judah. *Ḥiwi al-Balkhi: A Comparative Study*. Philadelphia: Dropsie College for Hebrew and Cognate Learning, 1949.
———. "*She'elot 'Atiqot ba-Tanak*." [In Hebrew.] *HUCA* 21 (1948): 29–91.
Rosenwald, Lawrence. "On the Reception of Buber and Rosenzweig's Bible." *Prooftexts* 14 (1994): 141–65.
Rosenzweig, Adolf. "Die Al-tikri-Deutungen." In *Festschrift zu Israel Lewy's Siebzigsten Geburtstag*, edited by M. Brann and J. Elbogen, 204–53. Breslau: M. & H. Marcus, 1911.
Rosin, David. "Die Zunz'sche Bibel." *MGWJ* 38 (1893–94): 504–14.
Roth, Cecil. "Jewish Antecedents of Christian Art." *Journal of the Warburg and Courtauld Institutes* 16 (1953): 24–44.
———. "The Marrano Press at Ferrara, 1552–1555." *Modern Language Review* 38 (1943): 307–17.
Rovner, Adam. *In the Shadow of Zion: Promised Lands Before Israel*. New York: New York University Press, 2014.
Rubenstein, Amnon. *The Zionist Dream Revisited: From Herzl to Gush Emunim and Back*. New York: Schocken, 1984.
Rubinstein, Aryeh. "Isaac Mayer Wise: A New Appraisal." *Jewish Social Studies* 39 (1977): 53–74.
Ruderman, David B. *The World of a Renaissance Jew: The Life and Thought of Abraham ben Mordecai Farisol*. Cincinnati: HUC Press, 1981.
Ryle, Herbert Edward. *The Canon of the Old Testament: An Essay on the Gradual Growth and Formation of the Hebrew Canon of Scripture*. 2nd ed. London: Macmillan, 1904.
Sabar, Shalom. "Torah and Magic: The Torah Scroll and Its Accessories in Jewish Culture in Europe and Muslim Countries." [In Hebrew.] *Pe'amim* 85 (Spring 2001): 149–79.

Sabar, Yona. *The Book of Genesis in Neo-Aramaic in the Dialect of the Jewish Community of Zakho.* Jerusalem: Magnes, 1983.

———. "Loyalty and Deviation in the Jewish Neo-Aramaic Translations of the Bible." [In Hebrew.] *Leš* 46 (1981–82): 124–40.

———. "The Pentateuch in Neo-Aramaic–Overview." [In Hebrew.] *Pe'amim* 83 (2000): 108–17.

Saebø, Magne, ed. *Hebrew Bible/Old Testament, The History of Its Interpretation.* Vol. 1. Göttingen: Vandenhoeck & Ruprecht, 1996–2000.

Safrai, Ze'ev. "The Origins of Reading the Aramaic Targum in Synagogue." *Immanuel* 24/25 (1990): 187–93.

Sagi, Avi. "Contending with Modernity: Scripture in the Thought of Yeshayahu Leibowitz and Joseph Soloveitchik." *JR* 77 (1997): 421–41.

———. "The Meaning of the *Akedah* in Israeli Culture and Jewish Tradition." *Israel Studies* 3 (1998): 45–60.

———. "Unity of Scripture Constituted through Jewish Traditions of Interpretation." In *One Scripture or Many? Canon from Biblical, Theological, and Philosophical Perspectives,* edited by Christine Helmer and Christof Landmesser, 186–216. Oxford: Oxford University Press, 2004.

Salomon, David A. *An Introduction to the* Glossa Ordinaria *as Medieval Hypertext.* Cardiff: University of Wales Press, 2012.

Salvesen, Alison. "A Convergence of the Ways? The Judaizing of Christian Scripture by Origen and Jerome." In *The Ways That Never Parted: Jews and Christians in Late Antiquity and the Early Middle Ages*, edited by Adam H. Becker and Annette Yoshiko-Reed, 233–57. Tübingen: J. C. B. Mohr [Paul Siebeck], 2003.

Sambursky, Shmuel. "The Term *Gematria*—Source and Meaning." [In Hebrew.] *Tarbiz* 45 (1976–77): 268–71.

Samely, Alexander. "Between Scripture and Its Rewording: Towards a Classification of Rabbinic Exegesis." *JJS* 42 (1991): 39–67.

Sandler, Peretz. *Mendelssohn's Edition of the Pentatuch.* [In Hebrew.] Jerusalem: Rubin Mass, 1940.

———. "On the Question of 'Pardes' and the Fourfold Method." [In Hebrew.] In *The Urbach Volume: Essays in Biblical Studies in Honor of Eliyahu Urbach at the Completion of 70 Years,* edited by A. Biram, 222–35. Jeruslaem: Kiryat Sefer, 1955.

Sandmel, Samuel. "The Haggada Within Scripture." *JBL* 80 (1961): 105–22.

———. *Philo of Alexandria: An Introduction.* New York: Oxford University Press, 1979.

Saperstein, Marc. *Jewish Preaching, 1200–1800: An Anthology.* New Haven: Yale University Press, 1989.

Sarna, Jonathan D. *JPS: The Americanization of Jewish Culture, 1888–1988*. Philadelphia: The Jewish Publication Society, 1989.

———. "When Jews Were Bible Experts." *Moment* 20, no. 5 (October 1995): 54–55, 80–81.

Sarna, Jonathan D., and Nahum M. Sarna. "Jewish Bible Scholarship and Translations in the United States." In *The Bible and Bibles in America*, edited by Ernest S. Frerichs, 83–116. Atlanta: Scholars Press, 1988.

Sarna, Nahum M. "The Anticipatory Use of Information as a Literary Feature of the Genesis Narratives." In *The Creation of Sacred Literature: Composition and Redaction of the Biblical Text*, edited by Richard Elliott Friedman, 76–82. Berkeley: University of California Press, 1981.

———. "The Authority and Interpretation of Scripture in Jewish Tradition." In *Understanding Scripture: Explorations of Jewish and Christian Traditions of Interpretation*, edited by Clemens Thoma and Michael Wyschogrod, 9–20. Mahwah NJ: Paulist, 1987.

———. "From Wellhausen to Kaufmann," *Midstream* 7, no. 3 (Summer 1961): 64–74.

———. "Hebrew and Bible Studies in Mediaeval Spain." In *The Sephardi Heritage: Essays on the History and Cultural Contribution of the Jews of Spain and Portugal*, edited by R. D. Barnett, 323–66. New York: Ktav, 1971.

———. *The JPS Torah Commentary: Genesis*. Philadelphia: Jewish Publication Society, 1989.

———. "The Modern Study of the Bible in the Framework of Jewish Studies." In *Proceedings of the 8th World Congress of Jewish Studies: Bible*, 19–27. Jerusalem: World Congress of Jewish Studies, 1983.

———. "The Order of the Books." In *Studies in Jewish Bibliography, History and Literature in Honor of I. Edward Kiev*, edited by Charles Berlin, 407–13. New York: Ktav, 1971.

———. "Psalm 89: A Study in Inner Biblical Exegesis." In *Biblical and Other Studies*, edited by Alexander Altmann, 29–46. Cambridge: Harvard University Press, 1963.

———. *Songs of the Heart: An Introduction to the Book of Psalms*. New York: Schocken, 1993.

Satlow, Michael L. *How the Bible Became Holy*. New Haven: Yale University Press, 2014.

Saulson, Scott B. *Institutionalized Language Planning: Documents and Analysis of the Revival of Hebrew*. The Hague: Mouton, 1979.

Saunders, Ernest W. *Searching the Scriptures: A History of the Society of Biblical Literature, 1880–1980*. Chico CA: Scholars Press, 1982.

Sawyer, John F. A. *Sacred Languages and Sacred Texts*. London: Routledge, 1999.

Schäfer, Peter. *Studien zur Geschichte und Theologie des rabbinischen Judentums.* Leiden: E. J. Brill, 1978.
Schapiro, Meyer. "The Angel and the Ram in Abraham's Sacrifice: Parallel in Western and Islamic Art." *Ars Islamica* 10 (1943): 134–47.
Schechter, Solomon. "Geniza Specimens: The Oldest Collection of Bible Difficulties by a Jew." *JQR* OS 13 (1901): 345–74.
———. "The Quotations from Ecclesiasticus in Rabbinic Literature." *JQR* OS 3 (1891): 682–706.
———. *Seminary Addresses & Other Papers.* Cincinnati: Ark, 1915; repr. New York: Arno, 1969.
———. *Studies in Judaism.* 2nd series. Philadelphia: Jewish Publication Society, 1980.
Schiffman, Lawrence H. "The Early History of Public Reading of the Torah." In *Jews, Christians, and Polytheists in the Ancient Synagogue*, edited by Steven Fine, 44–56. London: Routledge, 1999.
Schine, Robert S. *Jewish Thought Adrift: Max Wiener (1882–1950).* Atlanta: Scholars Press, 1992.
Schniedewind, William M. *How the Bible Became a Book: The Textualization of Ancient Israel.* Cambridge: Cambridge University Press, 2004.
———. *The Word of God in Transition: From Prophet to Exegete in the Second Temple Period.* Sheffield: Sheffield Academic Press, 1995.
Schoenfeld, Devorah. *Isaac on Jewish and Christian Altars: Polemic and Exegesis in Rashi and the* Glossa Ordinaria. New York: Fordham University Press, 2013.
Scholem, Gershom. *Kabbalah.* New York: Quadrangle/ New York Times, 1974.
———. *The Messianic Idea in Judaism and Other Essays on Jewish Spirituality.* New York: Schocken, 1971.
———. *On the Kabbalah and Its Symbolism.* New York: Schocken Books, 1969.
Scholer, Gregor. "Mündliche Thora und Ḥadīṯ: Überlieferung, Schreibverbot, Redaktion." *Der Islam* 66 (1989): 213–51.
Schoneveld, Jacobus. *The Bible in Israeli Education: A Study of Approaches to the Hebrew Bible and its Teaching in Israel Educational Literature.* Assen: Van Gorcum, 1976.
Schorsch, Ismar. "Coming to Terms with Biblical Criticism." *Conservative Judaism* 57, no. 3 (Spring 2005): 3–22.
———. *From Text to Context: The Turn to History in Modern Judaism.* Hanove NH: Brandeis University Press, 1994.
———. "Leopold Zunz on the Hebrew Bible." *JQR* 102 (2012): 431–54.
Schrire, Thedore. *Hebrew Amulets: Their Decipherment and Interpretation.* London: Routledge & Kegan Paul, 1966.

Schulman, Shoshana Jordan. *Diversity in Modern Jewish Bible Translations.* DHL thesis, Jewish Theological Seminary of America, 2000.
Schwartz, Baruch J. "On *Peshat* and *Derash*, Bible Criticism, and Theology." *Prooftexts* 14 (1994): 71–88.
Schwartz, Shuly Rubin. *The Emergence of Jewish Scholarship in America: The Publication of the Jewish Encyclopedia.* Cincinnati: HUC Press, 1991.
Seeligman, I. L. "The Beginnings of *Midrash* in the Books of Chronicles." [In Hebrew.] *Tarbiz* 49 (1979–80): 14–32.
Segal, J. B. *The Diacritical Point and the Accent in Syriac.* London: Oxford University Press, 1953.
Segal, Moshe Hirsch (Zvi). *Biblical Interpretation: A Survey of Its History and Development.* 2nd ed. [In Hebrew.] Jerusalem: Kiryat Sefer, 1971.
———. "The Promulgation of the Authoritative Text of the Hebrew Bible." *JBL* 72 (1953) 35–47.
———. "R. Isaac Abravanel as Interpreter of the Bible." [In Hebrew.] *Tarbiz* 8 (1937): 260–99.
Seidman, Naomi. *Faithful Renderings: Jewish-Christian Difference and the Politics of Translation.* Chicago: University of Chicago Press, 2006.
Shafat, Shoval. "The Legend About Offering the Torah to the Nations of the World and Its Alternative in the Tannaitic Midrashim and Amoraic Homilies from the Land of Israel." [In Hebrew.] *HUCA* 84–85 (2013–14): 1*–28*.
Shaked, Gershon. "Modern Midrash: The Biblical Canon and Modern Literature." *AJS Review* 28 (2004): 43–62.
Shaked, Shaul. "A List of Judeo-Persian Bible Translations." [In Hebrew.] *Pe'amim* 84 (Summer 2000): 12–20.
Shamir, Yona, and Mayer I. Gruber. "The Meaning of *Masoret* in Ezek. 20:37 and Rabbinic Hebrew." *Review of Rabbinic Judaism* 10 (2007): 210–20.
Shamosh, Amnon. *Ha-Keter: The Story of the Aleppo Codex.* [In Hebrew.] Jerusalem: Ben Zvi Institute, 1987.
Shandler, Jeffrey. "A Tale of Two Translators: Yehoash and Alter Take on the Tanakh." In *Geveb: A Journal of Yiddish Studies* (April 2019).
Shapira, Amnon. "Traces of an Anti-Moslem Polemic in Targum Yerushalmi A to the Story of the Aqeda." [In Hebrew.] *Tarbiz* 54 (1984–85): 293–96.
Shapira, Anita. "Ben-Gurion and the Bible: The Forging of an Historical Narrative." *Middle Eastern Studies* 33 (1997): 645–74.
———. "The Bible and Israeli Identity." *AJS Review* 28 (2004): 11–42.
———. *The Bible and Israeli Identity.* [In Hebrew.] Jerusalem: Magnes, 2005.
Shapiro, Marc B. "Is Modern Orthodoxy Moving Towards an Acceptance of Biblical Criticism?" *Modern Judaism* 37 (2017): 165–93.

———. *The Limits of Orthodox Theology: Maimonides' Thirteen Principles Reappraised*. Oxford: Littman Library of Jewish Civilization, 2004.
———. "Rabbi David Ẓevi Hoffman on Torah and Wissenschaft." *The Torah U-Madda Journal* 6 (1995–96): 129–37.
Sharpe, John L. III, and Kimberly van Kampen. *The Bible as Book: The Manuscript Tradition*. London: The British Library and Oak Knoll Press,1998.
Shatz, David. "Is There Science in the Bible? An Assessment of Biblical Concordism." *Tradition* 41, no. 2 (Summer 2008): 198–244.
Shavit, Yaacov. *Athens in Jerusalem: Classical Antiquity in the Making of the Modern Secular Jew*. Portland OR: Littman Library of Jewish Civilization, 1997.
Shavit, Yaacov, and Mordechai Eran. *The Hebrew Bible Reborn: From Holy Scripture to the Book of Books, A History of Biblical Culture and the Battles over the Bible in Modern Judaism*. Berlin: Walter deGruyter, 2007.
Shaw, Steve. "Orthodox Reactions to the Challenge of Biblical Criticism." *Tradition* 10, no. 3 (Spring 1969): 61–85.
Sheehan, Jonathan. *The Enlightenment Bible: Translation, Scholarship, Culture*. Princeton NJ: Princeton University Press, 2005.
Shelly, Chaim. *Biblical Research in Haskalah Literature*. [In Hebrew.] Jerusalem: Rubin Mass, 1942.
Shemesh, Yael. "Measure for Measure in the David Stories." *SJOT* 17 (2003): 89–109.
Shereshevsky, Esra. "The Significance of Rashi's Commentary on the Pentateuch." *JQR* 54 (1963–64): 58–79.
Sherrard, Brooke. "American Biblical Archaeologists and Zionism: How Differing Worldviews on the Interaction of Cultures Affected Scholarly Constructions of the Ancient Past." *JAAR* 84 (2016): 234–59.
Sherwood, Yvonne. "Binding-Unbinding: Divided Responses of Judaism, Christianity, and Islam to the 'Sacrifice' of Abraham's Beloved Son." *JAAR* 72 (December, 2004): 821–61.
———. "Textual Carcasses and Isaac's Scar, or What Jewish Interpretation Makes of the Violence That Almost Takes Place on Mt. Moriah." In *Sanctified Aggression: Legacies of Biblical and PostBiblical Vocabularies of Violence*, edited by Jonneke Bekkenkamp and Yvonne Sherwood, 22–43. London: T & T Clark International, 2003.
Shinan, Avigdor. *The Biblical Story as Reflected in its Aramaic Translations*. [In Hebrew.] Tel Aviv: Hakibbutz Hameuchad, 1993.
———. "Live Translation: On the Nature of the Aramaic Targums to the Pentateuch." *Prooftexts* 3 (1983): 41–49.
———. "Synagogues in the Land of Israel: The Literature of the Ancient Synagogue and Synagogue Archaeology." In *Sacred Realm: The Emergence of the*

Synagogue in the Ancient World, edited by Steven Fine, 130–52. New York: Yeshiva University Museum and Oxford University Press, 1996.

Shinan, Avigdor, and Yair Zakovitch. "Midrash on Scripture and Midrash Within Scripture." In *Studies in Bible* (ScrH 31), edited by Sara Japhet, 257–77. Jerusalem: Magnes, 1986.

Shmeruk, Chone. *Yiddish Biblical Plays, 1697–1750*. [In Hebrew.] Jerusalem: The Israel Academy of Sciences and Humanities, 1979.

Shochet, Elijah Judah. *Amalek: The Enemy Within*. Los Angeles: Cedarhurst; Jerusalem: Mimetav, 1991.

Shoham, S. Giora. "The Isaac Syndrome." *American Imago* 33 (1976): 329–49.

Shroyer, Montgomery, J. "Alexandrian Jewish Literalists." *JBL* 55 (1986): 261–84.

Signer, Michael A. "Rashi's Reading of the Akedah." *Journal of Textual Reasoning* ns 2, no. 1 (June 2003).

Siker, Jeffrey S. *Liquid Scripture: The Bible in a Digital World*. Minneapolis: Fortress, 2017.

Silberman, Lou H. "Wellhausen and Judaism." In *Julius Wellhausen and His Prolegomena to the History of Israel*, edited by Douglas A. Knight. *Semeia* 25 (1983): 75–82.

Silberman, Neil Asher. *Between Past and Present: Archaeology, Ideology, and Nationalism in the Modern Middle East*. New York: Henry Holt, 1989.

Silberstein, Laurence J. *History and Ideology: The Writings of Yehezkel Kaufmann*. PhD diss., Brandeis University, 1971.

———. "Religion, Ethnicity, and Jewish History: The Contribution of Yehezkel Kaufmann." *JAAR* 42 (1974): 516–31.

Silver, Daniel Jeremy. *The Story of Scripture, From Oral Tradition to the Written Word*. New York: Basic, 1990.

Simon, Charles. "Can the People of the Book Become the People of the iPad?" *Conservative Judaism* (Winter 2012–13): 10, 51.

Simon, Uriel. "Abraham ibn Ezra and David Kimḥi: Two Approaches Towards the Question of the Reliability of the Biblical Text." [In Hebrew.] *Bar Ilan* 6 (1968): 191–238.

———. "The Contribution of R. Isaac b. Samuel al-Kanzi to the Spanish School of Biblical Interpretation." *JJS* 34 (1983): 171–78.

———. *Four Approaches to the Book of Psalms: From Saadiah Gaon to Abraham ibn Ezra*. Albany: State University of New York Press, 1991.

———. "Peshat Exegesis of Biblical Historiography: Historicism, Dogmatism, and Medievalism." [In Hebrew.] In *Tehillah le-Moshe: Biblical and Judaic Studies in Honor of Moshe Greenberg*, edited by Moreechai Cogan, Barry L. Eichler, and Jeffrey H. Tigay, 171*–203*. Winona Lake IN: Eisenbrauns, 1997.

———. "The Place of the Bible in Israeli Society: From National *Midrash* to Existential Peshat." *Modern Judaism* 19 (1999): 217–39.

———. "The Religious Significance of the *Peshat*." *Tradition* 23, no. 2 (Winter 1988): 41–63.

Simon-Shoshan, Moshe. "The Tasks of the Translators: The Rabbis, the Septuagint, and the Cultural Politics of Translation." *Prooftexts* 27 (2007): 1–39.

Singer, David. "Debating Modern Orthodoxy at Yeshiva College: The Greenberg-Lichtenstein Exchange of 1966." *Modern Judaism* 26 (2006): 113–26.

Singh, Pashaura. *The Guru Granth Sahib: Canon, Meaning and Authority*. New Delhi: Oxford University Press, 2000.

Slymovics, Peter. "Spinoza and Biblical Criticism." [In Hebrew.] *Jerusalem Studies in Jewish Thought* 2 (1982–83): 232–54.

———. "Y. Kaufmann's Critique of J. Wellhausen: A Philosophical-Historical Perspective." [In Hebrew.] *Zion* 49 (1984): 61–92.

Smalley, Beryl., *The Study of the Bible in the Middle Ages*. Notre Dame IN: University of Notre Dame Press, 1964.

Smelik, Willem F. *Rabbis, Language and Translation in Late Antiquity*. Cambridge: Cambridge University Press, 2013.

Smend, Rudolf. "Die Mitte des Alten Testaments." *Theologische Studien* 101 (1970): 7–17.

Smith, Alison Moore. "The Iconography of the Sacrifice of Isaac in Early Christian Art." *American Journal of Archaeology*, 2nd series, 26 (1922): 159–73.

Smith, Jonathan Z. "Sacred Persistence: Towards a Redescription of Canon." In *Imagining Religion: From Babylon to Jonestown*, 36–52. Chicago: University of Chicago Press, 1982.

Smith, Lesley. *The* Glossa Ordinaria: *The Making of a Medieval Bible Commentary*. Leiden: Brill, 2009.

Smith, Wilfred Cantwell. "The True Meaning of Scripture: An Empirical Historian's Nonreductionist Interpretation of the Qur'an." *International Journal of Middle East Studies* 11 (1980): 487–505.

———. *What Is Scripture?* Minneapolis: Fortress, 1993.

Soloveitchik, Haym. "Rupture and Reconstruction: The Transformation of Contemporary Orthodoxy." *Tradition* 28 (1994): 64–130.

Soloveitchik, Joseph B. *Abraham's Journey: Reflections on the Life of the Founding Patriarch*. New York: Toras HaRav Foundation/Ktav, 2008.

———. "The Lonely Man of Faith." *Tradition* 7, no. 2 (Summer 1965): 10–18.

Soloveitchik, Menahem, and Zalman Rubashov. [In Hebrew.] *History of Biblical Criticism*. Berlin: Dvir-Mikra, 1924–25.

Soltes, Ori Z. *The Binding of Isaac: Genesis XXII and Its Progeny*. Washington DC: B'nai Brith Klutznick National Jewish Museum, 2005.

Sommer, Benjamin D. "Exegesis, Allusion and Intertextuality in the Hebrew Bible: A Response to Lyle Eslinger." *VT* 46 (1996): 479–89.

———, ed. *Jewish Concepts of Scripture: A Comparative Introduction.* New York: New York University Press, 2012.

Sorkin, David. *Moses Mendelssohn and the Religious Enlightenment.* Berkeley: University of California Press, 1996.

Spalding, Paul. "Toward a Modern Torah: Moses Mendelssohn's Use of a Banned Bible." *Modern Judaism* 19 (1999): 67–82.

Speiser, E. A. "ṬWṬPT." *JQR* 48 (1957/58): 208–17.

Sperling, S. David. "Israeli Biblical Scholarship: The Past Decade" *Jewish Book Annual* 51 (1993–94): 6–25.

———. "Judaism and Modern Biblical Research." In *Biblical Studies: Meeting Ground of Jews and Christians*, edited by Lawrence Boadt CSP, Helga Croner, and Leon Klenicki, 19–44. Ramsey NJ: Paulist, 1986.

———. *Students of the Covenant: A History of Jewish Biblical Scholarship in North America.* Atlanta: Scholars Press, 1992.

Spiegel, Shalom. *The Last Trial, On The Legends and Core of the Command to Abraham to Offer Isaac as a Sacrifice: The Akedah.* New York: Pantheon, 1967.

Sprinzak, Ehud. "The Politics, Institutions, and Culture of Gush Emunim." In *Jewish Fundamentalism in Comparative Perspective*, edited by Laurence J. Silberstein, 117–47. New York: NYU Press, 1993.

Staal, Frits. "The Concept of Scripture in the Indian Tradition." In *Sikh Studies: Comparative Perspectives on a Changing Tradition*, edited by Mark Juergensmeyer and N. Gerald Barnes, 121–24. Berkeley: Graduate Theological Union, 1979.

Staerck, Wilhelm and Albert Leitzmann. *Die Jüdisch-Deutschen Bibelübersetzungen von den Anfäng des 18. Jahrhunderts.* Frankfurt a.M.: J. Kauffman Verlag, 1923; repr. New York: Georg Olms Verlag, 1977.

Steiner, George. *After Babel: Aspects of Language and Translation.* New York: Oxford University Press, 1975.

Steiner, Richard C. *A Biblical Translation in the Making: The Evolution and Impact of Saadia Gaon's* Tafsīr. Cambridge: Harvard University Press, 2010.

———. "Saadia vs. Rashi: On the Shift from Meaning-Maximalism to Meaning-Minimalism in Medieval Biblical Lexicology." *JQR* 88 (1998): 213–58.

Steinsaltz, Adin. *Biblical Interpretation in 8th–16th Century Responsa Literature.* [In Hebrew.] Jerusalem: Keter, 1978.

Stern, David. "The First Jewish Books and the Early History of Jewish Reading." *JQR* 98 (2008): 163–202.

———. "The Hebrew Bible in Europe in the Middle Ages: A Preliminary Typology." *JSIJ* 11 (2012): 235–322.

———. *The Jewish Bible: A Material History*. Seattle: University of Washington Press, 2017.
Stern, Richard B. "Arnold B. Ehrlich: A Personal Recollection." *American Jewish Archives* 23 (1971): 73–85.
Stordalen, Terje. "The Canonization of Ancient Hebrew and Confucian Literature." *JSOT* 32 (2007): 3–22.
Sukenik, E. L. *Ancient Synagogues in Palestine and Greece*. London: British Academy, 1934.
Sundberg, Albert C., Jr. *The Old Testament of the Early Church*. Cambridge: Harvard University Press, 1964.
Sussman, Lance J. "Another Look at Isaac Leeser and the First Jewish Translation of the Bible in the United States." *Modern Judaism* 5 (1985): 159–90.
———. *Isaac Leeser and the Making of American Judaism*. Detroit: Wayne State University Press, 1995.
Swanson, Theodore Norman. *The Closing of the Collection of Holy Scriptures: A Study in the History of the Canonization of the Old Testament*. PhD diss., Vanderbilt University, 1970.
Sweeney, Marvin A. "The Emerging Field of Jewish Biblical Theology." In *Academic Approaches to Teaching Jewish Studies*, edited by Zev Garber, 83–105. Lanham MD: University Press of America, 2000.
———. "Why Jews Should Be Interested in Biblical Theology." *CCAR Journal* 44 (Winter 1997): 67–75.
Swete, Henry Barclay. *An Introduction to the Old Testament in Greek*. Cambridge: Cambridge University Press, 1902; repr. New York: Ktav, 1968.
Szyszman, Simon. *Le Karaïsme: Ses doctrines et son histoire*. Lausanne: Editions l'Age d'Homme, 1980.
Tal, Avraham. "The Samaritan Targum to the Pentateuch: Its Distinctive Characteristics and its Metamorphosis," *JSS* 21 (1976): 26–38.
Talmage, Frank. "Apples of Gold: The Inner Meaning of Sacred Texts in Medieval Judaism." In *Jewish Spirituality: From the Bible Through the Middle Ages*, edited by Arthur Green, 313–55. New York: Crossroad, 1986.
———. *David Kimḥi: The Man and His Commentaries*. Cambridge: Harvard University Press, 1975.
———. "Keep Your Sons from Scripture: The Bible in Medieval Jewish Scholarship and Spirituality." In *Understanding Scripture, Explorations of Jewish and Christian Traditions of Interpretation*, edited by Clemens Thoma and Michael Wyschogrod, 81–101. Mahwah NJ: Paulist, 1987.
Talmon, Shemaryahu. "The Bible in Contemporary Israel." *Judaism* 21, no. 1 (Winter 1972): 79–83.
———. "Martin Buber's Ways of Interpreting the Bible." *JJS* 27 (1976): 195–209.

———. "The Three Scrolls of the Law That Were Found in the Temple Court." *Textus* 2 (1962): 14–27.
———. "Yehezkel Kaufmann's Approach to Biblical Research." *Conservative Judaism* 25, no. 2 (Winter 1971): 20–28.
Tawil, Hayim and Bernarde Schneider. *Crown of Aleppo: The Mystery of the Oldest Hebrew Bible Codex*. Philadelphia: Jewish Publication Society, 2010.
Thackeray, H. St. John. "Psalm LXXVI and Other Psalms for the Feast of Tabernacles." *JTS* 15 (1913–14): 425–31.
———. *The Septuagint and Jewish Worship: A Study in Origins*. London: British Academy, 1923.
———. "The Song of Hanukkah and Other Lessons and Psalms for the Jewish New Year's Day." *JTS* 16 (1914/15): 177–204.
Thompson, R. J. *Moses and the Law in a Century of Criticism Since Graf* (VTSup 19). Leiden: E. J. Brill, 1970.
Tigay, Jeffrey H. "On the Meaning of *ṭ(w)ṭpt*." *JBL* 101 (1982): 321–31.
———. "On Translating the Torah." *Conservative Judaism* 26, no. 2 (Winter 1972): 14–30.
———. "The Torah Scroll and God's Presence." In *Built by Wisdom, Established By Understanding: Essays on Biblical and Near Eastern Literature in Honor of Adele Berlin*. Bethesda MD: University Press of Maryland, 2013.
Tishby, Isaiah. *Studies in Kabbalah and Its Branches: Researches and Sources*. Jerusalem: Magnes, 1982–93.
Toorn, Karel van der. "The Iconic Book: Analogies Between the Babylonian Cult of Images and the Veneration of the Torah." In *The Image and the Book: Iconic Cults, Aniconism, and the Rise of Book Religion in Israel and the Ancient Near East*, edited by Karel van der Toorn, 229–48. Leuven: Uitgeverij Peeters, 1997.
———. *Scribal Culture and the Making of the Hebrew Bible*. Cambridge MA: Harvard University Press, 2007.
Touitou, Eliezer. "Between 'Scripture's Straightforward Meaning' and 'The Torah's Spirit': Neḥamah Leibowitz's Relationship to Rashbam's Interpretation of the Torah." [In Hebrew.] In *Pirqê Neḥamah: Sefer Zikaron li-Neḥamah Leibowitz*, edited by Moshe Arend, 221–40. Jerusalem: HaSochnut HaYehudit le-Eretz Yisrael, 2001.
———. "On French-Jewish Biblical Interpretation." [In Hebrew.] *Tarbiz* 61 (1981–82): 522–26.
Tov, Emanuel. "The Rabbinic Tradition Concerning the 'Alterations' Inserted into the Greek Pentateuch and their Relation to the Original Text of the LXX." *JSJ* 15 (1984): 65–89.

———. *Textual Criticism of the Hebrew Bible.* Minneapolis: Fortress; and Assen/: Van Gorcum, 1992.

Trachtenberg, Joshua. *Jewish Magic and Superstition: A Study in Folk Religion.* New York: Atheneum, 1974.

Tschuggnall, Peter. "Der Gebundene Isaak: 'Isaaks Opferung' in der moderne jüdischen Literatur." *ZKTh* 114 (1992): 204–16.

Tsevat, Matitiahu. "A Retrospective View of Isaac Leeser's Biblical Work." In *Essays in American Jewish History,* 295–313. Cincinnati: American Jewish Archives, 1958.

———. "Theology of the Old Testament—A Jewish View." *Horizons in Biblical Theology* 8, no. 2 (December 1986): 33–50; "Response" from Bernhard Anderson, 51–59.

Twersky, Isadore and Jay M. Harris. *Rabbi Abraham ibn Ezra: Studies in the Writings of a Twelfth Century Jewish Polymath.* Cambridge: Harvard University Press, 1993.

Uffenheimer, Benjamin. "Buber and Modern Biblical Scholarship." In *Martin Buber: A Centenary Volume,* edited by Haim Gordon and Jochanan Bloch, 163–211. New York: Ktav, 1984.

———. "Cassuto as a Biblical Commentator." *Immanuel* 6 (1976): 20–29.

———. "Some Reflections on Modern Jewish Biblical Research." In *Creative Biblical Exegesis: Christian and Jewish Hermeneutics Through the Centuries,* edited by Benjamin Uffenheimer and Henning Graf Reventlow, 161–74. Sheffield: Sheffield Academic Press, 1988.

———. "Yehezkel Kaufmann: Historian and Philosopher of Biblical Monotheism." *Immanuel* 3 (1973–74): 9–21.

Ulrich, Eugene. *The Dead Sea Scrolls and the Origins of the Bible.* Grand Rapids MI: Eerdmans, 1999.

———. "The Non-Attestation of a Tripartite Canon in 4QMMT." *CBQ* 65 (2003): 202–14.

Urbach, Ephraim E. "The Role of the Ten Commandments in Jewish Worship." In *The Ten Commandments in History and Tradition,* edited by Ben-Zion Segal, 161–89. Jerusalem: Magnes, 1985.

Van Buren, Paul M. "On Reading Someone Else's Mail: The Church and Israel's Scriptures." In *Die Hebräische Bibel und ihre zweifache Nachgeschichte: Festschrift für Rolf Rendtorff zum 65. Geburtstag,* edited by Ehrhard Blum, Christian Macholz, and Ekkehard W. Stegemann, 595–606. Neukirchen-Vluyn: Neukirchener Verlag, 1990.

Van der Horst, Pieter W. "*Sortes*: Sacred Books as Instant Oracles in Late Antiquity." In *The Use of Sacred Books in the Ancient World,* edited by L.

V. Rutgers, D. W. van der Horst, H. W. Havelaar, and L. Teugels, 143–73. Leuven: Peeters, 1998.
VanderKam, James. "Authoritative Literature in the Dead Sea Scrolls." *DSD* 5 (1998): 382–402.
Van der Leeuw, Gerard. *Religion in Essence and Manifestation.* Princeton NJ: Princeton University Press, 1986.
Van der Zan, P. J. Abbink. "Ornamentation on Eighteenth-Century Torah Binders." *Israel Museum News* 14 (1978): 64–73.
Van Woerden, Isabel Speyart. "The Iconography of the Sacrifice of Isaac." *VigChr* 15 (1961): 214–55.
Vargon, Shmuel. "The Controversy Between I. S. Reggio and S. D. Luzzatto on the Date of the Writing of the Pentateuch." *HUCA* 72 (2001): 139–53.
———. "The Date of Composition of the Book of Job in the Context of S. D. Luzzatto's Attitude to Biblical Criticism." *JQR* 91 (2001): 377–94.
———. "The Identity and Dating of the Author of Ecclesiastes According to Shadal." [In Hebrew.] In *Studies in Bible and Exegesis* 5, presented to Uriel Simon, edited by Moshe Garsiel, Shmuel Vargon, Amos Frisch, and Jacob Kugel, 365–84. Ramat Gan: Bar-Ilan University Press, 2000.
Venuti, Lawrence. *The Translator's Invisibility: A History of Translation.* London: Routledge, 1995.
Verbin, John S. Kloppenborg. "Dating Theodotus (CIJ II 1404)." *JJS* 51 (2000): 243–80.
Vermes, Geza. "New Light on the Sacrifice of Isaac from 4Q225." *JJS* 47 (1996): 140–46.
———. *Scripture and Tradition in Judaism.* 2nd ed. Leiden: E. J. Brill, 1973.
Viezel, Eran. "R. Judah he-Hasid or R. Moshe Zaltman: Who Proposed that Torah Verses Were Written After the Time of Moses?" *JJS* 66 (2015): 97–115.
———. "Textual Criticism of the Bible in the Writings of Jacob Reifmann: A Re-Evaluation." *JJS* 68 (2017): 97–115.
Waddell, W. G. "The Tetragrammaton in the LXX." *JTS* 45 (1944): 158–61.
Waldman, Marilyn R. "Sacred Communication." Review of W. Graham, *Beyond the Written Word. HR* 30 (1991): 313–17.
Walfish, Barry Dov. *Esther in Medieval Garb: Jewish Interpretation of the Book of Esther in the Middle Ages.* Albany: State University of New York Press, 1993.
Wasserstein, Abraham, and David J. Wasserstein. *The Legend of the Septuagint, From Classical Antiquity to Today.* New York: Cambridge University Press, 2006.
Watts, James W., ed. *Persia and Torah: The Theory of Imperial Authorization of the Pentateuch.* Atlanta: Society of Biblical Literature, 2001.
———. "Ritual Legitimacy and Scriptural Authority." *JBL* 124 (2005): 401–17.

Waxman, Meyer. *A History of Jewish Literature*. New York: Thomas Yoseloff, 1960.

Weil, Gérard E. *Élie Lévita: Humaniste et Massorète (1469–1549)*. Leiden: E. J. Brill, 1963.

Weinberg, Werner. "Moses Mendelssohn's 'Biur,' Two Hundred Years Later." *Jewish Book Annual* 40 (1982–83): 97–104.

Weinberg, Yehiel Yaakov. "Towards the History of the Targumim." [In Hebrew.] In *The Abraham Weiss Jubilee Volume*, 361–76. New York: Schulsinger Bros., 1964.

Weinberger, Leon J. "God as Matchmaker: A Rabbinic Legend Preserved in the Piyyut." *JAAR* 40 (1972): 238–44.

———. *Jewish Hymnography: A Literary History*. London: Littman Library of Jewish Civilization, 1998.

Weinfeld, Moshe. "Biblical Interpretation in the Generation of the Revival in Israel." [In Hebrew.] In *Studies in Bible and Talmud*, edited by Sara Japhet, 9–15. Jerusalem: Hebrew University 1987.

Weingreen, Jacob. "Exposition in the Old Testament and in Rabbinic Literature." In *Promise and Fulfillment: Essays Presented to Professor S. H. Hooke*, edited by F. F. Bruce, 187–201. Edinburgh: T&T Clark, 1963.

———. "The Rabbinic Approach to the Study of the Old Testament." *BJRL* 34 (1952): 166–90.

———. "Rabbinic-Type Glosses in The Old Testament." *JSS* 2 (1957): 149–62.

———. "The Torah Speaks in Human Terms." [In Hebrew.] In *Interpreting the Hebrew Bible: Essays in Honour of E. I. J. Rosenthal*, edited by J. A. Emerton and Stefan Reif, 267–75. Cambridge: Cambridge University Press, 1982.

Weiss, Hillel. "Notes to the Analysis of 'The Binding of Isaac' in Modern Hebrew Literature as a Topos, Wonder, and Motif." In *The Akedah and the Rebuke: Myth, Wonder, and Topos in Literature*, edited by Zvi Levy, 31–52. Jerusalem: Magnes, 1991.

Weitemeyer, Mogens. "Archive and Library Technique in Ancient Mesopotamia." *Libra* 6 (1956): 217–38.

Wellhausen, Julius. *The Pharisees and the Sadducees: An Examination of Internal Jewish History*. Translated by Mark E. Biddle. Macon GA: Mercer University Press, 2001.

———. *Prolegomena to the History of Ancient Israel*. New York: Meridian, 1957.

Wellisch, E. *Isaac and Oedipus: A Study in Biblical Psychology of the Sacrifice of Isaac, the Akedah*. New York: Humanities Press, 1954.

Wellisch, Hans H. "Hebrew Bible Concordances, with a Biographical Study of Solomon Mandelkern." *Jewish Book Annual* 43 (1985–86): 56–91.

Wendel, Carl. *Der Thoraschrein im Altertum*. Halle: Max Niemeyer Verlag, 1950.

Werblowsky, R. J. Zvi. "Biblical Criticism as a Religious Problem: An Effort Towards Typological Clarification of Approaches and Solutions." [In Hebrew.] *Molad* 18 (1960): 162–68.

Werner, Eric. *The Sacred Bridge: Liturgical Parallels in Synagogue and Early Church.* New York: Schocken, 1970.

Wertheimer, Jack, ed. *Tradition Renewed: A History of the Jewish Theological Seminary.* New York: Jewish Theological Seminary of America, 1997.

Westerholm, Stephen. "Torah, Nomos, and Law: A Question of 'Meaning.'" *Studies in Religion/Sciences Religieuses* 15 (1986): 327–36.

White, William Charles. *Chinese Jews.* 2nd ed. New York: Paragon, 1966.

Wickes, William. *A Treatise on the Accentuation of the Twenty-One So-Called Prose Books of the Old Testament.* Oxford: Clarendon, 1887.

———. *Two Treatises on the Accentuation of the Old Testament.* New York: Ktav, 1970. Originally published 1881–1887; prolegomenon by Aron Dotan, vii–xlvi.

Widengren, Geo. *Mani and Manichaeism.* New York: Holt, Rinehart and Winston, 1965.

Wieder, Naphthali. *The Judean Scrolls and Karaism.* London: East and West Library, 1962.

———. "'Sanctuary' as a Metaphor for Scripture." *JJS* 8 (1957): 165–75.

Wiener, Leo. "The Ferrara Bible, 1 and 2." *Modern Language Notes* 10 (1895): 81–85; and 11 (1896): 24–42, 84–106.

Wiese, Christian. *Wissenschaft des Judentums und Protestantische Theologie im Wilhelminischen Deutschland: Ein Schrei ins Leere*? Tübinben: J. C. B. Mohr (Paul Siebeck), 1999.

Wigtil, David Norval. *The Translation of Religious Texts in the Greco-Roman World.* PhD diss., University of Minnesota, 1980.

Wilhelm, Kurt. "Benno Jacob: A Militant Rabbi." *Leo Baeck Institute Yearbook* 7 (1962): 75–94.

Wilhelm, Y. D. "The Orders of Tikkunim." [In Hebrew.] In *Alei Ayin: The Salman Schocken Jubilee Volume*,125–46. Tel Aviv: n.p., 1951–52.

Willey, Patricia Tull. *Remember the Former Things: The Recollection of Previous Texts in Second Isaiah.* Atlanta: Scholars Press, 1997.

Willi, Thomas. *Die Chronik als Auslegung: Untersuchungen zur Literarischen Gestaltung der Historischen Überlieferung Israels.* Göttingen: Vandenhoeck & Ruprecht, 1972.

———. "Thora in den biblischen Chronikbüchern." *Judaica* 36 (1980): 102–5, 148–51.

Williamson, H. G. M. *Holy, Holy, Holy: The Story of a Liturgical Formula.* Berlin: Walter deGruyter, 2008.

———. *Israel in the Book of Chronicles*. Cambridge: Cambridge University Press, 1977.

Wilson, Gerald Henry. *The Editing of the Hebrew Psalter*. Chico CA: Scholars Press, 1985.

Wineman, Aryeh. "The Akedah Motif in *In One Noose* by Hazaz." [In Hebrew.] *Bikoret Ufarshanut* 22 (July 1986): 75–88.

Wineman, Lawrence Joseph. *The Akedah-Motif in the Modern Hebrew Story*. PhD diss., University of California Los Angeles, 1977.

Wischmeyer, Oda. "Das heilige Buch im Judentum des Zweiten Tempels." *ZNW* 86 (1995): 218–42.

Witton-Davies, Carlyle. "Martin Buber's Contribution to Biblical Studies." In *Studia Biblica 1978* (JSOT Supplement 11), edited by E. A. Livingstone, 259–66. Sheffield: JSOT Press, 1979.

Wolfensohn, Avraham. *From the Bible to the Labor Movement*. [In Hebrew.] Tel Aviv: Am Oved, 1975.

Wolff, Maurice. "Zur Charakteristik der Bibelexegese Saadia Alfajjûmîs." *ZAW* 4 (1884): 225–46; and 5 (1885): 15–29.

Wolfson, Elliot. "Female Imaging of the Torah: From Literary Metaphor to Religious Symbol." In *From Ancient Israel to Modern Judaism, Intellect in Quest of Understanding: Essays in Honor of Marvin Fox*, edited by Jacob Neusner, Ernest S. Frerichs, and Nahum M. Sarna, 271–307. Atlanta: Scholars Press, 1989.

———. "The Mystical Significance of Torah Study in German Pietism." *JQR* 84 (1993): 43–77.

———. *Through a Speculum That Shines: Vision and Imagination in Medieval Jewish Mysticism*. Princeton NJ: Princeton University Press, 1994.

Wolfson, Harry Austryn. "The Veracity of Scripture from Philo to Spinoza." In *Religious Philosophy: A Group of Essays*, 217–45. Cambridge: Harvard University Press, 1961.

Wollaston, Isabel. "Traditions of Remembrance: Post-Holocaust Interpretations of Genesis 22." In *Words Remembered, Texts Renewed, Essays in Honour of John F.A. Sawyer*, edited by Jon Davies, Graham Patrick, and Wilfred G. E. Watson, 41–51. Sheffield: Sheffield Academic Press, 1995.

Wollenberg, Rebecca Scharbach. "The Book That Changed: Narratives of Ezran Authorship in Late Antique Biblical Criticism." *JBL* 138 (2019): 143–60.

———. *The People of the Book Without the Book: Jewish Ambivalence Towards Biblical Text After the Rise of Christianity*. PhD diss., University of Chicago, 2015.

Wood, J. Edwin. "Isaac Typology in the New Testament." *NTS* 14 (1967–68): 583–89.

Wyrick, Jed. *The Ascension of Authorship, Attribution and Canon Formation in Jewish, Hellenistic, and Christian Traditions.* Cambridge MA: Harvard University Press, 2004.

Yaari, Avraham. *The History of Simchat Torah: The Development of Its Customs in the Jewish Diaspora Through the Generations.* [In Hebrew.] Jerusalem: Mossad HaRav Kook, 1964.

Yarchin, William. "Were the Psalms Collections at Qumran True Psalters?" *JBL* 134 (2015): 775–89.

Yehuda, Zvi A. "Hazon Ish on Textual Criticism and Halakhah." *Tradition* 18 (1979–80): 172–80.

Yeivin, Israel. *Introduction to the Tiberian Masorah.* Missoula MT: Scholars Press, 1980.

Yerushalmi, David. "Judeo-Persian Bible Translations." [In Hebrew.] *Pe'amim* 84 (Summer 2000): 21–39.

Yoffie, Leah Rachel. "Popular Beliefs and Customs Among the Yiddish-Speaking Jews of St. Louis MO." *Journal of American Folk-Lore* 38 (1925): 375–99.

Yona, Shamir and Mayer I. Gruber. "The Meaning of *Masoret* in Ezek. 20:37 and Rabbinic Hebrew." *Review of Rabbinic Judaism* 10 (2007): 210–20.

York, Anthony D. "The Targum in the Synagogue and in the School." *JSJ* 10 (1981): 74–86.

Zac, Sylvain. *Spinoza et L'interpretation de l'Écriture.* Paris: Presses Universitaires de France, 1965.

Zafren, Herbert C. "Bible Editions, Bible Study and the Early History of Hebrew Printing." *ErIsr* 16 (1982): 240*–51*.

Zeitlin, Solomon. "An Historical Study of the Canonization of the Hebrew Scriptures." *AAJR* 3 (1931–32): 121–58.

Zenger, Erich. *Der Psalter in Judentum und Christentum.* Freiburg: Herder, 1998.

Zerubavel, Yael. "Back to the Bible: Hiking in the Land as a Mnemonic Practice in Contemporary Israeli Tourist Discourse." [In Hebrew.] In *Culture, Memory, and History: Essays in Honor of Anita Shapira,* edited by Meir Chazan and Uri Cohen, 497–522. Tel Aviv: Tel Aviv University, 2012.

Zetterholm, Karin Hedner. "Isaac and Jesus: A Rabbinic Reappropriation of a 'Christian' Motif?" *JJS* 67 (2016): 102–20.

Zevit, Ziony. "Jewish Biblical Theology, Whence? Why? and Whither?" *HUCA* 76 (2005): 289–340.

———. Matres Lectionis *in Ancient Hebrew Epigraphs.* Cambridge: American Schools of Oriental Research, 1980.

Zimmels, H. J. *Ashkenazim and Sephardim: Their Relations, Differences, and Problems as Reflected in the Rabbinical Responsa.* London: Oxford University Press, 1958.

Zinberg, Israel. *A History of Jewish Literature*. Translated by Bernard Martin. Cincinnati: Hebrew Union College Press; and New York: Ktav, 1972–78.

Zivion, Avraham. "Ben-Gurion's Attachment to the Bible." *Jewish Spectator* 43, no. 4 (Winter 1988): 8–12.

Zsengellér, József, ed. *Rewritten Bible After Fifty Years: Texts, Terms, or Technique?* Leiden: Brill, 2014.

Zucker, Moses. *Rav Saadya Gaon's Translation of the Torah: Exegesis, Halakha, and Polemics in R. Saadya's Translation of the Pentatech, Texts and Studies.* [In Hebrew.] New York: Feldheim, 1959.

———. "Towards a Solution of the Problem of the 32 Principles and the 'Mishna of Rabbi Eleazar.'" [In Hebrew.] *PAAJR* 23 (1954): 1–39.

Zuckermann, Ghilad. "Do Israelis Understand the Hebrew Bible?" *Bible and Critical Theory* 6, no. 1 (2010): 1–7.

Zunz, Leopold. "Bibel Kritische." *ZDMG* 27 (1873): 669–89.

———. *Die Gottesdienstlichen Vorträge der Juden, historisch Entwickelt*. Berlin: A. Asher, 1932.

Index

masoretes, 31–33, 81
masoretic text, 69
matres lectionis, 31
McGuffey Reader, xiii
Megillat Ta'anit, 30, 120
Meir, Rabbi, 26
Meir ibn Gabbay, 52
Meir of Rothenberg, 144n14
Mekhilta d'Rabbi Ishmael, 44
Meklenburg, Jacob Zvi, 66, 75
Melito, 27, 37
Menaḥem ibn Saruq, 98, 100
Menaḥem Recanati, 47, 160n21
Mendele Mokher Sefarim, 167n35
Mendelssohn, Moses, 44, 62, 63, 65, 67, 81, 99, 100, 103, 116, 117, 120, 122, 124, 130, 131, 133, 134, 136, 137, 168n52, 197n114, 199n134
Mendez, Henry Pereira, 195n80
merkavah mystics, 149n99
mezuzah, 1
Micah, 21
micrography, 2
mikhtam, 2
mikra' soferim, 26
Mikra'ot Gedolot, 37, 83, 158n114
Mikveh Israel, 71
minori ad maius, 84
Miqra LeYisrael, 175n11
Mishnah, 15, 18, 45, 125, 133
Mitchell, Stephen, 119, 192n51
Mohammad, 121, 142
monotheism, 70
Montefiore, C. G., 194n59
Morais, Sabato, 66
Morgenstern, Julian, 67, 68
Moses, 13, 22, 23, 24, 42
Moses ben David ben Naftali, 33
Moses de Leon, 94
Moses ibn Ezra, 100
Moses of Coucy, 5
Murabaat, 27
musaf, 8
Muslims, 103, 141
mystics, 8

Naḥmanides (Moses ben Naḥman), 57, 90, 97, 106, 160n19, 176n29, 180n120, 193n52
Naḥum of Gimzu, 86
naqdan, 33
Nasi, Doña Gracia, 116
Nathan, 21
Natronai Gaon, 59, 173n139, 199n135, 199n138
Nehemiah, 25
ner tamid, 147n61
Neumann, Erich, 109
Newman, Selig, 132
New Testament, xvi, 25, 141
Noah's ark, 1
notarikon, 96

Obadiah of Bertinoro, 14
Odyssey (Homer), 29
Oral Torah, 61, 76, 81
Origen, 114, 120, 123
Orlinsky, Harry, 119, 192n48
Ostriker, Alicia, 186n207
Owen, Wilfred, 188n242
Ozick, Cynthia, 133

Palermo, 14
parallelism, 87
parashot/parashiyot, 5
parathesis, 84
pardes, 82
parokhet, 147n61
Passover, xv, 7, 8, 10, 16, 75, 77, 83–84, 140

Paul, 90, 91, 93
Peel Commission, 73
Pentateuch, 28, 157n89
Perles, Felix, 170n79
Persian, 121
peshat, 97, 98, 100
pesuqei de-zimra, 8
pesuqim, 33
Petaḥ Tikvah, 71
Petuchowski, Jakob, 51
petuḥah, 33
Pharisees, 56, 61, 65
Philippson, Ludwig, 116, 170n79, 193n59
Philo, 22, 25, 42, 44, 80, 82, 87, 90, 91, 93, 94, 98, 99, 101, 107, 126, 193n53
Pirqei Rabbi Eliezer, 80
pishro, 80
Plato, 99, 140, 202n6
polyvalence, 81
Popper, Julius, 193n59
Potok, Chaim, 167n35
Prayer of Manasseh, 174n3
Preil, Joshua Joseph, 167n35
priestly blessing, 9
priestly source (P), 70
prophets, 23, 64
Prossnitz, Isaac, 117
Protestantism, xvi, 61, 62, 65
psalms, 3, 8, 9, 26, 61
Psalms of Joshua, 31
Pseudo-Eupolemus, 99
Purim, 7, 9, 17
Pythagoras, 99

qal vaḥomer, 84, 85
qameṣ, 156n80
qĕrei, 26, 59
Qirqisani, Jacob al-, 55–56
Qumran, 116, 121
Qur'an, xiii, 32, 61, 121, 137, 141, 155n14, 184n183

Rabinov, Yehoshua, 189n252
Rapaport, Solomon, 69, 70
Rashi, 36, 60, 81, 88, 108, 126, 180n126
Reagan, Ronald, 137
Recanati, Menaḥem b. Benjamin, 190n15
Reformation, Protestant, 64
Reform Judaism, 55, 63–64, 75–76, 140, 147n67
Reggio, Isaac Samuel, 69, 103, 191n28
Renaissance, 61
Res Gestae, 194n63
Revised Standard Version, 119, 131
Revised Version, 118, 119, 131, 135
rewritten Bible, 126
Rishon Le-Zion, 71
Roman Catholics, 61
Rosenberg, David, 119, 192n51
Rosenzweig, Franz, 47, 68, 118, 119, 120, 121, 123, 124, 126, 130, 133, 142
Rosh Hashanah, 8, 16
Rosh Ḥodesh, 9
Ruth, 42

Saadia Gaon, 44, 45, 75, 97, 99, 99, 116, 121, 122, 124, 127, 129, 131, 189n251, 197n111, 197n114
Sabbath candles, 75
Sachs, Michael, 117
sacrifices, 17
Sadducees, 60–61, 75, 174n144
Salmon ben Yeruḥim, 167n39
Salomon, Gotthold, 193n59
Samaria, 74
Samaritan, 26

Ingram Content Group UK Ltd.
Milton Keynes UK
UKHW041142020723
424318UK00011B/335

9 780827 615106